Intrepid Girls

Intrepid Girls

The COMPLICATED HISTORY *of the* GIRL SCOUTS OF THE USA

• • • • • •

Amy Erdman Farrell

A FERRIS AND FERRIS BOOK

The University of North Carolina Press
CHAPEL HILL

This book was published under the Marcie Cohen Ferris and William R. Ferris Imprint of the University of North Carolina Press.

Manufactured in the United States of America

Cover photograph of Girl Scout badges courtesy of the author.

Library of Congress Cataloging-in-Publication Data
Names: Farrell, Amy Erdman, author.
Title: Intrepid girls : the complicated history of the Girl Scouts of the USA / Amy Erdman Farrell.
Description: Chapel Hill : University of North Carolina Press, [2025] | "A Ferris and Ferris Book." | Includes bibliographical references and index.
Identifiers: LCCN 2025015473 | ISBN 9781469686837 (cloth ; alk. paper) | ISBN 9781469686714 (epub) | ISBN 9781469686844 (pdf)
Subjects: LCSH: Girl Scouts of the United States of America—History. | Girl Scouts—United States—History. | Feminism and racism—United States. | BISAC: HISTORY / United States / 20th Century | SOCIAL SCIENCE / Gender Studies
Classification: LCC HS3359 .F37 2025 | DDC 369.43/0973—dc23/eng/20250515
LC record available at https://lccn.loc.gov/2025015473

For product safety concerns under the European Union's General Product Safety Regulation (EU GPSR), please contact gpsr@mare-nostrum.co.uk or write to the University of North Carolina Press and Mare Nostrum Group B.V., Mauritskade 21D, 1091 GC Amsterdam, The Netherlands.

TO ALL GIRL SCOUTS, EVERYWHERE

Contents

Illustrations

ILLUSTRATIONS

Acknowledgments

My first thanks for this book, over a decade in the research and writing, go to the women who served as my leaders and the friends I made as a Girl Scout in Akron, Ohio, in the 1970s, especially my oldest and dearest friend, Laura Santilli. Girl Scouts gave me community, friendship, joy, and a tremendous ability to take on difficult tasks—I hope that this book serves as testament to the formidable education it provided, one that ultimately led me to ask the difficult questions that propelled this research.

I want to thank my Dickinson students who served as my undergraduate research assistants from the earliest stages of this book to its final steps: Maretta Sonn, Johanna Fleming, Emily Benson, Elizabeth Roy, Adena Cohen, and Alyssa Monsanto. Dickinson College, where I have taught for over thirty years, funded these Dana research assistantships and supported my travel to collections and the sites of Girl Scout history, including to Ohio to research the local archives and Camp Ledgewood; to the New York City national Girl Scout archives, to Pax Lodge in London; to Our Chalet in Switzerland; to the Juliette Gordon Low Birthplace in Savannah; to the (Boy) Scouting Museum in New Mexico; and to the Amache National Historic Site in Granada, Colorado, the site of one of the Japanese American incarceration centers during World War II. Funding from the Mellon Grant "Beyond the New Normal" project also allowed a timely course release for writing.

A 2017 National Endowment for the Humanities summer institute, Recognizing an Imperfect Past, was instrumental to this project. My thanks to many of our consultants, including David Blight, Karen Cox, and Vaugnette Goode-Walker (who graciously spoke to me at length about Savannah history); my colleagues at the institute, especially Brie Swenson and Nicole Maurantonio; and Stan Deaton, senior historian at Georgia Historical Society.

An American Council of Learned Societies Fellowship in 2019–20 was crucial to begin writing this book in earnest, as it allowed me to take a year's leave of absence from teaching at Dickinson. A National Endowment for the Humanities summer stipend in 2023 allowed me to write the chapter on Girl Scouting in the Japanese American incarceration centers. A Harvard Radcliffe

Institute Fellowship in 2021–22 provided an intellectual community and financial support for a robust year of research and writing in Cambridge. I particularly want to thank Claudia Rizzini and Sharon Bromberg-Lim, who managed our year so well, and the entire fellowship cohort of artists, writers, scholars, and scientists, especially Scott Stevens, Robin Mitchell, Ariela Gross, Merav Opher, Ralph Eubanks, Tiya Miles, David Cheng Chang, and Amanda Cobb-Greetham. Phil Deloria, Jane Kamensky, and Daniel Horowitz welcomed me to Cambridge with walks and tea. I also want to thank my Harvard undergraduate research assistants, Aisha Khan, Emerson Monks, and Anna Farronay, as well as Claire Yoo, who generously shared her work on Girl Scouting in Japanese American incarceration centers.

Archivists, librarians, and curators have been crucial to this research from the very beginning. I wish to thank Tamar Brown at the Schlesinger Library on the History of Women in America; Emily Anderson and Jamie Henricks with the Japanese American National Museum; and Malinda Triller Doran, Jim Gerenscer, and Jessica Howard at Dickinson College. I wish especially to thank all the volunteers and professionals at various Girl Scout sites and collections who worked with me, including Linda McBride of the Girl Scouts of Northeast Ohio Archives; Lynn Cutter at the Girl Scout Museum of Cedar Hill in Waltham, Massachusetts; Tanya Tulloch at Our Chalet in Adelboden, Switzerland; Liz Tranter at Pax Lodge in London; Lisa Junkin-Lopez at the Juliette Gordon Low Birthplace; Yevgeniya Gribov and Pamela Cruz at the National Historic Preservation Center of the Girl Scouts of the USA; Page Harrington, vice president of Cultural Assets of the Girl Scouts of the USA; and, most recently, Shannon Browning-Mullis, executive director of the Juliette Gordon Low Birthplace and director of archives. Jane Christyson, CEO of the Girl Scouts of North East Ohio, offered me a tour of Camp Ledgewood. And Frances Hesselbein, former CEO of Girl Scouts of the USA and over 100 years old at the time, graciously agreed to a lengthy interview.

At Dickinson I have a wonderful community of friends and scholars. I want to thank current and former members of my departments—American studies and women's, gender, and sexuality studies—Jerry Philogene, Darren Lone Fight, Jed Kuhn, Cotten Seiler, Anna Neumann, Katie Oliviero, Katie Schweighofer, Megan Yost, and Mireille Rebeiz, as well as my good friends and colleagues Sharon O'Brien, Regina Sweeney, Susan Rose, Adrienne Su, Carol Ann Johnston, Say Burgin, Nico Marini-Maio, Marie Helweg-Larsen, Magda Siekert, Claire Seiler, Wendy Moffat, Alyssa DeBlasio, Siobhan Phillips, Emily Pawley, Sheela Jane Menon, Sarah Kersh, Amanda Cheromiah, Barry Tesman, Sara Markowitz, Heather Flaherty, Andy Bale, Emily Pawley, Robert Pound,

Luca Trazzi, and Renée Cramer, who have shared writing with me, provided opportunities, helped me with teaching, provided last-minute photography, and generally cheered me on. Caroline Radesky, one of my wonderful former students who became a close colleague and friend, tragically died while I was finishing this book; I so wish I could send her the final edits for comments. Heather Ingram and Susan Serafin have been instrumental in helping me to run American studies and to bring this manuscript to a close. I am grateful to those who have supported my work, responded to my writing, and shared their ideas and friendship in such generous ways, including Carlisia McCord, Marie Tessier, Jacqueline Fear-Segal, Alison Kibler, Jennifer Helgren, Corinne Field, Kristine Alexander, Julia Mickenberg, Mara Baldwin, Tari McCormick Bergoine, George Lipsitz, Katie LeBesco, Perin Gurel, and Elaine May.

I'm grateful to those who keep my body and soul going, too—including Michele Landis at Simply Yoga and Fitness; my friend Johanna Tesman, who joins me there; Ruth Busko at Keystone Acupuncture; Jeff Wood from Whistlestop Bookshop, who keeps me stocked with books; and my Deep Listening Group, including Sharon O'Brien, Deb Stille, Virginia Jackson, Laura Rumley, Wendy Gebb, Carole DeWall, and Kim Stone. Kimine Mayuzumi and the Slow Down Circle have been especially helpful. Our writers' group and friendships at Ferry Beach have sustained me in more ways than one. And I will always share a grounding with my dear friends Laurie Santilli, Cindy Nicely, Sue Davis Mellin, Terri Glueck, Nancy Schneiderman, and Kathleen Dillon Narko from Akron, Ohio.

I am so very grateful to my agent Tanya McKinnon, who "got" my project right away and shared generative conversations about its purpose and shape, and to Carol Taylor, who keeps the details straight and who encourages us with her quotations on writing. My deep thanks to my editor Debbie Gershenowitz at the University of North Carolina Press, who immediately understood the stakes of this project. I am grateful to the entire team at UNC Press, including Dino Battista, Alexis Dumain, and Mary Caviness. To the art director Lindsay Starr, wow, I love the cover. Thank you for highlighting those badges I earned in the 1970s, complete with my own stitching. While I was researching and writing this book, my mother Lois Ann (Erdman) Farrell died; even though she was ninety, her feisty spirit, and our daily visits and frequent cocktail hours, made it seem impossible she would ever go. I share my deep grief with my sister Ann Farrell Midgley and brother Kirby Farrell. During this decade we lost so many elders besides my mom; my dad Jim Farrell died years earlier, and more recently we lost Sidney Bloom, Margery (Erdman) Orth, Robert Orth, Sylvia Griffin, and Jackie Farrell. It's hard to lose a generation! I am very grateful for the entire world of my extended family, my mother-in-law Maxine Bloom, my uncle Dick Farrell, my sister-in-law Laura, my cousins Lorraina and Kevin, my nieces and nephews, grandnieces and grandnephews, cousins, and kissing cousins who make a rich tapestry for my life.

My daughter Catherine and my son Nick never cease to amaze me with their creativity, their wit, and their deep and generous love. I am so amazed at the lives they have built for themselves and am ever grateful for our conversations, for our laughter, for our family meals, for sharing new plays and readings with Catherine and conferences and concerts with Nick. John and I are so lucky to have you. And I am so lucky to have John, who sustains me throughout, who is my first reader in everything, whose joy, friendship, and love carry me always.

Intrepid Girls

Chapter 1

Girl Scouts of the USA

RACE, FEMINISM, AND AMERICAN EMPIRE

Girl Scouts saved my life.

In March 1971, my family moved from Cleveland Heights to Akron, Ohio. I was eight years old. Moving to the new school midyear was absolutely dismal. The excitement that had come with my dad's new job at the *Akron Beacon Journal* wore off entirely once I had to actually go to school. I was shy, which made me a particular mark for the girls who called me "cow," taunting me to "push up those glasses," while the boys sitting behind me in class snapped my training bra. I finally told my mother about the boys, and the teacher changed my seat. But there was still enough bullying that when I broke my knee, ending up in a body cast due to complications, I really didn't mind. It meant I didn't have to go to school.

In fifth grade an announcement came that all girls were invited to an after-school Girl Scout troop meeting. I went—I'm not sure why. Joy of joys, none of the boys were there and none of the mean girls either! The leaders asked us if we'd like to go to summer camp, and I paired up with another girl—very skinny to my chubby—who also seemed shy. We stayed in the same tent, canoed together, faced latrine duty as a pair. I encouraged her swimming; she encouraged me to get up when the bugle went off painfully early each morning. We are still best friends. From fifth grade through ninth we attended weekly meetings, reciting the Girl Scout Promise and Law, making sit-upons and Bunsen burners, learning songs, working on badges for hiking, camping, first aid, cooking, skating, writing, travel, dramatics, home repair. I still have my sash and pins: Troop 811, Western Reserve Council, green pins for the years as Brownies, yellow for Juniors, white for Cadettes, and a gold ten-year pin I earned as a Senior. I've even kept a water-damaged photograph from our pilgrimage to the Juliette Gordon Low Birthplace in Savannah, Georgia.

As a girl, I knew I was part of a large organization, one that even stretched globally, as I proudly wore my World Association of Girl Guides and Girl Scouts pin. But my experience of it was small: my troop, my group of thirty or so girls, my loyal leaders. What I knew as I confronted an increasingly tight vise of white, middle-class feminine norms in my new school environment—even thought I wouldn't have used those terms then—was that I found refuge in my small Brownie troop. I could continue to be a child, free of the pressure to look good for boys, encouraged to continue "playing," only now with a road map of badges and outings. I mostly remember laughing—at our own jokes, at our canoeing accidents, at our mishaps starting campfires. Things that would have been a source of mockery and derision in the rest of my life—not having the right clothes or being clunky at physical activities—were not a big deal in Girl Scouts. Instead, my troop encouraged me to be curious and to embrace my desire to learn, so much so that as an adult when I learned that the American Portrait Gallery's 2017 special exhibit on Sylvia Plath had included her Girl Scout uniform and badges to illuminate her early ambition and inquisitiveness, I understood completely.

None of this did we call feminist. Feminism was certainly happening in the 1970s when I was a Girl Scout, but this name was never associated with our troop or the organization in general, at least as far as I knew. It was all about competence, curiosity, engagement in the Wider Opportunities, the name of the two-week Girl Scout trip I took to Washington, DC, in 1976, staying with scouts from all over the country, living in the George Washington University dorms, visiting the Smithsonian and various US government agencies. Of course, all those attributes—curiosity, competence, doing, opportunities—are feminist insofar as they challenge the world of feminine primping and male-dominated sexual harassment that I was escaping. But we never called it feminism. It simply felt like I had entered a parallel, more fun and interesting, and certainly safer world than I was part of at school. It was just an organization—for all girls, as we always learned in our troop, in the stories about the founder Juliette Gordon Low's expansive vision and on the boxes of Girl Scout cookies, which clearly featured pictures of girls of diverse ages, colors, ethnicities, and abilities.

Yet if the cookie boxes of the 1970s showed pictures of a multiracial cast of girls engaging in fun and exploration together, this wasn't my troop or my experience. Troop 811 in the west side of Akron was almost exclusively white.

No one ever talked about this whiteness to us children; it was simply so normal it was invisible, the very air we breathed, the stories we told. Camp Ledgewood, the Girl Scout camp where I spent weeks during the summer and many weekends during the school year, was almost entirely white; I remember one African American counselor. According to the records from Camp Ledgewood, the camp desegregated in 1947, but there was certainly no sign of this in my white world of the 1970s. Just a few miles away from Camp Ledgewood was Camp Mueller, an African American camp started by the Phillis Wheatley Association in 1941; there was no interaction between these camps as far I know, and I was completely unaware of this camp as a child.[1] When we visited the Juliette Gordon Low Birthplace, making the eleven-hour bus drive from northern Ohio to Savannah, Georgia, we stayed in a camp outside Charleston, South Carolina, that we called the "Girl Scout Plantation." We never discussed what it meant that the Girl Scouts had a plantation, never confronted the enslavement of people, never moved beyond a historic nostalgia evocative of *Gone with the Wind*. And we never once learned about the struggles for integration in the South (or North) or the battles over the Juliette Gordon Low Birthplace itself. And when Gloria Scott, the first African American president of the Girl Scouts, came to Akron in 1978, during a Girl Scout summit on leadership, I don't remember being encouraged to think about Scott or to understand the significance of her election to office. I don't remember ever being asked to think about race at all, except in the most superficial of ways, a nod to diversity on the boxes of Girl Scout cookies and in the "all girls" rhetoric of the Juliette Gordon Low lore.

In other words, Girl Scouts wrapped me in a cocoon. In the weekday meetings, the weekend trips, and the summer camping and excursions, Girl Scouts developed my confidence, taught me to be competent in so many things, and gave me respite before I headed back to the hostility I experienced at school. But it also never encouraged me to look sideways, to examine critically the bullying and sexual harassment going on at school, nor did it ever prompt me to cast a critical eye at the foundation below, at the problematic roots that made up the American project and that continued to ensnare people in the web of oppressive racial structures. There were others in the Girl Scouts—and you'll read many of their stories in this book—who did make these connections, and their "seeds of subversion" pushed this crucial organization to change and shift. But for me, as for so many million white girls and women, Girl Scouts carved out a space that discouraged our critical eyes, that cast the organization in a glow of benevolent history and innocent institution building. The approach allowed so many girls to experience an all-female world of empowerment and confidence building right under the watchful eyes of a patriarchy all too fond of keeping girls and women in check; even one of my colleagues told me her family would have never allowed her to join had they been aware of how implicitly feminist the organization was. But it was a dangerous cocoon, because it also taught so many of us, especially if we are white, not to look too closely at either the present systems of oppression or the foundational ones that continue to affect us today. It schooled us in a dangerous innocence.

Intrepid Girls is the story of how this organization that wrapped its arms around me—and tens of millions of other American girls and women—was fundamental to the history of the United States. It was a distinctly American institution, sanctioned by the US government; every First Lady since Edith

As a Junior and a Cadette I camped at Camp Ledgewood in Peninsula, Ohio, where we hiked, swam, canoed, ate at a mess hall, and cooked over open fires. Ostensibly the camp was racially integrated, but I only remember one African American counselor, and no campers, in the time I was there. While writing this book, I learned about Camp Mueller, an African American camp a few miles down the road started in 1941 by the Phillis Wheatley Association. Camp Mueller has closed, and Camp Ledgewood remains one of the few Girl Scout camps still open in Ohio. Courtesy of the author.

In 1975 I traveled with my Akron, Ohio, troop to the Juliette Gordon Low Birthplace in Savannah, Georgia. Here we stand on the stairs to the entrance, an iconic photograph still taken today by the thousands of Girl Scouts who visit the Birthplace annually. Courtesy of the author.

Wilson in 1917 has been the honorary president of the Girl Scouts, and Congress formally chartered the organization in 1950. It was also part of a bigger web, the World Association of Girl Guides and Girl Scouts, whose tentacles reached far, giving Great Britain and the United States a particular avenue to stamp their influence throughout their colonies and territories and in countries around the world. As this distinctly American institution, it was situated squarely in the middle of two major movements that marked the twentieth century: feminism and the fight to end racial oppression. When the founder of the Girl Scouts, Juliette Gordon Low, brought the idea of this new organization to Savannah in 1912, women did not yet have the vote. Most professions and jobs were closed to women. It was illegal even to send information about birth control through the mail. There was no such thing as marital rape, as the husband had a right to sex within marriage. The twentieth-century decades since 1912 saw a continual expansion of women's rights, fought for tenaciously by women across racial and class differences, from the Nineteenth Amendment in 1920 and job opportunities during World War II to a powerful feminist revolution in the 1970s that challenged restrictive laws and practices on every level. Girl Scouting was clearly part of this expansion of women's rights, even if it rarely said so explicitly, teaching girls how to be competent, how to be courageous, how to imagine a life for themselves outside of the narrow confines of domestic structures. And now, in 2025, Girl Scouts are still here, navigating yet a different terrain, one that seeks to roll back the gains they oversaw in the twentieth century.

As an adult, trained in US women's history and American cultural studies, about a decade ago I became profoundly curious about this organization that I remembered through a lens of nostalgic white innocence but now viewed with the eyes of a scholar and feminist. Despite the Girl Scouts' extraordinary reach, the organization has been relatively little studied.

Over 50 million women currently alive in the United States have been Girl Scouts, and the number of alums (the term Girl Scouts use for former members) grows exponentially if we go back to the origins of the organization. That is a staggering number of people who have been under the influence of this national organization. Coupled with its outsize iconic status—those Girl Scout cookies! Those little girls in green uniforms!—it's shocking how relatively little scrutiny this organization has received. Girl Scouting has such a cultural resonance that authors, activists, and pundits can draw on it with alacrity, such as Celeste Ng, who, in her best-selling novel *Little Fires Everywhere*, wrote that "a small crackling fire [had been] set directly in the middle of each bed, as if a demented Girl Scout had been camping there," knowing that her readers would quickly understand the reference.[2]

Yet even as I've won fellowships and awards to study the history of the Girl Scouts, when I describe my work to many people I'm often greeted with a quick laugh and change of subject, perhaps to save me from the embarrassment of having chosen to focus my scholarship on this cute but certainly inconsequential organization. Unfortunately, this response is part of a larger cultural perspective that still refuses to see girls and women as significant, that fails to recognize the centrality of girls and women to human history, that dismisses the study of struggles to loosen the grip of patriarchal power systems. The giggling at my project often turns to complete shock and horror, however, as I share the ways Girl Scouts were part of some of the most difficult chapters of American life: the forced indoctrination of American Indians in the boarding school system, the imprisonment of Japanese Americans, the brutal segregation of African Americans, and the McCarthy-inspired communist witch hunts.

Far from being an amusing or trifling part of American history, Girl Scouting was at the center of the struggles that shaped twentieth-century US life.

Girl Scouts both empowered girls and indoctrinated them to understand the outer limits to which they could push for their own self-determination. Girl Scouting was central to the progressive forces that fought for our highest ideals of democratic inclusivity *and* to the forces that dismantled the early promise of Reconstruction, built a system of Jim Crow, worked to indoctrinate American Indians, and imprisoned Japanese Americans. Those struggles played out in the lives of individual girls like me, in troop decisions, in council debates, and in the policies made by the national board. And these contradictions—the constant push and pull between democratic inclusivity and racism, feminism, and patriarchy—are why the story of the Girl Scouts is fascinating, rich, and crucial to tell.

In 1940, for instance, a white director of camping in the Massachusetts Girl Scout Council, Amy Brewer, asked the board to provide camping opportunities for "colored" girls. The Girl Scout camping director before Brewer had told the board that there was "no need" for the Girl Scout camps to be open to Black girls, as they attended segregated camps run by their own churches and organizations. Brewer, however, brought a new perspective to the table. Possibly it was because she grew up in New Bedford, Massachusetts, where many of the original troops, run by Emma Hall, a white woman who was a friend of Juliette Gordon Low's, were explicitly integrated. Brewer didn't think the Girl Scout policy of excluding Black girls from camps was legal. Isn't there a Massachusetts law, she argued, that said "colored children have the same privileges as white"? How would Black girls have the opportunity to be eligible to become Golden Eaglets, the highest rank in Girl Scouting, if they couldn't get camping experience? It wasn't that Black families were uninterested in sending their girls to Girl Scout camps; it was that the Girl Scout camps in Massachusetts were all-white, a policy so deeply engrained in everyday practice that it wasn't even written out. Black children went to segregated camps, unaffiliated with the Girl Scouts, run by other organizations or churches. But Brewer thought that if Girl Scouting was really for *all girls*, then the camps should be open to everyone. The board waffled, raising questions and concerns about Brewer's plea for Black camping. Brewer countered every objection with an answer. To the argument that there wasn't sufficient Black interest, she came up with the names of Black women interested in leading camping trips and Black ministers seeking opportunities for their girls. To the argument that white families would not like Black girls attending, she pointed out that, although she thought they should be able to attend at any time, the camps could schedule Black troops to attend before or after the regular season. To the question of who would ultimately be responsible, she offered her own time, saying she would be the primary leader. For three years, in meeting after meeting, the board debated and discussed. They suggested sending out questionnaires and asking more questions. They deferred making any decision. Finally, in 1942, the board voted: "It did not seem advisable to have a colored encampment at Cedar Hill," a camp near Boston that Brewer thought would work well and where, ironically, she would eventually have a pavilion named after her.

What happened in Massachusetts, with the fight between Brewer and the Massachusetts Girl Scout Council, was replicated across the country. Despite the voiced mandate of the national Girl Scout organization to bring scouting to *all girls*, the reality was that Girl Scouting was deeply segregated and excluded Black girls. Black troops could form only if there was a white council that would oversee them. Black girls had a right to join scouting, but only if a troop was willing to take them in. Girl Scout camps were white, a practice not always written out in policy but clearly apparent in the very fact that the Massachusetts council debated whether to open camps to Black troops. When camps did open their doors to Black girls, it was usually in one of two ways: either allowing an *individual* girl of extremely high social standing to attend or, as Amy Brewer suggested, allowing a Black troop to attend either before or after the regular camping season, in spring or very late summer. So even if the camps were ostensibly integrated, chances are that white girls attended sessions at the height of the summer, with Black girls "accommodated" during the cold spring or in the weeks just before or even after the school year had started. Girl Scout camp records all reveal segregation and exclusion, certainly in the Jim Crow South but also in the North, the Midwest, and the West. And when someone attempted to break this racial apartheid, the result was just as it had been for Amy Brewer: prevarication, endless discussion, deferral, and then rejection.

In the Girl Scouts, one of the most significant organizations of twentieth-century US history, we can see how racist policies were established and practiced, and we can see the actions of the girls and women who fought for inclusion and change. Significantly, the history of the Girl Scouts illuminates these policies and actions both on a micro level—the skirmish between Brewer and the board, the ways the "polite" delays and deferrals maintained a system of racial apartheid—and on a macro level, as the national board forged policies of racial segregation and as Black, Asian American, American Indian, Latina, and white women and girls fought for change.

As I surveyed the scholarly landscape when I began my research, I found many books on the Boy Scouts—but relatively little about the Girl Scouts.[3]

Much of what I found written about the Girl Scouts was produced by the Girl Scouts organization itself, especially on the 100th anniversary of its founding, and by a cohort of scholars whose work has been instrumental to the writing of this book.[4]

While there is limited work on Girl Scouting per se, there is, however, broad interest in US institutions—from historic sites such as Thomas Jefferson's Monticello to colleges, universities, and major cultural organizations—from scholars, writers, and activists who are examining in detail how the legacies of white supremacy, colonialism, and empire have shaped these institutions, what historian Martha Jones calls "hard histories." One of these has particular resonance for the history of the Girl Scouts: a statue of Theodore Roosevelt, the president of the United States from 1901 to 1909 and a leading conservationist, conqueror of new US territories, and known eugenicist. During the summer of 2020, when Black Lives Matter protests erupted around the world in reaction to police brutality and the killing of Black people, the Museum of Natural History in New York City decided to remove this statue from its front steps. In James Earle Fraser's imposing statue, Roosevelt, strong and virile, sits astride a forward-moving horse while an Indigenous man and an African man, both barely clothed, walk aside, behind, and beneath Roosevelt. The statue clearly illuminates a vision of humanity in which there are explicit hierarchies of civilization; it celebrates the victorious—and apparently benevolent—superiority of the white man, who conquers, explores, and moves forward. The museum removed the statue for its obvious racism, its celebration of the ways that white people extracted resources from Native Americans and Africans, its colonialist vision of conquering new lands and people, and its presumption that Native Americans and Africans are part of the "natural" world that white people civilized.[5] Juliette Gordon Low was formatively shaped by this vision of a British American imperialism, where the superior white worlds took hegemonic power over lands across the globe. This was not a hidden agenda but an explicit one, assumed to be the natural and ideal order of the world. The very first handbook for Girl Scouts was taken directly from Lord Robert Baden-Powell's book for Girl Guides in England, *How Girls Can Help to Build Up the Empire*. Low simply switched the title to the more American-sounding *How Girls Can Help Their Country*. While Low never saw this statue of Teddy Roosevelt, I think she would have been troubled by it, not for its racism or its vision of conquering and domination but for its total erasure of women. The absence of women in the action of the nation became a fire that spurred Low on. The Girl Scouts inserted themselves into this national story, imagining themselves not as guides who would help Roosevelt on a parallel but inferior track but as girls who themselves would go and save the world, as courageous pioneers, ready and able to move into unknown worlds—often men's worlds that had been closed to them. Like the critics of the Roosevelt statue, *Intrepid Girls* asks us to think about Juliette Gordon Low and the founding of the Girl Scouts in new ways. What did it mean for the Girl Scouts that Low brought with her the legacy of this white domination?

With the 100th anniversary of women's suffrage, scholars and others have challenged a narrative that typically focused on white activists such as Elizabeth Cady Stanton, Susan B. Anthony, and Alice Paul. These reconsiderations focus deeply on the experiences of suffragists of color and, in looking both backward and forward from the 1920 date of US women's suffrage, ask key questions about the lasting influence of the suffrage movement on the racial politics of national and international feminisms and on US citizenship in general. They see moments of racialized exclusion and discrimination not as unfortunate roadblocks in the overall positive history of women's suffrage but as integral to its endeavor from the beginning.[6]

Similarly, this book asks us to view an organization for girls that has lasted for over 100 years through a different lens, one that reveals how Girl Scouts fostered hierarchies of citizenship, of belonging, and of racialized and gendered orders, which resonate and percolate today. It weaves in new areas of inquiry that focus particularly on race, inclusivity, and whiteness. I am especially interested in Girl Scouting's promise to be an organization for *all girls*—though this is less a question of how its procedures and policies allowed for this adaptability than an exploration of how this goal was both a *promise* and a *threat*. To clarify, Girl Scouting's inclusive promise was often just that: a promise unfulfilled, limited by an implicit and sometimes explicit acceptance of white supremacy and by discriminatory practices and beliefs that prevented girls and women of color from fully participating. What did these struggles for full inclusion look like, both within the national organization and among girls and women of color who wanted to participate fully? Girl Scouting's inclusive promise could also be seen less as promise than as threat, an insistence, bolstered by US state power, on expanding into territories and cultures where it was unwanted—such as Indian boarding schools and World War II Japanese American incarceration centers—and where, even if wanted, it did the ideological and social work of an empire on the move. Its work of inclusivity was often that which Ibram Kendi calls "assimilationist" racism, the belief that people of color are inherently inferior—in culture and perhaps in biology—and need to be "raised" to the standard of white people. Assimilationist racists eschew the violence and meanness of segregationists, Kendi points out, but they maintain a belief in the superiority and normalcy of white people.[7] Girl Scouts clearly saw its mission—the helping hands, the sisterhood—as one in which the needy, the less privileged, ultimately the "inferior," could be assimilated to a better standard. It did this while nurturing empowering feelings—of joy, of patriotism, of confidence, of competence, of a belief in girls and an overarching sisterhood. How did this work out on the ground, I wondered, this mash-up of protofeminism, manifest destiny, and an impressive mix of what we might call affective engineering—the cultivation of what scholar Sara Ahmed would call a "culture" of emotions, in this case the "positive" feelings of sisterhood and helping others?[8]

To explore these questions, I immersed myself in the national archives of the Girl Scouts in New York City, which houses the records of the national organization from its origins to the present. I delved into the *Girl Scout Leader*, *American Girl* magazine, and Girl Scout novels and short stories. I traveled to the Juliette Gordon Low Birthplace in Savannah, where I also explored the archives of the Girl Scout First Headquarters and of the Georgia Historical Society. I visited Our Chalet in Adelboden, Switzerland, the first international Girl Guide–Girl Scout center, as well as Pax Lodge in London. I pored over oral histories and newspaper articles by people who had been students at federally sponsored Indian boarding schools and at Japanese American incarceration centers. At the Harvard Radcliffe Institute I delved into the records of the Massachusetts Girl Scout Council. I visited the archives of the Girl Scouts Commonwealth of Virginia, which includes the records of one of the first African American troops in the South. And I returned to Ohio, where I visited Camp Ledgewood, the camp I had attended in my youth, and studied the archival record of the Western Reserve Girl Scout Council, which had governed my own troop.

There are so many Girl Scout records scattered across the country and around the world—the Girl Scout national archive only houses the records of the national organization, not of councils or troops, which are kept (or not kept) at the discretion of each local organization. There will never be one complete work that can cover the history of the Girl Scouts in its entirety, and this book certainly does not even attempt to do that. The sheer *amount* of information precludes any completely definitive history. But the inability to ever tell a definitive story is about more than the vast amount of information. It's also about the archives one chooses to study, to curate, to amass. The archives a researcher chooses shape the very questions she asks, whose perspectives emerge, what stories come to light, and which remain hidden. Archival research favors written records, which is why oral history is so important to moving past the official story. Archival research also favors the records that were actually kept—perhaps an obvious point but one that is so important to keep in mind. Organizations can choose to destroy records and hide information, explicit attempts to cover up the past. But institutions may also choose never to record or to discard material about issues, people, and ideas they consider unimportant, which is why scholars who study women, people of color, and everyday life look to different kinds of sources to illuminate the past.[9] This book, drawing so heavily from the Girl Scout national records, is tilted toward the way the national organization thought and moved. As I read the material I looked for patterns, for changes, for the ways that the national organization narrated its policies and its decisions—and I also looked for gaps, for silences, for the ways that reading against the grain might allow us to consider more fully the significance of the Girl Scouts and the ways girls and women shaped and experienced those policies.

One of the major silences in the Girl Scout national archives is sexuality; there is very little about sex, about sexuality, even about reproduction. It's not surprising. The Girl Scouts wanted to get away from thinking of girls as solely sexual beings—the point was to remove girls from the constrictions of heterosexual, heterosocial life, to allow them to build and grow in other areas. Girl Scouts also used this narrative of "innocence" to protect itself from the various forces and organizations that worked to undermine the Girl Scouts: conservative Catholic organizations, the Boy Scouts (particularly in the early decades), and the American Legion. As sexuality, particularly women's sexuality, is inherently perceived as dangerous, not innocent, it's not unexpected that Girl Scouts rarely spoke about sex. But one also has to wonder about records that were deliberately hidden or destroyed—those that related to lesbian life among Girl Scouts, to leaders and girls whose sexual orientations were deliberately "overlooked" by Girl Scout officials, to the stories of leaders and girls whom Girl Scouting removed from the organization because of their sexuality. And while there was no evidence that I found of violence or wrongdoing, we know that other powerful institutions—religious, educational, sporting—have hidden records of sexual misconduct, harassment, and violence; thus, one has to note the absence of this discussion in the official archival record.

While sexuality is the most obvious example of an archival absence, there are certainly others, sometimes ones we don't even recognize as an absence. As I conducted my research over the years, I looked for places where the archives might lead us to the voices, experiences, and emotions of girls and women who were not necessarily archived in the national records, thus the oral histories, the local records, the scrapbooks, the newspapers, and the novels. There is *so much* these archives offer—the stories of particular time periods, of girls in so many different contexts, of complex, contradictory social histories. I urge anyone—scholars, journalists, writers, graduate students, former Girl Scouts—who wants to explore the lives and histories of girls, the nation, social organizations, bodies, and the empire at work to draw from this rich and largely unexamined trove of voices and actions kept in both large and small archives.

This book proceeds in a generally chronological direction, from the orgins of scouting through the present. Within each chapter there is some movement backward and forward, especially as I linger on the ways that Girl Scouts have represented these histories and the way that my own experience wove itself through these moments. Chapter 2 begins with the myth of the founder of the Girl Scouts, Juliette Gordon Low, contrasting the powerful, legendary stories about her with the more difficult facts about her life and the founding of the Girl Scouts, such as battles with the Boy Scouts organization and the controversial financial underpinnings of the organization, which ultimately stemmed from the enslavement of Africans and the taking of Indigenous lands. Chapter 3 explores the ways that early Girl Scout handbooks, novels, films, and camps created a sense of ideal white girlhood. This chapter particularly illuminates the ways that the Girl Scouts emphasized the heroism of the "pioneer" and used the concept of the "helping hand" to legitimate its protofeminism. It also introduces how white supremacy worked within the organization, both explicitly (the national organization used an extensive system of "segregated inclusivity") and implicitly (the national organization legitimated its exclusionary policies through presumptions of incompetence among girls and women of color). Chapter 4 turns to the work of the Girl Scout "field workers," who brought Girl Scouting to girls on reservations and in American Indian boarding schools. The chapter contrasts the implicit feminism of the white women who traveled alone through the West with their attempts to "give back" those Indigenous skills and crafts (i.e., camping and woodworking) that the US government had worked so diligently to destroy among American Indians. The chapter thus explores the ways that Girl Scouting was part of the US cultural genocide of American Indians even as it portrayed itself as a "helping hand." Chapter 5 situates the Girl Scouts more firmly as an international organization, one whose tentacles and ambitions reached far beyond the boundaries of the United States. The international sisterhood that the World Association of Girl Guides and Girl Scouts promised is particularly ironic when one turns to chapter 6, which focuses on the complex and often contradictory role of Girl Scouting during and after the forced relocation and incarceration of Japanese Americans.

Chapter 7 takes the long view of attempts by Black women to integrate Girl Scouting, challenging the separate inclusiveness that the national office condoned. In its first four decades, Girl Scout policy allowed Black troops to be organized only under the supervision of white councils and restricted camping opportunities for Black girls. African American leaders pressured the organization to change these policies by the late 1940s, but as the struggle over the founding of the Juliette Gordon Low Birthplace in 1954 illuminates, this fight was far from over even through the 1950s and 1960s. Chapter 8 explores the concerted right-wing attack on the Girl Scouts during the 1940s and 1950s, focusing on its "un-American" activities, many of those related to international sisterhood and antiracist educational efforts. Lingering on these accusations of communism, this chapter has us consider the subversive seeds carried within the Girl Scout organization. Chapter 9 focuses on the late 1960s through the 1990s, when Girl Scouting could no longer elude confrontation with the civil rights and women's movements. The organization rethought its policies toward girls of color, welcomed Betty Friedan to its national board, and elected its first African American board president, Gloria Scott, ushering in a new paradigm of "diversity." As the decades moved forward into the 1980s and 1990s, however, Girl Scouts faced a backlash, which resulted in decisions to retreat from its more progressive stances.

Chapter 10 changes course by turning to a significant moment of my own Girl Scout history, my troop's 1975 pilgrimage to the Juliette Gordon Low Birthplace and the Girl Scout Plantation. This chapter is the most autobiographical, taking a deep look at how my own story is implicated in the larger narrative of US history, racism, and feminism. It's also a difficult chapter, as it uncovers the painful stories of enslavement and brutality that were the bedrock of the very joyful trip I took to Savannah with my Girl Scout friends.

The book's penultimate chapter speculates about what the role of Girl Scouting is in an era that encompasses the #MeToo and Black Lives Matter movements, the decision by Boy Scouts to welcome girls, and transgender people's claims for inclusion. What does feminism mean when you don't speak it loudly? What does diversity mean when you don't attend to the past? And the final chapter reflects on why and how the Girl Scouts has had a complicated history since Juliette Gordon Low's day, which continues to the present.

Threading through all these chapters are a number of shared and contradictory observations: Ostensibly an organization devoted to democratic participation and a commitment to "all girls," the Girl Scouts nevertheless upheld discriminatory policies for decades. It also overlooked exclusionary practices and accepted excuses for racism and imperialism if they seemed necessary to maintain cohesion as a national and international organization. Even its protofeminist work to create new opportunities for girls was tightly linked to its ideals of white girlhood and womanhood. At the same time, girls and women of color drew inspiration from the Girl Scout promise of inclusivity, shaping Girl Scouting into meaningful activities both when it was thrust upon them, as it was in American Indian boarding schools and Japanese American incarceration centers, and when they had to fight for participation, as when African American girls and women pressured the national organization for opportunities for camping and troop formation.

While chapter 10 is the most autobiographical section of the book, there are echoes of my own experiences with Girl Scouting throughout: Those first summer camps I attended—Farm Weeks and Pioneer Week—are straight from the founding myths of the Girl Scouts. The encouragement to be outgoing, curious, competent, and a friend to other scouts—which courses throughout the history of the Girl Scouts—was so clearly central to my own experience. But other aspects were interestingly absent from my own experience, or at least my memory of it. For instance, I never remember doing any "good works" in our troop, an embarrassing omission—but perhaps a surprisingly good thing, considering the extent to which these good works were often performative masks that allowed unchecked beliefs in cultural superiority. But mostly these absences surround questions of race, which is typical of the privilege of whiteness, where whiteness goes unmarked and the struggles of people of color go unnoticed. This was, I realize now, typical of Girl Scout strategy on a national level—it was "fine" to include people of color, it was good to encourage girls to try out worlds that had historically been closed to us, but don't do it very loudly. That is, the Girl Scouts chose over and over to "take cover," to protect the organization from conservative forces by never explicitly "saying" "antiracism" or "feminism." While these silences may have sometimes shielded Girl Scouts from conservative attack, however, they also encouraged a complacent inability to see and a resistance to seeing their own complicity in racist structures, actions, and beliefs.

Girl Scouts, as I said earlier, saved my life. But it was also part of a complex set of institutions and structures that created and allowed systems of racism and white supremacy to flourish and that encouraged a type of quiet feminism that all too often did not speak directly about explicit forms of oppression and power structures. We need to be able to see how twentieth- and twenty-first-century Girl Scouts was both a force for change and an institution that implicitly and explicitly supported structures of racism and white women's ongoing racial privilege. The refusal to engage with these difficult and disappointing histories continues, unfortunately, to characterize much of white feminism in the United States. This book, then, is my own attempt to confront the past of Girl Scouting, to see the ways that the machinations of empire and of racism were closely intertwined with the development of mainstream feminism. I wrote this book as a model of the kind of complex feminist history that we need, history that recognizes the roots of the organizations that shape us and the ways that we participate in racialized power structures. Girl Scouting was an extraordinary gift in my life. Because of this, I feel a profound responsibility to confront and share its history—the complex, the difficult, and the inspiring—to see how we might live up to its potential to create the better world and the sisterhood that it promised.

Chapter 2

Origin Stories

THE MYTH AND MEMORY OF JULIETTE GORDON LOW

• • • • • •

Come right over. I've got something for the girls of Savannah, for all of America, and all of the world. And we're going to start it tonight!

—Juliette Gordon Low, 1912

Any consideration of the Girl Scouts needs to begin with its founder, Juliette Gordon Low—or, to be more exact, it needs to begin with the *story* of the founder, both what we know to be true and what we know about how this story shifted shape to serve different purposes. The *myth* of Juliette Gordon Low is grand and sweeping, standing in for the development and purpose of the institution itself—so much so that her birthplace is known within the organization as simply the Birthplace, creating an interesting collapse between the birth of Low herself and the birth of the organization, a merging between person and institution that remains to this day. This myth is also frequently misleading, obscuring difficult truths about the history of both Low and the Girl Scouts as an organization.

Surfacing most frequently in these mythic retellings of Low's life and the founding of the Girl Scouts are the supposed words she spoke to her cousin Nina Pape, which appear in nearly every biography and children's book about Low. On returning to Savannah from England in 1912, the story goes, Low quickly made a phone call to her cousin: "Come right over!" she exclaimed to

Pape, adding, "I've got something for the girls of Savannah, for all of America, and all of the world. And we're going to start it tonight!" It's no surprise the quotation gets repeated frequently. It evokes Low's burning enthusiasm—even impatience—for the gift of scouting to be given to girls everywhere. And even more important, the words speak to the promise of inclusivity that marked Low's vision and the foundation of this organization from its origins. Most girls and women familiar with the Girl Scouts will know this "I've got something for all the girls of America" quotation; I certainly did, as it had a prominent place in my well-worn *Girl Scout Junior Handbook* from the 1970s, just as it had in the handbooks from the 1940s, '50s, and '60s. And if you looked up the Girl Scouts in 2021, you would have found this same quotation on the Girl Scouts of the USA website. Explaining that Low "descended from a long line of strong and independent women," the website repeated the story about her call to Nina Pape when she returned to Savannah. After describing the first meeting in the United States, the text continued, "From that first gathering of a small troop of 18 culturally and ethnically diverse girls, Juliette broke the conventions of the time—reaching across class, cultural, and ethnic boundaries to ensure all girls, including those with so-called disabilities, had a place to grow and develop their leadership skills."[1] Of course this pithy quotation is repeated frequently—it evokes her enthusiasm, her passionate interest in girls, and above all, a vision of inclusivity of which the Girl Scouts organization is very proud.

There is one key problem, however. It's questionable whether the quotation is true. Like much of what gets repeated about Juliette Gordon Low, the original source is a 1928 collection of remembrances, *Juliette Low and the Girl Scouts*, compiled by Juliette's goddaughter and Girl Scout volunteer Anne Hyde Choate and Helen Ferris, an editor of the Girl Scout publication *American Girl*. The quotation shows up in an essay that Edith Johnston, the first Girl Scouts national secretary, wrote about Low for Choate and Ferris's collection. Apparently Nina Pape told Johnston about this conversation at some point, and sixteen years after the ostensible phone call, Johnston included it in her reminiscence about Low; significantly, Johnston had not heard the conversation herself.[2] After Johnston penned the memory of the quotation for the Choate and Ferris book, the lines began to pick up momentum, getting repeated in nearly every publication about Low's life and the origins of the Girl Scouts.[3]

Whether or not Juliette Gordon Low actually said these oft-quoted words to Nina Pape is a big question mark—it is literally a question of phone tag, someone's memory of a story about someone else's remembered phone conversation. And it turns out that Johnston did not even write the essay in the original 1928 collection! In 1952, she submitted a long, handwritten retraction to the Georgia Historical Society, in which she wanted to "set the historic record straight," most likely because she actually found Low a "most difficult person" despite the fact that she had been "put on a pedestal, and treated almost, as someone has said, as a saint." It turns out that Johnston had shared a few pages of memories with Ferris, but without any explanation or forewarning, Ferris wrote an essay under Johnston's name, drawing on some of those details but embellishing it with many others. It came as a complete surprise to Johnston, who wrote an impassioned letter to Choate soon after receiving a copy of the book, imploring Choate to take her name off the essay. Choate declined, apologizing but saying that Ferris had written or rewritten most of the essays, with "little stories" and details added to make the volume richer. "The purpose of the book is principally to keep Daisy's [i.e., Juliette's] memory bright for the oncoming generations of Girl Scouts," Choate explained. In other words, the purpose of the 1928 *Juliette Low and the Girl Scouts* was to create a mythic memory that might serve the movement for generations. It really had nothing to do with the "truth."[14]

It's important for us to establish how flimsy the historical record here is, especially as it has served as the basis for almost every biographical retelling of Low's life. Even if Juliette Gordon Low did actually say this line to her cousin Nina Pape, however limited the evidence for this actually is, was it true on a more abstract level? Is the spirit of that line authentic, even if its wording was off or such a phone call never existed? On the one hand, the evidence suggests that Juliette Gordon Low was indeed burning with a passion for the Girl Scouts that started when she led Girl Guide groups in England in 1911, which carried over to her decades of work for US Girl Scouts and international Girl Scouting and Guiding until her death in 1940. But was Juliette Gordon Low as inclusive as this quotation indicates? Did she really believe that all girls could and should become Girl Scouts? Was the Girl Scouts actually a democratic, integrated organization from its origins, which this telephone conversation suggests?

Juliette Gordon Low and the Question of Race

The powerful mythology and origin story of the Girl Scouts delineate an organization that was broadly inclusive and democratic, but the reality was something quite different. Juliette Gordon Low was very much a woman of her time, who did indeed imagine something expansive and fun for girls. Her vision, though, was firmly shaped by a racial context of white supremacy and extreme wealth. Her ideals might be described as inclusive, but that inclusivity meant that every group of girls needed to remain in its "appropriate" place, within a class, racial, and gender hierarchy that did not fundamentally disrupt the status quo. And even that inclusivity had limits. For instance, despite a very active feminist movement pulsating across the country by the early twentieth century, she did not believe in woman suffrage. For many white wealthy women—and that would include Low—suffrage meant an expansion of voting rights beyond their own elite families, something that would threaten their own class and racial privilege.[5] When early Girl Scout director Edith Johnston (the same one who gave the quotation about Low's phone conversation with Nina Pape) questioned Low on whether Girl Scouts would support suffrage, Low wrote back forcefully: "Girl Scouts are neutral. We will be left out of all political and religious controversies. . . . Our very existence in the community depends on the good will of every citizen. We can't afford to have any enemies or even any adverse criticisms—therefore we must hold aloof from politics and religion. . . . Neither you nor I nor any representative of Girl Scouts have any option about handling a question of suffrage because we have no right to vote at all."[6] As a wealthy, elite white woman who wielded power both in the city of Savannah and in national and international social circles, she could remain "neutral" on politics; this neutrality, however, was really a support for the status quo, because by not taking a stand *for* suffrage, she was allowing nonvoting for women to remain in place.

Not only did Low eschew the need for women's political power, she also had clear ideas about the whiteness of the organization. While she rejected her mother's urging to add the word "white" to the name of the Girl Scouts, she thought Black participation was dangerous—both for white girls and for the organization.[7] For Low, the aim was to grow the Girl Scouts, and this meant maintaining the support of white parents, many of whom would forbid their daughters to join if African American girls were there. Low likely never imagined Black girls as part of "everyone" when she said she had something for all the girls of America. At one point, when she was asked whether Girl Scouts should allow Black children to participate, she replied that every state should decide for itself—and then she added clarification that made her racist ideas clear: "Most of the Girl Scouts would resign, if Negroes were admitted at the South, and you know this is not prejudice as much as it is real knowledge of the harm negroes can do us, when beyond the eye of the leader, and the objections parents would feel to having negroes at the Rally, for many can and do corrupt other [i.e., white] children."[8] This quotation—with its emphasis on the "knowledge" about dangerous Black girls and its presumption that parents and girls were *white* parents and girls—gives a far different picture of Juliette Gordon Low than the "all the girls of America" quote suggests. And even small gestures, such as a journalist's photograph of First Lady Edith Wilson's meeting with a small group of Black girls—in their handmade Girl Scout uniforms—created controversy for the early Girl Scout organization and for Low, as it suggested national support for Black Girl Scouts.[9] Throughout Girl Scouting's history, African Americans worked hard to be part of it and to shape its future, but that is due to their own efforts and not to the vision of Juliette Gordon Low. When she said "for all the girls of America and for all the world," she certainly did not mean a fully inclusive organization for everyone but rather a clearly segregated and definitely limited inclusivity. There were different tiers of "everyone," and some people, depending on the context, needed to be explicitly left out if the organization were to flourish, according to its founder.

For generations of girls and women who have come to venerate Juliette Gordon Low as a model of intrepid and courageous womanhood, as a leader who fostered fun and competence for girls, as a founder who predicated her organization on ideals of inclusivity, friendship, and fairness, it's difficult to think that the fabled phone call might be untrue, both literally and on a more conceptual level. Girl Scouts have continually highlighted the story of Juliette Gordon Low as its founder, a sort of saint whose vision conjured and her work blossomed this growing organization; even the fact that her birthplace has come to be a stand-in for the origins of the organization itself is a crucially important point to note. Low became a kind of national saint, honored as we do the founding fathers: A Liberty ship was named in her honor, SS *Juliette Low*, in 1944; a stamp was made commemorating her in 1948; various elementary schools across the country were named in her honor in the 1950s; the National Portrait Gallery displayed a portrait of her in 1973; she was inducted into the National Women's Hall of Fame in Seneca Falls, New York, in 1979; a federal building in Savannah was named after her in 1983; and on the 100th anniversary of the Girl Scouts' founding, in 2012, President Barack Obama posthumously awarded her the Presidential Medal of Freedom.[10] But like most heroes and heroines, these narratives about her life might inspire, but they also obscure difficult truths. The frequently repeated stories themselves take on new meaning when explored through a lens of race, empire, and imperialism rather than one that emphasizes innocence, courage, and individuality.

Born in 1860, Juliette Gordon came from an extremely wealthy Savannah family, whose prominence in the city can still be seen in the name of Gordon Square, the imposing obelisk with her grandfather's name engraved on it, and the streets that still bear their titles. Her grandfather William Gordon was educated at Yale before he returned to the Savannah area, where he established Belmont plantation just outside the city, in Jefferson County, and founded the Central Railroad and Banking Company. Both of these lucrative enterprises were completely dependent on a system of chattel slavery. Most obvious, of course, the wealth procured from the cotton grown on the plantations was extracted from the labor of enslaved people, but also the sale of people themselves provided wealth, particularly after Congress legally terminated the transatlantic slave trade in 1808. In Georgia, the number of enslaved people grew rapidly even after Congress banned the slave trade, from about 189,000 in 1820 to almost 281,000 in 1840; while some of this came from the illegal importation of enslaved people, particularly in the Savannah port, it also came from the forced pregnancies of enslaved women and the continued enslavement of their children. In such a context, plantation owners' wealth grew not just from growing cotton but also from increasing their "stock" in enslaved people, who could be used to labor more on the plantation itself or could be sold for profit. The railroad system was integral to the profit-making in this system of plantation-based chattel slavery. William Gordon devoted his business acumen to the building of the railroad, a transportation system that could reach deep into Georgia, where the plantation system had grown, particularly with the expulsion of Creek and then Cherokee Indians. The railroad allowed the cotton grown on plantations to be brought to markets on the East Coast and in the North, movement necessary for the system to flourish.[11]

Juliette's father, William "Willie" Washington Gordon II, inherited shares in the railroad system as well as Belmont Plantation from his father. In addition, he built up a very prosperous cotton-brokering business, Tison and Gordon, in Savannah, in an industry completely dependent on the institution of slavery.[12] In the same year that Juliette was born, 1860, Georgia had over 462,000 enslaved people, more than 40 percent of the population of Georgia. The city of Savannah, where Juliette was born, had a population of 22,000; 700 of these were free Blacks, and 7,000 were enslaved. The Gordon family was integral in the system of enslavement. Besides the enslaved people on their own plantation and on those from which they bought and traded cotton, they had slaves in their Savannah home. The 1860 census records show Juliette's grandmother Sarah Gordon, who lived with Juliette and her family, as owning twenty-one enslaved people, ranging in age from a baby girl to a fifty-year-old woman.[13] As a prominent family, the Gordons were involved in governing this system: Juliette's grandfather was a lawyer, a legislator, and the mayor of Savannah, positions in which he could ensure the continuation of a system of brutal enslavement that made it extraordinarily dangerous and lethal for enslaved Black people to resist and where the liberty of the few free Black people was always in question. Juliette's father fought proudly for the South to retain the system of chattel slavery, serving as an officer in the Georgia Hussars, one of the Southern military regiments.[14]

The removal and genocide of Indigenous peoples was also key to the accumulation of wealth on both Juliette's father's and mother's sides of the family. In Savannah, the land on which the Gordons lived, farmed, and did business had previously been occupied by Creeks and Cherokees, who had been pushed out to the west, most famously on the 1838 Trail of Tears, in order for white settlers to use the land for the plantation system, which depended on enslaved labor.[15] Juliette's mother, raised in Chicago, grew up amid the wealth and property her grandparents had accrued through the roles they played in European expansion into the Midwest and dispossession of Native Americans, a process that Juliette's great-grandmother Juliette August Magill Kinzie immortalized in her 1856 book *Wau-Bun: The Early Day in the Northwest.*[16] While popular history often notes the Kinzies as the founders of Chicago, that title actually belongs to Haitian Jean Baptiste Point du Sable, the first settler, but his claim as the "first" often gets overlooked in favor of the white Kinzies.[17] *Wau-Bun* details, in particular, the period in the 1830s when Kinzie's husband dispersed annuity payments for the Ho-Chunk (Winnebago) people's lands that had been lost in various earlier treaties. Significantly, *Wau-Bun*, whose title means "the dawn, the break of day" in Ojibway, continues to be displayed and sold prominently in Girl Scouts of the USA gift shops—at least as of 2017—both at the national headquarters in New York City and at the Juliette Gordon Low Birthplace in Savannah. In those contexts, *Wau-Bun* signifies not genocide and obliteration, trickery and deception, or even the just rewards of a legitimate fight but rather a romantic vision of authentic pioneer adventures, friendly respect for Native peoples and cultures, and above all, the plucky spirit of the brave female narrator. What is not underscored, in either the book itself or certainly in its gift shop display, is the fact that Low's great-grandfather John Kinzie brought an enslaved person with him when he settled the Chicago area and was known as a fierce and hard-dealing man, unafraid to threaten life, plying Native Americans with liquor, and dealing fiercely with the various Indian tribes with which he "traded." Also unspoken is the fact that, as a result of the 1832 Sauk wars, the Winnebago ceded all land in what is now Illinois and Wisconsin. This meant that the Kinzies—Juliette's great-grandparents—laid claim to extensive land centrally located in the emerging city of Chicago, cementing their wealth and prominence.[18]

Edward Hughes painted this portrait of Juliette Gordon Low in 1887, soon after her marriage to William Low. It now hangs in the Smithsonian's National Portrait Gallery, a gift of the Girl Scouts of the USA. While this may be the most well-known image of Low, she much preferred images of herself in the Girl Scout uniform. Edward Hughes, National Portrait Gallery, Smithsonian Institute, NPG. 73.5.

Juliette's perspective on the world was shaped by her immersion in this elite American world, where she grew up moving easily between wealthy homes in the North and South, staffed fully with servants (enslaved or formerly enslaved in the South), and attending prestigious boarding schools. At age twenty-six she married William "Willie" Low, a very wealthy British American cotton factor with businesses in both the United States and England.

It's not surprising that Willie Low had a business in Savannah, as business enterprises had had close ties between this Eastern US port city and England since the advent of the transatlantic slave trade.[19] Although Juliette's family did not approve of her fiancé Willie due to his extravagant lifestyle, the union did mean a cementing of international wealth based on the vestiges of the transatlantic slave trade and racialized capitalism. For decades, Juliette largely lived among the British aristocracy, and the Lows owned expensive homes in Savannah, Scotland, and London, as well as stocks and properties throughout the United States and the British empire. She traveled regularly to outposts of the British empire, entertained by British officers and thrilled by the adventures these "exotic" lands afforded.[20] She enjoyed luxurious surroundings and depended on servants to care for these properties and for herself; after her marriage, relatives noted that "her main problem was with English servants, whom she found to be a very different breed from the happy-natured Negroes she had been accustomed to all her life."[21] In other words, she presumed that her status was both natural and deserved, she thought that servants should cheerfully take care of her, and she came from a family who perceived Black servants as particularly "happy" with their position.

The doubts that Juliette's family had about her marriage proved true, as Willie was an unfaithful husband who spent more time at racetracks and with his mistress than with Juliette. Before he was successful in securing a divorce, however, Willie died, leaving Juliette—after she successfully fought his will, which left the bulk of his estate to his mistress—a wealthy woman. She inherited their beautiful home in Savannah, money, land, and shares in the cotton factoring business. That, along with her yearly allowance from her own father and various business and railroad shares she owned on her own in the United States, meant that she was a *very* wealthy woman. Her social ties among the wealthy in the United States and the aristocracy in England made her cultural capital even greater.

In her late forties, childless and recently widowed, Juliette Gordon Low learned about scouting directly from its creator, Lord Robert Baden-Powell, an elite British military hero who feared the weakening of British white masculinity as Great Britain fought to maintain its global territories. Baden-Powell established scouting for boys and then, as an offshoot, guiding for girls, both of which were attempts to thwart racial degeneracy and ensure the longevity of the British empire with its colonial rule over India, South Africa, and territories throughout the world. Baden-Powell had made a name for himself as chief of staff and then major general of the British army in late nineteenth-century African wars, resisting both African attempts to reclaim lands in the Second Matabele War and Dutch attempts to overthrow British rule in the Second Boer War.[22] His various publications became quite famous, including his 1884 *Reconnaissance and Scouting* and then his series of articles, Aids to Scouting, first published in the magazine *Boys of the Empire* in 1900. Like Teddy Roosevelt in the United States, Baden-Powell thought physical toughness, outdoor acumen, and techniques of espionage could strengthen a British masculinity weakened by an overly urban, intellectual life; he encouraged the groups of boys who organized themselves into variously named "Baden-Powell" brigades and leagues.[23] Baden-Powell's wisdom about scouting and outdoor life came not only from his own experiences building empire and overthrowing resistance in Africa, and then India, but also from the information he gleaned from Frederick Russell Burnham, a military scout in the US Indian Wars in Western North America. Real-life "adventures" mixed generously with fantasy myth and storytelling, as Baden-Powell was fascinated not only with the "facts" of North American pioneer life and scouting but also with cowboy and Indian stories and *Buffalo Bill's Wild West Show*, which toured both the United States and Europe. According to Low's biographer Stacy Cordery, Baden-Powell even "adopted the trademark cowboy neckerchief and Stetson hat for use in Africa."[24] The ideological and cultural push for the scouts, then, emanated from two colonial impulses: that of the British empire's military expansion and imaginary and that of American expansion into Indian territory in North America and all the cultural ideology that accompanied and legitimated that conquest.

Low became enamored of Baden-Powell's scouting enterprises, both his own adventures as a military man and his formation of groups for youth. British military officers had long captivated Low—though she apparently eschewed any of their romantic advances after her husband died—and she was quickly smitten with Baden-Powell, his war heroics, and his plan for British youth. Baden-Powell encouraged her to take on the responsibility of leading some Girl Guide groups; Girl Guides had sprung up somewhat organically among British girls who wanted to join in on the fun of scouting. Baden-Powell was not particularly interested in an organization for girls, but he was happy for his sister Agnes to take on the responsibility, and he persuasively encouraged Low to become involved. Low agreed to lead a group of working-class girls in Scotland, teaching them to tie knots, drill, clean their teeth, and learn the laws and promise of Girl Guiding—but not scouting. When girls had first begun forming their own scouting organizations, emulating the boys' groups, they also named themselves "scouts"; a national outcry in Britain arose, however, claiming that these groups were unsuitable for girls, who were "aping" boys and becoming masculine girls. Agnes Powell made a case for a distinct organization, Girl Guides, which would be kept separate from the boys' groups (limiting the possibility of sexual encounters and gender impropriety) and whose purpose would include learning both the intrepid skills of scouting but also the domestic virtues demanded of young women. By 1912 the organization printed the first Girl Guide handbook, *How Girls Can Help to Build Up the Empire*, which in the United States would become *How Girls Can Help Their Country*. Both the "scouting" and "guiding" labels sprang directly from the experience of British imperial mission. "Scouts" were the British soldiers in Africa and India, who were literally scouting out areas for British colonial maneuvers; it's also the name given to white American settlers moving into North American Indian territory, something that also endeared Baden-Powell to the term. "Guides," in contrast, was the name Baden-Powell had given to Indians who had served under him in Northwest India in the 1870s, helping and "guiding" him in his expedition. In other words, he chose the word he used to describe his "loyal" servants, a racialized other, to describe the group of girl children who would join in his new endeavor; there was never a sense that either the Indian guides or the Girl Guides were equal to the British military scouts or the British Boy Scouts. The terms themselves both reflected and cemented gendered and racialized hierarchies.[25]

In 1912, Low returned to the United States, bringing with her a determination to introduce Girl Guiding. She was by all accounts a vibrant, energetic woman, whose interests and talents meshed perfectly with the ethos of Girl Guiding. She loved the out-of-doors, she'd had pets since she was a young girl (including parrots as an adult), and she loved the arts, both amateur playacting and the visual arts, in which she immersed herself. She was both an accomplished portrait painter and sculptor, even taking lessons in iron forging to learn the skills to create the gates at her home in Savannah. She was, according to so many remembrances of her, a "character," a description likely coming both from the fact that she did indeed fall outside the norm of the time, as she had no children of her own and a tumultuous marriage, and from the fact that she was sometimes distracted and erratic, someone for whom action was more interesting than contemplation. She also had a severe hearing problem in

Juliette Gordon Low (*right*) posing with the founder of the Boy Scouts and her inspiration for the Girl Scouts, Lord Robert Baden-Powell, and his much younger wife, Olave Baden-Powell, circa 1919. Courtesy of the Girl Scouts of the Commonwealth of Virginia and Commonwealth Council of the Girl Scouts of Virginia Records, 1910–2012, collection no. M 400, Special Collections and Archives, James Branch Cabell Library, Virginia Commonwealth University, Richmond

both ears, caused first by an infection she incurred as a young child in one ear and then by a rare and unfortunate accident during her wedding, when a piece of rice lodged in the other. The treatments she received appeared to make her hearing worse, rather than better. She never allowed this disability to stop her, however, generally moving forward confidently despite her hearing problem. This may have also added to her reputation as a "character," considering that her comments may not have always matched the topic of conversation. All of these traits—her enthusiasm for the outdoors, for learning new skills, and for confidence in the face of adversity—made her temperamentally quite well suited for this new organization, emblematic of the Progressive Era, with its optimistic energy for improvement and action.[26]

Popular stories about the origins of the Girl Scouts suggest that the idea of an all-girl US organization originated with Juliette Gordon Low, but actually there were many groups already in existence: the Camp Fire Girls, most notably, but also smaller groups that already called themselves Girl Scouts or Girl Guides.[27] Low, though, had extraordinary social ties—to Lord Baden-Powell himself as well as to various elite women in both the North and South—that gave her organization more currency than the others, most of which she disliked because of their greater emphasis on domesticity than the program she imagined. For years she fended off competition in order to claim hers as the "real" organization, whose name she had changed from Girl Guides to Girl Scouts because "girls preferred it." She particularly sparred with the founder of the Boy Scouts of America, James West, who initiated lawsuits against the Girl Scouts for using the name "Scouts," which would continue long past her death in 1927. Juliette had a particular knack for pulling in white society women to support her organization; in 1917 she even had First Lady Edith Wilson serve as the first honorary president, a practice that continues to this day.[28] Low herself served as the actual president until 1920, when she stepped down. As the organization grew it became increasingly frustrating for her volunteers and paid staff to work with Low's increasingly erratic behavior, according to her biographers. The move also allowed her to focus more fully on her work with the international World Association of Girl Guides and Girl Scouts. In her last fifteen years of life, she devoted herself to the Girl Scouts and lived her life almost entirely with other women except for her family members. She absolutely loved her Girl Scout uniform: a military-style belted suit in heavy serge, a tie pinned with a trefoil pin, a "state trooper"–style hat, and a blue-and-white ribbon around her neck with the Silver Fish, the prestigious British Girl Guide award. She wore the uniform most every day, and when she died in 1927 after suffering from breast cancer, she was buried in it.[29]

Almost immediately upon her death, the written memorialization of Juliette Gordon Low's life began with Anne Hyde Choate and Helen Ferris's 1928 *Juliette Low and the Girl Scouts: The Story of an American Woman, 1860–1927*. Choate, a wealthy East Coast socialite, was Low's goddaughter and had become the second president of the Girl Scouts after Low stepped down in 1920; Ferris, a graduate of Vassar College, was a prolific writer and the editor of the Girl Scout publication *American Girl*.[30] Together they compiled the 1928 text, a series of essays written by Low herself, her brother and sister, her grandmother, and various early leaders involved with the Girl Scouts. There is even a tribute by Lord Robert Baden-Powell himself. The tone of the collection is one of unbridled celebration of this idiosyncratic and forceful woman, filled with anecdotes about her childhood, her travels, and her unflinching support of the Girl Scouts even when others were less enthusiastic about her mission. There are endearing details about how she used her deafness to the Girl

In 1923 Juliette Gordon Low posed for this portrait in full Girl Scout uniform, an image she much preferred to the 1887 Hughes portrait. Courtesy Harris and Ewing Collection, Library of Congress.

Scouts' advantage, "pretending" she didn't hear when others objected to the way she was conscripting them into her cause. There are many anecdotes about her interactions with slaves and servants, shared not to problematize Low's life but to suggest what a warm, idiosyncratic woman she was. The entire volume is a love letter of sorts to Low and, because it also includes her own words, a love letter from the founder to the Girl Scouts.

Almost every story about Juliette Gordon Low in children's books or Girl Scout publications can be traced back to Choate and Ferris's collection or to a biography published three decades after Low's death, *Lady from Savannah: The Life of Juliette Low*. Gladys Denny Shultz, a professional writer and editor, wrote this biography with the help of Daisy Gordon Lawrence, Low's namesake and niece. (Low was known within her family as Daisy; hence the title of so many books about her and also the name of today's youngest group of Girl Scouts.) Lawrence is also identified as the "first" US Girl Scout, as Low had inscribed her name at the top of the list of the membership roster of the first Savannah troop.[31] Much of *Lady from Savannah* focuses on the "sweeping" history of the Kinzies and the Gordons, a kind of *Gone with the Wind* saga, though Shultz and Lawrence make a point of gesturing to her difficult marriage. Much of the earlier material had ignored this, as a wayward husband and an imminent divorce wasn't, in the eyes of early twentieth-century US culture, very ladylike. While Shultz and Lawrence draw from some of Low's letters and journals, *Lady from Savannah* relies heavily on family lore (including *Wau-Bun*) and the Choate and Ferris book for its details, many of which had already been reproduced in the early children's text *Juliette Low*, written by Mildred Pace in 1947. In other words, for the most part, the stories that make up the legend of Juliette Gordon Low and her founding of the Girl Scouts have largely relied on one source: Choate and Ferris's *Juliette Low and the Girl Scouts*, supplemented by the memories of her in *Lady from Savannah*.[32]

The Children's Mythology of Juliette Gordon Low

It's illuminating to look at many of the myths about Juliette Gordon Low, to see what parts of the history they soften, or emphasize, or redirect, in order to highlight aspects of the history Girl Scouts want to tell about itself and to downplay questionable aspects. The popular histories of the founding of the Girl Scouts and of Low's life, most of them children's books, emphasize a few key strands that are quite interesting to compare to the more general outline of her life, sketched above. The typical version, which shows up mostly in children's books and in some popular books, goes something like this:

Juliette was born just before the Civil War, in Savannah, where her loving family gave her the nickname of Daisy. Family allegiances torn between North and South (her mother was from Chicago, her father a true Southerner) meant that the war was particularly painful for her family, but it also meant she grew up with an all-American perspective that encompassed both regions, enriched additionally by her maternal grandparents' ties to the frontier and Indian communities. She even earned a second nickname, Little Ship under Full Sail, which had supposedly been given to her by Indians visiting her grandfather, in memory of her great-grandmother who had been given the same name by Indians who had captured her on the frontier. As a child she was adventuresome (like her great-grandmother!), loved the out-of-doors (which she largely encountered in expansive lawns in Chicago and on plantations her Southern family owned in Georgia), and was a true animal lover, even supposedly saving a kitten. She always took the side of the underdog. She often had silly reasoning and logic, but that just illuminated how truly pure she was inside. As a young woman she fell madly in love with an equally rich, dapper young man who had homes in both Savannah and England; unfortunately it turned out to be an unhappy marriage, as her husband, lacking the fine military and business qualities of her father, gambled, spent too much money at horse races, and took a mistress. (The children's books sometimes gloss over the mistress, but later biographies emphasize a life reclaimed after an unhappy marriage.) Her life faced additional challenges with the deafness she developed first through childhood infections and then when a piece of rice landed in her ear at her wedding—an omen of the troubles she would face in this ill-fated marriage. As a middle-aged widow with no children to give her purpose, her life felt particularly adrift. After securing the inheritance that her husband had tried to direct to his mistress, she met Lord Robert Baden-Powell, a British military hero who had just started the Boy Scouts and, with his sister Agnes, the Girl Guides. Throwing her life into the development of Girl Scouting (she changed the name once back in the United States) brought Juliette the meaning and direction she had been missing in her childless marriage and socialite widowhood. She had a vision of an organization for all girls, and she single-handedly grew the organization from its original small beginnings in Savannah to its new headquarters in Washington, DC, and then New York City. Finally, she devoted the last years of her life to the World Association of Girl Guides and Girl Scouts. Her intrepid vision, her sacrifice (she even sold her pearls to finance the Girl Scouts' growth), her joyful enthusiasm, and her inclusivity became the bedrock of this organization that transformed the lives of girls—from every race, religion, and region—in the United States and, because of her international work, in the world as well.[33]

What interests me about the Juliette Gordon Low portrayed in popular biographies and children's stories is the repetition of certain anecdotes, the erasure of others, and the ways the slippages and repetitions redirect attention from difficult truths or dangerous implications such as the histories of enslavement, racism, Indian genocide, and international British American imperialism that provided the foundational bedrock for the world Low accepted and inhabited. The stories also divert attention from the threat of explicit feminism or possible lesbianism. Above all, what these stories do is constitute what Robin Bernstein calls "racial innocence." In her powerful study of nineteenth-century US children's performances, Bernstein explores the ways that a cultural ideal of childhood innocence firmly took hold, "itself raced white, itself characterized by the ability to retain racial meanings but hide them under claims of holy obliviousness." "Childhood innocence," she explains, "provided a perfect alibi: not only the ability to remember while appearing to forget, but even more powerfully, the production of racial memory through the performance of forgetting."[34] In other words, these childhood performances—stories, dolls, toys—constructed a particular form of whiteness (and thus Blackness) at the same time that they denied they were doing anything of the kind. Childhood (that is, white childhood) and white children were innocent of race, so the argument went, and thus a form of plausible deniability—of the history of racism, of the responsibility for its creation—took firm hold that somehow gave cover to an entire culture and polity.

It's crucially important to note how many of the stories of the founder of the Girl Scouts emphasize her childhood: pure, innocent, and filled with her eccentric schemes and high jinks. One of the most frequently told stories is this: When the Union army came through Savannah, Gen. William T. Sherman came to call on Juliette's mother, Nellie Gordon, whose elite status in Chicago gave her a familial connection to the Union general despite the fact that the Gordons were a Southern family. Apparently young Juliette sat on the lap of one of General Sherman's officers, a man whose arm was missing, and told him that it was probably her father who had done it, as he "shot lots of Yankees." The officers, it seems, laughed at her cute naïveté, and Sherman ensured an escort for Juliette's family to get to Chicago safely. Before they were able to travel to Chicago, some of the earliest stories elaborate, the enslaved cook in their home dared to sell baked goods to the Union soldiers to make money for their strapped family.[35] In other words, Juliette was a sweet child, unaware of the significance of her words ("my father shot a lot of Yankees") whose household "servants" (actually enslaved people) risked their lives by selling goods to help the family. After the Gordons returned from Chicago, the children's books emphasize, Juliette led an idyllic childhood life surrounded by a nurturing family, spending summers in the countryside with her cousins, performing elaborate home-staged plays, and nursing small animals. It's important to note these stories about Juliette Gordon Low, which have circulated since her death in the late 1920s in biographies, stories, and children's picture books, and the way they have highlighted and constructed a myth of innocence. It's not, of course, that as a young girl Juliette would have necessarily known about complex racialized economic policies or that she would have had any control over the situation even if she was perceptive enough to grasp it, but the stories emphasize a kind of being "born into innocence" that is precisely what Bernstein discusses and that sociologist Tressie McMillan Cottom refers to as a problem of American history.[36] This being "born into innocence" is also a strategy that Girl Scouts would use for decades, both claiming a history that is free of complicated strands of oppression and taking cover under a "we are just girls" sentiment when actions seem to suggest a move outside of scripted roles.

These stories about Low's youth completely erase the reality of slavery and the dangerous, difficult, impoverishing conditions for African Americans after the war, during Reconstruction, and in the years following Reconstruction and instead emphasize an idealized childhood spent in Savannah and its countryside. Absent is any acknowledgment of the fact that the wealth of Low's family was based on enslavement. Her parents were enslavers, the family lived on a plantation, and her father was the owner of a cotton factor business, wholly dependent on the labor of enslaved people to grow and harvest the cotton. The family also enslaved the people who worked in their luxurious Savannah home. The "charming" stories that many of the early published works about Low tell about the enslaved people in the house may have diverted white readers, who were enmeshed in a romantic myth of the South, from the fact that these were indeed *enslaved* people, whose bodies, labor, and children the Gordons owned. Indeed, the stories that do allude to the Gordons' history of enslavement portray it as historically inevitable, familial, and kind and emphasize how grateful the enslaved were to their benevolent employers. The 1958 biography *Lady from Savannah* notes that cook Liza Hendry always called Nellie Gordon her "mother" and charmed the family with her misspoken, childish phrases. Helen Boyd Higgins's 1951 children's book *Juliette Low: Girl Scout Founder* describes the way that the cook hid sugar from the Yankees in order to save some for her "own family," meaning the white Gordons, cooking the first cake that Juliette had ever seen. "No wonder my family looks like plucked chickens! No biscuits, no butter, no cream, no nothing, because the Yankees came to Georgia."[37] Slavery is a benevolent system, according to these popular books, filled with grateful and loyal Black enslaved people who became loyal servants after the war. But this has much more to do with the mammy myth popularized in Margaret Mitchell's novel and then the film *Gone with the Wind* than it does with the reality of what it was like to be an enslaved woman working in a white person's kitchen.[38] These myths—originally written down in the 1928 book of reminiscences about Juliette Gordon Low and cemented in the 1950s—continued to be replayed and to reinforce the ideology of her innocence, as many of these first books and their spin-offs were still being sold in Girl Scout settings through the first decades of the twenty-first century.

The stories about benevolent slavery and the post-Reconstruction South did more, of course, than simply divert readers who were already enmeshed in a story of benign slavery; they worked to *generate* the idea of "soft" slavery. But the reality is that no amount of romanticizing or reminiscing about the Gordons' supposed compassionate care for the enslaved softens the fact of this history. And the difficult history of enslavement does not end with the Civil War. After the war, both of Juliette's parents were committed to rebuilding the cotton business that had allowed them to flourish economically. They both presumed the US government owed them monies and protection in order to do that, despite the fact that the South had seceded from the union. Juliette's mother, Nellie, immediately sold Northern land she had in her name in order to refinance their plantation and brokerage firm—land she had acquired because of her ancestors' deceit and claiming of Indian land. In addition to liquidating some of her Northern land, Nellie also successfully petitioned the US government to pay the Gordons for cotton crops destroyed or confiscated by the North.[39] It is crucial to note that at the same time Nellie was successfully petitioning the US government, newly freed African Americans were fighting for the right to landownership and for financial support for unpaid work and cost of life. Indeed, the work and lives of enslaved people had been fundamental to the flourishing of the Southern plantation system, to the northern economic industrial boom, and to the growth of the United States as an economic empire in the eighteenth and nineteenth centuries. The US government momentarily considered the claims of newly freed African Americans, establishing the Freedmen's Bureau and the mandate to give every Black family "forty acres and a mule," but by 1872 Congress had reconfiscated that land for white landowners and terminated the bureau, bowing to Southern white pressure and Northern determination to "unite" the country. For all intents and purposes, this brought an end to any possibility of compensation for the formerly enslaved. By the end of the period we identify as Reconstruction, a system of sharecropping and debt slavery replaced the physical enslavement of African Americans, ensuring the impoverishment of Black people and the continuation of white economic domination. It's crucial to note that this was not just a "natural" progression that followed the Civil War but a victory for white plantation owners and for the white business elite in the North and South, who had fought steadily, forcefully, and without chagrin for continued white domination in economic, political, and social arenas. So while Low's father, Willie Gordon, was reportedly generous to African Americans after the war, there is no evidence that he advocated for their political rights, landownership, or economic power.[40] The machinations of white capitalism after the war placed Low and her family at the top of society and allowed her family to hide their participation in an active system of oppression and extraction of wealth under a flurry of stories about friendly Black servants and a thriving business led by a charitable father. And while Low would likely have had little awareness of this system or the brutal existence that former enslaved people in Savannah faced (because her family would have explicitly hidden it from her), the continued erasure of this history in children's books and mythic biographies of Juliette Gordon Low is problematic.

One of the foundational myths about Low focuses on the marriage of her Northern mother, Eleanor "Nellie" Kinzie, and her Southern father, William "Willie" Gordon, who demonstrated a long-standing and powerful commitment to each other despite their different origins. The often repeated romantic story is that the "irrepressible" Nellie slid down a banister, landing at the feet of an "astonished" Willie, crushing his hat but winning his heart forever.[41] The story works well in the narratives Girl Scouts tell about themselves, as it evokes a sense of unbridled good nature, a can-do kind of attitude bridging the worlds of North and South, male and female, enjoyment and duty, that would later infuse Low and her endeavors in creating a new kind of fun, energetic organization for girls.[42] The story of this bridge between North and South—personified by the characters of Low's Northern mother and Southern father—gets repeated over and again in the popular writing about Low. It functions as a robust example of what historian David Blight calls the myth of reconciliation after the Civil War: the ways in which the "reunion" of the country was predicated both on a memory that ignored the profound injustices that propelled the war and on a memorialization by white Northerners and Southerners that focused on the idea of a just war with fine people of good integrity on both sides.[43] The experience and oppression of Black people gets erased in such narratives, with long-standing consequences in the United States' ability to face and address long-standing inequities. And the story of Low's parents, first articulated in 1928 and then repeated in nearly every subsequent remembrance of Low, follows this script of a melding of North and South that ignores Black suffering and white culpability. Their marriage, so the story goes, worked extraordinarily well, despite their differences in accent, in religion (she was Episcopalian, he Presbyterian), and in practices regarding slavery. Indeed, their differences regarding human enslavement were more a matter of marital squabbling than an existential question about oppression and humanity; apparently Willie agreed to quit teasing Nellie about her Episcopalian beliefs if she would stop mocking slavery, which she agreed to do.[44] Similar to the way Low's parents were able to forge a formidable union out of difference, the myths suggest, the Girl Scouts could be a powerful organization crisscrossing the North and South just like the United States had yoked the two regions. Indeed, *Lady from Savannah*, the major biography of Low from the 1950s, suggests that the union between Nellie and Willie produced something particularly wonderful in Juliette: "The truth is that the character and abilities and potentialities of Juliette Low were as variegated as the America that produced her. Puritan, bluestocking New England, the aristocratic South and the wild picturesque frontier had all gone into her making."[45] The problem was, of course, that this myth of Puritan Northern whiteness and aristocratic Southern whiteness—all with a bit of the "wild picturesque frontier" thrown in—relied on suppressing the history of African American oppression, or suppressing the history of the many enslaved people whose labor was fundamental to every creature comfort the Gordons experienced.

That myth, of course, also relied on suppressing the history of Native American genocide. Indeed, the comment about the frontier merits further attention, for the myth of Northern and Southern white unification coupled with Native American spirit figures prominently in the narratives about Juliette Gordon Low. The two pieces often coalesce, as in the 2013 children's book by Janie Lynn Panagopoulos *Little Ship under Full Sail: An Adventure in History*.[46] This adventure story goes something like this: While on the train ride from the South to the North to visit their Chicago relatives, Nellie tells Juliette and her sisters tales of her father and grandfather, who made deals with various groups of Indians in his role as the mayor of Chicago. Juliette's grandparents continue the story once the family arrives in the city, and the little girls listen with big ears as they learn about the Seneca's capture of their great-grandmother Nellie as a young girl and how she learned to live happily among them, earning the name Little Ship under Full Sail before returning four years later to her white family. Juliette earns the same nickname as her captured great-grandmother, filled as she is with a similar spunky spirit.

Countless picture books and children's biographies, from the 1940s onward, repeat the story. All of these stories originate in Low's grandmother's memoir, *Wau-Bun*, discussed earlier in this chapter. But that memoir is, of course, a celebration of settler colonialism, an imaginative act of remembering that paints the settlers as "friends of the Indians" and describes Indian resistance as an act of malicious aggression, as in the chapter on the Chicago massacre.[47] But it is also a text that constructs Indians as having a particular kind of special spirit that, because of their close contact with them, infuses the Kinzies with a remarkable energy and verve, a particular kind of "Americanness" located in the best of the frontier. This, I would argue, is why this story of Low's great-grandmother gets repeated so frequently in the tellings of Low's life—that brush with Indianness that her great-grandmother Nellie Kinzie experienced subsequently inscribed the Kinzies, and thus Low, and thus Girl Scouts themselves, with this vigor, this energy, this distinctive American identity.

The Shifting Stories about Juliette Gordon Low

As one peruses the myriad stories written about Juliette Gordon Low, it's illuminating to note which ones have survived for decades, which ones have disappeared, and which ones continue to exist but with a changing slant. The stories of the Kinzies on the frontier, of the Gordons' brilliant marriage, of the unfortunate accidents that created significant hearing loss for Low—these have all remained. One of the most apocryphal stories that has also remained is about Low's pearls. Apparently when faced with some unforeseen bills to be paid for the Girl Scouts' expansion, Low "sold her pearls" to make up the shortfall. It's a great story. In its first appearance in 1928, it suggested something of her eccentricity, her willingness to be a little less "ladylike" if it served her beloved Girl Scouts. As the story took hold in the 1940s and '50s, it suggested self-sacrifice for a bigger cause, a charitable act done in the name of securing a future for the girls of America. By the 1970s, the story became a way to demonstrate how she threw away the feminine entrapments that stifled her full participation in society. By the twenty-first century, the pearl story becomes emblematic of "throwing off" the taint of an overprivileged, wealthy family. Ironically, as historian Stacy Cordery discovered, it turns out that Low was quite irritated that she had to sell the pearls and was particularly peeved when she found out that other monies could have been used to pay the bills. But that factual detail did not stand in the way of decades of retellings of this legendary story that worked so well to "manage" the story of Low's extraordinary wealth.[48]

Stories of Low's life have also been adjusted and amended to thwart one of the most pressing accusations that the Girl Scouts faced: that it was an organization filled with and encouraging of lesbianism.[49] An all-girls organization, founded by an almost-divorced, widowed woman who loved nothing more than to wear her mannish uniform and Stetson hat, the Girl Scouts could certainly appear to encourage queer identities among girls. Indeed, writers such as Nancy Manahan have written eloquently about the ways that Girl Scouting—the actual experiences of girls and leaders, not the practices of the national institution itself—encouraged a space for lesbian exploration and community-building in the twentieth century.[50] By the twenty-first century, the Girl Scouts had a "hands-off" approach to sexuality, clearly stating that inappropriate sexual behavior toward children was never to be tolerated but that the sexual relationships of its leaders was none of the organization's business. But in the decades of the twentieth century that this book explores, the organization perceived lesbianism, even the possibility of lesbianism, to be an explicit threat to its survival. Of course, there were volunteers and professionals within the organization from its very founding who were lesbians, and many girls did find their experiences as Girl Scouts allowed them to explore same-sex attraction. But the stories and myths about Low worked to downplay the possibility of imagining *her* as a lesbian, despite the various markers—her final decades living and working in all-female worlds, her attraction to "mannish" clothing—that might suggest otherwise. Above all, the relentless emphasis on the marriage of her parents, besides illuminating a union of North and South as described above, also stands in as a model of successful, companionate, heterosexual marriage, something that the actual story of Juliette Gordon Low does not have, as hers was an unhappy marriage that ended with betrayal and a divorce averted only by the early death of her alcoholic husband.[51] Interestingly, it is in the 1958 biography *Lady from Savannah* that we begin to see explicit techniques to manage the implicit threat of lesbianism; included in the edition, for instance, is a photograph of the Edward Hughes portrait of a young Juliette Gordon, dressed all in ruffled pink, but not the portrait she herself preferred, in the uniform and Stetson hat.[52] The only picture we see of Juliette in her uniform in that book is with Lord Baden-Powell and his wife, Olave, also both in uniform, so she is appropriately linked with a heterosexual couple. And the biographers also conjure a maternal spirit, despite the fact that Juliette never had children, writing that in the Girl Scouts she would "find the children she had never had."[53] Most tellingly, it is in this biography that the story of her unfaithful husband comes into more focus, and one has to wonder whether, in the McCarthy era of intense fearmongering regarding homosexuality, it became safer for the Girl Scouts to lay out the details of a good-for-nothing husband than to allow insinuations about Low herself to grow. As the authors of *Lady from Savannah* write in their foreword: "We recognize that it would probably have been the wish of Juliette Low to omit all reference to the unhappy turn her marriage took. Her nieces and nephews believe she loved Willy Low to her dying day and would have wished to shield him. But the very silence that has been maintained on this subject heretofore has given rise to the impression that there may have been something shameful or disgraceful about it. Nothing could be farther from the truth as far as Juliette Low was concerned."[54] This is a fascinating note buried in the biography's introductory pages, with its allusions to shame and dishonor. Their emphasis that she loved her husband to her dying day and that she had done nothing disgraceful certainly pushes back against unsaid accusations of lesbianism. Fascinatingly, in the most recent biographical tributes to Juliette Gordon Low, in which she serves as a model of a "badass" woman, her troubled marriage has nothing to do with thwarting accusations of lesbianism; instead, it demonstrates a woman who was able to rise from the ashes of being dumped and who outsmarted the small-minded people who suggested her life was over as a middle-aged widow. Throughout the years, the outlines of this story about her unhappy marriage have remained, with writers filling in the meaning—from "not a lesbian" to "badass woman"—as they see fit.

What stands out the most in exploring the decades of stories about Low—all of which largely, as I said before, originate in the 1928 collection of reminiscences—is the manipulation and erasure of anecdotes about Black people. In the original 1928 text, Low remembers her nurse "Mormer," who worked as a "servant" in the house, and Low's sister Eleanor remembers playing with the children of the "Negro servants": "Pretty little black Hetty was my favorite," she adds. The nurse and Hetty, of course, were not always servants—before emancipation, they were enslaved, owned by the Gordon family. There is another story, frequently repeated, of Nancy, who is indeed described as an "old slave," who sells cakes outside the stately home to make money for the Gordon family despite General Sherman's orders for all Black people to stay off the streets. Another anecdote, told to highlight how eccentric Low was, tells of Low's decision to take their convalescing cook Eliza Hendry for a stroll in Low's personal carriage, where Hendry waves to surprised white people on the street.[55] Indeed, this is not the only time that a Black person shows up as part of Low's antics. Another is in the 1918 Girl Scout recruitment film *The Golden Eaglet*, in which Low orchestrates a stunt, a "game" with a Black cook who has a pitcher on her head.[56] The "silly" phrases of the enslaved and the servants show up in many of the reminiscences, such as when Eliza Hendry is purported to have chuckled that the Queen of England better not anger Miss Juliette. There are also some feel-good stories: Low standing up for the little girl Hetty when she was "unfairly" punished and giving a Black taxi driver a hefty tip so that he could give his skinny horse an extra meal.[57]

These stories, of course, demonstrate an unblinking understanding of a world where white people dominate, where the enslavement of Black people—from old women to young children—can be couched in familial terms and portrayed as benevolent and charming, a picture of the "old South." These stories are repeated in various forms in the children's stories about Juliette Gordon Low until the 1950s.[58] But at that point, with the rise of the civil rights movement, the narratives about Black enslaved people, about the stunts Low mischievously played on the formerly enslaved, and about enslaved children playmates who get punished by the mistress of the household no longer seem as innocent and endearing. And we begin to see not a confrontation with this difficult history but its disappearance. The 1958 biography *Lady from Savannah* refers to the "servants" in the household—even when the reference is to an antebellum time, when these were not servants but enslaved people. The fact that the Gordons bought, sold, and enslaved people never shows up. The newer children's biographies drop the stories about the little girl Hetty, about the nurse, about the cook, about Eliza Hendry. If they do show up, they show up as staff, not as the enslaved or formerly enslaved.[59] When I visited the Juliette Gordon Low Birthplace in the 1970s, I learned about household staff, but they were always referred to as servants—a part of her story that gets quickly dismissed compared to the attention lavished on the opulent living room, the interesting artwork, and the vision of Juliette Gordon Low. But for the most part, when it comes to the history of Black people and Juliette Gordon Low, what we find is erasure. Indeed, the most startling example of this is in the 1918 film *The Golden Eaglet*. We know from the 1928 reminiscences and from *Girl Scout Leader* articles and movie stills that there was at least one scene featuring a Black cook looking surprised with a jar atop her head, white Girl Scouts surrounding her, laughing.[60] But in the version of the film that I saw at the Girl Scout National Historic Preservation Center in New York City in 2015, shown in a small movie booth at the Girl Scout Headquarters, this scene was simply gone, and I could not find the scene in any of the extant versions of the film—all of which are marked as abridged—that I could locate. The damaging evidence was simply excised.

The shape-shifting of the Juliette Gordon Low story—the way it gained mythic status and is used to promote the Girl Scout movement—merits our close attention. This is particularly true as we think about the overarching narrative of inclusivity constructed by the continually repeated "phone call" quotation with which I began this chapter. What happens, though, when we put the excised parts back into the narrative? How does the myth of Juliette Gordon Low and of the origins of the Girl Scouts change if we actually address difficult histories rather than ignore them? What does the story look like if we put back, for instance, the picture of the unnamed Black cook, called on to play a bit part in *The Golden Eaglet*, that so aroused Low's enthusiasm? What shape does this fuller portrait take when we include new stories and put them side by side with the old? How does the picture change when we challenge a narrative of innocence? The following chapter will begin with an exploration of this iconic film, *The Golden Eaglet*, as we start to examine the "ideal girl" that the Girl Scouts set out to create in the early part of the twentieth century.

Chapter 3

Girl Scouting and the Intrepid Girl

• • • • • •

According to present policy, colored Girl Scouts are accepted at Camp Andree during the last two-week period. . . . There has been a colored unit at camp on only one occasion.

—1940 report on Camp Andree, one of the first Northern Girl Scout camps

The Golden Eaglet

In 1918, the Girl Scouts released *The Golden Eaglet.* Written and directed by the novelist Josephine Daskam Bacon and acted by Girl Scouts themselves in New York state, this silent film even included a cameo appearance by Juliette Gordon Low.[1] The film has held legendary status among Girl Scouts; it has even claimed its own special viewing booth at the museum of the Girl Scout National Headquarters, where I sat and viewed it countless times in the 2010s, giving up my spot when a group of young Girl Scouts would come for a visit. An early publicity article promoting the film describes its premise this way:

> Margaret and Dorothy are two small-town girls who are idling in the village street because they have nothing better to do. They are dressed in an attempt to realize the latest follies of fashion; they obviously have the chewing gum habit. As they are wondering what to do with themselves they hear the sound of fife and drum and through the village street comes

> marching a troop of sturdy little Girl Scouts. Business-like and happy looking, they present a marked contrast to the girls on the sidewalk. The two idlers are envious; they, too, would like to be as busy and happy as these little khaki-clad girls, and so the idea of becoming Girls Scouts takes root in their minds.[2]

And indeed, the film's protagonist, Margaret, loses her gum-chewing, fashion-loving ways and becomes a Girl Scout. Not only does the young, white Margaret's life shift away from the dangers of "idleness"; it moves directly into the energetic joy of mastery, of physical movement, and of helping those in misery. After joining a troop, she aids a bedraggled and sickly working-class mother whose husband is off to war, organizing her fellow scouts, who bring order to the dirty kitchen, nurse the ailing woman, feed the children, and even tidy the yard. At camp, she learns to swim, to semaphore, and to administer first aid. All these skills come in handy when she has to return home unexpectedly. She swims across a river after realizing the bridge is down and makes her way to the telegraph operator at the train station, who, in a bit of homage to the 1903 film *The Great Train Robbery*, has been robbed, beaten, and tied up.[3] She administers first aid to the man, messages the main office with Morse code, and upon returning home, earns the prestigious Golden Eaglet for her bravery and accomplishment. It's at the award ceremony that Juliette Gordon Low herself appears, pinning the coveted Golden Eaglet on Margaret's uniform.

Based on the laughter and gasps I heard when observing twenty-first-century Girl Scouts viewing the film, there is something totally engaging about this film and its spunky heroine, something both funny and inspiring to contemporary eyes. There is so much to note about this iconic film: the fact that Low herself was apparently over the moon about it, often suggesting new scenes for the harried filmmaker; the fact that Girl Scout Headquarters used it to publicize the movement, even sending it to soldiers stationed across the country and abroad; and the fact that it modeled a version of girlhood so different from traditional forms of heterosexually focused femininity, albeit one that was gaining some popularity in Progressive Era visions of girlhood that were starting to become popular in the serial fiction of the time.[4] Margaret is the model par excellence of what I call an "intrepid" girl—one whose energy and vitality both deeply satisfy her and make the world a better place. Note that I don't call her a feminist girl; though the film is made in 1918, at the height of the suffrage movement in the United States, there is not one suggestion that

Margaret is ever exposed to the world of suffragists or might herself desire to vote. Instead, she's part of an all-female world, seemingly outside the concerns of the public world even as, interestingly, this new community forges a way for her to be ultracompetent, active, engaged, spunky, and courageous—in other words, intrepid. It's a model that was offered to me when I was a Girl Scout; though I never saved a bound telegraph operator or waved down a train, like Margaret I learned so many skills, from swimming to whittling and hiking. I experienced such joy in the community of girls who gathered every week in the church basement where our troop met, and like Margaret, I felt a deep satisfaction when the leader pinned a new badge or award on my green sash. But no one ever called it feminist.

What one *doesn't* see in this film—or at least in all the versions I could find—is equally important. Still images from the film, published in the Girl Scout magazine *Rally*, show an African American cook, a hefty woman wearing a long work skirt and hair wrap, with a large white pitcher on her head. She is the only African American person in the film. Apparently, Low herself dreamed up some of these scenes, which she thought were amusing and fun for the actual Girl Scouts who were performing in the film.[5] Significantly, however, one doesn't see these scenes of the Black cook in the version available today. They have simply been excised from the record, at least as far as I could locate, except in this early published publicity material.

I'm not surprised that the Girl Scouts eventually chose to edit the film to remove these scenes. A scene with an African American woman dressed as a mammy figure who is mocked or patronized makes one deeply aware that the imagined "intrepid girl" is white and lives within a racialized society that actively promoted white supremacy and excluded Black people, whose only place was as servant, maid, and even butt of joke. With the scenes of the Black cook, Margaret's escapades look less sweet and the film no longer simultaneously innocent and daring.

The Golden Eaglet, then, raises two key issues that the rest of this chapter considers. First, considering that the Girl Scouts promoted a new kind of intrepid girlhood but didn't want to be labeled as a women's rights activist organization, what kinds of maneuvers did it have to use to dodge accusations of feminism? Second, what happens to our analysis when we refuse to separate racism from its portrayal of new possibilities for girls and women, a new way of living in the world? How can we think about this intrepid girlhood at the same time we consider the context of white supremacy and racism in which it emerged?

"She invented enough situations to have used up thousands of feet of film"—one situation from The Golden Eaglet, *devised by Juliette Low*

Juliette Low awarding the Golden Eaglet badge, in the first Girl Scout motion picture, The Golden Eaglet

Anne Hyde Choate and Helen Ferris's 1928 remembrances of Juliette Gordon Low include these two stills from Josephine Daskam Bacon's 1918 film *The Golden Eaglet*. The top image shows a Black cook interacting with a white scout, one of the "humorous" vignettes Low herself apparently imagined; in the bottom still Low herself makes a cameo appearance. The scenes with the Black cook have been excised from contemporary versions of the film. From Choate and Ferris, *Juliette Low and the Girl Scouts*.

Girl Scouts versus Boy Scouts

Although Juliette Gordon Low apparently referred to "something new" she had for girls in the apocryphal 1912 call she may have made to her cousin Nina Pape, there were actually a flourishing number of girls' and boys' organizations in the United States at the time. Indeed, the growing focus on youth and children, and their significance to the well-being of the nation, was fundamental to the Progressive Era, so much so that one sociologist, Ellen Key, termed it the Century of the Child.[6] Most of these organizations—religious, philanthropic, and patriotic—were sex, age, and race segregated, such as the Young Men's Christian Association (YMCA), the Young Women's Christian Association (YWCA), the Young Men's Hebrew Association, and the Young Women's Hebrew Association. Organizations such as Hull House in Chicago, the Henry Street Settlement in New York City, the Red Cross, and the National Association of Colored Women's Clubs formed special offshoots for children and youth. By the end of the nineteenth century, children and youth had gained a status demanding of protection (in child-labor and age-of-consent laws) and worthy of special development (in public schooling, youth organizations, and camps). Although Low spoke of the Girl Scouts as being unique, it was both typical of its era and similar in many ways to other organizations founded at the time. There were even other organizations that claimed the name of Girl Scouts. In 1910 Clara A. Lisetor-Lane created an organization she called the Girl Scouts of America. Lina and Adelia Beard also organized a group they called the Girl Scouts of America in the same year, later changing its name to Girl Pioneers. These were separate organizations from Low's, but like hers, they were also inspired by Lord Robert Baden-Powell and dedicated to instilling skills, confidence, and the ideals of citizenship in girls.[7]

Low proved herself a ruthless foe when faced with rivalry from these other organizations; in her letters defending her own organization as the first and real Girl Scouts, Low even suggested Lisetor-Lane must be a drunk or "insane."[8] But rather than the Beard sisters' or Lisetor-Lane's organizations, the most formidable rival to Low's organization was the Camp Fire Girls. Organized in 1910 by a number of children's development experts and educators—Charlotte Farnsworth (preceptress of Horace Mann School), Charlotte and Luther Gulick, G. Stanley Hall, and Ernest Thompson Seton—the Camp Fire Girls used the dominant educational and developmental psychological ideas of the time to bring the nineteenth-century cult of domesticity into the twentieth century. Highlighting the importance of the hearth to suggest an energy both domestic and pure, the motto of the Camp Fire Girls was "WoHeLo," or "work, health, and love." The Camp Fire Girls also emphasized Indian lore and dressed its members as Indian maidens, believing that such imaginary play would imbue its members with a naturalness and romanticism missing in modern life. When Low brought the idea of the Girl Guides back with her to the United States, the Camp Fire Girls already had a significant head start, with chapters across the country. One of the main resistances to the organization came from the Catholic Church, which for decades challenged what it saw as heathen worship of fire and a sacrilegious emphasis on beadwork that threatened to usurp the place of the rosary—accusations the Camp Fire Girls vehemently denied but which the Girl Scouts, and even First Lady Lou Hoover, reiterated.[9]

Secretary of the Boy Scouts James West resoundingly approved of the Camp Fire Girls, considering it the sister organization of the Boy Scouts of America. He found the twin foci of domesticity and Indian maidenhood a reasonable alternative for girls inspired by the activities of the Boy Scouts. His approval of the Camp Fire Girls was in sharp contrast to the *disapproval* he felt toward Low's new organization, which he didn't think presented a sufficiently domestic focus. His disapproval deepened once Low shifted the name from the original Girl Guides to Girl Scouts. As noted in the previous chapter, the term "guides" originated from the name given by the British to the Indian men who helped them colonize India; "scouts" was a term Lord Baden-Powell coined for his boys' organization, inspired both by the British men who "scouted" out land in India and by the American men who "scouted" out Indian territory in North America. To West's ears, "guides" was a much more palatable term for girls, suggesting a position clearly differentiated from and subservient to the boys'.[10] And he frequently quoted aspects of Lord Baden-Powell's rationale for use of the term, which Baden-Powell had published in the 1921 international Boy Scout *Jamboree*:

> Today, women have won for themselves a far greater share in the work of the world than was the case of old. Such a development is both new to them, and is a palpable gain to civilization.
>
> The Girl Guide training is framed to prepare the younger generation for taking on this increased responsibility. It is, however, to be hoped that their new activities will not so change their mentality that they forget they still have their special powers and duties as women. One of the greatest of these is the strong influence for good which they can, if they will, exercise over men.

> This influence can be strengthened by the better mutual comradeship that comes of widened experience: but it can be weakened by intrusion into what is definitely men's domain.
>
> The home-making and the character-giving abilities which are at once the privilege and the responsibility of women are needed to-day more than ever, as are also the tender sympathy, the patient pluck, and the quiet dignity which helps a man and raises the standard of his chivalry.
>
> Thus the value of a good woman in the world is higher than ever in her capacity as an adviser and helpmeet.
>
> The term "to Guide" seems to sum up in one word the high mission of woman, whether as a mother, a wife or a citizen. The Title of "Guide" therefore is the best applicable to the girl as an inspiring reminder to her of the ideal to which she is training herself. But the whole value were missed and the aim debased if one used the term "Scout."[11]

Baden-Powell evokes a very nineteenth-century sense of separate spheres, with a distinct domestic space for women, now defined as important for the twentieth century precisely because of its deferential, influential positioning in relation to men. Despite the fact that Baden-Powell prevaricated on this position, even later apologizing in writing to the Girl Scouts for interfering in their "fine program," the Boy Scouts quoted his words for decades.[12] What the Boy Scouts of America didn't do, however, was emulate his tone, which while patronizing was also outwardly respectful toward women. In its outrage at the Girl Scouts, the Boy Scouts of America, including James West, articulated its position in terms much more direct, angry, and misogynistic. In a 1924 report on the Girl Scouts, the Boy Scouts wrote that boys don't want even a reminder that they have anything in common with "mere girls." To associate with girls causes a "lowering of prestige," as "the word 'Scout,' is, and always has been, associated with *men* and with things and efforts intensely masculine and virile." Boy Scouts are "disgusted" at the "suggestion of femininity" that the Girl Scouts create, a Boy Scout leader from Cincinnati wrote, and now fear being "classed as sissies," as a writer from Spokane, Washington, explained. Indeed, another Boy Scout leader wrote that Girl Scouts make the entire endeavor of scouting a "sissy proposition." A Boy Scout leader in Baltimore was succinct: Girl Scouts makes boys "effeminate."[13] For decades the Boy Scouts railed against the term "Girl Scouts," claiming Girl Scouts was violating copyright by using the name, pleading with the organization to switch back to "Guides," and urging girls to join the Camp Fire Girls instead. The Boy Scouts argued that the Girl Scout program was "too boyish and masculine," "neither psychologically nor physically suited for girls." Not all local Boy Scout troops eschewed the Girl Scouts; some even organized events together. But in places where the Boy Scouts actually cosponsored outings, there was fear that all sorts of shenanigans would break out, as a Boy Scout leader in Tulsa, Oklahoma, complained: "They [Girl Scouts and Boy Scouts] get together on a social basis and the first thing you know there is a whole lot of doings between the Boy and Girl Scouts and the troops go to pieces."[14]

Just how significant and threatening was this new organization for girls? Considering that the Girl Scouts never claimed to be an organization promoting women's rights or feminism, the comments Boy Scout executives and leaders made—with their references to virility, to masculinity, to effeminacy—implicitly threatened violence, both to girls who step out of line and to any effeminate boys. And certainly they give us pause as we think about the painful history of sexual abuse within the Boy Scouts, to which I will return in the final chapter. The comments also speak to a 1920s world in which women are literally second-class citizens in both the law and in culture, with limited rights to property, to divorce, and to work. They speak to a world where pregnancy and sexual violence could derail a young woman without recourse and where the threat of pregnancy and sexual violence kept women narrowly in line. They speak to a world where almost every institution, organization, and law, where every form of popular culture, would steer girls and women toward what Adrienne Rich would call "compulsory heterosexuality" in the pathbreaking essay she wrote over a half century later, where women's lives are circumscribed and viscerally defined by looking to men for meaning, feeling, and purpose.[15]

At the same time that Low was learning about the Girl Guides in England and beginning her organization in the United States, there was a vibrant women's movement spreading across the globe that reached every aspect of women's oppression: economics, education, sexuality, birth control and reproduction, political rights, and property rights.[16] The aspirations of this first wave of feminism have never been fully realized, though activism, legal change, and cultural shifts in what is known as the second wave of feminism moved the goals forward in the 1970s. And the struggle certainly continues today. My point here, though, is to remind us that Girl Scouts did not emerge in a vacuum—there was a vital children's and youth movement and a burgeoning feminist movement that surrounded and propelled it, even if Low and her cofounders never explicitly referenced either. And the stakes were high, as girls and women faced significant cultural and legal oppression that the Girl Scouts simply seemed to flout. The girls and women who joined the Girl Scouts flocked to it in ways that the Boy Scouts found downright reprehensible. In their complaints to their organization, Boy Scout leaders wrote that Girl Scouts was "just a scheme to give the girls an excuse to wear bloomers and to indulge in boyenish [*sic*] activities." Did this writer mean "boyish"? Or "hoydenish"—meaning saucy, boisterous, loud? No matter, the girls didn't care and ran around with "merit badges on their sleeves and dressed up and were regular tomboys."[17] A regional Boy Scout director in 1921 wrote to the Boy Scouts: "From personal observation I am convinced the Girl Scout movement naturally draws to itself both the type of leadership and type of membership who are somewhat boyish in inclination. To state a definite case I noticed particularly a group of girl scouts in Indianapolis that the girls appeared to be very loud and swaggering in their deportment on the streets. Whether or not the 'clothes make the man,' the wearing of the sombrero hat at a rakish angle seems to make them feel that they must live up to the looks." One Boy Scout leader from Butte, Montana, warned: "We find that the Girl Scouts are endorsed by a woman's political organization, and I think that is general throughout the country if we go to the bottom of it. It is a political motive most of it." But then he seemed defeated in the face of the popularity of the Girl Scouts. "You cannot deal with the women on this subject," he conceded.[18]

What is fascinating is that the name "Girl Scout" did clearly evoke a feminist, pathbreaking mindset, although the organization itself never admitted it. Certainly Low understood the significance of the naming, even if she denied it. Indeed, when Baden-Powell began Boy Scouts in England, girls across the country joined in, starting ragtag groups of their own and pulling together makeshift uniforms. Baden-Powell's purpose in starting the Boy Scouts was to strengthen British masculinity and prowess in the world order; girls joining in did not fit his endeavor one bit. So he enjoined his sister, and then Low, to organize Girl Guides, the name evoking helpmates and subservience in both a gendered and racialized sense. So when Low brought the new organization to the United States and shifted the name to Girl Scouts, she may have been honest or she may have been disingenuous when she said that scouting just made more sense for American girls; either way, she certainly would have understood the rationale and the controversy that propelled the choice of the term "Girl Guides" in Great Britain. She was using a strategy that would be useful to the Girl Scouts throughout its history—a type of innocence, a denial of feminism—and that gave it a certain chameleon aspect, hiding behind a "we're just a girls' organization" framework that allowed the Girl Scouts to simultaneously claim and deny its progressive and challenging cultural aspects. Significantly, throughout her life Low apparently simply ignored criticisms of the name (and in the apocryphal stories, she used her deafness to her advantage here), and when asked more directly she simply said that "girls just prefer it" and "it makes more sense in the United States." And the Girl Scout organization refused to change it, even when facing charming pleas from Baden-Powell himself, decades of copyright legal challenges by the Boy Scouts of America, and even a push in the 1940s from First Lady Eleanor Roosevelt to join with the Camp Fire Girls.[19]

The archival records of the Girl Scouts don't really give any definitive explanation of why the naming shift occurred, though they give ample evidence of the decision to stick with the name Girl Scouts and to refuse any mergers with other organizations. The truth may be that US girls really did prefer the new term: "scout," with its generalized reference to games of cowboys and Indians, may have made more sense to American ears than "guide." One document even suggests that US (white) girls preferred the term "scout" over "guide" precisely because of the terms' racialized histories. "Guides were half-breed Indians or half-breed Negroes," the report explained as a reason (white) girls chose the term "scouts."[20] Though this was never publicly given as an explanation, this passing reference to "half breeds" certainly resonates with the dominant ideal of the "intrepid girl" as always white, an ideal we see in full force in Girl Scout novels and in the world of the Girl Scout camp.

Making the Girl Scouts Palatable

Although Girl Scouts never definitively explained its choice to use the term "scout," a number of maneuvers allowed the organization to claim the new "intrepid" girlhood while denying that it was a revolutionary or dangerous act: a strategy of cheerful helpfulness, an appearance of sexual innocence, and finally, an unnamed but crucially important whiteness, one that harkens back to its mythical pioneer. We can see all three of these tactics in *The Golden Eaglet* in Margaret, who is able to do all her daring activities precisely because she is helping others, a practice that places her squarely within an older model of feminine virtue. She marches, swims, knows Morse code, sets broken bones, and deals with dangerous robbers—but all this activity is focused on someone else in need, such as the bedraggled mother or bloody telegraph operator. Margaret never advocates for her own rights. She never voices dissatisfaction with the political or economic situation is which she is living. She never leads a union march or tells off a harassing boss. Instead, she throws herself into activities helpful to others and through that caring activity is able to engage in some stereotypically nonfeminine activities. Margaret leaves her own home to join a troop—but this is all right because the troop organizes itself to help the sickly mother and her children. Margaret learns how to live in the woods—like her pioneer forebears!—but this is all right because her wilderness skills allow her to treat a sister scout who broke her leg. Margaret learns to swim, tie knots, and master the newest telegraphic technology—but this is acceptable because it allows her to cross a raging (well, flowing) river to send a message home, untie the knots that have bound the gagged and beaten train operator, and send an SOS code to the stationmaster to flag down a train. And she does it all cheerfully, a desirable and acceptable emotional affect for girls in turn-of-the-century America.[21] This attitude of cheerful helpfulness was everywhere in the Girl Scouts—from the littlest Brownies, whose name came from a Christian story about a community of elves who secretly do good deeds, to the name of the first US Girl Scout handbook in 1913, *How Girls Can Help Their Country*, which frames the Girl Scout as a kind of helpmate to the nation.[22] Everything in the Girl Scouts necessitates this "needy other." That is, there needs to be someone to "help" (a feminine virtue) in order to legitimate the derring-do, the courageous acts, and the physical and mental prowess. This ideal of helping others motivates and legitimates so much Girl Scout activity in the twentieth and twenty-first centuries, masking and protecting from criticism of what might be seen as feminism, or at least as something unseemly, either among the girls themselves or the leaders, both volunteer and professional, who often devoted their lives to this all-female organization.

Not only did the Girl Scouts' unspoken feminism threaten a conservative, patriarchal culture, but the possibility that girls and boys might meet on equal terms, both as scouts, also raised alarm bells for Boy Scouts and other cultural commentators. These critics bristled at the possibility of a promiscuous mixing of the sexes, a heterosocial mingling with potentially disastrous results. *The Golden Eaglet* clearly addresses this fear, suggesting that it is life *outside* the Girl Scouts that is dangerous. Indeed, the first scenes of the film show Margaret and a friend dressed in the latest fashions, hanging around a soda fountain—the unspoken here, of course, is that they are prime for the plucking by predatory boys, saved just in time by the marching Girl Scouts. This was an explicit intention of the film, not just a consequence we can see in retrospect. In an article titled "A Gift from the Girl Scouts to Our Boys in Service," the Girl Scouts bragged that the film had been turned into a series of slides with captions, called a "Picturelook." The *Golden Eaglet* Picturelook was

Assisting others was often the rationale the Girl Scouts used to legitimate pushing past domestic confines, as this 1933 publicity image suggests. It also highlights the whiteness of the Girl Scout imaginary, with the rosy-cheeked scout and the blond curly-haired young girl. Poster Collection, Schlesinger Library, Cambridge, MA.

sent to the YMCA, which then ensured its availability in all the canteens (at military bases) in the United States and abroad. "The boys have 'Picturelooks' on many subjects, but this is the first Girl Scout one they have had, and we hope that it will make them anxious to get better acquainted with us and our work," the article stated. (One has to wonder if perhaps they would have been more interested in girly pictures sent from France than in the "Picturelook" of Margaret from the Girl Scouts.)[23]

This was not the first time that a suppression of sexuality was linked to the Girl Scouts. An issue of *Outlook* from 1918 described all the good works that Girl Scouts were doing for the country: working for the Red Cross cleaning out workrooms and knitting mufflers, leading canning demonstrations for the Food Administration, selling "close to half a million dollars worth" of Liberty loan bonds, and assembling care packages for convalescent hospitals in France. The article concludes, however, with the best work the Girl Scouts have done: diverting sexual energy.

> The organization of the Girl Scouts, acting under the direction of the Army and Navy Commission on Training Camp Activities, has found an urgent field for usefulness in the town adjacent to the camps. "The best service you can do," said the Army authorities, "is to keep the girls out of the camps." This is the task the Girl Scout leaders have set themselves. The work is now fully organized in the vicinity of Camp Devens, Massachusetts, and is being started near other camps. It puts into the life of the village girl so vigorous and constructive a programme of definite service and gives her a code of honor so completely within her comprehension that she has neither time nor desire to loiter around the camps. In this, as in every other activity, Girl Scouts serve "America First" in terms of everyday living.[24]

The "everyday living" that Girl Scouts espoused in the early decades was physically strong but explicitly asexual. The 1913 Girl Scout manual *How Girls Can Help Their Country* included a "Health" section, which began:

> To make yourself strong and healthy it is necessary to begin with your inside, and to get the blood into good order and the heart to work well; that is the secret of the whole thing, and physical exercises should be taken with that intention. . . . The Japs are particularly strong and healthy. They eat very plain food, chiefly rice and fruit, and not much of it. They drink plenty of water, but no spirits. They take lots of exercise. They make themselves good-tempered. They live in fresh air as much as possible day and night. Their particular exercise is Ju-Jitsu, which is more of a game than drill, and is generally played in pairs. By Ju-Jitsu, the muscles and body are developed in a natural way, in the open air as a rule. It requires no apparatus.[25]

Exercise, fresh air, minimal food, looking to the exotic "other" for hints on physical improvement (in this case the Japanese, referred to by a rude term, but more frequently American Indians and mythical pioneers): these were typical of the early Girl Scout discourse on bodily improvement. Genitalia, reproduction, and sexuality were referred to in the handbook in only the most general of terms, as something to be controlled. Quoting a "Miss Rogers," the handbook reads:

> Girls and boys should be comrades, so never do anything in word or deed to make a boy or man think less of you, and so lose his respect by

> making yourself cheap. Remember familiarity breeds contempt. Don't romp about with a boy whom you wouldn't like your mother or father to see you with.
>
> Don't let any man make love to you unless he wants to marry you, and you are willing to do so. Don't marry a man unless he is in a position to support you and a family. Moral courage is one thing that all Scouts keep a stock of. Don't be afraid to say you *won't* play at nasty, rude things. When mean girls want you to join in some low fun, when you think it is not right, ask yourself if mother would like to see you doing it; be brave, and have courage to say it isn't right. You will feel twice as happy afterward.
>
> Every time you show your courage it grows; it becomes easier to be brave after every time you have tried to be courageous.[26]

The key word in these three paragraphs is "comrade": Girls and boys should be comrades, should be friends in equal, so therefore don't doing anything to make them think less of you, which presumably means don't do anything "sexual." So Girl Scouting, then, can take away the "danger" of sexuality, replacing it with the "courage" to deny erotic energy and displacing that danger with the challenges and euphoria of *other kinds* of dangers.

The early Girl Scouts, then, laid claim to the term and possibilities of "scouting" by de-emphasizing its feminism and stripping and containing sexual energy. Of course, the organization deflected heterosocial eroticism by creating a tight community of girls and women, with extraordinary homosocial and lesbian possibilities. The Girl Scout memoirs I discuss elsewhere in this book certainly speak to this. But in the early part of the twentieth century, when female bonding could still be hidden under the mantle of "Boston marriages" and romantic friendships, the possibility of young men and women consorting was the biggest threat Girl Scouts considered.[27] And this was linked as well to the unspoken but crucially important whiteness of the organization. The possibility of white girls and boys socializing and dating was one level of trouble—but the possibility of girls and boys of different races meeting each other, dating, and having sex posed such a strong threat to a system of white supremacy that this danger was evoked far into the twentieth century as a rationale for segregated troops and camps. And indeed, almost everything in the early years of the Girl Scouts—even as it espoused a narrative of inclusivity—worked to ensure that the racial system was not shaken or challenged.

The whiteness of the Girl Scouts, while generally unspoken and unmarked, was critical to its ability to deflect and contain accusations that it was a dangerous organization. Maintaining whiteness meant that the organization was allowing for new experiences for (some) girls, but it was not fomenting a cultural, social, and political revolution. In *The Golden Eaglet* we can see this whiteness starkly—every girl in the film, in town, at camp, and at the award ceremonies, is white. The one African American, the cook, is a person to be patronized, teased, and maybe even liked—but she and any daughters she may have are not part of the Girl Scout movement, except as staff and servants.

Girl Scout Novels

The vision *The Golden Eaglet* constructs of a racialized world that champions "helping others" was repeated in several series of Girl Scout novels published from the 1920s through the 1950s. Some were actually officially approved and sold by the Girl Scouts and some were written by Girl Scout staff such as Edith Lavell, the director of Girl Scouts in Philadelphia, who penned a 1922 series based at the fictional Miss Allen's School in Pennsylvania. Other novels just used the Girl Scout name but did not have an official seal of approval. All the series, officially approved by the Girl Scouts or not, are listed in the *Girl Scout Collector's Guide* as "fun to collect," which gives them a stamp of nostalgia.

Each of these Girl Scout novels from the first half of the twentieth century can be classified as formula literature and generally follow the same narrative: the creation of a new Girl Scout troop, a particular adventure or mystery facing the troop, and a conflict among some of the girls that is always resolved by the end of the novel. Like in other girls' series such as the original Nancy Drew mysteries, the girls inhabit a world demarcated by race and class where the ideal is white, wealthy, and able-bodied.[28] Laundrymen are described as "Ch**ks"; Black men working in Pullman trains are referred to as "c**ns all dolled up in dish towels"; and the names of girls like Dagmar Bosika, the immigrant mill girl in *The Girl Scout Pioneers* by Lillian C. Garis, are referred to as "queer" and "foreign." Girl Scouts are picked up from troop meetings in a "big, spiffy limousine" with a chauffeur, often Black and speaking in dialect or a Chinese person speaking in broken English. Hostility toward the class system is met with scorn; for instance, Girl Scout leaders scold the mill girls for mocking the wealthy executives as "swells" and they disparage union organizing as not letting anyone "think for themselves."[29]

Sometimes the novels seem to suggest Girl Scouts might be an avenue for significant class mobility, assuming the character is white. In Edith Lavell's 1922 *The Girl Scouts Good Turn*, for instance, Marjorie persistently works to improve the situation of Frieda Hammer, "a poor, ignorant, badly brought up country girl," who is described as "uncivilized."[30] After running away and stealing Marjorie's canoe, Frieda goes through hard times, staying by herself in abandoned houses and finding work in mills under assumed names. Joining a Girl Scout troop channels Frieda's energy, and she finally returns to school. At first Marjorie invites Frieda to her own Girl Scout troop's summer canoe trip, and it seems as if this "country," "uncivilized" "mill girl" might be skipping over boundaries to join the exclusive Miss Allen's School Girl Scouts (exclusive because one must go to Miss Allen's School, earn an 80 percent grade average, and make the hockey team in order to join the troop). This awkward moment is resolved, however, when Frieda offers her services as the troop's cook. She can indeed join the exclusive Miss Allen's School Girl Scouts but as their servant.

The racial and class caste system had a foundational hold in all the early Girl Scout novels.[31] In the ideology of the Girl Scouts, individual transformation and "helping others in need," particularly sister scouts, was key. Usually these sister scouts in need of help were working-class or foreign-born immigrants, who were given assistance but never, like in the case of Frieda, enough to move into the highest social class. Indeed, part of the working-class girls' transformation was recognizing and accepting their place—as cooks, for example, or nonunionized workers who appreciate the helpfulness of the executive's daughter. The only example of wealthy girls needing to be "uplifted" focused on girls who were deemed too selfish and too inactive, traits represented by a chunky body. In Lavell's novel, another character named Lilly Andrews begins life at the prestigious Miss Allen's "extravagantly overdressed, noticeably fat, and crude in every respect." Over time, and with the help of her sister scouts, Lilly "put aside her extravagant taste, had resolutely trained herself down by self-denial, and had even done creditably in athletics." Vestiges of her old self remain (she still needs to fight her tendency toward "laziness," and she is described as "plodding"), but basically this white former fat girl experiences "uplift" through the program and character-building of the Girl Scouts.[32]

White girls—rich and poor—populate the Girl Scout novels. Just as in *The Golden Eaglet*, however, we see no girls of color as Girl Scouts in these popular publications of the 1920s. They are outside the parameters of the world of sisterhood, adventure, and "doing good" that the Girl Scout novels articulated. This exclusion was not just part of the imaginary story, however; this was also the reality baked into the heart of the first institution the Girl Scouts created: the Girl Scout camp.

Camping: Pioneer Mythology, Sexuality, and Racial Discrimination

Much of *The Golden Eaglet* takes place at what very early on in Girl Scout history established itself as the most sacred of institutions: camp. As did so many of the youth organizations that began at the beginning of the twentieth century, Girl Scouts viewed camping and camps as crucial to their program and to the development of girls and young women. Crucially important, camping gave Girl Scouts a vehicle to create an intrepid girlhood, an outlet for boyish activity, and a space to create the all-female communities of strength and adventure that so upset the Boy Scouts. And it is in looking at these camps in more detail that we can see how the Girl Scouts' white-centered policies and suppression of sexuality worked out in reality, not just in films like *The Golden Eaglet* or in Girl Scout novels.

The Girl Scout focus on camping was true of many girls' organizations at the time, including the Camp Fire Girls and the YWCA's Girl Reserves, all of which viewed getting girls outdoors as key to reclaiming a spirit and virtue that had been lost with urban and technological development.[33] Visits to farms, outings to parks, walks in the woods, and swims in outdoor bodies of water: these were both a salve for the degradations of modern life and a means to gain strength in a largely urban culture that no longer required the physical strength and activity of farm life. Boy Scouts particularly emphasized the importance of outdoor life; Lord Baden-Powell famously quipped that "woodcraft" was crucial to building young men, a reference to the ways that presumably primitive, natural crafts, preferably done in a camping setting, bolstered a masculinity weakened by industrial life. As Gail Bederman details in her pathbreaking work *Manliness and Civilization*, there was a tremendous emphasis in the early twentieth century on the importance of the outdoors as a way to capture white virile masculinity that had purportedly been eviscerated with the advent of the modern era. Politicians such as Teddy Roosevelt and organizations such as the YMCA all subscribed to this view.[34]

None of the girls' organizations, of course, as Susan Miller points out, wanted to suggest that the outdoors were a way to make girls permanently masculine. But they did give girls a chance to dabble in being a "tomboy," a phrase that the Boy Scout critics threw about so frequently in the criticisms detailed above. Being a "tomboy" gave girls a lot of freedom, at least for the years in which they were allowed to indulge in boyish, assertive, outdoorsy behavior. Significantly, however, class and race factored into who could safely act as a tomboy; only white upper- and middle-class girls had sufficient "femininity" to safely indulge in such temporary masculine play, at least according to dominant cultural critics of the time.[35] And that is precisely what we see in early Girl Scout camping: the girl as tomboy, encased in the privileges of whiteness.

When emphasizing the centrality of camp in the Girl Scout experience, the organization highlighted the importance of being outdoors—hiking (or tramping, as it was called in the early twentieth century), making nature crafts, swimming in ponds and lakes, and building campfires—as ways for girls to throw off the trappings of civilization, weakness, and decadence and enliven their overcoddled spirits. The Girl Scouts' rival group, the Camp Fire Girls, emphasized the importance of the hearth (the campfire), around which their members, all taking on fictional names and the dress of Indian maidens, would rekindle an energetic devotion to the domestic arts. Similarly, Girl Scouts often worked to stoke memories of the "Indigenous" in camping experiences, which became especially obvious—and convoluted—when the organization brought scouting to American Indian reservations and boarding schools. But compared to the Camp Fire Girls, Girl Scouts placed less emphasis on the hearth and the maiden and much more on the pioneer: the intrepid scout forging new paths, entering new territories, and drawing on the skills and fortitude of the ancestors, whether real or imagined.

The emphasis on outdoor life and the pioneer spirit meant that Girl Scouting pushed the development of camping for girls from its origins. One of Juliette Gordon Low's first Girl Scout endeavors was a two-week camping trip near Savannah, and by 1919 Girl Scouts had set up its first permanent camp outside Springfield, Massachusetts. In 1920, the Girl Scout National Headquarters published one of its first manuals, *Campward Ho! A Manual for Girl Scout Camps*, which was "designed to cover the needs of those undertaking to organize and direct large, self-supporting camps for girls."[36] In 1921, Camp Andree Clark opened in Briarcliff, New York, donated by the wealthy parents of Andree Clark, a Girl Scout who had died when she was only sixteen. Camp Andree first served as an experimental site to train leaders for Girl Scout camping and then as a residential camping site for Girl Scouts. Just adjacent to Camp Andree, the Girl Scouts opened Camp Edith Macy in 1926, which became the preeminent training site in the United States and the site of the first US International World Camp.[37] And by 1932, the World Association of Girl Guides and Girl Scouts, with monies from the American Helen Storrow, had opened Our Chalet in mountainous Adelboden, Switzerland, a center focused on international gatherings and outdoor adventure.[38] The focus on camping was extraordinarily successful: According to Girl Scout records, by 1932 there were 575 resident camps operating, with over 50,000 Girl Scouts attending every year. And importantly, just a few years earlier, in 1930, the Girl Scouts' intercultural committee had set up a "definite campaign to promote camping for *all* girls."[39]

Nearly every stream of thinking connected to early Girl Scout camping emphasized the ideal of the pioneer, a fact that is central to understanding how Girl Scouting imagined and circumscribed the ideal of the intrepid American girl.[40] In a 1930 internal memo titled "Program Building for the Permanent Camp," summarized in a 1987 Girl Scout report, Louise Price explained that "we are trying to restore to the girl her pioneer heritage through our outdoor program." Elaborating, she wrote that "our girls will be pioneers along their own frontiers which, in the future, will be the frontiers of education, social justice, home attitudes, arts and recreation. We will have much to contribute to the life of her family and community and there is nothing finer to the modern American girl who is geared to things that are worthwhile." Camping meant spending time in nature, identifying wildlife and plants, sleeping in tents or under the stars, learning to build fires, swimming, making group meals, doing chores, taking long hikes, and creating ceremonies (called "Scouts Owns") and sing-alongs. Scouting guidelines discouraged tennis (a game of the wealthy), basketball (an urban game), and jazz (music linked to loose morals and urban decadence); in 1925, the Girl Scouts even developed an official camping songbook "about pioneer and nature themes to counteract the influence of Jazz."[41] While the guidelines did not explicitly state that jazz was unwholesome because its roots were African American, certainly this was related to the rationale for discouraging it. Square dancing and folk music, hailing from Europe and with roots in the "pioneer days," earned center stage instead.[42] Ironically, Girl Scouts encouraged girls to imagine a rural past—of pioneers cultivating the land and pushing through the frontier, of Native Americans whose strength was impressive if doomed—but *actual* rural people and Native Americans were generally perceived as inferior, if quaint and interesting, folks who might be dangerous (in the case of a farmer protecting his land from intruding hikers) or were ignorant (as in the Native Americans who required the Girl Scouts to teach them).[43] At best, actual rural people and American Indians did not understand the theories, focus, and purpose of Girl Scouting.[44] Pioneering, instead, was a mythic construction, in which the imagined forebears (whether they would have actually been their ancestors or not) gave strength and a sense of purpose to young girls. This was true from the earliest days of scouting to the twenty-first century, where I recently saw tents designed to look like Conestoga wagons at Camp Ledgewood in Northeast Ohio, the camp I had attended in the 1970s. Indeed, one of the themed sessions I had attended was "Pioneer Week," where we slept outside, whittled, and cooked over campfires. For me as a white girl whose actual ancestors came to the very urban Cleveland, Ohio, in the late nineteenth century from Bohemia, Ireland, and Germany, fleeing forced conscription, poverty, and potato famines, the American pioneer, traveling in wagons to the West, was still, nevertheless, the ancestor to whom my imagination was supposed to cling.

What is key to recognize is the extent to which this emphasis on the *pioneer*, from its earliest usage, gave legitimation to girls pushing into territory that had been identified as male. Girl Scouts were "pioneers" and "frontierswomen," identities that gave license to act courageously and to demand rights but without the dangerous identification as feminists, woman's righters, or suffragists. It was much easier to create opportunities for girls by using this rhetoric of "pioneering," to keep "innocent" of the politics surrounding women's rights in the early twentieth century. The repercussions of this tactic cannot be underestimated, however. It meant that the articulation of opportunities for girls was linked to a both a myth and a reality in which white people assumed superiority and claimed dominance over land and people: Native Americans, African Americans, and colonies throughout the world. It meant, too, then, that who "girls" were to the Girl Scouts organization—even if it said "all girls"—was really white girls, the pioneer girls of yesterday. To be a Girl Scout meant adopting this mythic ideal of white, Euro-American, pioneer womanhood.

This ideal girl camper was also healthy, details of which were supposed to be documented before attendance by filling out a detailed physical form, signed by a physician. Indeed, with its focus on improving the health of the next generation, the entire project of camping can be seen as part of the burgeoning eugenics movement of the time, though this was not explicitly stated in the scouting publications.[45] Instead, the 1920 *Campward Ho!* manual couched these ideas in positive, cheerful tones: "Young girls are ambitious to do all that their fellows do," *Campward Ho!* read, "and very seldom are willing to admit any physical disability."[46] It was the responsibility of the troop leader, the physician, or the camp nurse to identify any underlying problems with weight (only underweight; being overweight was not mentioned as a possibility), anemia, flat feet, heart problems, or lice. The camper was supposed to have fortitude and heartiness, attributes that would increase with the camping experience, provided they had strong counselors and a good environment. The counselors were supposed to be no-nonsense and practical, because, as *Campward Ho!*

explained, "While patience and sympathy are both needed in group living, sentimentality is to be avoided."[47] A 1924 health report from Camp Andree noted that the biggest physical problems campers had during the summer were strained and sprained ankles, which could have been avoided had the girls had the "right kind of shoes." Otherwise, for the most part, the head nurse noted that there were too many cases of "hypochondrism," which would spread and cause "overanxiety." She explained that she tried to keep ill girls in the encampment rather than in the infirmary, as isolation seemed to make symptoms worse, but then, she wrote, "I frequently found the whole encampment attempting to render home nursing, hustling about in a frightened hysterical way, thus making the patient feel very sick." There were even "three cases of hysteria," which the nurse treated by threatening to kick the girls out of camp. "They were all girls of unstable or surly temperaments who needed to be handled firmly."[48] Camping scouts were supposed to be strong, sturdy girls, not wilting flowers flummoxed by minor ailments.

Within this ideal world of camping—with physical challenges, nature crafts, swimming in open water, challenging hikes, and daily chores—sexuality was only alluded to as a problem to be contained. The 1913 manual *How Girls Can Help Their Country* referred to genitalia, reproduction, and sexuality in only the most general of terms. "No girl must bathe [meaning going swimming] when not well," the handbook read, in what seems to be a veiled reference to menstruation.[49] More tellingly, on the rules of campsites:

> No Scouts allowed out of bounds without leave.
> No lads allowed inside bounds without leave.[50]

Girl Scout camps very rarely included mixed gatherings with boys' camps, and if they did, they were under limited and constrained circumstances. There was concern generally about policing girls' sexual and social mingling with boys but more specifically about the wrong groups of girls mixing with the wrong groups of boys. Certainly this was true about racial mixing, but in the early decades this was downplayed, because for the most part African American girls and boys were largely excluded from camping. Nevertheless, religious and class differences also played a part in concern about cross-gender mingling, especially because Girl Scout camps could certainly include Catholic girls, Protestant girls, Jewish girls, and girls from various ethnicities and classes. Indeed, even far into the twentieth century, an internal report explained that one of the only documented cases of mixed-gender camping, set up by National Headquarters in the New Hampshire White Mountains, was successful precisely because these were upper-class boys, from the "same type of families" as the girls. As the 1956 report read, "On the staff were three men from Dartmouth, experienced in mountain climbing; three women, also mountain climbers. There were 24 campers, 16–18 years of age. Campers came from same type families. All the boys selected were known to the councils who sent girls. . . . The camp was a *great* success—'Mostly because of the carefully selected campers.' But it was felt it was controlled, therefore, not repeated the next year."[51]

Of course, just because the camps excluded boys, it did not mean that sex was absent. Indeed, placing girls, teenagers, and young women in close quarters, in circumstances with no distractions from boys, in settings where they could explore their own sense of possibilities and challenges, certainly enhanced the possibility of girls imagining and experiencing each other as sexual and sensual partners. Despite (or perhaps because of) this, the Girl Scouts, as a national organization, kept a tight lid on any discussion or expression of lesbian or queer sexuality. In her 1925 report from Camp Andree, Jessica Rippin described her own work to curtail such sociality: "I strongly recommend that there be no after-taps parties at the Lodge or where it is possible either to hear the gayety or know that such things go on. Our girls at Andree, after all, average 16 ½ year and should be considered at all times. I believe that in my effort to discourage recreation among the councilors, I must have been rather irksome to them."[52] In Nancy Manahan's moving collection of essays *On My Honor: Lesbians Reflect on Their Scouting Experience*, women recount how much Girl Scouting, especially camping, created environments in which they could develop and act on sexual and sensual feelings. At most, however, there was a tolerance for such behavior if it was kept quiet and hidden—even if in plain sight. When lesbian and queer activity came to the attention of local councils, camp executives, the board of directors, or National Headquarters, however, and it could not be explained away or dismissed, it was quickly suppressed, even at great cost to the women involved.[53] Interestingly, though, archival records related to sexuality—lesbian, heterosexual, or queer—were extraordinarily sparse in the materials I examined at the Girl Scout National Historic Preservation Center. The records may be there, but they were not open to me as a researcher. Instead, what is available in light of this absence are oral histories and pieces of information that can be teased out from inference.

If sexual activity at the camps was seen as a problem to be silenced by the national organization (even if it was actually a wonderful possibility for many participants), the national archival record is much richer when it comes to discussions about race, in particular the participation of African American campers. Indeed, the archival record is so detailed about policies of exclusion and stigmatization in camping that a difficult and embarrassing history for Girl Scouting emerges, one which had lasting damage on African American girls and on the possibilities for truly diverse scouting. At the same time, African American women's continued insistence to be part of national training centers for camping and to create camping experiences for the girls in their communities demonstrates the powerful ways that outdoor excursions and nature immersion promised uplift and advancement; it was not something that African Americans themselves rejected.

As noted above, the very imaginary of "camp" and the pioneer girl was white. Indeed, the only explicit representation of African Americans in camping in these early decades was hired help, as a needed resource for developing a strong camping program for (white) girls. The 1920 manual *Campward Ho!*, for instance, listed all the chores the girls themselves should do and the work required of counselors and directors, all of whom were Girl Scouts themselves. It then added to this list of jobs three non–Girl Scouts: "A handy-man if the camp is large and there is much heavy work to be done; a cook and cook's helper."[54] Later in the manual there is a photo of a white girl in a Girl Scout uniform standing before a wood fire and an African American woman in turban and long skirt, definitely not a Girl Scout uniform. "The Sunday Dinner," the caption reads. "A serious and weighty undertaking. Sixty pounds of beef ready for the pot."[55] This African American cook, then, who doesn't even get a name, is *resource to* the camp but not *of* the Girl Scouts themselves.

While the African American woman as cook was seen as an indispensable resource for the camp itself, the Girl Scout national organization in the first half of the twentieth century viewed actual African American girls and leaders as largely incompetent interlopers in the camping experience.[56] If they were allowed to participate in the resident camps at all, it generally was for a limited time, for two weeks at the beginning or, more typically, after the end of the normal season. This timing ensured not only that Black and white campers would not mix but that the camps—sleeping quarters, latrines, and swimming pools—could be cleaned before white campers arrived or returned for the following year. If individual African American girls had their applications for attendance accepted, they were generally rejected once it became apparent to the camp that they were Black. In the rare instances that individual girls were accepted for attendance, the focus was on allowing only the "best type," ones whose class and educational status would ruffle few feathers among the white families. Accusations of low skill level and camping inexperience often were lobbed against African American troops who wanted to attend, despite the fact that the camps certainly accepted the skilled work of Black handymen and cooks. Girl Scouts was much more likely to accept African American girls for day camps, circumscribed ventures that went from midmorning to late afternoon. Frequently the rationale for day camps was that they were less expensive for campers, which was true. But day camp also meant that there was no specter of shared bathing and sleeping facilities, which were fundamental arenas for white fears and where white people enacted their discriminatory practices.[57]

A 1940 report from Camp Andree illuminates the reality African American girls faced through the early decades of the twentieth century—the limited access, the excuses used to rationalize discrimination, white board members' constrained attempts to battle the policies, and a culture where explicit discussion about race, racism, and discrimination was profoundly discouraged. "According to present policy," the report read, "colored Girl Scouts are accepted at Camp Andree during the last two-week period provided there are enough registrations to fill a unit. There has been a colored unit at camp on only one occasion when the Abigail Morris scholarships were granted to a group of Harlem Girl Scouts." In other words, Camp Andree allowed Black girls to camp the last two weeks of the season, but because there was *yet another* requirement that there be a large enough group, the reality was that only *once* in the camp's history since 1921 had there been African American girls. The report also indicates that individual African American girls may have applied for admission, but they would have been rejected once the camp officials knew they were Black. This may have happened via letter, if the officials found out quickly enough, but it also may have been a humiliating encounter at the actual campsite. In discussing the newer camp policies, the report noted that it was unlikely that an African American group large enough to fill a complete section of the camp, or what camp staff called a "unit," would sign up simultaneously. Someone suggested that perhaps there could be a solution: "Since the Andree folder is sent to all Senior troops, it is possible that applications may be received from colored girls, and since the units of interest at Andree are now based on choice, it is unlikely that twenty girls will choose the same unit of interest. The suggestion was therefore made that the staff be authorized to accept two or four colored girls, for whom a separate tent could be provided." Even this suggestion for limited integration was rejected: "The Program Committee, however, disapproved of changing the present ruling. Under the new set-up, this decision will make it impossible to accept applications from colored girls." The rationale then continued, drawing on the concept of African American incompetence: "It was the opinion of the staff that the colored girls could not keep pace with other campers and that it would not be fair to have them in camp together."[58]

The rationale of presumed incompetence was a frequent one in camping literature, one that certainly stands out as unreasonable considering that white girls did not need to pass any competency tests. Just as I did, the white girls would learn their camping skills while at summer camp or during the school year when visiting a Girl Scout camp. I was certainly never expected to have those skills before joining the scouts. This scrutiny of camping skills was a continual test for African American girls, whose leaders often had to provide evidence of hiking and outdoor cooking experience just to have the right to form a troop. For instance, historian Miya Carey notes that Gladys Ward led over fifty Black girls on rigorous hikes and outdoor cooking excursions in Maryland in the early 1930s in order to meet the requirements to register with national headquarters.[59] This is an important detail, as in other materials I read that would have been sent to white communities, there was no such skill testing prior to membership or troop formation.

Interestingly, to return to the situation at Camp Andree, one of the members of the advisory committee objected to this rationale of presumed incompetence; he basically pushed the Girl Scouts to be more honest about its discriminatory practices: "Dr. Osborne stated that scholarships could be granted to colored girls whose family background and schooling would make it possible for them to participate in activities on a level with the other campers. He thought it was a question of having the organization decide whether or not to accept colored girls at Andree." Osborne also pushed for the camp to actually integrate, though he did seem oblivious to the ostracism and loneliness this likely would have meant for the Black camper: "Dr. Osborne felt that if there are two colored girls, they should not be placed in the same tent. He thought it should be possible to find girls who would be interested in sharing a tent with a colored girl." The Camp Andree advisory council concluded by voicing its willingness to try Osborne's limited suggestion of allowing one or two Black girls, "as an experiment if the occasion arises, although it was pointed out that there may be parental [i.e., white parental] objection." One imagines that the occasion could easily be blocked, simply by the board not awarding any scholarships. And also of significance, the advisory council voiced reluctance to discuss race with the campers, meaning the white campers. "It was felt that the matter would have to be discussed with other camp policies, if at all." It's interesting, because discussion of race was something that made it into the official records (unlike, for instance, discussion of sexuality). But when it came to sharing this discussion with the girls themselves, it was presented as too difficult and too impolite for girls' participation. This, of course, was in a context where so much else was *expected* to be discussed by the girls themselves: goals, plans, responsibilities, schedules, priorities. This silencing encouraged white girls' ignorance and "innocence" about race, "normalizing" the all-white world they experienced as "natural" rather than as an environment that had to be carefully policed. It encouraged them to accept this social order without question and without, even, an ability to see it. The cost of this silence was profound and lasted for generations.[60]

African American communities, frustrated with the lack of access to official (white) Girl Scout camps and with the discrimination their girls faced, raised funds to create their own camps, and there are examples throughout the United States—in Savannah, Memphis, Cleveland, New York, and Oakland. Black communities used opportunities available to them for camping, frequently creating extensive day camps, such as the eight separate day camps celebrated in the Black *Pittsburgh Courier* newspaper in 1947.[61] Other Black community leaders, such as Virginia Richardson McGuire in the DC area and Josephine Holloway in the Memphis area, worked diligently for decades to ensure residential camping opportunities for Black girls. Their stories, which I will return to in chapter 7, illuminate how crucial the ideal of camping was to African American women, who pushed to open up this opportunity for their own daughters, nieces, and girls in their communities. For the most part, however, in the first half of the twentieth century the national Girl Scouts adhered to a policy of local rule that maintained a system that prioritized camping for white girls and that provided few opportunities for girls of color, especially African American girls. The focus on the "pioneer" created a prototype of the ideal Girl Scout: intrepid, white, and European. Excluding girls of color from this world normalized the idea that girls of color were indeed "incompetent" at camping and thus incapable of becoming Girl Scouts. This is ironic, of course, as white girls rarely had to come already equipped with the skills they would learn at camp, a fact that underscores how duplicitous the Girl Scouting was in its racial policies. For decades, as we will see in the following chapters, girls and women of color struggled with these exclusionary policies.

The Girl Scouts' iconic 1918 film *The Golden Eaglet* idealized Margaret as an "intrepid" girl, a tomboy who gets to revel in her strength, cunning, and adventure while being protected from accusations of feminism or pushing too far thanks to her whiteness and "innocence." This image of the "intrepid girl"—and the ways that the national organization used it to tamp down accusations of feminism, and the ways that it was linked so closely to a white ideal—will show up again and again in the following chapters, all of which explore moments when we see the Girl Scouts reaching toward, and backing down from, its promise to be an organization for *all girls*. Like the history of the United States in the world, it's a complicated story. The following chapter focuses on an area where the Girl Scouts thought they belonged, though many students and parents resisted and resented their encroachment: American Indian boarding schools. It begins with a young girl from the Caddo Nation in Oklahoma writing to the Girl Scout National Headquarters with her own application for the Golden Eaglet award.

Chapter 4

Girl Scouting and American Indian Girls

••••••

In comparatively few years her race is hurrying through those centuries which other races have taken at leisure in their gradual development. . . . There is an opportunity here for Girl Scouting to render a real service. . . . The modern Indian girl is faced with the necessity of making the difficult transition from the old Indian way of living to a modified form of our own civilization.
—Marguerite Twohy, *Girl Scout Leader*, 1932

On February 2, 1938, Hannah Whitebead wrote to the Committee on Awards at the Girl Scout National Headquarters in New York City. Applying for the Golden Eaglet award, the highest award a Girl Scout could earn, Whitebead explained she was a Caddo Indian girl who spent the school year and most of the summer at Riverside Indian School in Anadocko, Oklahoma, though she clarified that her "real home" was with her parents near Hinton, Oklahoma. A member of one of two Girl Scout troops at Riverside, Whitebead described in detail—following, one presumes, the "questionnaire" that she says the committee had sent her—the extraordinary number of activities and responsibilities she took on as a Girl Scout: chairman of her patrol, designer of a special scout room, and planner of many events, including a steak fry, a sing-around, and a wiener roast. Her group, she wrote, also managed to create an entire beauty parlor, with homemade furniture, decorations, and even a drain board for shampooing. She highlighted her work with the younger troop, the ways she helped them with their tests and games and the trails she set up with candy at the end. She joked about teaching an "official from Washington" how to cook over an open fire. She mentioned Armistice Day and the carrying of troop and US flags. She described fixing a "basket of food and toys to give to a family that needed cheerful Christmas greetings" and learning first aid, which she put to good use when a fellow scout sprained her ankle at Girl Scout camp. Additionally, she tended pigs, sheep, and chickens, worked as the matron's assistant in the girls' dormitory, kept house for a faculty member who lived on campus, and did housework for a Girl Scout committee woman who lived off campus. She also did her own laundry, ironing, and mending and made her own "Sunday dresses." "I think I am making use of my knowledges I learned in my Scout work and in school. I am proud to have been a Girl Scout. I think Scouting has helped me in many ways. I want to always remember the things I have learned and help others to learn them too," she concluded. Hannah Whitebead's detailed letter evoked a hardworking, caring, and outgoing girl—indeed, an intrepid one. It's also an unflinchingly uncomplaining letter—this is a girl who seemed to never stop working, whose daily schedule was so filled there was almost no time for rest. What little respite she did get, including at a camp she attended where she saw beautiful trees and learned about birds and flowers, she described with delight rather than resentment that there was so little time for such activities. Instead, the chores, responsibilities, and relationships with the younger girls are summed up as "making use of my knowledges," a sign of a star girl, eligible for a Golden Eaglet, rather than evidence of a school culture that was unrelenting and unforgiving.[1]

It's not clear from the archival record whether National Headquarters gave Whitebead the prestigious Golden Eaglet award. Girl Scout records frequently mention Betsy Benge, who attended Sequoyah School, an Indian boarding school in Oklahoma whose students were primarily Cherokee, as the first American Indian girl to win the Golden Eaglet—in 1937. Considering the similar timing, it may have been that Whitebead learned of Benge's award and thought it reasonable to apply for the Golden Eaglet herself.[2] Though we don't know whether Whitebead actually earned the Golden Eaglet, her letter gives us an important glimpse into the life of a girl at an Indian school in the early twentieth century and the ways that Girl Scouting framed and shaped her experience there. The 1912 origins of Girl Scouting coincide with a relentless government push of young Indian children off the reservations where they lived and into boarding schools designed to "educate for extinction," in the words of scholar David Wallace Adams.[3] The prototype for all the Indigenous boarding schools, designed to "assimilate" Indian children by forcing them away from home and into harsh, often military-style schools, was Carlisle

Indian Industrial School, founded in 1892 in Carlisle, Pennsylvania, the same town where I have spent nearly my entire adult life.

At the time Whitebead was writing in 1938, the boarding schools had experienced significant criticism for abuse and mismanagement (culminating in what became known as the Meriam Report in 1928), but thousands of Indian children still went to schools away from their homes and reservations, sometimes pressured by government officials, sometimes sent by their families who thought the schools provided their children their best opportunities. Riverside Indian School, which Whitebead attended, served Caddo, Delaware, Wichita, and Kiowa communities, all of whom had been pushed into Oklahoma Indian Country with President Andrew Jackson's Indian Removal Act of 1830.[4] Riverside was about thirty-five miles from what Whitebead notably differentiates as her real home outside Hinton with her family, despite the fact that she lived at Riverside nearly year round and likely saw her family very rarely. The distinction she made between home and school is important because, though the school's purposes in general were to engulf and reshape the students' identities and sense of home, clearly Whitebead resisted, calling her family her real home. Nevertheless, the rest of the letter notes in extensive detail the ways that the school, and particularly Girl Scouting, shaped every minute of her day, including whatever "leisure" the school provided.

Whitebead's letter to the Girl Scout National Headquarters should not have come as a complete surprise, as by this time the Girl Scouts paid considerable attention to American Indian girls. In 1932, the Girl Scouts published an entire issue of the *Girl Scout Leader* on American Indian Girl Scouts. Illustrated throughout with film stills of Indian troops, taken from a moving picture a white Girl Scout field agent shot in Oklahoma and Montana, the issue is also decorated throughout with "genuine" Indian designs and symbols. Clearly, white women, not Native, were the audience for this issue. The substance of its articles focused on the importance of Indians—and especially Indian arts and crafts—for enriching American life. As the US commissioner of Indian Affairs wrote to the Girl Scout National Headquarters in the early 1930s, "In Girl Scouting an Indian girl both gives and takes—she gets American idealism at its best, she can give of her Indian heritage in return."[5] Indeed, page after page in this issue of the *Girl Scout Leader* provides detailed information about making kachina dolls, bead-making, "primitive" design, and woodworking. There is also a list of forty-six books for further "Indian study," mostly related to folktales, nature study, music, dance, and some earlier anthropological work, including a book by Ella Cara Deloria.[6] In Girl Scout thinking, American Indians imparted to Euro-American girls beauty, nature, and a simpler life, unmarred by modern civilization.

Indian Girl Scouts in Oklahoma made their own uniforms (left, above); danced in Indian blankets (top of pages 50, 51). Girl Scouts of the Setting Sun Troop, Hardin, Montana (at right, above, left to right): Lucy Stray Calf; Phylis Plenty Hoops; Blanche Dawes; Annie Singer; Dorothy Big Lake; Edna M. Tobias, Captain; Edna Looks Back; Henrietta White Man, Mary Old Horn (face covered); Naomi White Fox.

Indian Girl Scouts play on a tom-tom made from inner-tubing.

An entire 1932 issue of the *Girl Scout Leader* focused on American Indian Girl Scouts. The issue included stills of Indian troops taken from a film a white Girl Scout field agent shot in Oklahoma and Montana. *From Girl Scout Leader*, May 1932

While the focus on Indian art and lore suggests an antidote to the problems of modernity for Euro-American girls, much of the special issue on American Indian Girl Scouts focused precisely on how Girl Scouts were helping Native Americans make the "necessary" transition to modern civilization. As Marguerite Twohy, a prominent Girl Scout field agent, wrote in the lead article:

> In comparatively few years her race is hurrying through those centuries which other races have taken at leisure in their gradual development. Her school days are her greatest opportunity to discover some sort of adjustment, not only for herself but for her race as well, and for translation of its rich and varied gifts. . . . There is an opportunity here for Girl Scouting to render a real service. . . . The modern Indian girl is faced with the necessity of making the difficult transition from the old Indian way of living to a modified form of our own civilization.[7]

Twohy's short message powerfully expresses the Girl Scout national organization's ambiguous ideas about American Indian Girl Scouting. Insisting on the relevance and importance of Girl Scouts, Twohy also takes note of what is being lost and hopefully how it can be retained. She ends by acknowledging the general white belief that the American Indians will never really achieve the status or ability of white people. These perspectives—an arrogant certainty of the necessity of Girl Scouts and its intrinsic benevolence, a belief in the inherent inferiority of American Indians, and a feeling of nostalgic lament that sometimes breaks through the certainty of the mission—marked the work of the Girl Scouts with American Indians from the 1930s until the 1970s. What stands out most about Girl Scout programming with American Indian girls is the staunch conviction that American Indian girls can learn to "feel good" about themselves by embracing their distinctive Indian cultures—their love of nature, their outdoor skills, and their art forms—as *Girl Scout culture*. As an article in the Girl Scout publication *American Girl* announced, Sacajawea and Pocahontas could have been thought of as the "original" Girl Scouts![8] In other words, Indian cultures needed to be rebranded as Girl Scouting.

Girl Scouts and American Indian Mythology

Much of the wealth that provided the original financial foundation for the Girl Scouts came from Juliette Gordon Low, whose familial assets came both from the enslavement of African people and from the dispossession and genocide of American Indians. In other words, as I underscored in the chapter on the mythology of Low, the financial foundation of the Girl Scouts was based on the seizure of Native American land and the eradication of American Indian people. While the Girl Scouts organization never discusses this fact, one can see traces of it in its naming practices and throughout its commemorative materials. For instance, the name of my own Girl Scout council in Akron, Ohio, the Western Reserve Girl Scout Council, was named after the area of land demarcated first as the Connecticut Western Reserve and then shortened to the Western Reserve. As the US government opened the Western Reserve up to white settlement, Native people, especially the Mingos and Seneca—were pushed inexorably to the west. A series of broken treaties, culminating in the Indian Removal Act of 1830, culminated in an area that the US government recognized as "free" of Indians, especially as it wanted to "cloak the acquisition in legality" and refused to recognize any Indians who remained as actually being Indians, particularly after the Indian Removal Act.[9] At my visits to Girl Scout gift shops, the Juliette Gordon Low Birthplace in Savannah, and the GSUSA headquarters in New York City and on the Girl Scout website, I've seen copies of *Wau-Bun*, the memoir by Low's great-grandmother about her life as a settler in the Midwest, prominently displayed, presumably because it celebrates the "pioneer spirit" of Low's forebears. It also clearly and without guilt demonstrates one fundamental economic basis for the Girl Scouts: the Euro-American domination, removal, and genocide of American Indians.

It wasn't just *Wau-Bun* that signaled the Euro-American conquest of American Indians in the lore of Juliette Gordon Low. On my multiple recent tours of the Juliette Gordon Low Birthplace, I met many Girl Scouts who would also visit Tomochichi's boulder across the street, touching it and sometimes holding hands and encircling it. Tomochichi was the Yamacraw chieftain celebrated in Euro-American history for working closely with Gen. James Oglethorpe in the first half of the eighteenth century to allow European settlement of what is now Savannah.[10] I'd never stopped at the boulder when I visited the Birthplace as a young Girl Scout, so I asked the visiting Girl Scouts why they were doing it. But even the troop leaders didn't actually seem to know why, just that it was an activity passed down to them from other troops, fitting in with the overall ritual of the visit to the Birthplace, an encounter with the "magic" of an American Indian they didn't even know for sure was a real person. They were nonetheless immersed in a settler colonial cultural experience that glorified relationships between Euro-Americans and Indians perceived as friends and even helpmates in the conquest of the United States. Like so much else in US culture, however, in Girl Scouting the domination that was central to our founding as a settler colonial nation was masked with a nostalgic yearning for the "purity" of Indian life and a desire for that energy to infuse contemporary lives.[11]

For the most part, as I noted earlier in this book, the "pioneer" was the fundamental model for the ideal Girl Scout, not the "Indian." In contrast, the leading competitor to the Girl Scouts at this time, the Camp Fire Girls, explicitly drew from the Indian maiden image. Girl Scouts, though, explicitly rejected the "hearth fire" and domesticity of the "Indian maiden" that the Camp Fire Girls encouraged. Instead, Girl Scouts were just that—scouts, the pioneers to the Indian maidens. Nevertheless, for Girl Scouts, Indians were still extraordinarily symbolically important. The very myth of the "scout," of the "pioneer," always included the presence of the Indian—as *inspiration* and as *challenge*, a threat to be overcome, a problem to be solved. The Girl Scouts chose the pioneer half of the pioneer/Indian equation, unlike the Camp Fire Girls, which chose the Indian half. "Pioneers" were intrepid and authentically *American*, but that pioneer spirit depended on "Indians" to construct this oppositional identity. Both parts are crucial to the same myth of adventuresome, intrepid white settlers who overcome the mythically noble if primitive and savage American Indians. Girl Scouts, rejecting the passive femininity implied in the Indian maidens, accessed the world of masculine courage and daring through an embrace of pioneer mythology. Indeed, one of the earliest Girl Scout badges was the Pioneer badge, which portrayed a set of crossed axes, presumably representing the clearing of the land and homesteading.[12] By 1938, the logo for the Pioneer badge had been changed to a teepee, in an interesting shift of iconography that suggests the blurry line between pioneer and American Indian in Girl Scout mythology.[13] An Indian Lore badge was developed in the 1960s, originating from a troop that had designed its own badge, which was then adopted by the national organization. Its purpose was to encourage Girl Scouts to "learn about the ways Indians lived" (note the past tense), and it pictured a kachina doll.[14] My own sash from the 1970s shows that I earned the Pioneer badge but not the one in Indian Lore.

For the Girl Scouts in the twentieth century, however, American Indians were more than the financial basis on which their origins rested and more than the mythology that lay behind their pioneer ideology. They were also the actual, sustained focus of decades of organizational campaigns and fieldwork with girls like Hannah Whitebead at Riverside Indian School. In a 1992 letter, the director of the Girl Scout National Historic Preservation Center wrote, "We seem to have more documentation for Native Americans in Girl Scouting than other groups."[15] According to the archival records, the Girl Scouts worked explicitly with the government to help organize American Indian troops, particularly in federally sponsored boarding schools. Even when funding was inconsistent and sparse and communication and direction often confused, the Girl Scouts explicitly hired a series of "field agents," whose work was to build up American Indian troops, train leaders, and send detailed reports of their lengthy trips, covering hundreds of miles, back to headquarters and to the federal Office of Indian Affairs. All of these exchanges among Indian Affairs officers and Girl Scout professionals resulted in reams of memos and reports, found in the Girl Scout National Historic Preservation Center.

No other group of girls that fell under a federal directive between the US government and the Girl Scouts in the first half of the twentieth century has a paper trail as long as that of American Indians. It's not that American Indians faced no discrimination within the Girl Scouts. As Charlotte Moton Hubbard wrote about a 1946 meeting she had with the education director of the US Office of Indian Affairs, "We should take . . . into careful consideration in extending the [American Indian Girl Scout] program . . . in those sections of the country" where there is a "problem of race. . . . Much of the same kind of attitudes are prevalent toward the American Indians as are prevalent toward American Negroes."[16] In other words, Girl Scouts, Hubbard suggested, should tread lightly in organizing American Indian girls if it causes problems among white troops. Nevertheless, Girl Scouts of the USA (GSUSA) concertedly organized American Indian girls into troops, mainly in remote areas located in federally sponsored boarding schools or on reservations not connected to councils in white areas. American Indian girls proved to be ideal sisters, who appeared to *need help*, a focus integral to the Girl Scouts. As noted in the previous chapter, in the early Girl Scout film *The Golden Eaglet*, the existence of needy people—often sister scouts—was integral to the very identity of Girl Scouts. To accomplish this goal among American Indians, Girl Scouts hired "field agents" to help organize Indian troops, particularly in the Southwest and across the nation in federally sponsored Indian schools. These Girl Scout agents worked with the Office of Indian Affairs and with tribal councils, encouraging Indigenous Girl Scout leadership (to an extent), organizing Indian Girl Scout rallies, and writing articles about Indian scouting for the national organization's publications. American Indian girls and women responded to the field agents in a variety of manners ranging from reluctance and dismissal to determination and desire.

Girl Scouting and the Office of Indian Affairs

In 1927, the *Syracuse Journal* published a photo of a Girl Scout troop in the Seneca Nation of Indians, Onondaga Reservation, noting that the troop had formed in

1921. Marjorie Kirk, a member of the National Camp Committee for twenty-five years and a Girl Scout organizer for over forty, later recalled that she was forming troops in the Syracuse area and she thought it was "a shame to leave out our Indians on the reservations near here. So I did go out and deliberately form a troop of Indian Girl Scouts at the Episcopal Mission there and I believe that was the first Indian troop in the country."[17] It's certainly possible, however, that there were other troops, formal or informal, among American Indians in the continental United States (and at least one troop of Indigenous Hawaiians) in the 1920s.[18]

By the 1930s, however, substantial discussion was taking place between the Office of Indian Affairs (which became the Bureau of Indian Affairs in 1947) and the GSUSA about resources, staffing, training, membership, and the purpose of scouting among American Indians, especially at federally sponsored Indian boarding schools.[19] The prototype for the Indian boarding school model originated in Carlisle, Pennsylvania, as the brainchild of Richard Henry Pratt, who believed in the systematic removal of children from their own communities. "In Indian civilizations I am a Baptist," Pratt wrote at one point, "because I believe in immersing the Indians in our civilization and when we get them under holding them there until they are thoroughly soaked." Pratt designed the Carlisle Indian Industrial School as a school where children were sent far from their homes and prohibited from speaking their own languages, wearing their own clothes, or practicing their own religions or customs. Daily life was busy, hard, and lonely, with morning classes, afternoon vocational lessons, endless chores, and severe discipline in cases of misbehavior. Students often got sick and even died while at school, ran away, and experienced sexual assault, especially during their outings, when they went to work in townspeople's homes and out on the farms of rural neighbors. Among white Americans, Pratt's focus on education was perceived to be more humane that the alternative of war and violence to control the "Indian problem," a systematic way to move American Indians from "savagery" to "civilization." But clearly, as activists, elders, scholars, and even the Bureau of Indian Affairs have argued, the school was its own form of genocide, designed to eliminate Indian sovereignty and cultures. Families sometimes purposefully chose to send their children to the schools—either out of desperation because of poverty and destroyed communities or out of a hope that the education could help their children and their communities. And some people remember their boarding school days with fondness and with respect for the education it provided. For the most part, however, the Carlisle Indian Industrial School, and the system of schools throughout the United States, Canada, Australia, and New Zealand for which it served as the model, created extraordinary intergenerational trauma and destruction throughout Indigenous communities that continues to have ramifications today. Yet throughout these decades of institutional life designed to eradicate Indian culture, communities, and religion, Native American students adapted strategies to survive and to ensure their own histories and futures would continue to live in the future. Girl Scouting was a part of this struggle.[20]

By the 1930s, when the earliest records of significant conversations between the Office of Indian Affairs and the Girl Scouts begin, the Carlisle Indian Industrial School had been closed for over a decade. The Office of Indian Affairs had established boarding schools throughout the United States, though, mostly west of the Mississippi or in the upper Midwest, and generally far from reservations so that children would be removed physically as well as spiritually and culturally from their own communities. Girl Scout records indicate that in 1932 there were thirty-five American Indian Girl Scout troops; in 1936 the number had grown to fifty-eight, many in Oklahoma boarding schools, as well as in New Mexico, North Dakota, and South Dakota.[21] Troops also existed in orphanages for American Indian children and on reservations run by the Office of Indian Affairs, sometimes in lieu of any public schools. Early records indicate that American Indian Girl Scout troops existed in New York, Wisconsin, Nebraska, New Mexico, Oklahoma, Arizona, Montana, Idaho, Colorado, Minnesota, North Dakota, South Dakota, Utah, Oregon, and Washington.[22]

By the time Girl Scouts began its work with the Indian boarding schools, there was significant competition by other organizations such as the YWCA, Camp Fire Girls, and religious groups that wanted to be part of the schools. Indeed, much of the correspondence between Girl Scouts and the Office of Indian Affairs focused on the need for more attention to be given to the Girl Scouts: money for a full-time director of American Indian Girl Scouting, uniforms, and supplies. Both the US government and GSUSA voiced their desire for additional Girl Scouting in the residential schools, but each thought the other entity should do more to foot the bill.[23] Girl Scouts were attractive to the Office of Indian Affairs because they provided that quintessential *image* of Americanness, which Pratt had emphasized since the origins of the boarding school movement, providing numerous occasions for public demonstrations and photographs of uniform-wearing girls taking part in flag ceremonies and demonstrating their "new" skills in homemaking, nature crafts, and citizenship that they had learned through their badgework. With a shift in the Office of Indian Affairs in the 1930s that emphasized some limited development of American Indian arts and language, the Girl Scouts also, as one

Girl Scouts organized troops throughout the United States in off-reservation Native American boarding schools. Pictured is a 1953 troop from Flandreau Indian School in South Dakota. Courtesy of Photographs 1936–1954, Records of the Bureau of Indian Affairs, National Archives, Washington, DC.

Girl Scout community adviser wrote in 1950, help "relate them [American Indians] to the rest of the nation and the world."[24] Girl Scouts organized national training sessions for leaders of American Indian troops in New Mexico and Oklahoma through the 1930s, '40s, and '50s and held multiple all-Indian camps in the 1930s in Oklahoma, with hundreds of Native American Girl Scouts attending.[25]

In the late 1940s, the Bureau of Indian Affairs' director of Navajo education, George Boyce, took a particular interest in Girl Scouting. When, in the 1950s, he became the superintendent of Intermountain Boarding School, located in Utah and one of the largest Indian boarding schools in history, he especially emphasized Girl Scouting, expecting his teachers to lead troops (even when they were extremely overburdened), setting up meetings with the national Girl Scout field agents, and offering training for leaders during a summer program.[26] Intermountain School is especially notorious in the history of American Indian boarding schools for its relentless focus on taking children hundreds of miles from their homes and systematically working to eradicate everything "Indian."[27] Boyce saw Girl Scouting as particularly beneficial to this enterprise, seeing it as a kind of translator helping to "relate them [Indian girls] to the rest of the nation and the world."[28] Much of Boyce's emphasis focused on getting his Navajo students to come into contact with white people, and thus he underscored the importance of integrated camping sites and intercultural exchanges, particularly where Intermountain students would visit white families in Brigham City, Utah, for a few days and then those white students would visit the Indian school for a few days. Girl Scouts would be the guides for the school portion of what Boyce called the Intermountain Indian School Community Visitation and Student Exchange Program. While the exchange may have hopefully fostered sympathetic feelings in the white families and youth toward the Intermountain students, the purpose was not deep teaching or mutual understanding between equal cultures. Instead, the purpose of the exchange was, as a 1953 Girl Scout report noted, "to help Indian youth anticipate and learn how to live in a white community in preparation for their eventual re-settlement off the reservation."[29] This perspective—eradicating Indianness and helping foster "white culture"—was key to the Girl Scouting mission at American Indian boarding schools.

American Indian Girl Scouts as the Foreigner Within

While the national board focused on American Indian girls as part of its mission to bring Girl Scouting to "all girls," it also saw American Indians as a foreigner within, an international arm of outreach.[30] Indeed, the funds used for Girl Scout campaigns among American Indians largely came from the Juliette Gordon Low World Friendship Fund, designed for "international understanding"; field workers often took their orders from the international office of the Girl Scouts, and Euro-American girls became pen pals with American Indian girls by sending their letters to the Girl Scout International Post Box.[31] Working with American Indians was as much an international mission, in Girl Scout ideology and organization, as the founding of the World Association of Girl Guides and Girl Scouts (WAGGGS) and Our Chalet, the international WAGGGS center in Adelboden, Switzerland. Field agent Marguerite Twohy ended her 1932 article in *Girl Scout Leader* this way: "This summer at the International Chalet, girls from many countries, with many languages, will come to understand one another. Here in America, despite the chasm that lies between our civilization and that of the Indian, Girl Scouts of both races are also coming to understand one another."[32] And as the reference to "both" races underscores, always in these early decades the presumption was that the white American Girl Scout was at the center, the one race, who would reach out and connect "despite the chasm" to the foreign Indian girl.

By the 1950s, some members of the board, however, began to question whether funds from the Juliette Gordon Low World Friendship Fund should be used for developing Girl Scouting among American Indian girls. The fund, after all, was designated, as the *Blue Book of Girl Scout Policies and Procedures* described, for the "promotion of Girl Guiding and Girl Scouting throughout the world as a contribution toward world peace and good will." As one board report noted, "Since the American Indians are U.S. citizens the Field Department must find some way to bring Scouting to these girls in the regular channels of the national organization."[33] Field agents, however, pressed their case to use international funds. "The culture of the Navajos is as foreign to the rest of the USA as that of Japan or Korea and probably more different than that of Germany. Their need for help is great," Ivalee Hobden wrote in a field report from her travels to Arizona and New Mexico in 1950.[34] In addition she added, "The Navajos were given the right to vote in the fall of 1948 and they do not know how to use it. The federal government gave them the right to vote a long time ago but Arizona and New Mexico did not extend voting privileges to Indians until 1948. I believe that our Girl Scout program, at its best, is badly needed to help the Navajos to understand their privileges and responsibilities as citizens." Thus, as a result of field pressure, through the 1950s the perspective prevailed that American Indian girls should be served through the international channel. Indeed, the threat of communism provided yet another level of urgency and rationale. As one field agent noted, "Increasingly, we are aware that our relations with other countries are seriously affected by the adverse publicity which the Communists are giving in their interpretation of our treatment of our racial minorities. Some of our Girl Scout adults traveling abroad have had to face open criticism that our much publicized democracy neglects its own racial minorities. . . . I believe this would be another step toward living the democracy we preach to other countries, and thus further our efforts toward international friendship."[35] While on the one hand highlighting the work of Girl Scouting among American Indian girls demonstrated to the world the force of democracy at home and abroad, on the other hand the Girl Scout national organization perceived it as somewhat of a conundrum: Were American Indians actually "foreign," or were they a domestic branch—a "foreigner at home"—within the organization?

Field Agents and the Girl Scout Helping Hand

Much of what we know about Girl Scouting among American Indians comes directly from the field agents, who generally were white, single, professional women. They traveled far and wide, meeting with troops and leaders, setting up conferences between the Bureau of Indian Affairs and the Girl Scouts, and attending investiture ceremonies and Girl Scout rallies. They wrote long letters, filled out forms, and made cases for more staffing and more resources. They clearly took satisfaction in their work, the knowledge they had accrued about American Indian nations, the ties they developed with the Indian school administrators and teachers, and the connections they made with the Bureau of Indian Affairs and reservation officials.

These women worked hard and prided themselves on their ability to withstand challenging circumstances. Many of their reports to headquarters spoke about difficult travel conditions. In her report on a weeklong trip to the Navajo Nation in 1944, Lucile Skewes noted how impossible it was to visit all the various schools, at one point even aborting a visit to Crown Point because "the valves on my car had reached such a bad state that I was fearful to get off the highway after dark."[36] A few years later, after a two-month stay on the Navajo reservation, Capitola Hill wrote that the Girl Scouts needed to provide more resources for "intercultural" work among the Hopi, Pueblo, and Navajo. The new staff member should be a professional woman, a leader in Girl Scouting, knowledgeable about "Western ways and ideas" (by which presumably she meant American Indian). But above all, she needed better transportation. She emphasized, "And, this is a must—she cannot do the work without a car, because there is no other way of reaching those schools. She must also be willing to drive great distances—some schools are over a hundred miles apart—over unpaved roads. Her travel allowance should be great enough to take care of major car repairs."[37]

These women, then, truly saw themselves as "scouts," for the most part working by themselves or in pairs, generally unmarried, reporting their adventures, their meetings, and their accomplishments back to the National Headquarters. They experienced a level of freedom and autonomy that would have been very uncommon among white women in the United States at the time. They also saw themselves as mini anthropologists, taking pride in the connections they made with the girls and working to translate the cultural knowledge they gained for national headquarters and white Girl Scouts through their articles in the *Girl Scout Leader* and *American Girl*. Marguerite Twohy, for instance, worked for over thirty years in the field department, beginning her work with the Pawnee Indian School north of Tulsa, Oklahoma, and over time working the entire area of Oklahoma, New Mexico, Arizona, and Utah. Numerous times Girl Scouts reference her story of attending an investiture ceremony at Pawnee Indian School, attended by parents and family members as well as teachers and other students. She noted how beautiful she thought their "Indian names" were—Little White Moon, Flying Cloud—wishing they had been able to keep them "throughout life," hoping in fact that they returned to their own names when they left school. And the girls then surprised her, after she handed out all their Girl Scout pins, by bestowing upon her an "Indian" name—Staditadaku, meaning "flower"—and giving her a beautifully beaded pair of moccasins.[38] Mary White was another prominent field worker, working her way up through the administrative ranks and authoring many of the reports and memos to the national office and the Bureau of Indian Affairs. Indeed, the *Girl Scout Leader* celebrated White as a "contemporary pioneer," whose life on her father's New Mexico cattle ranch translated well to her work as postmistress in a small New Mexico city and then to her leadership within the Girl Scouts. For decades, White penned letter after letter, responding to requests for information about American Indian troops in the Southwest and urging the national organization to provide more funds, especially for camping opportunities for American Indian girls.[39]

As a group, these field agents were sympathetic to the problems facing American Indians, particularly poverty and lack of education, and they often articulated an appreciation for their cultures, which they thought were worth saving, albeit in a modified form. Importantly, the Girl Scout field agents also saw American Indians as *inherently* needy, people whose lives were broken by their primitive culture, not by the centuries of genocide that had destroyed communities and pushed them onto impoverished reservations. Girl Scouts saw themselves as the antidote to that neediness. To add to the field agents' roles as adventuresome scouts and field anthropologists, their most vital was as missionaries for the Girl Scouts. And, like the white female Christian missionaries whose righteousness allowed them access to a full life of travel and independence, these Girl Scout field workers similarly had access to experiences far different than their more domestic sisters.[40] As Capitola Hill wrote in 1946 about her work with the Navajo Nation, being a field agent was "one of the most wonderful opportunities for intercultural work in the country," a way to "broaden their knowledge and to help" children who have "dire need" for the "bare necessities of life."[41] And the field workers also provided the paths for white troops to practice their helping hands, suggesting ways for them to provide assistance to Indian Girl Scout troops who had little to no money for national dues, uniforms, badges, or camping. Archival evidence indicates that some troops organized donations of used and outgrown uniforms, dresses, hats, and shoes, which they sent to Indian school troops. Some Indian school troops made contact with eastern white troops, who directly "helped" by setting up shops to sell the dolls and crafts made by Indian Girl Scouts, returning the money to Indian school troops, which frequently needed money to pay for dues, uniforms, and badges. In thanks for the donations of Girl Scout materials, one Indian troop sent a beautiful rug back to a troop in New York state.[42] And so in this way, white Girl Scout troops also benefited from this missionary point of view, broadening their own horizons through these pseudo-"international" exchanges with American Indian troops.

Sacajawea as the First Girl Scout: Girl Scouting and the Legitimation of "Indianness"

On a more complex level, though, the ability of white troops to help Indian troops went far beyond the simple provision of direct assistance or as philanthropic consumer. It also, more fundamentally, was the conferral of authenticity and legitimacy *back* to the "Indians." This is probably the most complex but also one of the most important part of the Girl Scouts' ideological engagement with American Indian Girls in the 1930s through the 1950s. As a 1934 *Girl Scout Leader* article noted, for instance, "Girl Scout camping is widely recognized as one of the most satisfactory of the Girl Scout gifts. It is a happy circumstance, therefore, that this gift is now being shared with true Americans whose ancestors taught the early settlers so much that they needed to know of stream, wood, and animal lore."[43] (By "true Americans" the *Leader* article meant American Indian girls.) The forms of dress, living practices, and community styles, which the earlier policies of Indian boarding schools had attempted to destroy and delegitimize, now were recognized by the national organization as authentic Girl Scouting and were "given back" to American Indian troops. In 1940, an *American Girl* article by the drama and arts director of the Girl Scouts, Oleda Schrottky, reported on a pageant performed by Girl Scouts at the Santa Fe Indian School. A total of twenty-three girls from many tribes and pueblos—"Mescalero Apache and Hopi tribes, and the pueblos of San Joan, Santo Domingo, Nambe, Zia and Acoma"—were members of two troops, one named "Sacajawea," the guide for Lewis and Clark, and the other "Nampeyo," a renowned female pottery maker. In the pageant, the troops decided to portray the lives of eight famous women whom they had researched in the school library: Pocahontas, Betsy Ross, Molly Pitcher, Sacajawea, Dolly Madison, Julia Ward Howe, Clara Barton, and Juliette Gordon Low. All the women the girls chose to portray were explicitly linked to the nationalist project of the United States: as Indian "friends" to the explorers, creator of the flag, helpmate to her husband in war, wife of the president who saved the Declaration of Independence, author of the "Battle Hymn of the Republic," nurse to the troops, and founder of the Girl Scouts. Schrottky's article about the American Indian girls' pageant fits them into an ideal of white intrepid girlhood: young women yearning to break free of male constraint.

Schrottky's descriptions of Pocahontas and Sacajawea merit particular attention for the ways they illuminate the process of turning American Indian girls into leaders who defy male authority, whose work and talents could be shaped into meaningful narratives about Girl Scout achievement. "In reading the life of Pocahontas—who was the first character to appear—the girls found that she was a tomboy, and often turned handsprings with her brothers, to the dismay of her father, who was chief of the tribe. In fact, she was romping with her brothers when the runner came with news that Captain John Smith had been captured," Schrottky wrote. Pocahontas, then, was a tomboy, just like Low, who loved physical activity and defied patriarchal authority and limitations. But, importantly, she used those skills to be a brave peacemaker: "Pocahontas, who was then just twelve years old, stood erect and resolute before her father, and when the prisoner was brought in and his head laid upon the two huge stones, she flung herself upon him and save him from death. This was the beginning of a great friendship between the Indians and the Colonists. This little girl was a peacemaker and, through her understanding of people and ability to mediate, she save both sides much bloodshed." Again, there is much to note here, including the gyration upon which Indian-colonialist history is now portrayed as a "great friendship," navigated by the courageous and emotionally savvy work of a twelve-year-old girl, the typical age of the Girl Scouts in the Santa Fe Indian School. Sacajawea is actually portrayed as the "original Girl Scout," predating Low. Schrottky explained, "Sacajawea, the bird woman, guide of the Lewis and Clark exploring party, is known to all of us. We think of her as a guide and trail blazer, but she was a mother and homemaker and interpreter to the Indians, as well." The next part of Schrottky's description is especially noteworthy because it illuminates how Girl Scouting allows Indians to understand their own lives:

> *Had she been given a badge for each of her skills, she would have had her sleeve appliqued with them.* On the long trek through the wilderness, when food was scarce, she boiled and roasted roots and wild onions, showed the men how to get grease from elk bones to use for butter, and knew every edible seed and berry in the wilderness. Sacajawea did not need a compass. She used the sun and the stars to steer by. The journey was full of dangers and hardships, but she led the Lewis and Clark expedition safely to their goal, the Pacific Ocean. Girl Scouts like to think of her as the first Girl Scout, and are proud of her loyalty, courage, resourcefulness, and service for posterity.[44]

Like Pocahontas, Sacajawea could be thought of as the "original Girl Scout."

Even American Indian languages were co-opted by the Girl Scouts to become an achievement, a badge to be sewn onto a sleeve. A *Girl Scout Leader* article noted in the 1930s that Girl Scouts who attended a camp in Oklahoma helped a social worker speak with a neighboring Indian family. "One of the girls volunteered to help the social worker, and gave an intelligent and helpful demonstration of her ability to converse alternately in Cherokee and English," thus earning her Interpreter badge. Camping in particular played an important role in trying to teach American Indian girls to see themselves as Girl Scouts. A 1953 article on Girl Scouting in "Navajo Country" reported on a meeting at Intermountain Indian School:

> "You say you want to be Girl Scouts?" she [the leader] asked. "Do you know what it means to be a Girl Scout? Well, I'll tell you. How many of you sleep on a bed when you are home?" Few hands went up. "How many of you sleep on a blanket or sheepskin on the ground?" Many hands went up. "Well, that's being a Girl Scout!" "How many have gas ranges in your kitchens at home?" No hands. "How many cook over a campfire?" All hands. "And that's being a Girl Scout!" And on she went, down the list of things that we in Girl Scouting call pioneering and most of these girls knew only as "living." Girl Scouting wasn't so strange, after all.[45]

There is so much that is fascinating in this passage—most obvious, of course, the introduction of something strange to the girls (Girl Scouting), then translated as familiar (sleeping on the ground, cooking over a campfire) and identified not as living, and certainly not as Navajo, but as "pioneering" and "Girl Scouting." Those practices—sleeping on the ground and cooking without a stove—were translated not as "primitive," something to be eradicated, but rather as the legitimate Girl Scout activity of camping. The article goes on to summarize the problems Navajo Girl Scouts faced: They don't speak enough English. They don't have enough money for uniforms. They return to reservations with horrible health problems and poverty. Yet the article doesn't point out what is perhaps the most obvious point: These Navajo Girl Scouts are different from their "sister scouts," for whom sleeping on the ground and building campfires are only *temporary* practices. The gift, then, that Girl Scouting provides, the helping hand of sister scouts, is teaching Indian girls the temporary and liminal nature of pioneer and Indian ways. American Indian girls could learn from white girls the ways to a civilized life, learning to return to the ways of their ancestors and communities as temporary play or as a Girl Scout badge.

Hearing the Pain despite the Girl Scout Propaganda

Amid the celebration of the helping hand that the Girl Scouts lent to American Indian girls and the celebration of the authenticity of the latter, extraordinary stories of despair and poverty abound. A 1932 *Girl Scout Leader* article titled "Navajo Nuggets—The Pinon Nuts" describes the ability of Navajos in New Mexico to find this "delicious nut" where "white men saw none." The author, a white woman who ran a small-town post office, describes in detail the suffering of this Navajo community during a particularly harsh winter:

> During the days that followed [the storms] it was tragic to see the half-clad women and children coming and going with their little sacs of nuts that they had picked before the storms; some had their feet tied in rags; some had thin canvas shoes for which they had traded their nuts. . . . Their children, huddling about the camp fires to keep from freezing, were badly burned. Babies were born, only to die of exposure. Men were crippled with stone-bruises and chilblains; pickers were tortured with infected fingers. We gave what we had of food, clothing, canvas shoes.

The article ends by noting that finally help from the Indian Service came to ensure they were "carried safely back to the Reservation." It's hard to understand what it means to be "safe" here, considering the story the author has just told. But there is more: After the conclusion of the piece, we have an editorial note, which ignores entirely the story of suffering we just witnessed.

"It is little wonder that the pinon of New Mexico, to the Navajo the one crop that through the years has made living possible, should be called the Navajo Nugget. The pinon nuts picked by their toilers among the western mountains have been made available for distribution; they should form a desirable addition to a list of camp supplies. Attractive one-pound sacks, at 25 cents, may be ordered direct from the agent." This is an amazing ideological sleight of hand, in which the witnessing of genocide is turned into a celebration of the authentic, and the purchase of the nuts allows a white Girl Scout to simultaneously be a friend to every other scout (though it's not clear that the money is even going to the Navajo girls) and to demonstrate her "real" experience of the wild.[46]

The Eradication of "Shyness"

Girl Scouts, then, largely ignored the forces of the poverty and annihilation they were seeing, focusing instead on their work of helping American Indian girls transition to a new form of civilization. The main obstacle in the way of transitioning to a civilized state that Girl Scouts seemed to focus on was a matter of affect: girls' *shyness*. Girl Scouts perceived American Indian girls to be excessively modest and unwilling to assert themselves, qualities that were the antithesis of the "cheerful" attitude demanded and prized by the organization.[47] In her lengthy article in a 1932 issue of the *Girl Scout Leader*, for instance, Marguerite Twohy wrote, "A new girl in any camp has to adjust herself socially to the group as a whole, if she is to be happy. To the shy little Indian girl, that adjustment is doubly difficult." She witnessed the "first efforts of Indian girls in the Southwest to bridge that gap between themselves and their white Girl Scout sisters" at Camp Mary White in Roswell, New Mexico, in the summer of 1930. "At first our little Indian visitors were silent and shy and did not mingle with the other girls, despite friendly advances. Then, one day, discovering the other girls' interest in bead work, in which they excel, they started helping with an impromptu class taught by the girls themselves. At camp fire one night, in colorful blankets and moccasins, they did their Corn Dance, played an Indian game, and sang Indian songs for an awestruck audience." In describing the fifth annual rally of American Indian Girl Scouts in Oklahoma, field worker Mary White wrote, "It was gratifying to see that we have accomplished at least one of the purposes for which the first and subsequent rallies were held—that of affording an opportunity for the girls of the various schools and tribes to become acquainted. Only a very few instances of shyness between the various school groups were noted."[48] The field workers' and leaders' perspectives on shyness were almost uniformly negative: Shyness was never seen as a possible sign of politeness, modesty, thoughtfulness, or reluctance to engage in an activity seen as hurtful or irrelevant—but rather as a sure sign of an inherent feeling of inferiority, of a lack of confidence. A field report from Mary Littlefield in 1942 about the Crowe Indian Agency described the need to divide the troops into a white one (for the staff members' children) and an Indian one, so that the "Indians would be stimulated to do a better job." As evidence of her belief that the "Crowes are a very inferior tribe," she wrote that "my presence seemed to have such an effect on them that they could hardly talk at first, but got over some of their shyness later. The children are entirely undisciplined."[49]

The American Indian girls held up as successes were those who had "overcome" this "shyness" so that they could "make friends," "be a good member of the group," and act in and upon the world. When nominating two Navajo girls to attend an International Camp, George Boyce first described the young women's family background, including the fact that their relatives were leaders in the tribal council and spoke good English. One of the girls, Georgia Anne Wauneka, "last year attended the Navajo Intercultural Girl Scout Camp at Toadlena, New Mexico, where she showed ability to make friends easily and was an active member of every group in sharing ideas and making contributions." The other, Barbara Jean Brown, was "ambitious," and though she "will appear shy when first introduced to strangers," she will "make friends and be a good member of the group." Most important, they were willing to be generous with their own heritage: "They will be ready to tell other girls various Navajo folk stories and other aspects of Navajo life. They both speak the Navajo language as their mother tongue, and will bring some articles for display, including their native costume, in addition to their Scout uniform."[50] A year earlier, a field report noted that the leaders of the Toadlena Intercultural Camp had said how much the event had helped the girls, noting how they now "take the lead in singing, dramatics, etc., in the troop" and organized a Thanksgiving tea for the teachers.[51]

Girl Scout reports suggested that camping experiences could pull young Indian girls out of their sequestered, premodern lives, introducing them both to contemporary amenities and to a demeanor appropriate for modernity. In 1954, for instance, 110 girls from the Navajo reservation and their leaders traveled to the Grand Canyon for a weekend event. Due to a heavy snowstorm and cold, the girls were placed in cabins rather than camping. "You should have seen their eyes as they were assigned only 4 to a cabin, with a light switch, real bed and a key to the door. This was the first time many had touched a key, let alone had it for the whole weekend to keep and be responsible for," the field agent's report read. In the morning, she added, "the light switches [were] being flipped on and off from about 5 o'clock on. They were fascinated by being able to touch them." Their awe at being given the "key" of modernity was highlighted along with their affective change: "At the campfire a representative from each troop told what they had done during the year. It is something for these children to stand up and talk. Usually, two stand together, but this time not one faltered. You could see the faces of the leaders beaming. They let them sing some of the Navajo songs, which pleased me."[52] Ironically, the Girl Scouts brought Navajo girls to the Grand Canyon, a place of sacred importance to Navajo and many other tribes in the area (Hualapai, Havasupai, Paiute, Hopi, and Zuni), as a place to be introduced to keys, lights, and public speaking. The ability to sing some Navajo songs apparently bridges the gap between what the Girl Scouts saw as a sequestered, inferior life and the inevitable transition to a modern, meaningful, "outgoing" life.

We can see this imperative to be "outgoing," cheerful, and confident in the letter Hannah Whitebead wrote to the Committee on Awards when she applied for the Golden Eaglet award. In asking her to list all of her accomplishments, the questionnaire was in itself a practice antithetical to shyness—it required her to throw away modesty and basically brag about all she had done. It was, indeed, a required manipulation of affect, challenging some of the most fundamental attitudes that many American Indians encouraged in their children: modesty, generosity, and a keen ability to listen rather than to showcase one's own ideas or accomplishments. From the archival record, we have no way of knowing how this felt for Whitebead, but we do know from the oral histories of other American Indian children growing up in Indian schools that this forced outgoing and cheerful affect was grueling, unsettling, and often destructive, and it created significant problems when they returned home.

Resisting the Girl Scout Mission

As one reads the official Girl Scout archival record—the "Indian" issues of the *Girl Scout Leader*, the detailed reports from white field agents, and the memos that flew back and forth from Girl Scout National Headquarters to the field agents and the Indian Service—hints and slippages emerge, voices and perspectives that deny the overarching narrative of authenticity, Girl Scout sisterhood, and helpful modernization. Above all, one hears the arrogant certainty of the Girl Scout mission and a complete inability to see beyond its shuttered eyes. Throughout the record, for instance, one hears hints of Native resistance, as in a memo from 1950 noting that it was difficult to establish Girl Scouting in Navajo country because "the Tribal Council has been known to make the National Commissioner of Indian Affairs wait a day or two to make an appearance" and in a report from a Maine council that Penobscot women have historically refused to take part in Girl Scout leadership training.[53] One hears the pain, confusion, and anger caused by this "difficult transition from the old Indian way of living to a modified form of our own civilization" in an early 1930 article that explains, "Upon being pressed for their Indian names, the girls reluctantly admitted having them. A few had forgotten—or pretended to forget—entirely, and had become Mary Jones and Anna Smith."[54] One hears the calls for a more complex sisterhood dismissed, as in a 1940 memo about the work of the principal of the Creek Indian Orphanage, who wanted to get integrated troops organized with the local public school. "Frankly, I am somewhat skeptical about the success of this venture," the field agent wrote.[55] A 1951 memo recounting the ideas generated during a brainstorming session about American Indian Girl Scouts notes that Marguerite Twohy, the field agent who had been working out west for over two decades, "brought up the point that we must be careful not to exploit the Indians by bragging about what we are doing—which isn't much. She would like to see us not give publicity to the efforts we are making until more has been accomplished."[56]

And in the sparse reporting we hear from girls themselves, we get a glimpse of their very difficult lives and the changes foisted upon them by the state and the exigencies of settler colonial life. Hannah Whitebead, for instance, the Caddo girl whose letter opens this chapter, states from the beginning that her *real home* is with her parents; the school, and life away from her family, is a temporary moment no matter if she spends the bulk of her time there. And that letter, listing of all her accomplishments, ending with the fact that she also works endlessly as a domestic—in the dorm, for a dorm matron, and for a woman away from the school—suggests that Girl Scouting might have just added to her load.

A report from the 1950s draws our attention to one particular instance of outright resistance among Native American girls. In the summer of 1954, the Gila County Girl Scout Council in Arizona created an "experimental workshop in intercultural relations," allowing two Apache girls to attend an otherwise all-white Girl Scout camp. "They got along very well for the first week and seemed to be enjoying the experience," the report read. But then, "toward the middle of the second week they got upset over restrictions and regulations on freedom to go hiking, etc. They threw knives, wash basins and other movable articles at the girls in the unit and caused a real disturbance. They wanted to go home. They were sent home, but the damage done to the feelings and attitudes of the girls, both Apache and Anglo, was extensive." Interestingly, there seems to have been no real attempt to talk to the Apache girls, to find out why they were so upset: Had something happened? Did someone say or do something offensive? Had they been physically threatened? Did they feel they were singled out for unfair restrictions? Why the shift after everything had gone so well? Were they extraordinarily homesick? We know none of this, and no one seems to have thought to ask.

The rest of the report also highlights a theme that emerged frequently when white Girl Scouts spoke about the "problem" of girls of color: They were simply inferior and incompetent. The report noted, "In discussing this with the council, CA [community adviser] discovered that the money for the Apache girls was provided by a club to the two girls who wrote the best composition of 'why I want to go to camp.' The troop leader knew that there were other girls in the Indian troop more ready for the experience. We discussed future selection and preparation of these girls for future established camping opportunities." One imagines that the concept of "ready for the experience" did not in this case refer to camping *skills*, something also frequently noted as a problem for girls of color, but rather to *attitude*. These girls did not exhibit a pleasing demeanor, a thankfulness, a willingness to obey, but rather got angry and threw things when they felt they had been mistreated! And perhaps they got what they may have wanted all along: to go home! It's useful to think about this completely as an event staged for the benefit of the Apache girls themselves, a way out of a painful, boring, or simply unwanted experience.

The report concluded, "Those present who had been at camp felt the Anglo girls were very frightened by the experience and would not go to camp again if the Apache girls were there."[57] The wording of this sentence is worth pondering. "Those present" seems to exclude the Apache girls, as it's clear that no one has actually spent much time talking to them. And the emphasis, in the end, is on the perception of the white girls' fear: It's a moment when the white girls are allowed, perhaps even encouraged, to feel fear, something that is otherwise highly discouraged among the Girl Scouts, who emphasize competence and courage. And the consequence also seems clear: The Apache girls will not be "invited" back, as the perception is that they are so dangerous that the white girls "would not go to camp again if the Apache girls were there." One imagines that only a Native girl who could be counted on to be unthreatening, acquiescent, uncomplaining, and grateful would be welcome in this "intercultural" experiment.

Reading Participation

In the stories that American Indian girls and women told, we see multilayered recounting of their Girl Scout experiences, accounts that are complex and sometimes contradictory. The work of scholar John Bloom, in his book *To Show What an Indian Can Do: Sports and Native American Boarding Schools*, helps us think through these layered accounts. Bloom interviewed former students who had attended Indian boarding schools in the 1930s, '40s, '50s, and '60s. They told stories describing the myriad ways they created joy, pleasure, and resistance through their sporting experiences in an environment that was otherwise designed to break them. Some of this resistance showed up in what he called "hidden transcripts," ways that students told stories and shared histories that could look like acquiescence from one angle but spoke refusal and resistance from another.[58] And certainly we see this in Hannah Whitebead's letter, which is on the one hand a recounting of her many achievements but on the other hand could also be a letter of protest: How could one young woman be expected to do all this? We see this as well in a story from the 1930s, where one of the white field agents describes a multischool rally where students spoke dozens of languages and came from as many tribes. The girls worked to teach each other and the "white staff members" salutations in their own languages. "The earnest efforts of the latter were the cause for much merriment among the campers, but everyone achieved at least the Indian grunt of approval, which is 'How!'"[59] The field agent seems blithely unaware that "how" was an Anglo-American invention, a modification of the Lakota-Dakota/Sioux greeting *hau*, popularized in TV shows, Westerns, and children's games. One can easily imagine that the girls who greeted each other this way were laughing hilariously *at* the leaders—a moment of humorous comradery fostered at the expense of the Girl Scout leaders, who were clueless. A lengthy 1953 report on the history of the Girl Scouts among American Indians written by Mrs. Edward Hughes, a regional committee member, illuminates a similar perspective, a false modesty with an incisive edge. Hughes, presumably an American Indian herself, wrote in the introduction, "At the risk of giving you information that may be obvious to many of you, please permit this aborigine to give you, my more civilized counterparts, some of the historical background!"[60]

What is interesting about Hughes's lengthy history is that she is actually quite positive about the role that Girl Scouting can play in the life of American Indian communities. As she writes, "We have the great opportunity to embark upon an adventure in shared responsibility, as part of Scouting and as part of the noble democracy in which we live—the responsibility to aid in the self-determination of a people." She sees it as reciprocal relationship—not one in which white America simply "helps" American Indians. Girl Scouting for Hughes is a means for dominant US culture to become educated about Native American life and histories *as well as* a useful set of opportunities for American Indian girls. She frames her report with the clarity that her readers will incorrectly presume they are the "civilized" ones, but then she moves on to explain why this is a positive relationship for both the white American Girl Scout institution and for girls and women in American Indian communities.

Throughout the archival record of the GSUSA we see glimpses of many American Indian adults, like Hughes, who took part in Girl Scouting. Of the fourteen leaders who attended the second all-Indian summer camp in Oklahoma, for instance, five were American Indian women.[61] Bertha Bird, quoted in the article on Girl Scouting in "Navajo Country," herself was a member of a Pueblo tribe and a counselor at the Intermountain Indian School. And sometimes mothers of American Indian girls took part, if they lived close enough to the schools or if the troops were on reservations. In 1941, for instance, field agent Katharine Shankland reported that an "Anglo and Spanish-American" troop in Taos, New Mexico, invited a Pueblo troop to attend a tea. She first explains that the Pueblo troop was not particularly active; the Indian schoolteachers were too busy and the Pueblo mothers largely uncooperative. But then she described the tea: "They invited the Indian troop and mothers from the Pueblo, but did not expect the mothers to attend. The entire group of twenty Indian girls attended and about half of their mothers. These latter were very colorful in their best blankets, wrapped to their eyes. . . . It was definitely an effort for the Indian mothers to get away since they were required to bake extensively for the next day, which was a festival day to celebrate the planting of the corn—with dancing and religious ceremonies in the kivas and on the grounds of the pueblo."[62] Knowing how much Girl Scouting was pushing its zealous message of Americanization and its complicitous rewriting of American Indian histories, one could understand why American Indian women would be reluctant to act as leaders or attend events. Yet from another perspective, there are numerous reasons for their participation: curiosity about the work of this organization, interest and hope in the ways that Girl Scouting might actually help their communities, a desire to protect their daughters, and a chance to be with their daughters within a colonial context that pulled their children away from them. If the white women who became Girl Scout Indian field agents did so for a variety of reasons—adventure, protofeminist impulse, missionary zeal—the Indian women who took part did so for a range of compelling reasons as well, even if the official Girl Scout record gives us fewer records of their thinking.

In the 1950s, the GSUSA records indicate that the Navajo Nation was particularly interested in working with the Girl Scouts. Uranium, oil, and gas had been discovered on their land, and the tribal council wished to spend some of these monies on supporting Girl Scouting within their nation. The GSUSA reacted extraordinarily positively to this offer, especially since it came with a financial incentive. As a 1957 Girl Scout quarterly report exclaimed, "In this budget [the one augmented with the uranium, oil, and gas monies] went an item for Girl Scouting! Upon meeting with the Education Committee of the Tribal Council the far-sighted planning of its leaders was evident. The Navajos want a Girl Scout program, gradual as it will be, that will develop indigenous leadership; a program to develop citizenship and consciousness of the importance of the community and a program that will integrate the Indian territory and the Indian girls into the nearby towns."[63] Significantly, the Navajo council asked the GSUSA to deal with it directly, *not* with the Bureau of Indian Affairs or the government school system.[64] Indeed, the council appeared to see Girl Scouting as a way to help Navajo girls, an investment in their girls' and nation's future, but only if done with autonomy, from their own leadership and without the control of the Bureau of Indian Affairs.

American Indian adults and tribes may have had their own reasons for encouraging scouting. As John Bloom's oral histories with former Indian school students suggest, they were looking for ways to bring pleasure and meaning into the drudgery and loneliness of their school lives. And as Margaret Archuleta, Brenda Child, and K. Tsianina Lomawaima describe in their rich collection *Away from Home: American Indian Boarding School Experiences, 1879–2000*, the students used the avenues available to them to create some space within their lives and to carry on Indian arts, cultures, and traditions: "Students were resourceful and ingenious—they found ways and means, times and places, to speak their own languages, eat their own food, and exercise religious practices." In particular, as Lomawaima points out, the students gravitated toward patriotic holidays as ones in which the white teachers and administrators would allow them to dance—even if they had to be, as she put it, "literally and figuratively wrapping themselves in the American flag." We can certainly see this in the Thanksgiving teas and the Girl Scout rallies, for instance, where girls could share stories, dances, and language all under the guise of "badgework." Indeed, those stories, dances, and language could be marked as accomplishments, not as something to be eradicated. And the myriad activities planned by the troops—visits to town, trips to the movies, camping trips outside the school, even the dedication of a particular room in the school for scouting activities—meant that girls could experience a bit of freedom, something in sore shortage at the schools, particularly, as Lomawaima points out, for the girls.[65] Throughout the GSUSA archival record we hear that American Indian girls are yearning to wear their Girl Scout uniforms and longing for more resources to buy materials or for donations of cast-off pieces. While this may have been the wishful writing of agents trying to legitimize their own work, we could also imagine that in a school setting where children had few clothes and little status, the uniforms provided them with a bit of both, another clothing option amid scarcity and a way to stand out among the sea of homogeneity that the school worked to impose. Moreover, the fact that Indian troops were encouraged to make "authentic" crafts to sell to eastern troops in order to make money to pay national dues can be seen in a different light. While the Bureau of Indian Affairs was working assiduously to teach American Indians that they had to shed all Native attributes to participate in the modern world, the girls themselves were proving otherwise. As Lomawaima pointed out, "'Indianness' became more lucrative than virtually any government assimilation program that Indians could adopt."[66] In other words, these Girl Scouts were demonstrating the ways that their very identities were crucial *to* their economic and cultural survival.

And of course, we also need to consider joy. Girl Scouting might have been a space where girls could forge their own fun, connection, and pleasure. Hannah Whitebead's letter in 1938 gives us a real sense of this: "We had many good times with our captain and our committee women. They took the whole troop of Scouts to a picture show and a treat after the show. We enjoy having our picnics and parties together." And she especially emphasizes how much she liked her time at Camp Tom Hale in Wilberton, Oklahoma: "I never enjoyed my camp days as much as I did during the time I was in Camp Tom Hale," she wrote, adding: "The thing I enjoyed the most was nature study. I took nature study under Mrs. Bohard of Sequayah [another Indian school]. We went on hikes early in the mornings to study the different kinds of birds, flowers, and trees. In the evenings we went on hikes to study the land and water insects and the different kinds of nature musics. A scout or any one could not help but enjoy nature in the camp. The tall pine trees were so beautiful they stood so high and pretty and made you want to grow big and straight as they were." This is a particularly poignant passage coming from a young Caddo woman who lived most months of the year at a boarding school far away from her own community, which had fought the allotment and destructive policies of the Office of Indian Affairs, but which had decided (or had decided for it) that a boarding school option would be best for their young daughters. In this moment we see Whitebead breathing in fresh air, enjoying the close study of nature, and imagining a future that is positive and strong.

A Continuity in Policy and Perspective

From the 1930s through the 1960s, the GSUSA generally perceived its work with American Indian girls as useful and worthy; the primary question was whether its programming and ideals were actually helpful to or for American Indian girls. In the early 1960s, the Girl Scout national executive director requested that the field department prepare a report to be shared with the US Commissioner of Indian Affairs regarding the status of Girl Scouting and American Indian communities. The field department requested information on the work of individual councils, Indigenous leadership, adult participation, Indian school troops, regional activities, and integrated troops.[67] While individual councils did report back with specifics—regarding activities, membership numbers, and problems ranging from lack of interest to inevitable troubles with transportation—the overall assessment of the Girl Scouts was that the organization was achieving its goal: integration. That may have been the ostensible goal, but as we have seen throughout this chapter, the reality was that troops were generally segregated, on reservations and in boarding schools. And of course, the goal of integration was largely one-way, with American Indian girls expected to move into "civilized" life, even as Girl Scouting "allowed" them to remember that which their parents had "forgotten." As the *Girl Scouts Professional Newsletter* reported:

> Today the Indian is in transition. The old culture is dying out. Whether American Indians wish it or not, they are losing their tribal ways of life and becoming a part of the communities in which more and more of them work and live. The children are learning to speak and live the white man's way. Girl Scouting has helped to make the transition easier for Indian girls from Maine to California.
>
> Girl Scouting is close to the old Indian way of life: cooking out, sleeping under the stars, learning to know and live with nature. People who live as members of a clan or a tribe, in any group larger than a family, think mostly in terms of the larger group. Perhaps this is one of the reasons why Indian girls today find group activities like Girl Scouting so understandable and satisfying. Girl scouting offers American Indian girls the chance to learn new things and to relearn many old things

> that their parents have forgotten. Scouting teaches these youngsters a greater pride in being Indian.
>
> Through Girl Scouting, Indian girls gain concepts of citizenship, respect for the democratic process, and moral and spiritual values. No matter what their cultural background or economic status, girls everywhere can understand and accept the Promise and Laws as their own pattern for living as good women and useful citizens.[68]

As this passage indicates, in the 1960s the Girl Scouts as an institution largely held to the same ideals about American Indians as it had in its first concerted efforts to reach out to tribes and Indian schools in the 1930s. Girl Scouting, the national organization believed, provided a useful bridge from the inevitable transition from primitive, old-fashioned traditions to civilized, modern ways. The terms "primitive" and "civilized" may have disappeared by the early 1960s, but the general sentiment had not. Girl Scouting worked as a transition, the organization's national leaders believed, because much of scouting was already familiar to Indian girls: camping, outdoor life, and nature study. Indeed, Girl Scouting could teach Indian girls what their parents seem to have forgotten to teach them and could encourage them to take pride in their culture and history. And finally, Girl Scouting, according to the national leaders, could teach American Indians the superiority of US democracy and governance (even though this hadn't worked out so well for American Indians up to this point!) as well as spiritual and personal values. Left unsaid, but still very clear, was the presumption that their own Indigenous communities had failed to teach them those values.

The problem articulated in this *Professional Newsletter* article was that there were few American Indian women who participated as scout leaders. "In all regions, the need for more indigenous leadership is constant. We know that in recruiting leaders among the Indians we must reach them through someone they trust. They need help in overcoming seemingly insurmountable obstacles—poverty, poor command of English, a sense of inadequacy. They must be shown the way until they can feel secure on their own; the Girl Scout professionals and volunteers must keep in constant touch, offering training and on-the-job help."[69] Yet as we saw in the exchange between National Headquarters and the director of the Navajo Nation Indian Service in the 1950s, Native Americans had pushed for more Indigenous leadership themselves. It was the Girl Scout organization that, in doubting the "professionalism" of Native American women, seemed to have a clear sense of the "inadequacy" of American Indian leaders.

Throughout the GSUSA record about American Indians, the field agents, white leaders, and Girl Scout administrators lament the shortage of Native American participation among adults and write about their desire for more Indigenous leadership. At least in one case, however, it becomes clear that the Girl Scouts wanted more local-level adult participation but doubted whether Native women could actually be successful with higher-level responsibility. In 1951, the director of Navajo Schools, Hildegard Thompson, worked closely with the Girl Scouts to encourage the organization to provide a full-time staff member for the Navajo Nation. Thompson voiced her opinion that the position should go to a Navajo woman. Marguerite Twohy responded, "It seems to us here at headquarters that it would be easier to secure a white professional worker for the project than to find a Navajo who would have the necessary qualifications for this professional job." It's not clear from the record whether such a woman was ever hired, but Thompson responded to Twohy with a very clear defense of the need for a Navajo employee to "develop understanding of the Girl Scout program among Navajos, to train Navajo leadership, and then to turn the full responsibility over to the Navajos for carrying out the Girl Scout work. . . . To be entirely effective, such a person should have a clear understanding of the culture and a thorough speaking knowledge of the language. I think that it would be impossible to recruit a person with these qualifications on the outside and of necessity, therefore, such a person should be a Navajo." She then went on to counter what she anticipated was the doubt that any such person existed: "I believe we could find a few Navajo girls who would meet the qualifications outlined in your professional bulletin. Last year, a Navajo girl graduated from college with a degree in social work. We also have a few Navajo college graduates in the teaching profession."[70] For Thompson, Girl Scouting was important, but it had to be on Navajo terms, done for and by Navajo people. And Navajo leadership was integral to this.

Thompson's perspective would take hold by the end of the 1960s. Indeed, the seeds of rebellion had been growing since the early days of Girl Scouting's forays into American Indian communities. The sense of joy that Girl Scouting seemed to offer, as Hannah Whitebead expressed, the push for more Native American Girl Scout professionals that Thompson articulated, and the possibilities that Girl Scouting offered to their communities, which the Navajo council voiced—these calls for Indigenous participation on Indigenous terms would all germinate by the end of the decade, though not without struggles and obstacles.

But for the first fifty years of Girl Scouting, the national organization was strongly confident that its mission was to "lend a helping hand" by offering

Girl Scout programs in Indian boarding schools to "civilize" American Indian girls. Its presumption of Euro-American superiority and its programming in these boarding schools were closely in line with its global practices as Girl Scouting established troops internationally. In the following chapter we turn to considering Girl Scouting not just as a force of empire within the boundaries of the United States but also as reaching far outward, as the tentacles of Girl Scouting extended into territories and countries throughout the world.

Chapter 5

The Arsenal of Democracy

GIRL SCOUTING IN AN AGE OF EMPIRE

As our country has served the world as the arsenal of democracy, let us now use the storage battery of this organization to enliven and quicken its work carried on for youth around the world.
—Constance Rittenhouse, 1945 Girl Scouts of the USA memo

Although the children's stories and mythology about Juliette Gordon Low tell a tale of a small group of girls in Savannah blossoming over time into a huge national and global organization, the Girl Scouts had been part of an international web since its founding, when Low led Girl Guide groups in England that had sprouted up as Lord Robert Baden-Powell's Boy Scouting was catching on.[1] The name of the first Girl Guide handbook in 1912, *How Girls Can Help to Build Up the Empire*, leaves nothing to the imagination—the point of Girl Guiding was to aid the British empire in its imperial ambitions. Girl Guides and Girl Scouts followed the same global trajectory as the Boy Scouts, sharing a presumption that it was the good and right thing to move quickly and confidently into the same regions where their male counterparts were making inroads. Girls' groups sprung up organically wherever Boy Scouts established outposts and then moved forward quickly, with more deliberate organization and separate from the Boy Scouts, as Girl Guiding and Girl Scouting gained stronger footing. Whether those new groups became Girl

Scouts or Girl Guides depended on whether Great Britain or the United States held the strongest imperialist tie to the region or sometimes was just a result of who reached the territory or country faster.[2] Sometimes Christian missionaries from the United States and Great Britain brought Girl Scouting or Guiding to other countries, such as the Philippines, where American missionaries brought Girl Scouting in 1918.[3]

Juliette Gordon Low was extraordinarily interested in this international development. She was enamored with the romance and power of the British empire and saw the United States as a playful rival in this rightful and even God-given domination of the world. A close friend of Rudyard Kipling, she was deeply moved by his novel *Kim*, in which the protagonist, a mischievous British boy, befriends a cast of "exotic" characters in India, bringing them amity and the benefits of a superior culture.[4] Girl Scouts, she thought, should take on, in their own way, the "white man's burden," a phrase Kipling coined in his poem of the same name. In this poem, he exalted the United States' role in the turn-of-the-century war against the Philippines as a mission to civilize the "sullen peoples, half devil and half child."[5] The US war in the Philippines was extraordinarily long-standing and brutal. While the war began as an alliance between the United States and the Philippines against Spain, after the United States defeated Spain it paid Spain $20 million, refused to include Filipinos in peace negotiations, and began a protracted and deadly three-year war to maintain power. The death toll was grim. Over 20,000 Filipinos and more than 4,200 Americans died. Even more extreme, the US government had no regard for the civilian population, which suffered far over 200,000 deaths from famine, disease, rape and assault, torture, destruction of homes and communities, and warfare. Even after the end of the official war, US forces continued to use brutal methods to contain any possible insurrection, such as the notorious 1906 Bud Dajo massacre, where American soldiers killed almost 1,000 people, mostly women and children. This kind of violence could only be legitimated—or "ignored"—if one believed in the "rightful" power of white people's global dominance the way Kipling described in his 1899 poem. Like Kipling, Low made the same assumptions about the rightful and necessary dominance of white Americans to claim as theirs territories and lands, outposts, and countries in North America and around the globe. By this logic, US dominance was perceived not as brutal, coercive, and cruel but as part of the necessary ordering of rightful ownership, governance, and "civilization"—in other words, the "white man's burden."[6]

After resigning her position as the president of the US Girl Scouts in 1920, Low turned her full attention to the Girl Guide and Girl Scout International

Council. Founded a year earlier, in 1919, the council held its first meeting in Oxford, England, to discuss Girl Guiding and Scouting worldwide.[7] By 1925, in Shanghai, China, the Girl Scouts of the USA had organized its first Lone Troops on Foreign Soil, an organization devoted to the daughters of American military members, diplomats, and business leaders who were abroad, though members of the local and international communities in the area might also join.[8] That same year, Low approved the charter of a new Girl Scout patrol in Puerto Rico.[9] Internationalism, then, became her new mission. In 1926 she supported the establishment of Thinking Day, on the birthday of Lord Baden-Powell, a day set aside for Girl Scouts and Girl Guides to think of each other across the world.[10] (This is still celebrated today.) A year before her death in 1927, Low presided over the Fourth World Camp of Girl Scouts and Girl Guides at Camp Edith Macy in upstate New York. It was at the Fifth World Camp, in Hungary, that the International Council voted to form the World Association of Girl Guides and Girl Scouts (WAGGGS), with twenty-six countries represented: Australia, Belgium, Canada, Czechoslovakia, Denmark, Estonia, Finland, France, Hungary, Iceland, India, Japan, Latvia, Liberia, Lithuania, Luxembourg, Netherlands, New Zealand, Norway, Poland, South Africa, Sweden, Switzerland, the United Kingdom and Northern Ireland, the United States, and Yugoslavia. While each of these countries was an official member of WAGGGS, however, the United States and United Kingdom held center stage.[11]

The reality, then, is that Girl Scouts emerged out of the cradle of empire. I say this not as a vague gesture toward the timing of its origins—1912, a moment of British hegemony and US ascendancy in the world order—but as a factual reference to its origins. And these origins shaped the foundations of this organization, from the very imaginary that set the group into motion to the monies that provided its resources and the people who shaped its direction. Girl Scouts have played a key role in the workings of US empire, from the settlement of North America and the containment of American Indians to the colonization of the Philippines, Guam, and Puerto Rico, the annexation of Hawai'i and Alaska, and the establishment of over 800 US military bases worldwide today. Girl Scouts has consistently ridden this wave of US power, establishing itself as the "soft" side of the workings of American empire, one whose effect was crucial at legitimizing and carrying out the processes and practices of US hegemony through culture and friendship.

The United States doesn't like to think of itself as an empire. The history that most of us learned in school emphasizes our revolutionary roots: We were founded as an anticolonial project, rejecting the imperial constraints

From the beginning, Juliette Gordon Low was keenly interested in establishing Girl Scouting in all the states and territories of the United States. In 1925 she chartered the first troop in Puerto Rico. Here pictured is a troop in San Juan in 1945. Wikimedia Commons, CC BY-SA 4.0.

and ambitions of England. We rejected tyranny. We are a beacon of democracy, shining a light of freedom wherever we venture. This is false. Unlike Great Britain, which reveled in its status as an empire so vast that the "sun never set" on it, the United States, as historian Daniel Immerwahr so aptly puts it, has worked hard to "hide" its status as an empire. For the most part, Americans don't perceive the United States as an empire, and even the maps we use to discuss our past and present history hide our global presence. Yet our history is all about empire. The United States pushed its way across North America, pressing Native Americans farther westward and onto smaller and smaller areas, breaking treaties, allowing for explosive white settlement such as the Oklahoma Land Rush of 1889 into former Indian territory, and using the bloody and ruthless force of massacre and war to encroach and protect white settlement. In 1848, we ended our long war with Mexico with the Treaty of Guadalupe Hidalgo, which ceded over 50 percent of Mexican land to the United States: present-day Texas, California, Nevada, Utah, New Mexico, and parts of Wyoming, Kansas, and Oklahoma. Through war, force, and international pressure we claimed dominance over the Philippines, Guam, Puerto Rico, Cuba, Hawai'i, Alaska, and a host of small islands; in the early twentieth century we occupied Cuba, Haiti, and the Dominican Republic. Even as the United States dropped its ravenous desire to physically occupy and formally incorporate other countries and lands after World War II, its desire for dominion has continued unabated, seeking a prime position of influence, decision-making, and unconditional access to land, resources, communication, and position. Today the United States has over 800 military bases around the world; that is a shocking number considering that all the other countries of the world have a total of thirty military bases outside their own political borders.[12] We have what Immerwahr calls a "pointillist empire," an empire that seeks and maintains power through "points" of access, military bases in particular, that allow for unimpeded access to all that the empire demands. And this access is further accelerated by the fact of American culture spreading itself everywhere—from the ubiquity of English (and programs like the Peace Corps to enforce its acquisition) and popular culture and media to US brands and styles. All this paves the way for US political power, for commercial interests, and even for the ease of Americans using the world as a tourist resource.[13]

The US footprint, then, is important to recognize when considering the global reach of the Girl Scouts. When I was a Girl Scout in Ohio in the 1970s one of my most prized pins was the World Association one, signaling friendship and sisterhood around the world. Girl Scouting has supported peaceful international relations so much so that it has been the source of longtime conservative critique of the Girl Scouts, from the Red Scare of the 1950s to the MAGA movement of today. Yet the international movement of Girl Scouting has also supported American dominance and hegemony, legitimating and even hiding the violence, brutality, and force necessary to enact and maintain US power. International friendship in this context, then, is another form of dangerous innocence, a perspective that can encourage relationships and empathy between disparate people but also one that can serve as the cultural—as opposed to military—force of American domination.

We can see a prime example of American hegemony mixed with international sisterhood in the decision-making regarding the first world center of Girl Guides and Girl Scouts. The money to establish the center came from a key figure in American philanthropy and Girl Scouting, Helen Osborne Storrow, a very well-to-do Bostonian who was the chair of the World Association at the time. Storrow agreed to fund the first international center, but only if it was built in Switzerland, a country she had been enamored with ever since she met her Bostonian husband James Storrow there while they were both on European tours.[14] Swiss scout Ida Von Herrenschwand found a property located in the Bernese Oberland area of the Swiss Alps, which was not only beautiful but offered key opportunities for adventure, including camping, hiking, and skiing. The architect who traveled with Storrow and Von Herrenschwand to locate the new center apparently ran ahead of them and triumphantly planted an American flag in the spot where it would be built. With the planting of the flag, Storrow and her architect marked a spot as belonging to the US movement, a symbolic act of ownership that would define the center from its origins. In 1932 the center, called Our Chalet, opened, a beautiful lodge designed in the rustic style of the Swiss German Alps, with a mini chalet nearby that would serve as Storrow's home base when she visited the world center.[15]

The Boston-area philanthropist and World Association leader Helen Storrow apparently planted an American flag with her architect on the mountainside in Adelboden, Switzerland, to mark the location of the first international center for Girl Scouting and Girl Guiding, Our Chalet. Here pictured in the 1940s is a group of American Girl Scouts and international Girl Guides in front of the iconic structure, a center of pilgrimage to this day. Courtesy of the Girl Scouts of the Commonwealth of Virginia and Commonwealth Council of the Girl Scouts of Virginia Records, 1910–2012, collection no. M 400, Special Collections and Archives, James Branch Cabell Library, Virginia Commonwealth University, Richmond.

Our Chalet is still a world center for Girl Guiding and Girl Scouting, one of five that were eventually established around the globe, the others in the United Kingdom, Mexico, India, and Africa. I visited Our Chalet as part of my research for this book during a crisp, sunny week in June 2018, staying with my family in a nearby town and hiking each day up the tremendously steep (for me) mountainous road to get to the lodge. There I met with troops from across the United States and England who had made the pilgrimage to Our Chalet, just as my troop had made the pilgrimage to Savannah, Georgia, in the 1970s. Troops hailed from Los Angeles, London, and Chicago, with some staying at the lodge in preparation for extended adventures and others just there for the day to see where international scouting had begun and to attend a workshop. Staff came from around the world, but everything was conducted in English, a solid chunk of America in the middle of the Swiss Alps. I took part in a pinning ceremony on that first day, where we all received special Our Chalet pins to go with the distinctive blue-and-gold trefoil pin denoting membership in WAGGGS that every Girl Scout receives on joining. It was quite moving, as I had, to be honest, always dreamed as a girl of traveling to Our Chalet, which was out of reach for our Akron, Ohio, troop. After the raising of the WAGGGS and Swiss flags, a representative from every country present placed a small flag in a log made especially for this ritual so that by the end we had a medley of flags, a mini United Nations. I spent hours talking with the girls and leaders who had made the trip, I listened carefully to the staff's and director's views of the current center, and I sat in the dining hall during some of the workshops—ones on body self-confidence and gender-based violence—all while observing the engraving high on the wall, "For the promotion of guiding and good will between nations." It was chilling to remember it was carved in 1932.

I spent most of my time at Our Chalet in the basement World War II bomb shelter that had been repurposed as the center's archival repository. I immersed myself in materials from the 1930s, '40s, '50s, and '60s, diving into boxes of old uniforms, photos of Helen Storrow, and countless scrapbooks from throughout the years. For decades, participants in the weekly programs at Our Chalet would create elaborate scrapbook entries, usually demarcating participation through sketches and drawings of the countries they represented, along with little quips and jokes that only insiders to the camp would have understood. One gets a feeling that staying at Our Chalet, either before World War II or in the decades immediately following, might have felt a bit like the all-women utopias imagined by lesbians in the 1970s land movement or even evoked by Charlotte Perkins Gilman in her 1915 novel *Herland*, a liminal space outside the parameters of nationalistic patriarchy, where girls and women could create alternative communities. The rhetoric of Our Chalet stressed international friendship and sisterhood, realized through shared scouting and guiding identities and activities. And, indeed, so many of the anecdotes in the scrapbooks suggest that Our Chalet was a place where women made deep friendships, found lovers, imagined world peace, and created a moment of heaven on earth. In Nancy Manahan's collection of essays by lesbians in Girl Scouting, Rachel Wetherill described her teenage dream of going to Switzerland: "That's what Our Chalet was all about. High up, high on the mountain in Adelboden, Switzerland, was a building where scouts and guides from all over the world could learn to know each other. If President Kennedy and Premier Khrushchev had such a place, I thought the world wouldn't be so dangerous. I made myself a vow that one day I would get to Our Chalet."[16] When Girl Scout leadership, staff, and troops came to Our Chalet in 1932, the world order was one in which the power of the United States and Great Britain were clear and relatively unquestioned, and their interests, especially US interests, presumed to be synonymous with a beneficent set of relations among nations and among the girls and women themselves. The English language ruled. American styles predominated. The extraordinary unequal relations between US and British powers and the colonies were neither addressed nor challenged. US dollars and cultural hegemony made Our Chalet a reality, a space for girls and women to imagine sisterhood. Yet it was not a community outside of patriarchal nationalism, even if American and British participants could sometimes imagine it was. And, indeed, the space is so beautiful, the rituals so powerful, that it's easy to pretend; as I described earlier, I was moved myself, despite my own perspective on American empire and the problems of a false innocence.

As one gazes around the globe, one can see the footprints of Girl Scouts everywhere, particularly where the United States has settled, claimed jurisdiction, or maintained the empire of influence. In the Philippines, as noted above, the first troops were established in 1918. In Hawai'i, the first troops began in 1917. In Guam, 1935. In Alaska, 1925.[17] The national Girl Scout archives list over eighty countries with explicit Girl Scout ties, from Afghanistan to Zambia.[18] Focusing primarily on the experiences of "mainland" Girl Scouts, this book does not address the complexity of reasons girls had for joining the Girl Scouts internationally or what I am sure were layers of often contradictory experiences, both among American girls who were part of troops off the mainland and certainly among girls who experienced Girl Scouting as part of the colonial and expansion missions of the United States. It's important to underscore, however, that none of the scouting or guiding movement presumed equality when it began its internationalist thrust; the underlying presumption was white superiority. Early on in the movement, Lady Olave Baden-Powell, in vaguely lamenting the problem of racism in Girl Guiding and Girl Scouting across the globe, concluded, as historian Tammy Proctor described, that "to retain egalitarian sisterhood within the movement, some girls must be kept out." Better to exclude than to acknowledge the reality of the unfairness and inequity that racism caused. In other words, the problem of racism was handled by eliminating the presence of those deemed to be trouble: girls of color. When it came to Boy Scouts mingling with Girl Guides or Girl Scouts, the organizations were even more concerned about interracial mixing, giving even more fodder to the argument for either the segregation of girls and boys of color or their complete exclusion.[19]

During World War II and in the decades immediately following, the Girl Scout international movement articulated, as Jennifer Helgren so carefully outlines in her book *American Girls and Global Responsibility*, a world made "safe" by the twin forces of US hegemony and a vision of international sisterhood and friendship.[20] Particularly after the war, US Girl Scouts organized pen pals and friendship boxes, even with former enemy countries Germany and Japan, where an outstretched hand of sisterly warmth could, presumably, bring everyone back into the fold of a world ordered by US interests. After the Korean War, US Girl Scouts organized a well-documented effort of "Kits for Korea," small pouches of items, that, like other friendship packets, contained school supplies, toys, fabric, and food. It's not clear how useful all these items were, but the sheer quantity collected and sent was tremendous.[21] This was the "soft" side of the military and economic force of the new postwar era and order, the opposite of muscular diplomacy and what Helgren calls "intimate diplomacy."[22] There was so much focus on this international activity that at one point the US Postal Service had to curtail the pen pal scheme, as it threatened to shut down certain branches. And indeed, all these international gestures by Girl Scouts were a "vehicle for sharing the American way of life," as the styles were American, the foods were American, and the language was English. American girls did learn about other cultures and other girls, but the presumption was always, at the foundation of these initiatives, the superiority and "normalcy" of US culture.[23]

After World War II, WAGGGS gained an even stronger international footing, beginning in 1945 when it gained observer status with the newly established United Nations. It also continued to open new centers. Our Ark (now called Pax Lodge) opened in London in 1939; Our Cabana in Cuernavaca, Mexico, in 1957; Sangam in Pune, India, in 1966; and an African center that rotates locations around the continent in 2011.[24] The fact that the United States does not have one of these centers might indicate that US Girl Scouts are not at the center of this world movement, but I believe it indicates that these centers provide locations of excursion, immersion, and tourism primarily for American girls and women. Sometimes this has manifested in extremely ugly instances of US misbehavior, such as in 1958 at Our Cabana, where a group of "rowdy" Girl Scouts "openly flirted with locals, used foul language, and condescended to other travelers." They also refused to acknowledge the authority of the local Mexican leaders who were running the center. It was enough to "impair international relations," as one Girl Scouts of the USA staff member warned.[25] It also gave a prime example of the way the centers could be as much about American pleasure, a touristic "cutting loose," as about any international friendship and understanding.

In the years after World War II, a fascinating dynamic of dual forces emerged. As girls in former colonies throughout Southeast Asia, Africa, and India increasingly shed their association with Girl Guides and Girl Scouts (even as the world centers were established), the United States consistently grew its overseas Girl Scout presence in other ways. The Lone Troops on Foreign Soil program grew quickly, due to an increase in both military bases and US businesses.[26] Communist countries eliminated their scouting and guiding activities, while the United States worked to build up these activities throughout the "free" world. The Girl Scouts of the USA funded field agents to travel to Tokyo and other sites in Japan for six-month slots, to build troops, foster "miniature democracies," and "practice the essentials of decent living." They were very successful, with over 125,000 girls joining in 1950.[27] In places such as Okinawa—where after bombing and conquering the island, the United States installed a military base that took up almost a quarter of the island—mostly segregated troops formed, some with Okinawan girls and some with American girls, the daughters of servicemen and military officers. For at least some of the American girls on Okinawa, it seems to have been a site of adventure, rather like for the white women who traveled through hard territory to visit Girl Scout troops in US Indian reservations. In an essay called "I Live on Okinawa," published in 1947 in the Girl Scout publication *American Girl*, a teenage American girl recounts how she wears army boots and pants because of the mud, prepares a cake for her father with a two-burner stove, befriends a monkey as a family pet, enjoys the beauty of the landscape (much of it hibiscus growing over the remnants of bombed villages), and helps teach English to the "natives," whose clothing is largely "cast offs" made from "old Army things" and "parachutes" they found after the war. It's all exotic, a form of adventure, a protected view of the "other" from the safety of the army base rather than an immersion in the extraordinary trauma and destruction left from the war.[28]

Three scrapbooks from an American Girl Scout troop on Okinawa in the 1950s suggest how significant the Girl Scouts were to the creation of "soft diplomacy," the practices of friendship and cultural sharing that support global domination. In the scrapbooks we see pages of newspaper clippings, with pictures of Girl Scouts meeting with servicemen in hospitals, having fun in troop meetings, camping, horseback riding, and taking part in ceremonies with visiting dignitaries. There are stories about the training of army wives to become troop leaders, the events planned between American and Okinawan Girl Scout troops, and excursions planned on US ships and planes. We see the American girls in US Brownie, Junior, Cadette, and Senior uniforms, and we see the local Okinawan girls in a slightly different uniform, a white blouse with a colored kerchief. We see American and Okinawan girls taking part in "international dances, wearing costumes from around the world—dirndl skirts, hulu skirts, Indian headdresses." We even see an American girl feeding an Okinawan girl a piece of "southern fried chicken." By the 1960s, according to information in this scrapbook, more than 1,100 daughters of American military families and 730 Ryukyuan girls were part of the Okinawa chapter of USA Girl Scouts Far East. And throughout these scrapbooks we see the choreographed moments of intimacy between the two groups, though with a decided presumption of American centrality.[29]

The line between international friendship and international domination in the global movement of Girl Scouting is a fragile one. Every statement and overture of kindness and understanding was surrounded by an aura of US power, presumption, and arrogance. For instance, in a *Reader's Digest* story, we learn about a 1960 Roundup in Colorado, with over 10,000 attendees, mostly mainland Americans but also girls and leaders from the new states of Alaska and Hawai'i and from Western Europe, South Korea, India, Argentina, Israel, and Japan. The article highlights the sharing of languages (Aleut, Portuguese, Finnish, Danish, Korean) and the rituals of "swaps," a friendship exchange of small tokens among different troops. The scouts even talked about some of the pressing issues of the era. At one of the youth forums they discussed segregation, asking "Are parents' attitudes really the problem in human relations?" and "How can I be proud of my heritage if I deny this same right to others?" The author of the article, Mary Bard, notes that the girls seemed "unaware of the race, creed, or color of the girls participating in these discussions." The whole event ended with a teary rendition of a Roundup song and a symbolic

After World War II, the United States established a military base on Okinawa that took up almost a quarter of the island. Girl Scouts quickly launched dual troops, some with American girls of US families, others with girls from Okinawa. Here, American troops visit US servicemen in their military hospital in the late 1950s. Courtesy Girl Scouts of the Nation's Capital.

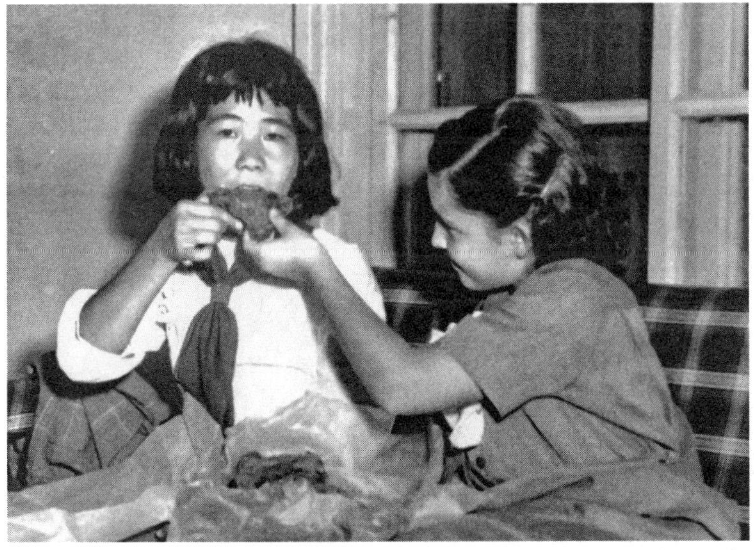

During a 1957 Ryukyuan-American "Girl Scout Get Together," girls taught each other American and Okinawan dances, then shared a picnic lunch. The photo shows an American girl feeding a local girl a piece of "southern fried chicken." Courtesy Girl Scouts of the Nation's Capital.

In 1957, Girl Scouts from the United States whose families were stationed on Okinawa and Okinawan Girl Scouts presented an international folk festival. Here, Okinawan Girl Scouts danced dressed up as American Indians. Courtesy of Girl Scouts of the Nation's Capital.

US Girl Scouts dressed up as hula dancers from Hawai'i at their 1957 international folk festival in Okinawa. Courtesy Girl Scouts of the Nation's Capital.

burning of a scroll in honor of "international friendship, peace and tolerance." These are powerful moments, ones that would fuel the beliefs and practices of so many girls and women in fighting for global equity and feminism. But this entire event is also a moment clearly illuminating the ties between US political power and the Girl Scouts. The site for the Roundup was prepared by the US Army, which had "converted the rolling prairie land to a well-ordered campsite, providing roads, a water system, sanitary facilities, religious equipment, buses, ambulances and trucks, a field hospital." While American girls paid their own way through troop fundraisers, the Juliette Gordon Low World Friendship Fund helped subsidize (and select) the international attendees. Indeed, the presence of the international girls was key to the experience of the American girls, who would be enriched by these encounters and taught, as would the girls from around the world, that the United States was the greatest—and the most benevolent—power in the world. It might have been that the girls didn't see "color" or "creed" when they met in their small discussion groups, but African American girls had a strictly limited presence at the Roundup. It was another instance where US white girls were taught to be innocent, to "not see" power, racism, discrimination, or history. At one point, Bard recounts that a "tiny" girl from Seoul, Korea, leaned over to tell her "blond" companion that "this was the first time I ever left Seoul. Now I will no longer fear foreigners." It's as if this is just the story of a sweet, naïve Korean girl who learns the benevolence of a world run by US power through the community of international, though mostly American, sisters. No one asks why she feared foreigners, whether it had to do with the war that destroyed her city when she was a young girl or the ubiquitous presence of American military men in South Korea after the war. The article, and the Roundup itself, ignores the Korean War completely, leaving us in a haze of sweetness that doesn't deal with historical realities.[30]

In June 1945, the Girl Scouts outlined its plan for what it considered com bined international-intercultural work: "As our country has served the world as the arsenal of democracy, let us now use the storage battery of this organization to enliven and quicken its work carried on for youth around the world."[31] The phrase "arsenal of democracy" jumped out to me in the reams of documents the Girl Scouts produced, especially as I thought of the wing of the Girl Scouts doing its "international" work at home during World War II in the Japanese American incarceration centers. The girls' experiences at those centers were complex and layered, part of the contradictory and even byzantine web of nationalistic and global Girl Scout policies in the 1940s. It's a difficult but necessary story to hear. In the next chapter, I turn to these stories, of Girl Scouting at the Japanese American incarceration centers.

Chapter 6

Japanese American Incarceration and the Myth of International Sisterhood

••••••

We followed the Girl Scouts to the end.
—Janet Sui Matarai Misaka, remembering her experiences at Heart Mountain

In spring 1944, the twelve members and three leaders of Intermediate Troop 2 at Rowher Evacuation Center in southeastern Arkansas—one of the ten centers incarcerating Japanese Americans during World War II—inscribed their names on an official form from the Girl Scouts of the USA. A large yellow trefoil takes up the center of this green "Girl Scout Troop Certificate," one of the featured items at the Japanese American National Museum's exhibit on coming of age in the World War II incarceration centers. Circling the trefoil are the images of four white girls: a curly-headed brunette (looking very much like Shirley Temple) as the Brownie; a blond Intermediate; a Senior with the distinctive scarf; and a Mariner, blond and curly-haired liked the Intermediate but wearing the seafaring blue and looking up as if she's reading the sky for navigational signs. All are smiling; all have rosy cheeks. They are the picture of the ideal Girl Scout: cute, competent, healthy, enthusiastic, innocent—and white. Two preprinted signatures stand out in the lower left: a facsimile of Juliette Gordon Low's and that of Girl Scout president Helen Means. Along the center trefoil are preprinted lines for troops to write in their information: city, state, year of membership, leader, assistant leader, members. This is the same document that troops across the country would have used. But in the section for city and state on this particular certificate, the information stands out: Rowher, Arkansas. And as if the writer experienced an afterthought, or a sense that no one outside the community would even know where they were, someone had penned in "Relocation Center" in parentheses after "Rowher."

This green sheet—probably a ubiquitous part of Girl Scout life in the 1940s—is full of contrasts. We see the "wholesome" vision the Girl Scouts had idealized since the 1910s, a vision of "free," "intrepid," and "innocent" white girls, and the reality of the imprisonment young Japanese American girls and their leaders were experiencing. It leads us to consider the complicity of the

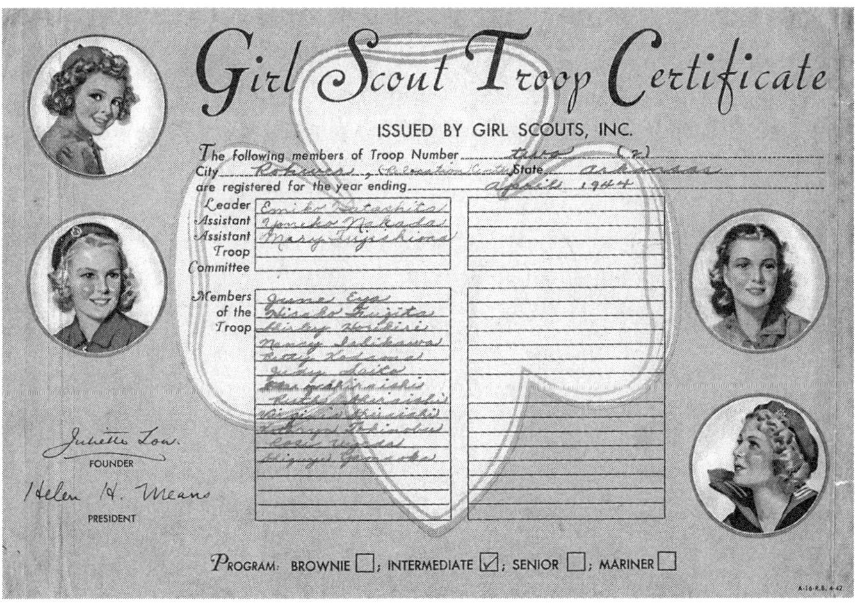
Girl Scout Troop Certificate

ISSUED BY GIRL SCOUTS, INC.

The following members of Troop Number two (2)
City ____ State Arkansas
are registered for the year ending April 1944

Leader
Assistant
Assistant
Troop Committee

Members of the Troop

Juliette Low.
FOUNDER

Helen H. Means
PRESIDENT

PROGRAM: BROWNIE ☐; INTERMEDIATE ☑; SENIOR ☐; MARINER ☐

A 1944 Girl Scout enrollment form from Rohrer, Arkansas, where over 8,000 Japanese Americans were incarcerated between 1942 and 1945. Significantly, the sheet reads "(Relocation Camp)" next to the location. The images of the white, smiling Girl Scouts are in stark contrast to the reality of incarceration facing the Japanese American girls. Japanese American National Museum, Los Angeles (gift of R. Ruth Shiraishi, 2007.50.34).

Girl Scouts of the USA (GSUSA) in the imprisonment of Japanese immigrants and Japanese Americans, or Nikkei, during World War II, and it forces us to ask how the US government used the concepts of Girl Scout "courage" and "innocence" to hide the horrors of its imprisonment and treatment of Japanese Americans and Japanese in these incarceration centers.[1] That list of names does something else, too: it pushes us to ponder what Japanese American girls and their parents made of their membership in this national organization that brought its badges, parades, troops, and pictures of cheery white girls into the incarceration centers.

Girl Scouts in Incarceration Camps

In February 1942 President Franklin D. Roosevelt authorized the US Western Defense Command's order to remove and incarcerate over 100,000 people of Japanese descent. Girl Scouts immediately became involved in this effort. Soon after the removal was ordered, the Seattle Girl Scout Council requested monies from the Girl Scout International Fund to help with what was euphemistically known as "evacuation" of girls in their area, one of the largest regions of forced relocation. At first the Girl Scout National Board voted to table the vote on Seattle's request until they could gather more information from the American Red Cross, the Foreign Policy Association, and a scholar from Western Reserve University, Grace Coyle, who was, as the board put in its minutes, "making a study of the Japanese evacuation centers for the government."[2] Eventually, however, Constance Rittenhouse, the president of the national board, signed an agreement with the War Relocation Authority (WRA) to provide Girl Scouting in all the camps. Because the US government wanted to encourage "evacuee identification with groups typically American in concept," it would help carry out a full Girl Scout program for girls ages seven to eighteen. In signing this official agreement with the WRA, the Girl Scouts was complicit in the business of indoctrination and incarceration.[3]

Yet even before the national board made any decision, local councils were getting involved. At the Fresno Assembly Center, a temporary detention center in operation from May through October 1942, where Nikkei were taken before being sent to the permanent, more inland incarceration centers, the executive secretary of the Fresno Girl Scout Council gave lectures on leadership to the leaders of the newly formed troops in the assembly center.[4] By September of that year, the national board had approved the decision to organize girls in incarceration centers as "lone troops," meaning they weren't affiliated with local councils and regions. The troops would be run under the direction of each center's community service director, a WRA position, who would appoint troop leaders from among their own employees and from those imprisoned. The community service director would also serve as a permanent member of the troop's advisory council.[5] Girl Scout field directors, the same paid professionals that had made forays into the American Indian reservations and boarding schools, regularly visited the incarceration centers, giving talks on Girl Scouting and "leadership," that ubiquitous yet somewhat unclear trait that Girl Scouting promotes throughout its history. Interestingly, by February 1943, the national board carried a motion that "national and local publicity on Girl Scout activities in Japanese relocation centers be permitted, emphasizing, however, that Girl Scouting had been undertaken in these centers at the request of the federal government."[6] In other words, all publicity was to obfuscate the Girl Scouts' own agency in participating in the centers, deflecting responsibility to the government.

It's not at all clear from these brief archival records what prompted the decision to avert responsibility. Was there concern about participating in the imprisonment of innocent people? Certainly by 1943 there was a national outcry about this injustice, even if it wasn't mainstream, and one of the major sister organizations that the Girl Scouts recognized, the YWCA, had explicitly stated that the removal of Nikkei was about "race" and "war hysteria."[7] Was there concern that the quality of the programming would not be up to national standards, a frequent rationale used to legitimate discriminatory practices and segregated troops? Was there worry that Girl Scouting would somehow be tainted as an activity for unworthy "needy" girls, even enemies of the state? Would participation in the removal efforts somehow distract from Girl Scouts' efforts to expand, as the national board of directors had approved the program "A Million or More by '44" in 1942?[8] While we don't know the answers to these questions, we do know that the Girl Scouts agreed to participate in the incarceration centers, and unlike the YWCA, it came with no voiced disinclination to join in a racist endeavor. According to GSUSA records, by 1943, all the incarceration centers had Girl Scout troops.[9] Giving the girl prisoners a taste of a group "typically American in concept," the Girl Scouts played a key role in indoctrination at the incarceration camps, indoctrination that was in line with American foreign policy, with dominant ideals of white girlhood, and with a patriotic commitment to the nation. It was also an indoctrination rife with hypocrisy and contradiction. One of the first points of hypocrisy was the very term used to describe the prisoners—"evacuees"—suggesting that the imprisonment was for their own protection. Yet as one former prisoner noted, "If we were put there for our protection, why were the guns at the guard towers pointed inward, instead of outward?"[10]

Girl Scout participation in the incarceration centers was very much in line with the history of the GSUSA. The arm of the Girl Scouts funding its program in Japanese American incarceration centers—the National Field Committee—had, up to this point, largely focused on bringing Girl Scouting to American Indian girls, as we saw in chapter 4. Moreover, the fact that the Field Committee asked that monies be donated from the International Committee of the Juliette Low Memorial Fund also makes sense, as Japanese American girls were definitely understood by the national Girl Scout organization as "international," not "domestic." Girl Scouting could be brought to these Japanese (American) girls within this logic just as it was brought to the Chinese (American) girls in New York City and what they called Spanish (American) girls in the Southeast. I place "American" in parentheses because Girl Scouting definitely saw all these ethnic groups—Chinese, Japanese, Latina—as the foreigner within national boundaries. Working with the US government to create Girl Scout troops in incarceration centers also connected to the way the organization saw its mission as lending a helping hand and bringing an outlook and way of life designed to build character and health. As an institution it would legitimate and make sense of its work with incarcerated Nikkei girls as outreach and assistance, just as it had construed its forays into American Indian boarding schools as civilizing and uplift. This rhetoric of beneficence both protected the organization from examining the deleterious effects of its work and lent legitimacy to the many, mostly white, women who were able to carve out interesting lives as field workers and professional staff.

Whatever the rhetoric, however, one must also see the Girl Scout work in American Indian boarding schools and Japanese American incarceration centers as part of the long arm of US imperialistic practices. American Indian girls themselves may have had complex experiences with Girl Scouting at the boarding schools, from alienation to enjoyment and pride as we saw in chapter 4, but the Girl Scout policy itself of establishing troops at the boarding schools was a continuation of the policies of the US settler state, policies designed to eradicate and contain Indianness so that the nations could be claimed as Euro-American states. Similarly, the decision to move into the incarceration centers, at the behest of the WRA, was also a decision in line with the presumption of the Girl Scouts as a "patriotic" organization whose priority was protecting Euro-American dominance both at home and abroad.

I turn now to one particular incarceration center in Arizona, known as Poston (officially, the Colorado River Relocation Center), one of the largest incarceration centers of Nikkei during World War II.[11]

Girl Scouting and Poston

A 1943 article in the *Poston Chronicle* noted that members of a Girl Scout troop in Poston had decided to compile songbooks and make adobe bricks as "community service."[12] This short article seems to be just a puff piece, printed literally to fill up empty column space and perhaps to demonstrate to readers outside of the prison that, as Girl Scouts, the incarcerated could still engage in civic and community endeavors, just like their patriotic counterparts throughout America.

When I first read the news clipping about the adobe bricks, I thought, "Was the Girl Scout organization at Poston trying to teach Japanese American girls Indian crafts as a means of uplift, just as they were teaching Indian crafts to Indian girls?" This seemed entirely plausible, as the camp, which eventually would imprison over 18,000 people on three different sites, was located in southwestern Arizona, within the boundaries of the Colorado River Indian Reservation, where Mohave and Chemehuevi Indians had lived for centuries and where Hopi and Navajo people had been forcefully relocated. The Colorado River Indian Council had voted against the creation of the incarceration center within their boundaries, refusing to take part in the kind of forced resettlement and persecution that had happened to them. The US Bureau of Indian Affairs overruled the council, however, agreeing to jointly run Poston with the WRA. The commissioner of Indian Affairs, John Collier, envisioned Poston as a kind of experiment, where he could see whether skilled Japanese American farmers would be better able to cultivate the arid Arizona land than Native Americans, whom he saw as failing because of their lack of skill (rather than the bad conditions). He brought in experts—psychiatrists and sociologists—to examine how to manage populations under federal control, including Alexander Leighton, a psychiatrist and member of the Navy Reserve Medical Corps, to lead the studies.[13]

My initial thought about adobe brickmaking as arts and crafts quickly proved wrong. One of the first tasks Collier and the WRA had male prisoners do was build adobe bricks, ostensibly for schools for the incarcerated girls and boys. This was extremely difficult work: hot, muddy, and physically exhausting. Leighton wrote a lengthy analysis of why prisoners disliked making adobe bricks. While he adopts a patronizing tone, the details on the difficulty of the work are clear:

> Adobe buildings were unfamiliar and were looked upon as inferior. The labor involved was arduous, with the temperature now between 115° and 124° in the shade. Furthermore, dabbling in mud was considered degrading, and ruined their clothes which the Government would not replace. The wages of $12 per month made this an important matter, and the wages were in themselves no incentive to work. The non-Japanese fore-men in charge of construction seemed too bossy and superior, or too condescending. Finally, it was believed that the schools were really not for the residents, but were for the Indians or were to be hospitals for invalid soldiers, and that the whole plan was a scheme to get labor for next to nothing.[14]

Interestingly, the wording in that last line, "it was believed," suggests that unfounded rumors resounded within Poston, undermining morale. Even Leighton, however, mentions elsewhere in his study that the Bureau of Indian Affairs had indeed planned to have the buildings made of adobe so that they could be used on the reservations later.[15] The US government and the Bureau of Indian Affairs were indeed getting buildings built for "next to nothing," with imprisoned labor doing physically exhausting and dehumanizing work. Collier apparently attempted to quell the rumors by saying that it was important for the schools to be built with long-lasting bricks, as the Japanese might be interned for many, many years, setting off another round of anger among the imprisoned, who were regularly being promised that life in the "relocation centers" was just for the duration of the war.

Poston is well known for being one of the incarceration sites where the imprisoned explicitly resisted through strikes and uprisings; the best-known strike lasted weeks, set off by the imprisonment of a detainee who was accused of killing an informer. Less discussed, however, is a strike in 1942 by fifty-six adobe brickmakers, which, according to Brian Niiya, was quickly "settled," presumably meaning put down.[16] After the strike, perhaps in an attempt to prove how docile the prisoners had become, the *Poston Chronicle* published many articles in 1943 about the myriad "volunteers" who were competing to see which unit could make the most adobe bricks. One article noted that "among those industriously making 'mud patties' were doctors, councilmen, surveyors . . . bigwigs, blocks managers, the press, doctors' wives, [and] others representing various departments."[17] Another gave a big thanks to "the women . . . [who] deserve credit for taking strong initiative in aiding construction of the adobe bricks. . . . The school buildings will soon be a reality."[18] While not completely clear, it seems that after the strikes *everyone* was expected to chip in and that these "volunteers" were working after their other shifts, doing work in the center's offices, laundries, mess halls, and infirmaries. Even the *Chronicle*, however, which gives the most saccharine and censored view of the centers, provides hints of continued resistance. While the adobe brick strikes may have ended, mischief designed to upset the government's plans continued. One article, for instance, noted that "costly and irreplaceable lumber has been reported missing from the Poston Two school building project." (This was the same one that the adobe bricks were used for.) The article also shines a light on the threat always hanging over the prisoners, quoting project director W. Wade Head, who "made it clear that firm, drastic action will be taken, if necessary (such as a house-to-house search) if such actions are continued."[19]

Making adobe bricks was no easy arts-and-crafts project, so when the troop decided to make them, were they being coerced to volunteer? Or did they in fact decide to pitch in, doing this arduous labor to ease the burden on their mothers, fathers, and older siblings who were taking this on in their extra hours? Or were they doing it, in fact, in the hope that the schools might actually be built? Or—a real possibility—were they actually accomplices in the very mischief that the article above derided, as being a Girl Scout would be a wonderful cover for resistance workers? While there are no definite answers to these questions, the news clipping makes one thing clear: Girl Scouts, all of whom were detainees in the prison, were making the very adobe bricks that would imprison them at Poston.

Girl Scouting and the Duplicity of Good Citizenship and Patriotism

The Poston adobe brick project starkly illustrates how Girl Scouts asked its incarcerated members to act in ways complicit with their own imprisonment but to see that work as "service." The records give us many other examples. A scrapbook from the Fresno Assembly Center mentions twice that Girl Scouts served ice water at the reception center, working with their "troop leaders" to "afford maximum comfort and prompt attention" to visitors. (The reception center at Fresno allowed visitors, "Caucasian and Japanese," from 2:00 to 4:00 p.m. each day.) One can imagine the harried, painful, and desperate meetings in this very hot and crowded "reception" center as the already incarcerated met with those on the outside to gather news, to plan strategies, and to make hurried decisions about the homes, businesses, and farms they had been forced to leave.[20] It is bitterly ironic to imagine Girl Scouts, presumably in uniform, serving ice water and giving comfort to detainees and their visitors when they themselves were prisoners, not only witnessing the distress and confusion of the adults, community leaders, and elders but also being called on to bolster and console their elders, keeping the chaos and grief in check.

In a photo taken by Bud Aoyama at Heart Mountain, an incarceration center in Wyoming, we see Girl Scouts greeting prisoners as they are coming off the train. Flanking the white male soldiers with billy clubs on their hips, the Girl Scouts look on as the women prisoners step down off the train. Here, again, we see Girl Scouts called on to witness and to help, though their empty

In 1943, Bud Aoyoma captured this moment in a photograph titled *Incoming*, of Girl Scouts, themselves incarcerated, and soldiers greeting newcomers at Heart Mountain Relocation Center in Wyoming. Bud Aoyama, "INCOMING—Arrivals leaving train assisted by Girl Scout with their baggage," Heart Mountain, Wyoming, War Relocation Authority Photographs: Japanese-American Evacuation and Resettlement, BANC PIC 1967.014 v.66 HG:103—PIC, Bancroft Library, University of California, Berkeley.

hands suggest it was unclear what exactly they could do to help the women unloading themselves and their few belongings off a dusty train onto an even dirtier landscape.[21] They are asked to become the hostesses of their own imprisonment, positioned in a liminal role, part police officer, part prisoner, part girl, part superior to the women exiting the train.

Girl Scouting did not just ask girls to think in disjointed ways about the work they were doing in the service of their own imprisonment. It also asked girls to feel loyal and to perform loyalty to a country that was imprisoning them. In both its philosophy and its programming, the Girl Scouts was at heart a patriotic endeavor, and this was drilled into scouts in the camps. Eva Koyama, a young girl imprisoned at Minidoka, in Idaho, tells her father about joining the Girl Scouts, adding, "Here is the Girl Scout Oath":

> On my honor, I will try
> To do my duty to God and my country
> To help other people at all times
> To obey the Girl Scout laws.[22]

Duty to God and to country are in the same line, given equal weight, so for the imprisoned who felt it was constantly necessary to try to prove their loyalty to the United States, visible evidence of patriotism was very useful. Interestingly, both the visual and the written archival records of the incarceration centers provide many examples of Girl Scouts doing patriotic things. We learn about Girl Scouts planning Flag Day and Fourth of July events. We see them taking part in flag ceremonies, serving in bugle corps, and marching in parades. We learn that they raised money for veteran groups.[23] For the girls and young women who were Girl Scouts, encouraged to take part in these motions of service and allegiance to country, the participation must have elicited extraordinarily conflicted feelings and mental dissonance as the incarceration centers and the Girl Scouts emphasized the necessity of embodying honor, respect, loyalty, and enthusiasm to the country that had imprisoned them and their families. Any examination of the Girl Scouts in the twentieth century must emphasize how duplicitous the organization was in asking girls and women to demonstrate their "good citizenship" and their "patriotism" in a context where the United States had forcibly taken their homes and businesses, imprisoned them in often brutal conditions, and given them no particular reason to hope for their futures. It was a low moment for the Girl Scouts of the USA.

"We Followed the Girl Scouts to the End"

As Valerie Matsumoto illuminates in *City Girls: The Nisei Social World in Los Angeles, 1920–1950*, second-generation Japanese American girls and women had a robust social life before the war, which included membership in many girls' organizations; they built rich networks of friendships, challenged many social norms, created their own ways of being Japanese American, and they had fun! Matsumoto details the many ways they brought these organizations into the incarceration centers: journalism clubs, dance clubs, the YWCA's Girl Reserves, athletic leagues, and of course, the Girl Scouts.[24] This suggests that Girl Scouting in the incarceration centers may have been both an endeavor foisted on unwilling participants and a strategy of survival, sometimes even pleasure, or possibly resistance—as the adobe brick anecdote suggests—within the confines and danger of the camps.[25]

Emily Anderson, curator of the *Coming of Age* exhibit at the Japanese American National Museum, explained that for many families Girl Scouting was a particularly attractive organization before the war as it provided so much flexibility: The girls could be both "American" and "Japanese," they could be both Buddhist and American, and they could be loyal to family and cultural traditions but also express their American patriotism and learn American cultural norms. Janet Sui Matarai Misaka, who was interviewed for the exhibit, provides a powerful example of the ways young women brought Girl Scouting into the incarceration centers. Ten years old when her family was forced to leave Mountain View, California, Misaka described herself as one of the "first Japanese Americans to join the troop in Mountain View," a Brownie troop that was all white. With her mom's help, she even won the cookie sale contest for the entire council. Movingly, she brought her *Girl Scout Handbook* with her to the camps; this detail really stands out, considering how little her family was able to bring and how difficult their relocation was. First they had to move to Santa Anita Assembly Center, a racetrack where she and her family were forced to live in converted horse stalls, and then to Heart Mountain in Wyoming. Within a month of her landing in Santa Anita, adults in the assembly center had begun Girl Scouting. Misaka recounted that the adults "got everything going fast to keep us out of trouble." At Heart Mountain she remembered going with her troop down to the river, where they made little stoves out of cans and cooked some treats. She remembers making a memory album and learning how to build a stool. And they repeated the Girl Scout Promise, something she could do basically by heart even over sixty years later: "On my honor, I will try to do my duty to God and my country, to help other people at all times, to obey the Girl Scout laws." When she finished reciting the Promise during the interview with Anderson, she started laughing wistfully and then reflected on the irony of her and other girls' experiences with the Girl Scouts while imprisoned: "Well, we did all that. That's what we did. We followed the Girl Scouts to the end."[26]

Newspapers from the prisons and oral histories from women who had been incarcerated provide many details about what the troops did, a mind-boggling range of activities including doing construction, greeting new prisoners, caring for young children, camping, and hosting sing-alongs and parties. At the Fresno Assembly Center, physician and prisoner Joseph Sasaki and his wife Katherine Sasaki formed nine Girl Scout troops, from young Brownies to teenage girls over age sixteen, who were trained in leadership.[27] Reading the official scrapbook from the assembly center, written by prisoners, we learn that Girl Scouts worked to plant and maintain a center garden, including potted plants that had been donated by the Brownies. The older Girl Scouts taught the littlest children in the center. In one troop, eight Girl Scouts, with their two leaders, planned daily after-school sessions for preschoolers. Meeting outside behind the laundry, they split into small groups, with the Girl Scouts doing health check-ups and leading games, music, and art.[28]

Adults may likely have encouraged Girl Scouting to provide evidence of loyalty in a context that threatened their children with statelessness, but they also voiced concern that even if their US citizenship were safe, they would end up with no country for which to feel loyalty. Indeed, the editorial board of the *Heart Mountain Sentinel* wrote in their piece "A Salute to the Scouts," "Now more than ever before there is a need for guidance for boys and girls in the formative ages. Embittered by evacuation, exposed to abnormal conditions of camp life, it is too easy for youth to acquire a warped, unsocial attitude."[29] Many of the adult prisoners, concerned about the depression, apathy, anger, and despair from which their children might suffer, may have seen Girl Scouting as a respite. Mary Taukamoto, writing in the Fresno Assembly Center's *Vignette*, expressed the anguish of being a parent:

> Already four months within Army Centers, I feel old in this experience of evacuation. Since that fateful March morning when the destiny of 150,000 people were suddenly altered . . . there were a thousand fears that gripped the hearts of the mothers. . . . We are evacuating for the duration, but what of our children's training, and cultural background, education, spiritual guidance—could they be put away for the duration?

> We are overwhelmed by the tremendous responsibility, and frightened as we are, we realize there is no room for tears. No time for confused hesitation. Right now every opportunity must be ingeniously utilized toward the good. Idleness and bitterness will deaden character and make our children worthless citizens.[30]

In the same publication, Sam Nakano wrote:

> We who have grown up with the outside world must bide our time and take matters in stride, but our children who have been suddenly cut off from the world and thrown together in this "foreign atmosphere" deserve any sacrifices we can make, so that after the duration, life can be made easier and more comfortable for them. Let's teach them that even in a life such as this, our hearts do not despair, that, although we left behind many material things, we did not leave our courage, our fortitude, and our ability to do the best with the least.[31]

The focused concern about the long-term implications for children gives us a hint of why families might spend their limited funds to donate to Girl Scout troops and pay membership fees to the national organization. It also helps explain why mothers would spend more of that limited money to buy material from the canteens to make the Girl Scout uniforms themselves, guessing at the style as there were no official patterns available, something that many women recount in their oral histories about life in the centers.

Some of the oral histories collected in the Densho Digital Archive give us a sense of the importance of Girl Scouts for providing some relief—safety within the camps, recreation and social activities, and even opportunities to leave the prisons on outings and camping trips. Marion I. Masada, for instance, was first imprisoned with her family in the Salinas Assembly Center and then moved to Poston, traveling with her family and grandmother on a very rickety old train, black curtains covering the windows the entire ride. She recalls her life in Poston as being very hot and dusty with absolutely no privacy. A neighbor sexually molested her, but fear kept her from reporting it. Her mom had a baby while imprisoned, so Masada had to take on more home chores and the family laundry. The memories we can hear on the recording are hard to dredge up, difficult to recount. But when the interviewer asks her, "Are there people who stand out . . . who were important in Poston?" she visibly relaxes and says, "My Girl Scout leader." "She was fun," she says simply.[32]

In another interview we learn about more adult women who remember the Girl Scouts fondly, the reunions they've had, and the experiences they can recount. Growing up in La Puente, California, Margaret Saito had first been taken with her family to the Pomono Assembly Center and then moved to Heart Mountain for the remainder of the war. Both her parents were second-generation Japanese Americans. She has no good memories of anything from the prisons except for the Girl Scouts. "Oh, I was in the Girl Scout troop, I think I was fourteen, and Aya Nishimura was our leader. And it was mostly people my age, maybe a year older, and those people are still around and come to the reunions. So we take Girl Scout pictures of all the Girl Scouts at Heart Mountain, there were many troops. We take those pictures and it's nice we're still able to." "What kind of things did you do?" the interviewer asks.

> Oh, I remember two summers we camped in Yellowstone. Those were really fun times. And one of those Girl Scout members, she reminded me that during one of the times one of the girls was in the outhouse and there was a bear so they couldn't come out [*laughs*]. So they were trying to get help, get the bear away. It's things like that, and I remember the wild strawberries that were growing by the building that we stayed in. It was beautiful. I couldn't, you couldn't ask for a nicer place to camp. It was really a nice memory.

And then she adds something interesting, especially with our knowledge of how many Girl Scouts were called on to do hard labor, both physical and emotional, for the prisons. The interviewer asks, "I know some of the boys who went up there did projects that they worked on. Did you work on projects?" Saito responds, "No, no projects. I don't remember doing any good for anybody [*laughs*]. You know, like repairing. I don't recall anything like that." Instead, she recalls hiking, earning badges, and camping, all ways to both metaphorically and physically leave the prison.[33]

A set of letters among members of the Koyama family also shows the sense of relief that the Girl Scouts brought, though we need to read these thoughtfully, as the envelope in which the letters were sent was marked "censored," and the writers clearly knew their letters were being read. Dr. Keizaburo "Kei" Koyama was imprisoned at the Department of Justice detention facility in Camp Livingston, Louisiana, when his wife Teru and his daughter Eva wrote to him from the Minidoka Relocation Center in Hunt, Idaho, in October and November of 1942. Eva writes about a surprise visit from a friend, a soldier who was on furlough; the weather; and her boredom. Then she adds, "I joined the Girl Scouts and its lots of fun we have Ruth Mishino (sp?) for our leader and she's very good." Teru writes about their son, William, whose birthday it is and who is away picking beets in freezing Idaho weather. She notes how her neighbors in the camp aren't sharing coal, and their lack of human decency seems to bother her even more than the cold. She worries that her husband isn't writing. "Are you ill?" she writes, adding that she knows the dampness in Louisiana must be horrible. And then she writes, "Eva joined the Girl Scouts and today a scout field master came so the committee and the scouts' mothers went to the meeting and I enjoyed the field master's message very much. There were only two mothers present, just Mrs. Matishi and myself. Miriam joined the Brownies, same as cub scouts and she is enjoying it too. I'll be one of the busy mothers with all my children in the scout activities. I want to keep myself busy so I will not allow myself to worry about our future too much."[34] There is something extremely poignant about this passage, in which Teru imagines herself as a busy scout mom, a popular culture image far from the reality she was facing, imprisoned, her husband far away in a different, dank, prison, her son sent on a work detail, all of them freezing with insufficient coats and heating fuel. While she would have been writing this knowing the censor's eyes were on it, the pain and pathos of imprisonment certainly come through, as well as the relief that scouting engendered if not a sense of hope then at least a momentary reprieve from anxiety.

Scouting may have been one of girls' only opportunities to actually physically leave the camp. Yasuko Ikeda, imprisoned at Heart Mountain in Wyoming, remembered going to Yellowstone. But for her, the pleasure contrasted sharply with the racism she faced; indeed, the trip underscored their own imprisonment. She remembered that she and other Girl Scouts traveled "in army trucks" to Yellowstone, where on one of their sightseeing day-trips they passed "a car full of sailors that came by and they yelled out the window, 'Go home Japs.' And so, we did not answer back, but among ourselves, we also [said], 'We'd like to go back to California, or Oregon, or Washington.'"[35] But they couldn't. They were prisoners.

Leaving the Camps

Toward the end of the war, government officials began a policy of moving people out of the incarceration centers to communities across the United States, in areas far from the West Coast. They turned to young women they

Girl Scout troops of all ages at the Minidoka Relocation Center in Jerome, Idaho, where over 13,000 people of Japanese descent were incarcerated from 1942 to 1945. *Girl Scout Troops in Minidoka*, Hunt, Idaho, ca. 1942–45, NARA ID: 210-CMB-SP2–1875, National Archives, Washington, DC.

identified as "exemplary" to safely serve as ambassadors throughout the country. These young women often went alone or in very small groups, as the point of resettlement was to break up what the government saw as a dangerous concentration of Japanese communities on the West Coast.[36] Here, too, the Girl Scouts became involved, promising to have the various Girl Scout committees in the camps write to the councils where the girls and young women were moving, to encourage local troops to get in touch with and welcome the newcomers. The policy never seems to have been enacted in full, however, as the archival record includes statement after statement from the national board that the GSUSA will help resettle Japanese American girls, but there is no evidence that the GSUSA actually did it or that regional councils or local troops welcomed any of the girls. Before the war, the troops in California were largely segregated by ethnicity and class. After the war, however, GSUSA seemed particularly uninterested in creating any new troops for Japanese American girls, allowing only for the "possible assimilation of individual

Girl Scouts." This may seem progressive, as it would likely mean Nikkei girls integrating into already existing white, Black, and Mexican American troops, but it was probably more about ensuring that Nikkei communities did not reconstitute themselves after the war and instead dissolved into the nation.[37]

Apparently, however, despite whatever publicity and letters the Girl Scout National Headquarters sent, local councils did not always welcome those who returned from the camps. A particularly painful example of this comes from Sally Kitano, who moved back to Bainbridge Island, Washington, after she and her family were imprisoned at the Manzanar concentration camp. She recalled:

> When I got back to the island, a lot of the kids were, belonged to the Rainbow Girls. And that was, that was the thing to belong to. Okay, and then the other thing was joining the Girl Scouts. 'Cause I was in the scouting program before the war. And so I went up to the lady who ran the scouting program and I said, "Can I get back into the scouting program?" And she said, "Well, the kids are too far advanced now so I don't think that you would fit in." And I says, "Okay." I mean, I accepted it. I was disappointed, very disappointed, but I said, "Okay. I understand that." And then, but it wasn't too long after that I found out that anybody can go join the Girl Scouts at any time.

After Kitano shares that she never rejoined the Girl Scouts, the interviewer asks her if any Japanese Americans joined. "Not at that time, no," she answers. After which she adds, "I remember Remo, my classmate, said, 'Well, let me see what I can do.' You know, so she, so she had her mother call headquarters. And they said no, Japanese are not accepted. And that's when I practically broke down and cried, 'cause I couldn't get into anything. That was, that really hurt, I think."[38]

Considering the Imprisonment of Girl Scouts

At the same time that Sally Kitano was unable to get any troop to welcome her—with their unfounded excuses—the national Girl Scout organization and the World Association of Girl Guides and Girl Scouts were moving forward with their intercultural-international programs, creating pen pal programs, setting up world conferences, and orchestrating the collection and dispersal of resources to be sent to European and Japanese war-torn areas. The continual press of the rhetoric was international friendship and global sisterhood. There seemed to be no such concerted effort when it came to the girls whose imprisonment Girl Scouts countenanced and supported. Indeed, there didn't even appear to be a recognition of the organization's own collusion decades after the prisons closed. In 1992, in a response to someone asking about the history of girls of color in the Girl Scouts, the director of the GSUSA National Historic Preservation Center, Mary Levey, responded: "Girl Scouts had Girl Scout troops in the Japanese-American internment camps and there was no national policy of discrimination. Firsthand accounts represent the experience of the person giving the account. I had recently heard a staff member here talking about someone who had been in one of those camps, had been in a Girl Scout troop and had had a positive experience."[39] Not only does this short note occlude the fact that local troops and councils excluded Nikkei girls, with absolutely no repercussions from the national organization, but it also suggests a level of magnanimity and generosity in allowing girls to join troops while they were incarcerated. It also obscures the fact that these troops at prisons and camps like Poston and Manzanar did not just "happen" but were established with an official agreement between the GSUSA and the US WRA, under the auspices of employees from both organizations. It is far from the (what many of us consider still limited) acknowledgment provided in the 1988 Civil Rights Act, which recognized that the government acted from "race prejudice, war hysteria, and a failure of political leadership," rather than from any necessary security considerations, in incarcerating Nikkei. The involvement of Girl Scouting in the incarceration of Nikkei during World War II clearly reveals the intertwining of gendered, national, and racial histories; the machinations of white nationalism; the complicity of this national, protofeminist organization in the incarceration of Nikkei girls; and the duplicitous and convoluted gyrations necessary for the organization to legitimate, and even celebrate, its "goodwill." But listening to the girls' stories themselves, and those of the parents who encouraged their involvement, we also see how girls and women who were incarcerated in the camps often used Girl Scouts for their own purposes, for their own survival, envisioning and creating new forms of relationships from within the structure that had emerged directly out of empire, so much so that they even found joy decades later in sharing memories and traveling far to reunite and recollect with their sister scouts.

The next chapter will pick up some years after the last Japanese American incarceration center closed, to follow the story of African American girls and women who fought to integrate the Girl Scouts. Their story is at the heart of the ways that Girl Scouting simultaneously purported to be an organization for "all girls" yet systematically excluded girls of color and denied their full participation. It illuminates clearly how the Girl Scouts colluded in the systemic racism that runs through the center of the history of the United States, despite a rhetorical belief in freedom and opportunity. Like the history of Girl Scouting in Japanese American incarceration centers, it is a difficult story.

Chapter 7

Girl Scouting and the Color Line

AFRICAN AMERICAN GIRL SCOUTS IN THE TWENTIETH CENTURY

••••••

Our relationships with racial or interracial groups must be openly and honestly discussed if we really intend to be as democratic as we say we are.

—Charlotte Moton Hubbard

In 1952 the African American magazine *Ebony* published a five-page spread celebrating the Girl Scouts as an "interracial" organization. Among *Ebony*'s many photos of mixed-race groups of scouts and African American leaders, there was one that the Girl Scout national organization frequently publicizes, showing Birdsall Otis Edey, one of Girl Scouts' early founders and presidents, at a Girl Scout rally in Central Park. Taken sometime in the 1920s, the photo shows Edey in the middle of a group of eight girls, two of whom appear to be African American, the rest white. The image suggests an inclusiveness and welcoming attitude toward everyone, and to a certain degree it's accurate: There have been African American Girl Scouts from the early days of scouting, led by Black women including Lolette Crutcher, Doris Worthy, Charlotte Moton Hubbard, and Ethel Harvey. The *Ebony* article explains that segregated troops still existed in the Jim Crow South but that Girl Scouts were making "slow and steady progress toward surmounting racial barriers . . . so quietly it has escaped much attention of the press."[1]

Ebony's comment that Girl Scouts' antiracist work had "escaped much attention of the press" was more than a casual observation—it was an intentional policy of the Girl Scouts, and the archives are filled with memos reminding staff members to only selectively publicize efforts at integration, especially working to avoid notice where Jim Crow policies were in place. The concern that Black girls' participation would hurt the reputation of Girl Scouting and drive white girls away shaped Girl Scout policy for decades in both the North and South. The priority was to create a national organization that would please everyone, and for the most part this meant pleasing white members, acquiescing to fears over Black membership, downplaying Black Girl Scouting in the media (the praise the national council gave in the *Ebony* article was atypical), and implementing explicitly discriminatory policies. Through the 1960s, the national organization generally refused to intervene when discrimination was brought to its attention, instead allowing local councils to carry out policies of their choice. Even the work of more progressive councils to form Black troops or support integrated troops was sometimes discouraged for fear that this would lead to white fear and anger, problems that the organization regarded as more important than inclusivity. Black leaders and girls had to challenge and navigate complex and duplicitous policies of segregation and discrimination in order to form their troops, create their camps, and insist that the Girl Scouts live up to its promise of a democratic sisterhood.

In his 1903 *The Souls of Black Folk*, W. E. B. Du Bois wrote, "The problem of the twentieth century is the problem of the color line." This was certainly true of the Girl Scouts of the USA in the twentieth century, whose mission statement demanded it be for "all girls" and whose national files are filled with initiatives, policies, and plans to offer Girl Scouting to predominantly Black communities, to recruit more Black girls and leaders, and to hire more Black staff.[2] But the organization also perceived Black membership as dangerous, the intermingling of Black girls and white girls as impossible, and the mere fact of Black recruitment as threatening to the growth of the organization in white communities. The white leadership saw the organization from the perspective of other white members, so much so that its discrimination was normalized and even invisible to itself. African American girls and women never stopped claiming Girl Scouting as their own, however, despite the myriad ways that the Girl Scouts created and maintained systematic, organizational racism despite a rhetoric that stated the opposite.[3] This was true not just in the Jim Crow South but also in the North. Girl Scouting was central to the ways that discrimination and racism threaded itself through every aspect of American life in the twentieth century.[4]

Girl Scout Racial Policy

While the Girl Scout national organization claims to have always welcomed African American girls, the reality was much different. Two primary policies—the local rule policy and the lone troop policy—deeply curtailed the ability of African Americans to organize as Girl Scouts. The first of these, the local rule policy, did not explicitly exclude or name African Americans, but it allowed Girl Scout councils to exclude, segregate, and discriminate. In its early years, someone wanting to start up Girl Scouts in their area would write to national headquarters. They would likely receive in return an enthusiastic letter from the Girl Scouts, such as this 1916 recruitment letter that concluded: "The first and most essential step in organizing a Troop is securing an intelligent, vigorous young woman over 21 years old to act as Captain. . . . We ask you to do your share in hastening the time when every American community shall have its Troop of Scouts. Let us bring this opportunity for health, happiness and helpfulness within the reach of every American girl. None are too poor to meet the necessary expense and none too rich to need its benefits."[5] What the letter did not spell out, however, was that this welcoming attitude was only directed toward white young women. After recruiting the "captain" (the early name for a Girl Scout leader), the organizer was referred to the local council, which would conduct the final troop approval. Two points are key here: *All* local councils were white in the first decades of Girl Scout history, and *all* authority for approving the formation of a troop resided with the local council. This "local rule" is extremely important to understand and to underscore, as it gets at the heart of how discrimination worked in the Girl Scouts. Because the national organization vested so much authority within local communities, it meant that exclusionary policies could be practiced largely with impunity for decades. Local councils could slow or stop the formation of African American troops or move African American girls from integrated troops to all-Black troops. Certainly there are examples of local (white) councils that approved all–African American troops and integrated troops, but there is significant evidence of local councils blocking the ability of African Americans to create a troop. Council members throughout the country could fail to authorize an African American troop simply by not responding to the request or could outright refuse to authorize the troop.

In the South, local white councils forbade the formation of African American troops for decades; not until the 1930s is there a record of the first African American troop, in Richmond, Virginia.[6] Emma Watson, the dean of women at Virginia Union University, a historically Black institution, wrote directly to the national Girl Scout organization about starting a troop at her school.

Apparently the national organization wrote back favorably, which incensed the local white Richmond council when the item came before them for approval. The white council passed a unanimous motion to register a "protest against National for taking up and deciding many matters which are local, especially where a race question is involved."[7] Nevertheless, one of the white directors was persuasive in her insistence that the Black troop was important, and the white council approved its formation on the grounds that all "unwritten rules of the community" be followed. These were actually written down, however, in a document between the white council and the three Black women—Mrs. Emma Watson, Dr. Lina Jones, and Mrs. A. V. Binga—who would lead Troop 34, the first troop of African American girls south of the Potomac. The rules included strict racial segregation, separate award ceremonies, and no representation on the main (white) council.[8] What this meant was that for decades there was basically a council within the council, a separate group of African American women leaders who for the most part

Around 1950, this group of Richmond, Virginia, Brownies and Intermediate Girl Scouts prepared to embark on a trip; in a time of intense Jim Crow travel and lodging restrictions, Black communities used Girl Scouting to forge opportunities for their daughters. Courtesy of Girl Scouts of the Commonwealth of Virginia and the Commonwealth Council of the Girl Scouts of Virginia Records, 1910–2012, collection no. M 400, Special Collections and Archives, James Branch Cabell Library, Virginia Commonwealth University, Richmond.

In an undated photo from the late 1940s or early 1950s, Richmond Girl Scouts pose in front of a display of African American literature and culture at Rosa Dixon Bowser Public Library. Courtesy of Girl Scouts of the Commonwealth of Virginia and the Commonwealth Council of the Girl Scouts of Virginia Records, 1910–2012, collection no. M 400, Special Collections and Archives, James Branch Cabell Library, Virginia Commonwealth University, Richmond.

made autonomous decisions but always within the ultimate control of the white council. For instance, it was the white council that denied the request of a priest from a local Black Catholic school for an additional troop, citing that there were already as many "colored troops as we could handle" and suggesting there was need for "more study," the convenient and typical way white councils deferred, deflected, and decided against integration.[9] Closer to where Juliette Gordon Low's earliest troops were growing and flourishing, Sarah Randolph Bailey, a teacher, a principal, and one of the founders of the Negro Training School for Girls in Macon, Georgia, faced an even less receptive audience than Watson had in Richmond. In 1935, Bailey requested permission to start a troop for girls under her direction, but Georgia councils refused her efforts to start any troop. Undeterred, Bailey turned to the YWCA, and within two years she had formed fifteen YWCA Girl Reserve groups. Not until 1945 did the Girl Scouts of Georgia invite her to organize Black troops.[10]

Sometimes in its refusal to organize African American troops, a local council would cite national policy forbidding the formation of non-white troops, despite the fact that such a thing didn't exist. If a potential leader wrote to inquire about or challenge the exclusion of African American girls, the national organization would usually respond by clarifying that Girl Scouts was for "all girls" but explain that the authority to determine the creation of new troops resided in the local council. In 1946, for example, the district director from the San Francisco Girl Scout Council wrote to Constance Rittenhouse, president of the Girl Scouts, to gain the support of the national headquarters in challenging the discrimination Black girls were facing in troops in her city. Rittenhouse replied that Girl Scouts was "open to all girls," an "objective" that the organization "works toward as fast as is possible within given communities." But that was all the support she gave, concluding, "I am sorry that you have a problem of discrimination on your hands but at long range it is, as I am sure you will understand, not possible to try to give you advice in the matter."[11] Headquarters had spoken: It would deny having a national policy of discrimination but allow it to happen unchecked. It was an ugly policy that deflected responsibility for the practices of white supremacy.

The Lone Troop Policy and Racial Exclusion

Local councils were not completely off the mark when they alluded to a nationally mandated racial exclusionary policy, however. There was one articulated clearly in the *Blue Book of Girl Scout Policies and Procedures*: the lone troop policy. The lone troop policy forbade the formation of lone troops of a constituency "other than the white race." A lone troop existed without the oversight of a local council. These usually occurred in geographic areas where there weren't enough troops to form a council. Lone troops had no overseeing body except for the regional council or the national organization itself. Once a sufficient number of lone troops organized in a particular geographic location—usually at least four troops—the area would then be eligible to form a council. Clearly there was concern at the national level about what the lone troop policy might have meant for the growth of African American troops, because it made it possible for African American troops to ostensibly form without any direct supervision by white Girl Scouts, and if there was a sufficient number of African American troops in a particular area, they could actually form a fully autonomous African American council. Neither of these possibilities was acceptable to the national organization. In 1928 the board of directors adopted a policy toward "Girl Scout troops of other races": "Girl

Scout troops of other races may be formed only where there is a Local Council, this Council to have full autonomy over all local troop organization."[12] While some historians note this moment as a time when scouting officially included non-white girls, the reality was that before this date Girl Scouting was so loose that African Americans could organize themselves into troops if they found a way to do it.[13] Indeed, many girls simply "declared" themselves Girl Scouts in early years. But the 1928 decision codified the racial hierarchy of Girl Scouting, officially placing white girls and leaders at the helm, with all the power to determine whether any particular girl of color or troop of color would be able to become scouts. "Other races" makes clear that the standard race was "white," so it was unnecessary to even name it as such. This discrimination continued for decades, entrenched in capital letters in the *Blue Book of Girl Scout Policies and Procedures* as the "RACIAL POLICY": "Girl Scout troops of other races may be formed only where there is a Girl Scout local council, this local council to have full authority over all local troop organization." Or as one document explained, "There are no lone troops of races other than the white race."[14]

The lone troop racial policy meant that in areas where there were no local councils, no Black lone troops could form. In other words, a local white council had to be available and willing to authorize and supervise a Black troop. It didn't matter if there were girls wanting to form a troop and captains (whether white or Black) willing to lead them. If there was no local (i.e., white) council available or if the (white) local council said no, that was the end of the matter.

Around 1940, the national board sent a letter of explanation to anyone who was inquiring about starting a lone troop; the interpretive remarks noted that Girl Scouting was nonsectarian and that troops could be formed in orphanages and institutions for the physically and mentally disabled. When it came to the rule that forbade "lone troops of races other than the white race," the letter explained:

> A local council represents a cross-section of the whole community and serves as a protection for all its troops and gives them the backing of the entire community. The national organization believes that by this policy it is protecting its lone leaders by not asking them to carry the full responsibility of initiating troops of other races. It is felt to be essential that troops of other races have community understanding, interpretation and sponsorship in keeping with the spirit of a given community. At present, therefore troops of other races may be formed only where such sponsorship exists in the form of a local council.[15]

There are interesting layers of legitimation in this explanation for the whites-only lone troop policy. Above all, it sets up the policy as one of "protection" for the leaders, who presumably are insufficiently competent to lead new troops if they aren't white. The leaders of white girls, no matter the girls' religion, nationality, or economic status, do not require this protection because they already have the "spirit of a given community." The white community is, within this logic, the community. And also within this logic, Black leaders are de facto considered "incompetent."

In addition to the presumption of Black women's incompetence, there was another layer of rationale as well, one that was not so explicit in the explanation in the 1940 document. It was assumed that too many Black troops would hurt the reputation of Girl Scouting, both nationally and within a region. The national organization feared that white girls would avoid joining, or white parents wouldn't let them join, or the Community Chest (similar to today's United Way) wouldn't fund Girl Scouting if it gained a reputation as a Black-friendly organization. The archival record abounds with reminders to ensure that white scouting gain a foothold before approving Black troops, to wait to approve Black troops only when there are sufficient white troops, to deny Black troops if there aren't enough white troops, and even to ensure that the percentage of Black troops never exceeds the percentage of Black people in a geographic region. A member of the Committee on Negro Girl Scout Troop Organization, Mrs. Plant Osborne, wrote in 1940 that the racial policy regarding lone troops may limit the good work Girl Scouting could do for "Negro girls" but that it serves as a "check on the reputation that Negro troops give Girl Scouting in any community. It seems well for white troops to be well organized and rather secure before any Negro groups are launched."[16] And in consulting with a council from Beloit, Wisconsin, that wrote to national headquarters to inquire about forming Black troops, a field representative wrote it was necessary to recruit the "highest type of Negroes in the community," avoid "mixed camping," and "limit the number of Negro troops."[17] The fear of racial mixing and of Black membership smearing the reputation of Girl Scouting and limiting its growth among white people ran deeply through official channels in the national Girl Scout organization.

At the same time that members of the national staff were penning their letters warning about the dangers of Black membership, the Girl Scout national organization was also, ironically, trying to broaden its reach. In 1935, the national board requested a program study to draw attention to the need for a "wider base of membership."[18] In the early 1940s, during World War II, the Girl

Scouts launched a campaign for "a million more by '44"; the 1944 annual report noted that by July of that year it had passed the million membership mark, with Girl Scouts in the United States, Alaska, Hawai'i, Puerto Rico, and Panama. The report emphasized that the organization's Black membership had grown to 26,003 girls as part of its efforts to "extend the program to all racial groups."[19] Both international and domestic pressure pushed the organization to extend membership to African Americans. It was becoming increasingly embarrassing for the Girl Scouts to articulate its vision of a democratic world and to espouse its own democratic governance when there were clear barriers to African American membership. As one internal memo quipped, "Other races are asking—democracy for whom? The white race?"[20]

While the national organization was becoming increasingly determined to increase membership and sensitive about the image its racially exclusive policy projected, African Americans were pushing steadily to become Girl Scouts. Indeed, the continual pressure African Americans placed on the Girl Scouts became difficult for the organization to deflect or deny. As a result, the national organization formed the Committee on Negro Girl Scout Troop Organization. In 1940, the committee presented the national board with a lengthy compilation, titled "History of Requests for Negro Girl Scout Lone Troops" from 1936 to 1940. The report listed more than sixty-five requests from across the country where a request for a Black lone troop had been made and, with only a few exceptions, denied. The lone troop policy had done the work it was intended to do: prevent Black troops from forming. According to this report, the Girl Scout national organization had denied membership to Black troops in the Northeast (Connecticut, Massachusetts, and New Jersey), the mid-Atlantic (Maryland and Pennsylvania), the Midwest (Indiana, Illinois, Iowa, Ohio, Missouri), the South (Virginia, Kentucky, Florida, Georgia, North Carolina, South Carolina), and the West (Texas, Arizona, and New Mexico). Sometimes a troop would be admitted only to have its charter rescinded once the national headquarters realized the troop was Black. Usually, however, National Headquarters simply returned the request with a notice about the "racial policy" and told the group to inquire again if a (white) council was formed. If the organizers wrote back articulating the injustice of the racial policy, National Headquarters sometimes responded with what they called a "sympathy letter" (as they did in response to organizers in Staunton, Virginia, for example), but it stood firm by the policy that excluded all but white lone troops. The report also noted cases where Black girls had been denied membership in white troops; the response was always that this was a "local problem" and that the (white) local council president should "use her own judgment."[21] As one staff member wrote in 1942, "No widespread activity which will jeopardize our white girls should be undertaken."[22]

The rejections for lone troops were directed to girls and leaders not just in sparsely populated areas without a white council, however. There was precedent, as we saw in earlier chapters, for organizing singular troops in Indian boarding schools and Japanese incarceration centers. But Girl Scout National Headquarters rejected requests from respected African American institutions for higher learning, such as Fisk University, Tuskegee Institute, and Hampton Institute. Indeed, in 1928, Girl Scouts' Dixie Regional Committee, which had jurisdiction over the areas where these schools were located, refused to organize Girl Scouts in these schools despite repeated requests. The committee wrote in a detailed memo that these institutions should have "separate organizations," even suggesting the possible name of Booker T. Washington Girls.[23] A decade later, teachers at Hampton requested a charter to begin Girl Scouting, which National Headquarters denied. Only in 1941, when the town of Hampton, Virginia, had sufficient white troops to form a white council, does it appear that the school began its Girl Scouting program. Officials at Tuskegee Institute began writing National Headquarters about forming a Girl Scout troop as early as 1927. A National Field Committee official visited Tuskegee, but she decided that the school should create a separate, non–Girl Scout program for girls. In 1928, the institute made another request for Girl Scouting. The response read: "Until the experiments being made with St. Louis, Cincinnati, and New York, re: Negro Scouting prove successful, National's policy [regarding] Negro Scouting would have to be enforced." Interestingly, this suggests that the Girl Scouts fundamentally saw "Negro Scouting" as experimental, as something "extra" and problematic, not core to the purpose or goals of the organization. The "History of Requests for Negro Girl Scout Lone Troops" report adds that in 1937 a Girl Scout commissioner from Wisconsin visited Tuskegee and was dismayed to find out that there were no Girl Scout troops. She wrote to the Girl Scout president and First Lady Lou Hoover. Still, however, National Headquarters denied the request for a troop at Tuskegee on the basis of a field representative's recommendation that "unless there is a very real demand for Scouting in white families there, it should not be started in Tuskegee."[24] The fear of Girl Scouting gaining an African American reputation is strong, palpable, and largely unquestioned in the national record of these early decades of scouting.

African Americans Creating Girl Scouting

Crucial to African American women's activism was the right for African American girls to be defined as *girls*, not as little adults. In her examination of Black Girl Scouting in Washington, DC, Miya Carey describes how the first African American woman to be on the National Capital Council, Virginia Richardson McGuire, "believed that giving girls a happy and healthy childhood and a chance to develop into leaders was as much a civil rights issue as racially restrictive covenants and lynching." McGuire's work in the Girl Scouts, Carey argues, was as political as her work in the NAACP. And this impetus—to create spaces where African American girls could enjoy experiences and grow as children—underscores the impetus for African American leaders to simply move ahead with Girl Scouting without approval from National Headquarters. In Bordentown, New Jersey, for instance, Mrs. Lee wrote in 1936 and 1940 to request forming a lone troop of African American girls. After the second denial, Lee responded that "the troop would go on anyway." She "could not understand why white girls could have troops and not Negroes." Similarly, in the 1930s Josephine Holloway attempted to get a Tennessee council to approve the African American troops she had formed. The white council founder Letitia Morgan urged the council to recognize Holloway's troops, calling upon the rhetoric of inclusion in the Girl Scout handbook and the Girl Scout promise. Despite Morgan's vehement support, the white council refused to accept the African American troops. Disgusted, Morgan insisted that a record be made of the refusal in the minutes, evidence of their discrimination. Holloway, like Lee in New Jersey, simply disregarded the no and led the troops on her own. Historian Elisabeth Israels Perry suggests that "contemporary economic conditions" were as much to blame as racial prejudice for the Nashville council's decision to exclude African American girls.[25] While it's true that the Black communities were poorer than the white ones and that the white council did not have endless resources, it's difficult to see "economic conditions" as anything more than another excuse by the white community, considering that Holloway was able to make the troops happen without any financial support from the white community at all.

The Tennessee council eventually recognized Holloway's troops in 1942. Perhaps the council's change in perspective came from a visit by First Lady Eleanor Roosevelt, a close friend of African American educator and activist Mary McLeod Bethune, who had worked to begin African American Girl Scouting in Washington, DC, even taking one of her troops to the White

House. Though the Nashville council finally acquiesced to pressure to include Black troops, it emphasized that Black troops must remain below 25 percent of the total Girl Scouts in the area. Again, Holloway simply ignored the demands of the white council and continued, with friends and colleagues, to form Black troops. By 1944, the central Tennessee council pulled Holloway into the professional staff, hiring her as the "field advisor for Negro troops," a position that illuminates both Holloway's perseverance and the deep segregation of the Tennessee council. Holloway has become a real heroine in Girl Scout lore. In March 2022, Girl Scouts of the USA posted a picture of Holloway on its Facebook page, celebrating her "duty, dedication, and creating opportunities for Black Girl Scouts" as part of Women's History Month.[26] One Facebook reader commented angrily that the Girl Scouts should stop "whitewashing" history. And indeed, this reader is correct; what the Girl Scout post failed to point out is that Holloway didn't "create opportunities" for Black girls—as if Black people didn't know how to generate good options for their kids. White people regularly and systematically barred Black people from good opportunities. Holloway had to persevere in the face of explicit refusal, she had to run "rogue" troops when the council refused to approve, and it seems she even needed to mastermind some political influence to finally embarrass the national organization sufficiently that it would put pressure on the local entities to recognize her troops.[27]

Knowing that Girl Scout troops often formed simply because girls showed up and started "doing" Girl Scout things, and knowing that white councils often refused to recognize Black troops, one has to surmise that there were many unrecognized but active Black Girl Scout troops throughout the United States. One of the questions that these unauthorized troops raise is how they were able to acquire all the troop paraphernalia—insignia, badges, uniforms, and camping equipment—if they weren't registered as official troops. One way around this was the fact that many girls—white and Black—actually sewed their own uniforms with fabric that was sometimes just a close approximation of the official dress. Indeed, Holloway purchased gingham cloth that she used to teach the girls how to sew their own uniforms. Camping equipment would have been easier for troops like Holloway's that were forming without council approval, as it could be ordered by mail from various companies; it did not have to be "officially endorsed" gear. But some of the items needed to become a Girl Scout were official: badges, handbooks, pins, and other forms of insignia. These were vital objects, fundamental to being a Girl Scout, as they symbolized both membership and the detailed achievements and challenges

Josephine Holloway (*top left*) with one of her Nashville troops in the 1940s. Courtesy of the Girl Scouts of Middle Tennessee.

Josephine Holloway with her granddaughter, now Dr. Nareda DeCleene, in the 1960s in Nashville. Courtesy of the Girl Scouts of Middle Tennessee.

In an undated photo, Josephine Holloway on a tractor at the camp eventually named after her, Camp Holloway, outside Nashville. Courtesy of the Girl Scouts of Middle Tennessee.

An undated portrait of Josephine Holloway, including a photograph of her in Girl Scout uniform. Courtesy of the Girl Scouts of Middle Tennessee.

met by the girls. These items were only available by mail order to the national headquarters, which required proof of membership, or at registered Girl Scout stores, usually a counter in a department store, where Black leaders would have been turned away in communities that knew Black girls weren't welcome in Girl Scouts. Sometimes department stores barred Black girls' and leaders' entrance to the store in its entirety. Black leaders used ingenious methods to acquire the items fundamental to Girl Scout membership. One of the ways was to travel to an area with fewer restrictions to purchase the materials. Holloway sent her husband to purchase and send her Girl Scout handbooks when he was in Chicago as a medical student. Another was to have a recognized troop or organization, sympathetic to the cause of Black troops, order the materials. As late as 1940, for instance, National Headquarters continued to deny troop formation at the Tuskegee Institute. The American Red Cross stepped in and ordered materials for Tuskegee in 1941 without mentioning their final destination.[28]

While camping equipment was not a difficult acquisition for African American Girl Scouts, actual campsites were, which was unacceptable to African American Girl Scout leaders. Camps, they argued, were central to a happy and healthy childhood, as they meant vigorous outdoor activities, access to safe swimming areas (most municipal pools excluded African Americans, forcing them to use dangerous swimming holes), and fun, leisurely summers and weekends.[29] If Black communities didn't have access to white residential camps, they sometimes opted for some of the few integrated day camps that had been set up by the 1940s in the North.[30] Other African American Girl Scout leaders worked diligently to create their own residential camps. Part of Holloway's ongoing focus was finding places for her scouts to camp; at first they traveled from Nashville to Indiana to find a camp willing to accommodate them. Not until the 1950s did the Nashville council purchase land for African American scouts, though it was in rugged shape and the white council refused to include it in its infrastructure plans for the development of camps.[31] Holloway's situation in Nashville was replicated across the country, with African American camps generally much more poorly funded and developed than the white council camps. Nevertheless, they were theirs to use as they saw fit, and they were highlighted as goals for Black philanthropy and development. After they officially formed their own troops, Black Girl Scout leaders in Maryland founded Camp Pinoaka in 1936 on the grounds of Pocahontas State Park. Every summer the camp hosted over 100 girls, with a staff of counselors, lifeguards, a nurse, and a director. A Camp Pinoaka staff report from the 1940s remarked how little outdoor experience the girls had during the school year; their goal for girls was to "experience fun and adventure" and gain skills to live comfortably out of doors. Most of the girls were not swimmers; they coaxed the girls to take their lessons seriously by offering canoeing and kayaking, very sought-after activities, only to the girls who had passed their swimming lessons. Girls learned skills in open-fire cooking and hiking, passing them on to younger ones through songs, games, and demonstrations; they planned their own menus and chore rotations as much as possible. The camp director emphasized how successful their camping summers were, despite the fact that the state park itself, where the camp was located, had failed to make promised necessary improvements to the lake. Photos from Camp Pinoaka show girls doing archery, building campsites, hiking, and most of all, laughing and having fun. The unimproved lake was an obstacle, but like with the other impediments facing Black Girl Scouts, they pushed forward.[32]

Changing the Lone Troop Racial Policy

The lone troop racial policy, which allowed only white troops to form autonomously, eventually caused national and international embarrassment for the Girl Scout National Headquarters. Finally responding to the press for Black lone troops, the Girl Scout national board voted in 1940 to initiate an experimental period that would lessen the restrictions placed on African American troop formation. Rather than requiring a white local council that would oversee "lone troops of other races," the board approved a policy whereby "Negro lone troops be permitted to form, safeguarded by community endorsement and supervision equivalent to that supplied by councils. By this is meant that Negro troops shall not be formed until careful investigation of the sponsoring group and leaders is made by members of the regional committee or persons designated by them." In other words, a community organization—perhaps a civic or philanthropic group—could "approve" the lone troop if there wasn't a local council available. It wasn't much of a shift in policy. If white racism was rampant in the local councils, there is no reason to think that it wouldn't be the same in the civic groups approved by a regional council. Nevertheless, fearing that this might mean an increase in African American Girl Scout leaders, the board asked regions to create a plan for training schools for Black leaders, but that "where possible northern Negroes be assigned to northern training schools and southern Negroes to southern training schools." And finally, the board asked that "communities consider the population ratio of Negroes to whites and not let the percentage of negro Scouts overbalance the population percentage." After two years, what was then called the Racial Relations Committee reported that during the experimental period, Girl Scouts accepted sixteen African American lone troop applications and refused "more than twice that number." The national organization explained its refusal of African American troops on two grounds: There was no local (white) organization that was willing to sponsor the group, or there was not yet a sufficient number of white troops in the area.[33]

The fear that Girl Scouting might be seen as a Black activity was a continual threat for the white national organization, but the organization knew it went against its explicit rhetoric of inclusivity. Just a month earlier, Girl Scout executive director Constance Rittenhouse wrote a memo to another staff member, Sibyl Newell, explaining that "the more I thought about the criticism that come to us about our policy on organization of Negro troops which is inconsistent in our statement that Girl Scouting is for all races and creeds, I wonder if we could not eliminate that policy entirely and have an accepted organization procedure which would give us the protection we need."[34] That phrase, "give us the protection we need," nebulous as it is, refers to the worry that African American troops will hurt Girl Scouting. Newell's follow-up memo explains this more explicitly:

> It is my hope that we can secure the approval of the Field Committee and Board in eliminating our present policy which says there are no lone troops of races other than the white race. . . . In discussing Negro troop organization with the staff we want to make sure that they realize that a negro lone troop is as acceptable to us as any other, provided it would not interfere with the future development of Girl Scouting in the community. In any lone troop organization we must make sure that we are not hampering the development of Girl Scouting for all girls in that community. . . . We must also be sure that our troop organization meets with the approval of the leading citizens of the community so that we may count on their moral and financial support for the future development of Girl Scouting.[35]

In other words, the Girl Scout national organization wanted to eliminate the racial policy so that the organization wouldn't face public recrimination, and Girl Scouts was happy if that meant that a few more of the "best" African Americans could have access to the organization. Numerous, strongly worded qualifications surround this shift in policy, however; there is concern about "hampering the development of Girl Scouting for all girls" (which meant white), and there's a requirement that Black troops have "the approval of the leading [white] citizens" as well as their "moral and financial support." In other words, nothing really changed in Girl Scout policy. Girl Scouts wanted to include Black troops to extinguish criticism about discrimination but only insofar as the inclusion didn't upset white members.

In 1942, the Girl Scout national organization voted to rescind the lone troop racial policy completely. Not much had changed for Black membership, however; despite training sessions and documents that encouraged "extending Girl Scouting to other races," there was still extraordinary resistance to Black membership.[36] Black girls and women who wanted to form a troop continued to have to gain the approval of a local sponsoring organization or a local council, which would be approved by the regional council. One member of the Racial Relations Committee noted that the attitudes of "local councils" were more of a barrier to Black membership than the lone troop rule; she urged the national organization to "encourage a more liberal attitude among local groups." On a national, regional, and local level, the Girl Scout organization voiced a desire to attract only the "right" kind of Black leaders, "good potential Scout material . . . whose major interest is not crusading for the Negro race."[37] And throughout the 1940s there was consistent deferral to the practices and policies of local regions and councils, whether they were practicing implicit or explicit discrimination. Girl Scouts could explicitly engage in discriminatory practices, but by deleting the phrase "Girl Scouts of other races" from the *Blue Book of Girl Scout Policies and Procedures*, as the organization had done in 1942, it could hide behind a mask of innocence.

Deferring to "Local Standards"

In 1940, the Gainesville, Florida, local council wrote to the Girl Scout National Headquarters with its plan to respond to African American community members who wanted to start Black troops in the area.[38] It appears that before this date, there were no Black Girl Scouts in Gainesville. The white Gainesville council listed twenty-four proposed policies to govern the inclusion of Black scouts, the primary of which was a requirement for there to be a "group of leading colored citizens" who would govern the "colored Girl Scout troops," "subject to the rules and regulations of the Gainesville Local Council." In other words, there would be a Black council within the white council, and all new troop formation would have to be approved by the white council. This was a typical arrangement in the South until the late 1950s. In addition, Black Girl Scouts were to be strictly forbidden from wearing their uniforms on days other than official meeting days, uniforms were to be returned to the council when a girl left scouting, and a separate Court of Awards was to be coordinated for Black scouts. Above all, the plan read, "if Scouting for colored girls is to succeed, *there must be strict racial integrity*." Mrs. De Westfelt, a staff member in the Girl Scout National Field Division, noted that the "plan of organization sounds good"; her only intervention was to discourage the Gainesville council from insisting on the return of Girl Scout uniforms. "I think you should have some statement saying that negro Girl Scouts who drop out of Girl Scouting must never wear their Girl Scout uniforms, but once girls have purchased uniforms, I do not see any way we can prevent the girls from keeping them, if they wish. . . . I believe that this policy would be more trouble and would cause more hard feelings than any other. I know that this has been tried by several councils, and do not believe that it has been too successful."[39] The exchange between the white Gainesville council and the National Headquarters is significant insofar as it illuminates in stark terms the extent to which Girl Scouting deferred to local discriminatory policies. The plan to require the return of uniforms by Black scouts was the only item the national organization criticized, but it was actually Girl Scout policy not just in some Southern councils but also in schools, orphanages, institutions, and Northern councils, all of which legitimized the practice by voicing fear about the reputation of scouting if Black girls wore their uniforms except on carefully prescribed terms. Notably, the Gainesville council made a statement about "strict racial integrity" for "colored scouting to succeed," which the national field director failed to challenge at all. By "integrity" they mean segregation and racial purity, maintaining spheres so separate and unequal that there was no chance of any spillover or mixing. This response was typical as the national Girl Scout organization began to make scouting more open to all girls: Move slowly and never challenge a white council's fundamental assumptions about race and white supremacy. Above all, this exchange illuminates the ways that Black Girl Scouting, particularly in the South, was completely segregated. The white councils had ultimate control and significantly longer purse strings than the Black councils. At the same time, however, the Black councils created a sphere of influence and decision-making that prioritized Black empowerment and Black sisterhood. White Girl Scouting failed to take this into consideration once pressure to desegregate gained steam, as there was no interest by the white councils to maintain African American staffing and priorities.

Hosting the National Conventions

A look at the Girl Scout national conventions in the 1940s gives a sense of how the national organization's thinking about race began slowly to transform during this time. The national conventions were extremely important events, not just because of policy that was articulated during the meetings but also as a crucial gathering of the multiple regional groups of Girl Scouts into a national whole. The national conventions served as an enacted symbol of what the Girl Scouts stood for, the ideals and practices that made it a formidable national and international organization. Struggles over the form and shape of the national conventions also give us a sense of what the organization sacrificed in order to create and maintain unity as a national organization. One of the primary areas of "compromise" was the question of race. This phrasing, however, is problematic as it suggests a fair middle ground, where each side gives a little. The reality was, however, that "compromise" meant leaving Black members behind. Just as Northern white people sacrificed the cause of Black people after Reconstruction and into the twentieth century in order to create harmony with white Southern (and Northern) segregationists, the Girl Scouts regularly sacrificed and abandoned Black girls and women in order to maintain a national organization.[40]

In early 1941, planning began in earnest for the national convention to be held in November of that year in Dallas, Texas. Only after the planning efforts were underway, however, did the convention manager write what she called an SOS letter to a member of the Girl Scout Dallas office. What would the conditions be for a "visiting Negro delegate volunteer or professional"?[41] She received a terse response from Dallas: "[We] have Jim Crow law. No housing for Negroes available. Marian Anderson had to be placed in a Negro home."[42] National headquarters began to worry that African American delegates would not even be allowed into the convention hall; the Girl Scout national office considered moving the conference. But in mid-April the convention manager explained that Black Girl Scouts would be admitted to the convention floor provided they "use service entrance and elevators." They would not be able to eat in the public dining room or lodge at the hotel. Accommodations in area African American homes would have to be arranged. "This will, no doubt, be satisfactory as it seems to be a great concession for the South," one of the members of the organizing team wrote.[43] What this meant, of course, was that it was a great concession for the white South. This very limited allowance for partial participation by Black Girl Scouts was enough for the Girl Scout national organization.

In 1947, five years after the national organization eliminated the lone troop racial policy, the Girl Scouts faced a similar dilemma to that of the Dallas convention. The conference now was to be held in Long Beach, California. While the conference hotel would allow African American delegates to be part of public spaces during the event, none of the hotels in the city—including the conference hotel—would allow Black guests to register as overnight guests. The Long Beach Hotel Convention Bureau "assured" the Girl Scouts that it could "handle this problem . . . without any embarrassment to the Negro delegates" by setting up alternative housing in Black people's homes and the few hotels in Los Angeles that would take them.[44] Unlike during the 1941 convention, however, this response no longer satisfied the Girl Scouts. The aftermath of World War II had created an atmosphere where African Americans insisted on full participation in the mainstream of American life, and in the Girl Scouts, pressure by African American scouts, growth in African American membership, and increased organizational emphasis and rhetoric around democracy and inclusive membership meant that the national (white) organization took notice. As the Girl Scout convention manager wrote to headquarters, they were "running the risk of criticism because we are going to a city where the best hotels will not accommodate Negroes."[45] Once the national director of Girl Scouts, Constance Rittenhouse, heard about the housing problem for Black Scouts, she requested that Margaret Murray, a white Girl Scout field worker in Los Angeles, work on ensuring "a satisfactory nondiscriminatory housing plan for the Negroes attending convention." "We do not feel it advisable," Rittenhouse continued, "to accept the proposed arrangement that Negro delegates be asked to commute to Los Angeles. This, as you know, involves both expense and effort and is not a fair arrangement."[46]

Rittenhouse's note began a flurry of activity—and a detailed education about racial discrimination—for Murray. Meeting with convention bureau officials and hotel owners, Murray first tried two main tactics she thought would take care of the issue: minimizing risk and articulating civil rights law. She told white hotel owners that "very few" Black people would actually be traveling to Long Beach, even though she had no way of knowing how many Black Girl Scouts would be attending, and that they would all be Girl Scouts, an identity that was recognizable and respectable in white communities. And when she met with white hotel owners, she waved a copy of the newly passed California Civil Rights Bill, forbidding discrimination in public places, including hotels.[47] Neither of these tactics convinced the hotel owners to take Black guests; indeed, the manager of the Lafayette Hotel, J. B. Miller, yelled at Murray that she should stop listening to "Mr. Roosevelt and the Communists in the country" and that he wouldn't have any "so-and-so's" (Murray's phrase for the racial epithet) in his hotel.[48] Moreover, no Long Beach hotel would put its racial policy in writing, stating that it would or would not accommodate African American delegates. The Girl Scouts knew, then, that its African American delegates might likely be refused housing, but the organization had no explicit evidence to bring to the Civil Rights Agency of California.[49] Despite consulting several attorneys, the national headquarters concluded that it had no legal recourse to pressure the hotels.[50]

Girl Scouts also didn't really want the controversy or publicity that would accompany a lawsuit. The organization wanted a convenient and quiet solution and was willing to accept incremental change if that was the best route to resolving the problem. Just knowing that there were a sufficient number of hotel rooms available satisfied the national organization, even if most of the hotels would refuse Black delegates. The Girl Scout national organization had called in Murray to intervene in the situation because it didn't want the embarrassment that would result if it became public knowledge that the organization had knowingly scheduled a conference in a place where African Americans faced hotel and restaurant discrimination. The organization realized quickly that the local Long Beach Girl Scout liaison, a white woman named Mrs. Jesse Holton, was herself a problem, "prejudiced," in the words that Murray wrote back to the national headquarters. Murray told headquarters that Holton "was sorry that we were making an issue of it—that she had found out that the YWCA would take approximately ten Negro delegates and thought that that should take care of the situation very nicely."[51] The national organization asked Murray to "work around" Holton; they didn't want to confront her, they just wanted to find hotels that would work for Black delegates. So Murray met with the recalcitrant hotel managers, talked to the convention bureau, and reached out to whatever local organizations she thought might assist.

The most helpful resources, she reported, were the executives she met from the Urban League, the NAACP, the Los Angeles Civil Rights Commission, the Booker T. Washington Community Center, and the Federal Public Housing Authority of Los Angeles. One adviser for the housing authority, Bernard Ross, responded quickly when apprised of the situation, "Well, you certainly aren't going to have the convention there then, are you?" He added that if the Girl Scouts chose to hold the convention in Long Beach, "it would lose whatever progress it had made here on the Coast and people would lose confidence in the organization."[52] Charlie Bratt, also with the Federal Public Housing Authority, informed Murray that the Congress of Industrial

Organization (CIO), the union organization, had recently withdrawn its conference from Long Beach for the same reason—it could not ensure housing for Black delegates—and moved it to San Jose, where housing was secure for all its members.[53]

It's important to note that had the all-white Girl Scout Board thought to question the availability of lodging for Black delegates before signing a contract with the Long Beach Convention Office, this problem could have been avoided; certainly had there been African American leadership on the national board, the issue of housing would have been on the table from the beginning. As it was, not until March 1947, about six months before the conference, did the issue become a pressing one. After two months of negotiations with hotels that went nowhere, and discussions with representatives from the African American communities in the area, Murray became discouraged about the outlook for the conference. At a regional conference meeting, she apprised the committee of the situation, suggesting that they give a full explanation to the entire Girl Scout community. She also suggested that the "best thing would be to take the convention out of Long Beach" or, if necessary, cancel it.[54] On May 2, 1947, the Convention Program Committee voted that the conference be "withdrawn" from Long Beach unless the hotels in Long Beach could, in a written contract, "assure housing of Negro delegates."[55]

At a regional committee meeting on May 14, 1947, Murray reported that the committee deliberated extensively about the housing situation for Black delegates. Its conclusions: The Girl Scout membership should have "full information" about the problems the Girl Scouts were facing regarding racial discrimination.[56] By this, the committee meant that the organization should share information about the problems of discrimination with the entire body of the Girl Scout organization; it also had better be ready with an explanation as to why Long Beach had ever been chosen, considering that the CIO had pulled out.[57] "We should take a courageous rather than a conservative stand," the regional committee concluded.[58]

Once all these resolutions from the Convention Program Committee and the regional committee, as well as Murray's full report, moved to the national office, however, things slowed down significantly. Constance Rittenhouse, the executive director, wrote to Murray that "one or two hotels" in Long Beach would likely take African American delegates.[59] As to Murray's suggestion that the matter of discrimination be brought up on the convention floor, Rittenhouse also declined: "No plans have been made for taking up the subject before the whole convention," she wrote, agreeing with another comment made by a staff member that "we should not otherwise make an issue of the race question."[60] Rittenhouse ordered Murray to stop her interviews of the hotels and her discussions with African American community members.[61]

Bitterly disappointed, Murray continued to discuss the housing problem, writing to national staff member Charlotte Moton Hubbard, one of the organization's only African American employees. Hubbard would later serve as the first African American woman to become a deputy assistant secretary of state of the United States. At the time, however, she was a woman in her thirties, the daughter of the former president of the Tuskegee Institute, and a former educator at Spelman College. Hired to advise the Girl Scouts on intercultural and international affairs, Hubbard worked tirelessly throughout the 1940s at the national headquarters, writing "intercultural reports" that articulated best practices for creating a diverse membership in terms of integration, recruitment, language use, and terminology. Officially an adviser of the Girl Scout Community Relations Department, she led problem-solving in regional and local councils. These years of work, and the fact that Murray seemed not to have read any of the materials Hubbard had written, may have made her particularly impatient with Murray's "realization" that African American people faced discrimination. Hubbard scolded Murray for being so naïve, writing that she could "visualize and imagine the many difficulties" that Murray faced in her work trying to accommodate African American delegates but that "as a member of a minority group such situations are faced daily."[62] Hubbard also voiced her exasperation at the national office's decision to keep the situation hidden from the general body of the Girl Scouts:

> It may present some difficulties for there are many people in our organization who feel that such a discussion may be unladylike and that such issues as involve this kind of discussion and questions, border on the unladylike. This, to me, is ridiculous for I think that in this whole area of misunderstanding and misconception as regards our relationships with racial or interracial groups must be openly and honestly discussed if we really intend to be as democratic as we say we are. . . . I do think that it would be tragic if the organization failed to face squarely the many implications that are involved in this entire matter.[63]

Hubbard's plea for honesty went unheeded and would return to haunt the Girl Scouts straight into the twenty-first century.

Ultimately, the regional and national leadership of the Girl Scout national organization decided to move forward with the Long Beach national convention, despite the discrimination they knew Black Girl Scouts would face, and they wrote to Margaret Murray and Charlotte Hubbard with their apologies. "[I] can only hope you won't be too disappointed in me," Mrs. Louis Martin, the regional director of Girl Scouting in the Los Angeles area, wrote to Hubbard, after Martin had rescinded her earlier decision to cancel the convention. "We have made such gains in parts of the country where I never dreamed it possible that feel as an organization we should be proud of our record. I can also see us going much farther if we will but continue to interpret and feel our way just as rapidly as possible but not too rapidly."[64] Rittenhouse told Murray she was "proud of her" for her "valiant efforts," even though she knew that Murray would not be "satisfied" with the result.[65] In other words, Martin and Rittenhouse wanted to be content with incremental change, one that would inch the organization—and the nation—toward integration, providing encouragement but not insistence.

In the end, 2,000 delegates from across the country, leaders, local and regional council members, and girls themselves, came to Long Beach for the annual Girl Scout convention. First Lady Bess Truman, the honorary president of the Girl Scouts, wired the convention her greetings, noting the "esteem" in which the organization was held "across the nation."[66] The *New York Times* described the convention as one of racial harmony: "Race is no barrier to scouting," the headline read, quoting the Girl Scout president Harriet Ferguson as saying the organization was "making notable progress in extending scouting to all girls, 'regardless of race, creed, or color.'"[67] The Black press also took note of the convention. The *Pittsburgh Courier*, for instance, lauded its local women who were elected as delegates to the convention.[68] The *Chicago Defender* explained that the NAACP, the National Council of Negro Women, and the Urban League would all have representatives at the conference, which would be held, the article explained, at the Wilton Hotel in the "beautiful Pacific oceanside city" of Long Beach, California.[69] This beautiful town, however, had been anything but welcoming to the Girl Scouts' African American membership. In the end, the Girl Scouts took a conservative, not a courageous, stand, one that tried to accommodate Black members but only so far as it would not make any white delegates uncomfortable or embarrassed.

At the end of December 1947, convention manager Katie Lee Johnson and the director of the Girl Scout public relations department reported on the 1947 convention, noting the "unusual conditions" and difficult work that the "biracial subject" caused and explaining that "the problem of housing Negro delegates was almost insurmountable." Even during the conference, one of the hotels, the Buffam, turned back forty-seven hotel reservations once it realized the guests were Black. The Girl Scout organization had to plead with the hotel to take them. At four other hotels, a white Girl Scout had to check in every Girl Scout guest, as the hotels would otherwise not take African Americans. And the main conference hotel, the Wilton, ordered the Girl Scouts midconference to check out all the African American guests, claiming that two of its permanent (white) guests had checked out because of the African Americans. The Girl Scouts, the report noted, "persuaded [the hotel] to keep the Negro guests." The report concluded, "Housing of Negro delegates and guests was a constant issue—the strain on the Housing Bureau and Convention Staff who fought with hotels and motels to get them to take Negroes cannot be overestimated."[70] While that was certainly true, it's notable that the summary of the conference mentioned the pain and difficulty faced by only the white staff and volunteers. The embarrassment, anger, humiliation, and trouble faced by the Black delegates themselves merits no attention in the summary report.

While the report was a halfhearted response, one that certainly did not center the experience of African American scouts, it did have one explicit consequence. In 1950 the board of directors approved a new "intercultural policy on nation-wide gatherings," which was added to the *Blue Book of Girl Scout Policies and Procedures*: "Gatherings planned and held by the national Girl Scout organization for nation-wide attendance shall be held in communities where the individuals attending will have freedom of choice in seating, eating, and living accommodations in hotels and buildings engaged by the organization." This policy was still limited: It allowed for regional and local meetings to be held in segregated spaces, and it only promised that the specific places reserved by the Girl Scouts would be open to all. And regional and local councils could continue to host events at places that barred African American participants. Nevertheless, it was a fundamental shift in policy that underscored the organization's commitment to inclusivity. The pressure that African American leaders such as Charlotte Hubbard, white allies such as Margaret Murray, and the entire community of African American organizations had placed on the Girl Scouts had a definite effect on the organization's policy. As the history of the Girl Scouts throughout the remainder of the 1940s, the 1950s, and the 1960s attests, however, both the national office and regional offices were able to circumvent this new policy if it made white scouts uncomfortable or resistant.

Pressure within the Girl Scouts: Charlotte Moton Hubbard

Throughout the long history of the Girl Scouts, despite institutional pressures that slowed and maintained policies of exclusion and discrimination, there were staff members who consistently and powerfully advocated for change.

One of these women who particularly stands out was the figure who became so exasperated by the Girl Scouts' reluctance to speak up about race at the 1947 national convention: Charlotte Moton Hubbard. In 1945, Hubbard joined the Girl Scout national staff as a community adviser. Just a year after the end of World War II, during which the motto of the Girl Scouts had been "A million or more by '44," the Girl Scouts were keen to increase membership across the nation and to demonstrate its democratic inclusivity in a world that had just beaten fascism and was now squaring off against communism. As a Girl Scout community adviser, Hubbard would suggest ways to improve what the organization called its "intercultural" relations, a term that encompassed race, ethnic background, and religion. The daughter of the second president of the famous African American university the Tuskegee Institute, Charlotte Moton had grown up in a world that preached the uplift rhetoric of Booker T. Washington, Tuskegee's founder. When she was a child, the Ku Klux Klan had threatened the life of her father, Robert Russa Moton, when he used his position as Tuskegee president to advocate successfully for an African American medical staff for a new Black veterans hospital. The KKK hated the fact that their Alabama town would now have an additional influx of educated, proud African American men and women, unbowed by white intimidation. Charlotte's mother, Jennie Dee Booth Moton, was a tireless advocate for Black freedom, working closely with leaders such as educator Mary McLeod Bethune and the white antilynching activist Jessie Daniel Ames. After graduating from Boston University, Charlotte accepted a position with the US Army, traveling around the country to troubleshoot problems soldiers were having in the local communities where they were stationed, many of them race based. As that job came to end when she was in her early thirties, newly married and living in Washington, DC, the Hampton Institute offered Charlotte Moton Hubbard a job teaching, but she declined, saying an offer she had received from the Girl Scouts was more attractive and much more lucrative.

At the Girl Scouts, Hubbard's mission was to strengthen intercultural relations. On the one hand, the Girl Scouts were determined to increase Black membership, open up camping opportunities to everyone, and be a demonstrated beacon of democratic inclusivity. On the other hand, Girl Scouts still maintained extensive discriminatory practices and policies, as we have seen throughout this chapter.

Hubbard thus found herself in the middle of this contradictory world, advocating for the rights of Black girls and women in an organization that wanted change but also wanted to play it safe. In Alabama, for instance, the KKK threatened violence against an interracial training the local Girl Scouts were planning. Hubbard was keenly disappointed that Constance Rittenhouse, the Girl Scout national director, called to shut down the training. Hubbard's discouragement with Rittenhouse's tepid responses to racism was so great that at one point she seriously considered resigning, only to be convinced by Alice Carney, a white staffer who had become a close friend, to stay and fight for the change they were all seeking. And she did stay for five years, making inroads as well as she could. She even managed a bit of radical infiltration, directing a play at the 1949 national convention based on Langston Hughes's poem "Let America Be America Again." With her advocacy, the national organization changed its policy; now, national meetings were allowed to take place only in localities where hotels and restaurants would be open to everyone. And one of her proudest lifetime memories, Hubbard said in a 1980s oral history that spanned her life from childhood to her storied career in the US State Department, was the Girl Scout intercultural report she wrote that challenged everything from the organization's policies on Black troops to the racist lyrics in the Girl Scout songbook.[71]

Brown v. Board of Education and the Challenge to Segregation

When the US Supreme Court issued its landmark 1954 decision in *Brown v. Board of Education of Topeka*, ruling that it was unconstitutional for states to establish segregation in public schools, the Girl Scouts began to face increased scrutiny—from both within and beyond the organization—about its own policies and practices. The Girl Scouts hiding behind "intercultural" committees was not sufficient for those who questioned the organization's perspective on *Brown*; they wanted an explicit statement from the Girl Scouts. After some deliberation, however, the leadership of the Girl Scouts concluded that they would not make any public statement about the ruling. As one national internal memo explained, "It is generally felt that for Girl Scout people there is no need for anything *special* on this subject, because it is expected that progress along established lines will continue."[72] Previous guidance from the national organization reminded staff and volunteers that "we do not condone involuntary segregation." But it also equivocated about exactly how the "involuntary segregation" should be undone: "We work towards the time when each individual will be accepted for herself," one national staff memo read. "This will have to be a gradual process and may be time-consuming and variable according to current local mores, individuals concerned, and geographic factors, to name only a few."[73] Desegregation efforts would be slowed if local and regional councils did not want to change.

When pushed to articulate its response to *Brown*, the national organization noted in particular three policies in the Girl Scout *Blue Book* that spoke to the "basic policy and belief" about race and Girl Scouting:

> Membership in the Girl Scout movement is open to all girls and adults who subscribe to the Girl Scout Promise and Laws.
>
> Race, religion, national heritage, or economic status shall be no barrier to membership in the Girl Scout organization.
>
> The Girl Scout organization believes that girls and adults of all faiths, of all races, and of all national heritages should have equal opportunity to experience democracy in Girl Scouting through participation in its program and administration.[74]

These fundamental statements about race and Girl Scouting, from the perspective of the national organization, made any additional remarks about the Supreme Court decision unnecessary and superfluous, despite the fact that they were just general statements without any teeth and didn't address the specific court ruling at all.

The decision to avoid making a statement about *Brown* clearly echoed the organization's earlier choices to be silent about race and to underpublicize its attempts to create a more inclusive institution. Part of this hesitation stemmed from a belief that publicizing the Girl Scouts' inclusive policies caused dangerous backlash. It was fine to advertise Girl Scouts' inclusivity to audiences of color and in certain circumscribed publications, but it was dangerous to air the idea in areas or to audiences that were hostile. On a local level, when Black and white Girl Scouts mingled, they did indeed experience violence and recrimination. In 1948, for instance, in Richmond, Virginia, neighbors called the police on a group of Black women who were going into a white neighbor's house for a Girl Scout training session.[75] The very association of Girl Scouting with desegregation—whether or not a particular council was actively interested in desegregating—sometimes brought out threats from white community members, both financial and physical. A case study of a Southern town (possibly Columbus, Mississippi, according to the document) described the Community Chest's refusal to fund the Girl Scouts; a Citizens' Council, a group dedicated to the "preservation of racial separation," was active in the area, and its presence evoked the possibility of violence toward Girl Scouts. Ironically, in that situation the local Girl Scout council was not even actively desegregating. The funding refusal—and the implicit threat of violence from the Citizens' Council—occurred because the Girl Scouts had a reputation for liberal leanings.[76] A few years earlier, when Girl Scouts in Memphis, Tennessee, took some small steps toward desegregation, the local council reported with relief that both the Black and the white newspapers used "discretion" in reporting about the Girl Scouts. "A good lively article on what the Girl Scouts have achieved in racial integration could be the death of the integration process in its present incarnation," the Memphis council reported. It added, "It could arouse the dormant emotions of the racially reactionary whites whose number in the area is still great, through probably declining. It could subject the organization to violent verbal attack and frighten off contributors, volunteers, and parents who are themselves as yet wavering and indecisive in the new practice."[77] The parents this note refers to were white parents who may not have wanted their girls associated with an interracial organization, though there certainly may have been African American parents who doubted their girls would be safe and welcome in a white environment. But the threat of violence was also real, in this case verbal. Other cases were more explicitly physical. These moments of explicit danger to Girl Scouts strengthened the belief among some staff that keeping desegregation policies quiet promised more safety for the girls. Doing the work unobtrusively meant that segregationists may not have been alerted to—and incensed by—Girl Scouting and its inclusive promises. Quiet and slow meant that change could happen imperceptibly, with no backlash. But quiet and slow also ensured a level of comfort for white people, both liberal and conservative. It could work as a screen to slow down change; to make excuses for tolerating programming in segregated communities that excluded African Americans; to continue underfunding programs for African American girls; to prevent African American girls from joining camps, troops, and rallies; to pay African American Girl Scout employees significantly less than their white counterparts; and to maintain all-white governing councils.

The *Brown v. Board of Education* decision nevertheless brought attention to the Girl Scouts even as it tried to keep its interracial work under the radar. An exchange about a 1955 Girl Scout calendar photo that featured Asian American, white, and Black Girl Scouts along with their fathers illuminates the way that *Brown* heightened anxiety among some white Girl Scouts. A worried Girl Scout leader from Tulsa, Oklahoma, wrote to Olivia Layton, president of the Girl Scouts: "I question the judgment of including such a picture in the calendar. . . . Quite apart from the sensitivity toward desegregation at this time . . . is it wise to publish to the south as well as the north, a picture which can be interpreted by the rabid segregationist as suggesting a trend toward boy and girl relationships interracially?"[78] Layton responded forcefully:

> Your own question about the advisability of including an interracial picture in our calendar is one we have pondered many times. We feel that the calendar pictures should truthfully represent our organization . . . which is open to all girls. This particular picture seemed eminently suitable as it shows an actual event attended not only by a Negro father and daughter but also by an Oriental father and daughter as well. . . . We realize that there are people who will object to any photograph showing white people working or playing with members of the Negro race. We do not believe, though, that we should be controlled by extremists.[79]

Layton's comment about the photo showing an "actual event" was crucial to this exchange, as part of the method that Girl Scouts used to manage the question of interracial representation was to clearly identify where events had taken place. That is, Girl Scouts who segregated could not become "ruffled" by pictures of mixed groups if those pictures were clearly identified as taking place in regions of the country where segregation was not the rule and custom. Layton's point about "extremism" was core to the Girl Scouts: Excluding African Americans was "extreme," but so was pushing the ramifications of *Brown* onto councils that weren't quite ready. Above all, the national organization wanted to encourage "a climate of opinion where maximum harmony will exist in this transition period."[80]

The case studies, workshops, and trainings on intergroup relations were all focused on creating an uneventful transition from segregation to desegregation. But sometimes a voice emerged that expressed impatience with this slow and quiet movement. At a regional workshop, one of the national council members presented a discussion of a difficult situation in Wichita, Kansas. A young African American woman who was a longtime volunteer for the Girl Scouts was not hired by the council. There was apparently "no question concerning the applicant's ability. Rather, the Girl Scout staff and council volunteers said that the 'local community [Wichita] is not yet ready.'" After some back-and-forth, the national staff member wrote in capital letters, getting to the crux of the matter and indicating her anger and impatience at the Girl Scouts for its ongoing support and tolerance of discrimination: "DOES ONE WAIT FOR THE CLIMATE TO BECOME FAVORABLE? LET OTHERS DO THE WORK? DOES THE GIRL SCOUT COUNCIL HAVE AN OBLIGATION IN MAKING THE CLIMATE

BECOME MORE FAVORABLE BY TAKING STEPS WHICH AT THE TIME MAY SEEM TOO PREMATURE? The community adviser believes the latter."[81]

Not only had some national white staff become frustrated with the Girl Scouts' reluctance to take a stand on segregation, but Black and white women on the local level began to push the national organization to be more explicitly progressive. "Custom" was no longer an acceptable excuse. On July 19, 1955, six women from Natchez, Mississippi, wrote to Dorothy Stratton, the national executive director of the Girl Scouts, about the formation of a new council in their area. They wrote that they were "sure you realize what a great service the Girl Scout Organization is rendering in this fight for justice for all mankind. Here in Mississippi we need every agency available to help our people live as true Girl Scouts." They pointed out that, while they had had success with a leadership training given to white and Black leaders simultaneously, there were numerous instances of segregation, among them a parade in which white Girl Scout troops insisted they be separated by a "mobile unit" from Black troops; well-funded camps for white Girl Scouts and none for Black girls; and the fact that the regional director had visited Natchez and planned the leadership meeting in a hotel "where Negro leaders dare not go." The six women requested that moving forward all of these issues be addressed by the national staff, including the formation of a council with both Black and white members. The national staff, they argued, needed to understand that "meetings will be held only in places that will allow leaders and committee members of all troops to attend."[82] It's not clear from the record whether the national organization intervened in the ways that this group requested, but their expectation that the Girl Scout organization would "fight for justice" was clear.

Throughout the 1950s, regional councils in every part of the country sent in extensive reports to the national organization about the state of segregation and desegregation within their troops and councils. They usually showed a jumbled compilation of details demonstrating both the continued machinations of structural racism in scouting and attempts to change. A field worker from Wheeling, West Virginia, for instance, reported that Wheeling council members—all white—believed that "Negros should prove their ability to help themselves" before being "allowed" to participate more fully in council activities. There was still a "Negro Central Committee," which worked "as a council within a council." The report explained that this committee was "responsible for organizing Negro troops, seeing that leaders take training, arranging for the short (five day) camping period at the established camp after the regular established camping season is over." Yet the report also noted changes, particularly the mixing of white and Black troops in leader training courses and in planning boards created by the girls themselves. Part of the change was likely due to the action of the executive director (a paid, professional position) of the Wheeling council, who simply "assumed" that both groups would attend major events, such as the Kits for Korea campaign and the leaders' recognition ceremony. She did this by ignoring the instruction she had received previously to "delete" certain key pages of the council newsletter before they were sent to Black troops, a very effective yet subtle and hidden way that white scouts in Wheeling had previously excluded Black scouts. By sending the entire newsletter, the executive director ensured that all Girl Scouts and their leaders were aware of and invited to every event happening in the region, which also meant it created solid ground for African American troops to complain if they found they had been excluded.[83] Other councils took similar actions, such as the Foothill Area Girl Scout Council in California, which developed an in-depth "Experimental Workshop in Intercultural Relations," inviting white, Black, and Latina members; the reading list for the workshop included works by some of the country's deepest thinkers on race, including W. E. B. Du Bois, Charles Johnson, Hortense Powdermaker, Richard Wright, and Sterling Brown.[84]

Desegregating Girl Scout Camps

When I was a young girl in the 1960s, my family would travel from Cleveland and Akron to camp at a park in West Virginia called Oglebay Park. It wasn't too expensive, and it was a lot of fun: a well-stocked cabin, other families who had traveled from northern Ohio and Pittsburgh, lots of drinking for the adults so they were in a good mood, time to explore outside. I remember only white families camping there. This makes sense now as something that happened by design, not by chance, as it turns out that it was one of the segregated campgrounds that prevented Girl Scouts of color from attending. When I came upon a Girl Scout report on intercultural relations in West Virginia and Virginia, I found a note that local council members felt that "Oglebay Park would not like it" if they let Negro troops camp there, as "the park does not open its facilities to Negroes." It was a detail that was just left hanging, as if it were a moment and place of acceptable, inevitable segregation, a place where the "maximum harmony" of desegregation would be disrupted if one pushed too hard.[85]

Around the same time that this council was reporting that segregation was inevitable at Oglebay, other councils were working actively to desegregate their campsites. Sometimes a white camp would break the boundary of segregation by inviting one or two girls of color, a token inclusion; they were then surprised when no one wanted to take up their offer. One of the national community relations experts, Besse Kranz, noted this problem along with the qualms some African American parents might have with sending their girls to white camps. "Special interpretation of Girl Scout intercultural policies should be given to the Negro parents," she wrote. "They might need to be assured that their children will be well received and cared for properly, since it might be their first experience. I feel this would be a good precaution since other councils, when they first established interracial camp programs were disappointed when only a handful of Negro girls participated."[86] When camps did desegregate, it seems that the model was to pretend everything was as it had always been. Mentioning race was considered bad form, sure to cause a problem where color blindness might otherwise rule. In 1955, for instance, staff at Baltimore's Camp Deer Creek, the first camp in the area to be open simultaneously to white and African American Girl Scouts, reported that "staff was given no indication as to the race of their campers until they arrived. This philosophy of 'making no difference' resulted in the quick bridging of any assumed problems. There was not a single problem that could be traced to a difference of races." The only issues they noted were "cute" ones: Black girls' concern over the red and sunburned faces of the blond girls, who in turn were surprised by the hair care methods of the African American girls. Other than that, innocence and goodwill got the girls through the summer, according to the report.[87] There are no voices in that report from the actual Black campers, who likely had a different experience.

By the late 1950s and into the 1960s, most councils chose to desegregate their camps, in large part as a consequence of persistent pressure from frustrated African American activists. The opening of white Girl Scout camps to African American campers frequently meant that African American camps were closed down or were collapsed into the white camps. The closure of the Black camps is a sure sign that the white councils perceived the Black camps as inferior and ancillary to the white camps. One of the unexpected and unfortunate results of the Girl Scouts' closure of its Black camps meant that African American scouts lost the autonomy and community they had built in their own camps. The desegregation of Girl Scouting in Memphis, Tennessee, in the early 1950s illuminates this loss, both of African American autonomy as a whole and of the possibilities provided by the camp in particular. A very explicit report explained that after the Black Memphis council was eliminated, only one or two Black volunteers and staff served on the now integrated Memphis council. As a result, the report read:

> There was also a falling off in Negro volunteer personnel and consequently a temporary drop in troops registered. There was overt expressions among Negroes of distrust as to their camp money. They had raised $11,000 for a Negro camp site. Now the whites had the $11,000 and no camp site had been purchased. The picture aroused a great deal of suspicion. The new Executive was a native Southern local white. She said she meant integration, but was not *their* "Executive" (Senior Negro field worker) being reduced to a mere field worker? Was not their committee of management dissolved while still not a single Negro was on the white Board? Were not all their committees disbanded while only a Negro or two had been placed on some of the otherwise all-white committees? "Integration" looked very much to them like being swallowed up and reduced to subordinator by the whites.[88]

The national Girl Scouts' response to such problems was to encourage more "intergroup communication" and to address the surprise of white leadership that Black people were not "enthusiastic" about the merger and continually voiced mistrust of white scouts. But nowhere did the national response address the losses that African American scouts experienced—of autonomy, of leadership, of community, or even of the $11,000. Orchestrated by white people, with a presumption that the resources and autonomy of Black people should be folded into the white organization, with no attention paid to what would need to happen to ensure Black members had access to resources and decision-making, Girl Scout desegregation sometimes actually resulted in losses for African American people and a decrease in membership. Desegregation in Memphis, for instance, is an illuminating moment of how integration could result in the maintenance of racial hierarchy rather than its destruction.

The Juliette Gordon Low Birthplace

In 1956, two years after *Brown* declared that segregation in public schools was unconstitutional, the Girl Scouts of the USA held a celebratory event marking the opening of the Juliette Gordon Low Birthplace in Savannah, Georgia. The Girl Scouts had purchased Juliette Gordon Low's childhood home three years earlier after a push by Low's family members and Southern regional Girl Scout members to turn the house into a commemorative site honoring Low's life. Long stripped of furniture and period features, the home had been broken into apartments and was in need of serious repair when the Gordon family began the drive for the Girl Scouts to purchase the building. The Girl Scouts began a well-publicized national campaign urging every Girl Scout in the United States to give at least a small amount of money so that the Birthplace could "belong" to everyone.[89] The June 1954 cover story of the *Girl Scout Leader* included a picture of a young white girl, sporting braided pigtails and a beret, gazing at Low's home with blueprints to the side stamped with a trefoil reading "It's Ours." The three-page article urged all members to send in a donation—from $1 to $1,000—to refurbish "the house, with its gardens, carriage house and servants' quarters [*sic*] . . . to preserve this example of a typical mansion of a bygone era, of gracious living," and to help create a center "where girls from all over the world can come together to find friendship and inspiration."[90] A photo marking the 1956 dedication of the Birthplace portrays the festive occasion: Flags wave from the front of the mansion, and girls in uniform line up on the dual staircases and across the sidewalk. It's a similar photo to one that I have from my trip to Savannah with my Girl Scout troop in 1975; though mine is now water damaged, I can still make us out on the staircase, standing proudly in our uniforms. When I traveled to the Birthplace to do research in the late 2010s, I saw lots of troops marking their pilgrimage to the birthplace of Girl Scouting by posing for a photo in the same style: girls lined up on the staircase, faces beaming. What especially makes the 1956 photo stand out, which the Girl Scouts had on its website until 2022, is that the girls lining up in front of the building are a diverse group. While in the minority, African American girls are clearly in the front, at the right of the photo.[91]

The photo underscores how important Girl Scouting was in many African American communities, which pushed hard to create opportunities for their girls. But it also conceals the very specific discrimination that Black Girl Scouts were facing at the Birthplace at the moment that photo was taken. Concern about the "mixing" of troops ran so high that a schedule was tightly maintained for the dedication to ensure that no Black troops would be in the house at the same time as white troops. Although sleeping quarters had been built for the Birthplace (and funded by Girl Scouts across the country), they were closed to everyone, because local people did not want African American girls sleeping there. Even the suggestion of a "camp-out" was nixed to prevent

Black girls from staying at the house. Instead, Black troops had to find places to stay in Black community members' homes, as no hotels would take them.[92] But the celebratory picture does not show any of these problems, which were tolerated and even created by the Girl Scout organization itself.

Controversy swirled as planning for the 1956 dedication began, when it became clear to the national organization that Black troops would not be welcome at the Birthplace. Certainly the question about Black participation could not—or at most should not—have been a surprise to the national organization, which had been deeply enmeshed in the question of race for years. The committees on "Negro scouts" had given way to Intercultural and Human Relations Committees as the Girl Scouts considered ways to increase African American girls' participation and overall racial understanding both internationally and nationally. After the debacle of the 1947 national convention in Long Beach, California, the policy was changed in the *Blue Book* in 1950 to ensure that no national Girl Scout event could be held unless all participants could be guaranteed equal access to the restaurants, lodging, and meeting centers engaged by the Girl Scouts. By early 1954, the national organization was carefully deliberating how the *Brown* decision impacted Girl Scout organizing. And on a grassroots level, African American leaders and girls pushed relentlessly for an end to substandard opportunities, especially in camping and campgrounds.

Despite all this, the national Girl Scout organization decided to move forward with the purchase and establishment of the Juliette Gordon Low Birthplace in an area known to refuse to follow national policy. In 1953, the board consulted a lawyer to see whether the Birthplace would be legally required to follow local segregation policies. His opinion: "If the Girl Scouts owned the Gordon residence they would be perfectly free, as a matter of law, to admit both white and colored Scouts to the house at the same time. Whether you did so or not would be entirely for you to say. If you did, I do not think the white children would come. If you held national or international meetings in it, attended by Negro women, I do not think the white women in the South who are interested in Scouting would come."[93] The Girl Scout national organization also knew that Black troops would not be able to find places to eat and sleep when visiting the Birthplace. "Infinite and delicate handling will be required as to eating and living accommodations," a Savannah priest replied to the national organization's query about the atmosphere in Savannah. He added, "As to key-Negroes on the Scout National level, I think most satisfactory accommodations could be provided for them in homes locally. Among

Savannah Negroes, there are many beautiful homes and their owners well educated and socially-correct."[94] The situation was the same as it had been in Long Beach in 1947, when Black delegates could not find housing; what had changed now, though, was that the national organization had a policy *against* this kind of discrimination. The national organization was in a quandary, as it had decided to move forward with the house and the dedication, despite knowing it went against its own policies. The solution? To declare the national dedication a regional event, in a region where discrimination was still tolerated. At least one national staff member, Agnes Leahy, felt uncomfortable with the possibility of skirting the national rules on nondiscriminatory lodging and dining in this way: "The Juliette Low Birthplace is being created as a national shrine. It surely cannot be interpreted as a regional operation, or having attendance from a limited area."[95]

Despite Leahy's pleas, the national board acquiesced to white Southern demands. While it was clearly a national event (even the First Lady was invited), the Girl Scouts technically called it a "regional" conference of Southern states. This allowed the organization to appease white Southern scouts while technically following its national policy regarding inclusivity. Rather than having a celebratory "camp-out" at the Birthplace, it would be a day-only event. Troops would go in one by one; thus there would be no "mixing" in the house itself. Black troops could come, but they would be separated from segregated white troops. The sleeping quarters were eliminated, so that there would be no possibility of African American girls spending the night at the Birthplace.[96] It was easier to shut the house down for everyone than to make a case that Black and white girls should be able to stay there together. And for years, despite recognizing the lie that it was, Girl Scouts allowed the staff at the Juliette Gordon Low home to permit white-only events, under the guise that they were "private" events, not "Girl Scouts" endorsed.[97] It was another situation where the Girl Scouts acquiesced to discriminatory policies in order to accommodate the wishes of white supremacists.

Not surprising, the attempts to mask the discrimination failed to convince African American leaders, staff, and girls, many of whom raised the issue with the national organization. Nell Hamm, a national African American staff member, heard that Black Girl Scouts would never be allowed in the Birthplace if there were white scouts there, even if they were part of an interracial troop. A Northern regional committee member asked the national organization, "If such rumors . . . are incorrect perhaps it needs a positive statement of policy on the matter to clear the air and not just assume that Girl

Scout practices are being followed."[98] Yet no such public declaration followed, despite repeated requests for a definitive statement from the national headquarters.[99] Instead, throughout the 1950s and 1960s, the Savannah local council worked to keep Black and white troops separated, created white-only events under the auspices of "private" groups doing the inviting, and ensured that the sleeping quarters remained closed. As one national staff member explained, the Birthplace was a real problem, as it clearly was not a place "where all girls can work and play and *live* together." "I am sure," she wrote in 1963, "that some of the Negro organizations, such as the NAACP, etc., will at some time in the near future *demand* that the national organization take some kind of stand or action." Throughout the 1960s, though, Black troops had significant difficulty finding lodging and food if they made a pilgrimage to the Birthplace, and national staff deflected their questions when they tried to pin down housing plans.[100]

In the 1970s, my white Cadette troop made the pilgrimage to the Juliette Gordon Low Birthplace. We had really worked hard for the trip, selling as many cookies as possible and taking part in endless car washes on the weekends to raise the funds. We planned meticulously, calling bus companies to get financial estimates, writing to hotels in Savannah, making arrangements with a local camp, and scheduling a detailed itinerary. Our leaders fostered tremendous independence in us in planning the trip, which still stands out to me today. After an eleven-hour ride on our chartered bus, we stayed at a local hotel in Savannah. The next morning we dressed in our uniforms and had our picture taken on the steps of the Birthplace, in a style very reminiscent of that original picture at the 1956 dedication ceremony. I was so happy as that camera flashed. Throughout that entire trip, we never learned about any discrimination at the Juliette Gordon Low Birthplace, we never discussed Jim Crow, and we certainly never learned about the exclusion of African American scouts. I don't remember seeing any African American girls at the Birthplace, and this absence prompted no discussion among us. I keep a copy of that troop photo, now crumbling, close by as I think and write about the history of the Girl Scouts. I think about the ways that the organization, when confronted with a choice between full inclusion and the demands of its white membership, acquiesced to the demands of white supremacists. I think about the ways that African American girls and women fought for inclusion in Girl Scouts in general and at the Juliette Gordon Low Birthplace in particular. I think about the ways the organization worked to school white girls like me in innocence, and the ways that it lied to Black girls and women as it deflected their inquiries about troop formation, camping opportunities, and the Birthplace itself. I also think about what I didn't know when I traveled to Savannah in 1975, both that the Girl Scouts had been under attack for being "too liberal," communist even, and that the white hegemony of the Girl Scouts had begun to crumble by the 1960s under pressure both from outside the Girl Scouts and from the membership itself.

Chapter 8

Even the Girl Scouts

COMMUNISM AND THE SEEDS OF SUBVERSION IN THE GIRL SCOUTS

• • • • • •

The Girl Scout Handbook . . . sell[s] the young, the innocent, and the unsuspecting on a totalitarian world government.
—*Los Angeles Herald and Express* columnist, 1954

In 1954—the same year that the Girl Scouts were quietly debating the ramifications of the *Brown v. Board of Education* decision and announcing the organization's national campaign to buy the Juliette Gordon Low home despite the racial segregation in Savannah, Georgia—a national controversy blew up in the organization's face. Robert LeFevre, a far-right-wing, anticommunist, anti–United Nations activist from Florida, published a diatribe in the conservative publication *Human Events*. His March 1954 article, "Even the Girl Scouts," accused the Girl Scouts of being a dangerous, un-American organization. Specifically, he wrote that the Girl Scouts encouraged its members to honor the United Nations above the United States, to believe in the Universal Declaration of Human Rights, to trust the League of Women Voters, and to find racial prejudice morally repugnant. He concluded his article by advising "all American mothers to discourage their girls from joining that organization, until it stops the U.N. and world government propaganda and becomes what many think it is, a real American organization." At first the national Girl Scout staff dismissed LeFevre's article, published as it was in a rather obscure journal by an obviously fringe regional journalist. They were wrong, however. His article set off a chain of events that required Girl Scouts to act publicly and definitively, events that illuminate how precarious, tenuous, and difficult was the Girl Scouts' claim to be an international organization "for all girls," especially when it chose to appease its ultraconservative critics. This same controversy, though, asks us to question whether there were seeds of subversion—if not actual communists—in this nationalistic organization.[1]

The 1954 Communist Controversy

The Girl Scouts became embroiled with the Fort Lauderdale radio personality Robert LeFevre after a botched invitation to a regional event in Florida. A member of the Broward County Girl Scout council had invited LeFevre to the Girl Scout event without knowing his extreme anti–United Nations views; concerned that he would stir up controversy, the council reminded him that they were a nonpolitical group and asked him to temper his remarks. Angered at being "censored," LeFevre apparently refused to appear (though he said the invitation was withdrawn) and set out on a fact-finding mission about the Girl Scouts. He dove into the 1953 *Girl Scout Handbook*, where he found many "startling" details, which he laid out in his *Human Events* article. He attacked the Girl Scouts' full endorsement of the United Nations and of the 1948 Universal Declaration of Human Rights, singling out the human rights of citizenship, property, housing, fair working conditions, and education as particularly problematic. He derided the *Handbook*'s comparison of the Universal Declaration of Human Rights with the US Bill of Rights. He came down especially hard on merit badges Girl Scouts could earn such as My Community, My Country, International Friendship, and World Neighbor, because they supported the importance of government agencies and represented "questionable viewpoints." He specifically singled out a reference to the League of Women Voters, which the *Handbook* described as a useful "nonpolitical organization" encouraging civic engagement. And among his accusations about the United Nations, the League of Women Voters, and the merit badges was a paragraph focused entirely on the Girl Scouts' antiracism work. He wrote:

> The handbook emphasizes prejudice by setting up a chart of questions for the girls to answer. One question suggests that when discrimination is practiced by members of one race toward members of another race, prejudice against race is multiplied. The chart encourages members of certain races and countries—specifically the Chinese, the Negroes, and the Italians—in thinking that they are looked down upon by

> Americans, that Americans have been unfair toward them. The questions suggest that the Girl Scout who does not associate freely with all members of all other races, regardless of their individual merit, is morally deficient.

LeFevre's sweeping accusations pointed to three main subversive elements that the Girl Scouts apparently supported: a world government, feminism, and a society that both recognized racism and worked against it. And though the article never used the word "communism," it quickly got picked up by right-wing commentators across the country who used LeFevre's words as evidence of the Girl Scouts' seditious philosophy. As one pundit noted in the *Los Angeles Herald and Express*, "The Girl Scout Handbook . . . sell[s] the young, the innocent, and the unsuspecting on a totalitarian world government."[2] Local community groups across the nation, alarmed by LeFevre's accusations, threatened to cut off financial support and blackball the Girl Scouts. One regional Girl Scout staff member reported rumors running wild that Girl Scouts were "Communistic from top to bottom."[3]

The controversy gained additional steam when Illinois representative Patrick Sheehan, a Republican and Joseph McCarthy sympathizer, decided to enter LeFevre's article into the July 1954 *Congressional Record*. A month later, with pressure from its Anti-Subversive Commission, the Illinois chapter of the American Legion voted to censure the Girl Scouts as a "subversive and un-American influence." As evidence, the chapter cited the 1953 *Girl Scout Handbook*'s discussion of the United Nations and "one-world" citizenship just as LeFevre had laid out. But it also noted that "an official Girl Scout magazine" had "highly recommended . . . the writings of certain pro-Communist authors." These attacks focused on the February 1953 issue of the *Girl Scout Leader*, which had featured very short (one paragraph each) positive reviews of books by the children's book author and women's rights activist Dorothy Canfield Fisher and the Harlem Renaissance author Langston Hughes. Both had been called before the House Un-American Activities Committee and their names were eventually cleared. Their mere appearance before the committee was enough to tarnish the Girl Scouts by association, however, and the topics of their books fueled the fire. According to the *Girl Scout Leader* review, Fisher's book *A Fair World for All* describes the United Nations and the Universal Declaration of Human Rights "in terms of the everyday experience of young people." The fact that the Girl Scouts recommended this book provided more evidence for its support of an internationalist viewpoint in general and the United Nations in particular. The 1953 *Leader* review describes Hughes's

The First Book of Negroes as a "charming book about Negroes," introducing the "history, achievements, and present-day life of Negroes in different part of the United States and in other lands. It is a children's book written by a distinguished man of letters whose style will charm adults as well. Both Negro and white readers are likely to find here facts that are unfamiliar and interesting."[4] Today this review sounds extremely condescending and placating, but for the many conservative white groups who had targeted the Girl Scouts, the fact that the *Leader* praised both Fisher and Hughes and encouraged Black and white readers to read and learn from them was an extraordinary challenge to a culture and system of white supremacy and thus to what they saw as the American way of life. In other words, it was anti-American to be antiracist. As a writer for the *Southern Conservative* wrote about the Hughes and Fisher reviews, "If American parents want their children's views on citizenship influenced by black male Communist Fronters or white female subversives, that seems to be what they are getting but if they don't, they had better take a good long search look into what is going on."[5] The Illinois American Legion, picking up on the charges of feminism, internationalism, and antiracism, voted to censure the Girl Scouts and forwarded the motion for a national vote by the body of the American Legion as a whole. Its charges noted that "J. Edgar Hoover, Director of the FBI," had "warned that subversive and un-American influences" were "attempting to capture the minds of our youth"; that the 1953 *Girl Scout Handbook* gave precedence to the United Nations "over American citizenship"; and that other Girl Scout publications promoted the writings of "pro-Communist authors." It demanded changes in both the *Handbook* and other publications before the American Legion would reinstate its support.

A Long-Standing Battle

Internal memos from the Girl Scouts suggest that staff members were caught off guard by LeFevre's 1954 attack, misreading it as an element of a fringe movement rather than the spearhead in an attack that dominated Congress and community groups throughout the country. It's somewhat surprising that they initially dismissed the LeFevre attack, considering that the Girl Scouts had been quietly but firmly removing suspect Girl Scout leaders and thwarting accusations of communism since the late 1940s. Popular memory often points to the "McCarthy era" as a time of heightened fear about communism, when Wisconsin Republican senator Joseph McCarthy rose to prominence in 1950 with a speech alluding to widespread infiltration of the government by communists and then gained even more notoriety when he took the helm of hearings interrogating the army in 1954. The state-sponsored interrogation of "un-American" activities, however, first began in 1938, when the House of Representatives established the first Un-American Activities Committee to investigate suspected Nazi sympathizers and then, after the war, suspected communist infiltrators. In 1947 President Harry S. Truman compelled all federal employees to take a loyalty oath. For years, the government circulated a list of organizations considered subversive, and membership in one of those (which ranged from bona fide Communist Party organizations to others that simply leaned to the left) or even past attendance at their meetings could land a person in front of the House Un-American Activities Committee for interrogation. Being called before the Un-American Activities Committee, even if eventually exonerated, could cause one to be blacklisted forever, with jobs, relationships, and housing opportunities drying up. The concerted effort of the US government to crack down on any dissent cost many people everything they had, and the chilling effect of the political witch hunt, particularly on the arts, cannot be underestimated.[6]

In the wake of President Truman's 1947 call for a federal loyalty oath, Girl Scout personnel began to pressure their national director, Constance Rittenhouse, for a response from the national office. "The questions are quite persistent" about "un-American activities," one senior staff member wrote in a 1948 memo.[7] Rittenhouse initially voiced reluctance to engage in "witch hunting."[8] She eventually relented in 1949, signing off on a lengthy notice to all staff members about what to do when a member was accused of being a member of the Communist Party. The memo urged everyone to avoid public statements about communism, instead redirecting the conversation to how scouting helped "girls become happier better people as well as responsible homemakers, wage earners, and citizens." It reminded staff that "we need not resort to political definitions in order to judge . . . a person. We have our own standards. It is against those standards that any member may be measured." In this way, the policy suggested that the Girl Scout Promise and Law were the organization's own "loyalty test" but one that still resided outside the world of politics. It was crucial that the Girl Scouts present itself as an organization unsullied by and disengaged from the political realm.[9] Nevertheless, the memo also included a "Guide on the Release of Leaders," which walked staff step by step through a "tactful" way to ascertain whether a leader was problematic; the memo never mentioned the word "communist" but rather suggested that if a person's work was not in line with the Girl Scout Promise and Law—which assumed loyalty to God and country—she should be let go.[10]

While the national Girl Scout organization had been highly aware of the threat of communism well before LeFevre's attack, it seemed less concerned about actual infiltration by communists than about any negative publicity that might blow its way. And the organization did take action, generally requiring that any potential communist activity among the Girl Scouts be reported to the national organization.[11] Not every investigation of a suspect Girl Scout resulted in dismissal. One 1953 report to the national organization noted that a Southern California council was "in sympathy" with a woman who was a former Hollywood cartoon artist and Communist Party member and voted to keep her as a troop leader.[12] And in another situation, national staff urged a Colorado troop to allow a young girl to join the Girl Scouts, dismissing as irrelevant the fact that her father was accused of being a "liberal professor."[13]

But in other cases, the national organization supported forceful and decisive moves to contain what it called potentially "explosive" situations. Most of these related to race and civil rights, echoing the extraordinarily fierce attacks on civil rights organizations throughout the twentieth century that accused the Girl Scouts of "communist" activity whenever the organization fought actively for the rights of people of color.[14] In 1952, for instance, the local council in Orange County, California, refused to incorporate a group of lone troops in the agricultural town of Costa Mesa. Why? A conservative group called the Associated Farmers thought the Costa Mesa area was a "hotbed of subversive groups." Though Girl Scout records do not explicitly refer to union activity among farmworkers or the races of the lone troops, the condemnation from the Associated Farmers suggests that these were Latina girls whose parents were involved in farm union organizing.[15] Indeed, so many of the cases where the Girl Scouts became embroiled in controversy had to do with troops or individuals whose politics espoused an antiracist point of view. A 1951 internal memo noted possible "Communist activity" among what appeared to be Black troops in the Rockaways, New York, who opposed the national sponsorship program, a policy that required non-white troops to have a council or local organization sponsor them. "This may be honest conviction but its persistence bears watching," the memo added, presuming that if the struggle for racial inclusion continued, these troops must be subversives. By contrast, more conservative political activism by troops was tolerated, if not always encouraged. In 1953, for instance, a group of right-wing New Mexican Girl Scout troops organized themselves to protest the shooting of the migrant rights film *Salt of the Earth*. The national organization supported the protests, only urging local leaders to shift their sign from reading "Help Fight Communism Through the Girl Scouts" to "Girl Scouts—a Force for Freedom," in order to avoid mention of communism.[16]

We have no way of knowing how many Girl Scout leaders were quietly asked to resign due to their organizational affiliations, their political activism, the clubs they joined, or the relationships they had. We know that lesbian relationships came under extraordinary scrutiny by the Un-American Activities Committee, and while I did not find any record in the national organization archives regarding lesbian leaders and communism, it's likely they were a target, urged to leave quietly before scandal arose. The national organization reminded its staff to dress "correctly and neatly" when dealing with the public, explaining, "People are judged by externals, and women, particularly, by their appearance. . . . We can be called 'un-American' by the way we look and act. . . . Remember the social graces—they are just as important as what we have done or haven't done."[17] This was a call to act in a dignified and feminine manner, to dress appropriately, to ensure that there would be no taint of mannishness or lesbianism to tarnish the image of the Girl Scouts and bring charges of un-Americanness. It's probably safe to assume that there were indeed women who found themselves face-to-face with a council member or another leader, urged to leave scouting quickly and quietly, whether because of their liberal ideas, left-wing organizational affiliations, or relationships with other women. The threat and shame of scandal was so great that the pressure to leave without a trace would have been tremendous, especially for anyone accused of lesbianism or communism.[18] And for these same reasons of shame and scandal, it's likely that councils who "took care" of any problems locally might have been reluctant to report the situation to the national organization, despite the policy requiring it, in order to avoid further scrutiny and embarrassment for the accused leader or the troop or council as a whole.

Not everyone left quietly when being pushed out of the Girl Scouts. Jeannette Shepard, a Brownie leader from Mamaroneck, New York, was considered a fine leader until her name appeared in the newspaper. She was a plaintiff in a case being brought against the American Legion and the Roger Smith Hotel for canceling a race relations conference, one that apparently was going to feature the well-known African American activist and actor Paul Robeson. As an officer of the Westchester Committee on Human Rights, Shepard became a "source of concern" for the local council, which met with her individually, asking her to resign. Defiantly, she responded, "I refuse to resign. You can expel me." After significant cajoling by the council staff about the welfare of the children, Shepard relented and signed the resignation papers. But then the letters started pouring into the Westchester council, as well as to national offices, expressing anger at what appeared to be a forced resignation. The Westchester Committee on Human Rights wrote that it was "shocked" by the attack on the leader, considering that they thought the Girl Scouts stood for "free speech, equal rights without discrimination, racial and religious tolerance, and all democratic principles."[19] Despite the pushback from liberal groups and community members, the Girl Scouts refused to reinstate Shepard. Perhaps it was her connection with Paul Robeson, a figure too Black, too leftist, too sexual, and too outspoken to be linked with the organization. Instead of rethinking its approach to her case as the Girl Scouts had done with others, national staff pulled rank, dismissing her as a troubling "cause célèbre," deciding to "practically say nothing" to anyone who questioned them, simply repeating that they had accepted her resignation. And then the national organization resorted to an old tactic of smearing the individual, questioning not only her "controversial activity" but her "emotional stability." It simply waited out the protesters who wanted her reinstated until they grew tired of writing and the controversy eventually died down.[20]

The 1954 Attack

In the years preceding LeFevre's 1954 "Even the Girl Scouts" attack article, the national Girl Scout organization had been quietly thwarting accusations of communism and subversive activities, even if there were moments, such as the situation with Jeannette Shepard, when a case became more prominent and controversial. Girl Scout national director Constance Rittenhouse had been trying to thread a line, never veering into "witch hunting" but keeping a tight lid on any activity too leftist, too feminist, too queer, or too antiracist. It's especially important to note that these attacks on the Girl Scouts were happening simultaneously with the push by African American women and girls discussed in the previous chapter for full inclusion in the organization, for integrated camps and troops, and for a national Birthplace that actually welcomed everyone. Right-wing white groups called these antiracist initiatives for integration and inclusion "subversive" and "un-American." Instead of challenging the groups on the substance of their accusation (Is it un-American to push for integration?), the Girl Scouts responded by never pushing "too far" or "too hard," just going as far as "local circumstances" (among white people and white groups) would permit.

Perhaps it was what they considered their relative success at dealing with right-wing attacks, perhaps it was their own confidence in the organization as the preeminent girls' patriotic organization in the United States (remember, the Girl Scouts encouraged both American Indian girls and Japanese American girls to highlight their Girl Scout membership to prove their patriotism!), or perhaps it was that the organization was spending a lot of its energy trying to appease the white segregationists while navigating the changes demanded by the new civil rights movement, but whatever the reason, the Girl Scouts allowed the LeFevre attack to blow up into something big before putting its forces behind defending the organization. Letters poured in to national headquarters from around the country, demanding to know why the Girl Scouts had come under the sway of subversive forces. LeFevre's close yet selective reading of the 1953 *Girl Scout Handbook* as a seditious tome prompted thousands to return the newly issued book to the publisher. The *Saturday Evening Post* worried that "somebody has slipped some dubious propaganda into the manual of a patriotic organization for young people."[21] Councils throughout the nation wrote to the national headquarters with heightened concerns; in Wheeling, West Virginia, for instance, the council reported that it asked for guidance and reassurance from the national organization, some proof of "Americanness" it could wave to ensure its organization would not be blackballed and its local funding—known as the Community Chest—cut off.

It wasn't until the Illinois American Legion voted to censure the Girl Scouts, however, that the national organization sprang into definitive action. The first thing the board chose to do was send a telegram to councils and staff across the country. The author of the telegram was Marguerite Twohy, the same woman who twenty years earlier had been working as a field agent in American Indian boarding schools and who went on to organize scouting internationally; she was now a high-level staff member in the national office. "If necessary," the telegram read in a typical shorthand style, "answer newspapers about American Legion charges. . . . Girl Scouts USA stand on record of 42 years service to girls our country. Promise taken by every girl and adult in Girl Scouting is: On my honor I will try to do my duty to God and my country. In that promise we believe and on those principles we act."[22]

The national organization enlisted Lillian Gilbreth, a longtime Girl Scout supporter and the inspiration for the mother in *Cheaper by the Dozen*, to write an article for the *Girl Scout Leader*, titled "Girl Scouting: One Answer to Communism."[23] Significantly, this article marked the end of a pretense of "nonpolitical" stance, considering that it named communism and Girl Scouts in the same sentence, a practice that had been explicitly discouraged in previous years. The Girl Scouts even brought former First Lady Eleanor Roosevelt into the fray, encouraging her to use one of her very popular My Day columns to focus on the controversy. "The Girl Scouts have always emphasized the value of getting to know young people in other areas of the world," Roosevelt explained calmly, before she went on to blast the Illinois American Legion.

"If things like this were not so ludicrous, they would be tragic," she bluntly stated.[24]

Although Eleanor Roosevelt referred to LeFevre's charges as ludicrous, the Girl Scouts explicitly backpedaled in its public positions, most notably in the changes it decided to make in the *Handbook*. While in later discussions the Girl Scouts often said these changes were just small points of clarification as the book was already going through some revisions, this was only technically true. When the American Legion made its attack, the *Handbook* was indeed up for reprinting, which usually meant a time to correct any inaccuracies or typographical errors. But the Girl Scouts used this moment to make more than fifty wholesale changes in the materials, following the suggestions of councils across the country, which had sent in recommendations for revision of "problem" passages.[25] While the national council chose to retain much of the material on international friendship and even on the United Nations, it toned down certain points, further highlighted patriotic texts such as the Bill of Rights, and changed the names and requirements for many merit badges. Most of these omissions and revisions took away any explicit charge to "make the world a better place," with one of the phrases amended to read "make your contribution to the world." It was as if any vision of international harmony or girls' agency in social, cultural, or political betterment was itself "un-American." In a section titled "Citizenship Here and Abroad," the national council changed the sentence "You are preparing yourself for world citizenship" to "You are preparing yourself to be an active citizen and a 'friend to all.'"[26] Mention of the League of Women Voters as an organization devoted to "the education of women of political action" was deleted completely, instead encouraging girls to find a nonpartisan organization in their own town.[27] The One World badge became the My World badge.[28] The words to "The Star-Spangled Banner" were added to the preface of the book.[29] And a section on "international friendship" lost any explicit references to racism and prejudice. In the original version, the text was surrounded by sketch drawings of five girls, roughly drawn to "look" white, Asian American, Black, and perhaps American Indian (she has long braids).[30] The original text explained that it was natural to like some individuals and not others. But then it went on to push girls to face their own group prejudices: "However," it explained, "you can learn that every group of people has its own way of life. You can try to understand and respect that way even though it is quite different from your own. You can practice good will toward all races, creeds, and national backgrounds in your home town. It is easy to be friends with people you like. Start now by making new friends among those you *think* you do not like. Develop wide interests and right attitudes." The revision kept much of this same text but removed the admonishment to challenge one's own limited and dangerous beliefs. "Start now by making new friends among those you *think* you do not like" was changed to "Start now by making new friends."[31] The original text had urged girls to think for themselves, to begin questioning the ways that cultures and ideologies of prejudice had shaped their likes, dislikes, friendships, and communities. This new phrase simply suggested adding someone new to their friendship circle. Later in the same chapter, both the original and revised text included a questionnaire: "How Do You Rate as a Friend to All?" One of the first questions was "Do I use such expressions as 'd**o,' 'n****r,' and 'c***k'?" The original text spelled out these derogatory phrases, which we certainly recognize as problematic today. The revised version eliminated any mention of ethnic groups. "Do I call names that might hurt people's feelings?" was the new question, completely taking the teeth out of the explicit question about racism and prejudice.[32] The final part of Marguerite Twohy's telegram to the Girl Scout community focused on these changes: "We have reviewed our handbook to see where we may have given false impression by poor choice of words and where there is possibility of misinterpretation changes have been made and these changes are now on the press. We believe in the sense of fair play of citizens our country and are confident that they will find us worthy of their continued support."[33]

In case the anticommunist *Girl Scout Leader* article, Eleanor Roosevelt's column, and the *Handbook* changes were not enough to remove the taint of subversion from the organization, the Girl Scouts also began quickly after the LeFevre and American Legion attacks to remove anyone who seemed at all likely to be identified as "subversive." A troop leader in Detroit quickly and quietly resigned the same year as the LeFevre attack, after being convinced by the regional Girl Scout staff that her appearance (even if acquitted) before the Un-American Activities Committee was detrimental to the girls and the organization. The regional and national staff separately conferred to ensure that this leader would never be able to re-register as a Girl Scout in any capacity.[34] On a visit to the Seattle region, Marguerite Twohy reported that the entire city was a "hot spot for Communism," with many Girl Scout leaders called before the Un-American Activities Committee; she collected the names of the women so that none would be "inadvertently . . . re-registered or registered."[35] Similarly, when a leader in Dayton, Ohio, was investigated before the Un-American Activities Committee, the national organization encouraged the regional council to have this woman immediately put on temporary suspension, though, in the effort to appear neutral, not to put anything in writing; it seemed doubtful she would be reinstated.[36] There was no generous response of support as there had been a few years earlier for the cartoon designer accused of communist leanings.

"What Happened to the Girl Scouts?"

As the Girl Scouts pulled ranks to thwart any accusations of communism, forcing resignations, publishing anticommunist materials, and revising the *Handbook*, a public backlash ensued. One of the most vocal critics was the journalist Ben Bagdikian, who published an article titled "What Happened to the Girl Scouts?" first in his local paper, the *Providence Journal*, and then—despite the national Girl Scout organization's attempts to stop publication—in the newsmagazine the *Atlantic*.[37] Significantly, Bagdikian began his essay by quoting Juliette Gordon Low's infamous (if perhaps inaccurate) sentence, "I've got something for the girls of Savannah and all America and all the world," reminding readers that Low was one of the first "true internationalists." But then he recounted all the changes made to the *Handbook*, describing it as a result of the Girl Scouts going into a "panic," and concluding, "The Girl Scouts of America was and is a fine organization which still encourages idealism, good citizenship, and international friendship. What happened in 1954 was that the Girl Scouts in the forty-second year of their existence decided it was no longer safe to say so too plainly."[38] Of course, the Girl Scouts organization had always been very circumspect about its words; that chameleon aspect was what allowed it to exist in the North and the South during Jim Crow, to appease white segregationists while purporting to be an organization that welcomed African Americans, and, at its very origins, to change the name from "guiding" to "scouting," pretending that it was "just what girls wanted" rather than a statement about feminist leanings. But the changes to the *Handbook* struck many people as having gone too far to appease right-wing conservatives. The changes got the attention of Louis Lyons, a Nieman Fellow at Harvard, who called the *Handbook* changes a troubling "sign of the times" that should cause a "sardonic, bitter laughter."[39] And when columnists across the country got wind of the American Legion's accusations, the mockery was palpable; the *Chicago Daily News*, for instance, described the American Legion's charges and the *Handbook*'s changes as "berserk patriotism."[40] The *Denver Post* called the American Legion "big bullies," while the *Chicago Daily Sun-Times* railed, "How screwy can the Legion get?"[41] In his *Harper's* column, Bernard DeVoto derided, "The Girl Scouts flee from mention of the United Nations."[42] When the Girl Scout president, Olivia Layton, wrote to *Harper's* "correcting" the accuracy of DeVoto's words, the columnist had none of it, responding, "Your letter is disingenuous. . . . You know this very well."[43] And as with all the councils and leaders who had written to headquarters worried about subversion within the Girl Scouts, now a new onslaught of letters came to New York, in which the writers wondered why, as one woman from Cleveland wrote, the "opinions of a few dangerous reactionaries justifies taking one's ideas into hiding—no matter to what degree." She added, "The hint of a lack of courage on the part of the Girl Scout organization is disheartening."[44]

Perhaps because of this backlash, when the national American Legion voted on the censuring charges, it voted that the changes made to the *Girl Scouts Handbook* satisfied its concerns. Nevertheless, the Girl Scouts stayed alert to the accusations, visibly appeasing conservatives throughout the rest of the 1950s with active anticommunist statements. As late as 1961, the Girl Scouts sent out J. Edgar Hoover's pamphlet *Communist Target—Youth!* to all councils, even writing Hoover for more copies when their initial supply ran low.[45] And members of the American Legion and other conservative groups still voiced questions: What about the other Girl Scout publications? Did they have subversive elements? And who had actually authorized the original wording in the 1953 *Handbook*? For many people like the editorial writers who dismissed the charges as "screwy," the attacks on the Girl Scouts were simply outrageous. Not only was Girl Scouts a quintessential "patriotic" organization, but Girl Scouts were just that—*girl* scouts—meaning they were children, innocent of any wrongdoing. The syndicated cartoonist Herb Block's "Stand Fast, Men—They're Armed with Marshmallows" exemplified this point of view. The cartoon pictured a group of fat soldiers, holding an Illinois American Legion banner, a book titled "How to Detect Subversion and Witchcraft," and a picture of Joe McCarthy. Fumbling through the woods, they come upon a trio of blond, pigtailed girls roasting marshmallows over a fire. For Block, these charges, like the men in his cartoon, are absolutely ridiculous.[46] And the Girl Scouts themselves are sweet, innocent, white girls, the epitome of American national spirit.

When the national American Legion met in 1954 in Washington, DC, over Labor Day weekend to vote on the Illinois chapter's charges, there were still rumblings wondering who had actually written the 1953 *Handbook* that troubled them so much. Margarite Hall, an Intermediate Program adviser for the Girl Scouts, was the person who had led the revision of the *Handbook*. In a 1990 oral history she described being investigated during "the McCarthy days." She dismissed the charges about the *Handbook* itself—the changes had been prompted by the girls' likes and dislikes, including, she said, the small print about the Bill of Rights, which Hall replaced with a flow chart of the US government. But it was a "real heated time," she explained, and despite the innocuous nature of the *Handbook*, she had to list all the other organizations she had ever belonged to. "Well, I did belong to the First Baptist Church . . . and the American Camping Association . . . and the Girl Scouts." "Good God, what a dull life," the interviewer responded. In other words, it was preposterous for

A 1954 political cartoon in which Herb Block mocks the Illinois American Legion for its accusations of communism against the Girl Scouts, who are portrayed as young, innocent white girls roasting marshmallows. Herb Block, "Stand Fast, Men—They're Armed with Marshmallows," Herb Block Foundation, Washington, DC.

the Girl Scouts to be accused of communist infiltration—they were simply too "innocent."[47]

That story of innocence—exemplified by the blond, white girls by the campfire in the political cartoon, by a staff member so "dull" her only activities were church and camping—certainly came in handy as an attractive cover for an organization under siege. It's not that the archival record suggests any actual infiltration of the Girl Scouts by a communist world association, but the question of whether there were subversive elements in the Girl Scouts is complicated. Indeed, the woman from Cleveland who wrote to national headquarters voicing her disappointment in the Girl Scouts' "lack of courage" is telling, for there were seeds of feminism, of antiracism, and of peace-driven internationalism within the Girl Scouts—all positions that required a tremendous amount of courage because they challenged traditional notions of patriarchy, racial segregation, and militaristic nationalism. Think of the encouragement that girls consider themselves "scouts," not "guides," the push for confidence, the encouragement to enter the world of politics through the League of Women Voters. Think of Josephine Holloway forming her own African American troops in Nashville, and the Black "councils within councils" throughout the South that worked tirelessly for opportunities for African American girls. Think of the young white woman Margaret Murray waving her civil rights pamphlets in front of hotel owners in Long Beach, California, and working side by side with African American Girl Scout staff member Charlotte Moton Hubbard to ensure housing for Black delegates during the 1947 national convention. Think of Hubbard herself, who for over a decade pushed for changes to the racial policy and to Girl Scout materials like the *Songbook*. Think of the national organization pushing—even if too delicately—councils across the nation to recognize the implications of the 1954 *Brown* decision, as a moment when segregated camps and councils would finally have to come to an end. Think of the girls and women who traveled to events sponsored by the World Association of Girl Guides and Girl Scouts, learning about human rights and forging bonds with girls from around the globe. These international gatherings certainly supported the hegemony of the United States as a "benevolent" force, but they also provided girls with ideals of pacifism, a complex and difficult US history, and international sisterhood.

In the period following World War II, there was extraordinary fear about the dangers of communists and left-wing agitators. Some of this was an authentic fear of communist nations sending in spies to foment rebellion and take over the United States; much of it, however, was a resistance to the vision of an alternative world in which every human being had access to health care, housing, and education, in which human beings were not defined or limited by race or sex, and where the profit motive of capitalism did not determine every interaction. Certainly many of those who were agitating for the possibilities of human rights, civil rights, feminism, and socialism in the 1920s, '30s, and '40s had actual contact with and were members of communist groups in the United States and internationally. More common than actual communist membership, however, was an overall inspiration by the vision of leftist groups—whose voices gained urgency during the economic depression and labor unrest of the 1930s and in the postwar era in the aftermath of a world war fought for democracy abroad. Girl Scout leadership in the 1950s thought it quite farfetched for their organization to be accused of communist affiliation. For sure, the organization's status as patriotic seemed unquestionable; it was an organization par excellence born out of American empire, one seen as so inherently "American" that it was foisted on American Indians and Japanese Americans as evidence of patriotic allegiance. But in the early years of the Cold War, groups such as the American Legion called the Girl Scouts communist, un-American, and subversive based on wording in the *Handbook*, recommendations of books and authors, and invitations extended to speakers. I certainly look back on my Girl Scout days as offering me some very fertile seeds of subversion, even as it also wrapped them up in a package of patriotism and innocence. And in the 1960s and 1970s, those seeds would riotously bloom, pushing the boundaries of the Girl Scouts' history and future.

Chapter 9

From Revolution to Backlash

GIRL SCOUTING IN THE LATE TWENTIETH CENTURY

• • • • • •

We never used that word ["feminism"].
—Frances Hesselbein, 2017

The opening festivities at the 1969 Girl Scout National Convention in Seattle showed no signs that the organization had responded to the series of landmark legal decisions challenging racial discrimination in the last fifteen years or to the growing pressure from within to broaden its base. Instead, everything about the opening ceremonies spoke "whiteness." Debbie Reynolds launched the ceremony with a rendition of "Let the Sunshine In"; the self-help humorist and TV personality Art Linkletter spoke about his daughter's recent death to LSD and the importance of Girl Scouts in leading away from "temptation"; and most glaring, an all-white choir of 100 girls sang and carried the flags for the World Association of Girl Guides and Girl Scouts. In response, a group of thirty-eight African American women at the convention quickly delivered a statement to the national board explaining that they were "appalled, shocked and extremely embarrassed at the lack of obvious, active, and full participation of black Girl Scouts in this convention."[1] The African American newspaper *Chicago Daily Defender* noted the "concern over the limited representation of minority group girls" and explained that the outgoing Girl Scout president made an appearance mid-conference to note that it was an "error . . . that we cannot allow to go unacknowledged" and that "plans are afoot to make sure that no such misrepresentation ever occurs again at any nationally sponsored Girl Scout event."[2] "The immediate widening of the circle," the *Girl Scout Leader* reported, was a "small, integrated choir" that opened one of the final sessions of the convention with renditions of "Kum Ba Yah" and "We Shall Overcome." This quick attempt to patch over decades of misrepresentation and exclusion did nothing to assuage the anger of many of the delegates. Dorothy Baker, a spokeswoman for the group that had complained to the national board, noted, "They've said to us, 'We've given you breakfast, lunch and dinner, what more do you want? Maybe what some of the girls need is dignity. Sure the Girl Scouts are integrated, but it's time now to look at how they are integrated. Like this choir? I wouldn't want my daughter to sing in that choir now—it's tokenism."[3]

Rumbles of Discontent

The leadership of the Girl Scouts may have carefully chosen this white tableau to begin the conference as a way to fend off accusations of communism and radicalism that had so shaken the organization in the 1950s and 1960s. But it may have also been a reaction to significant pressure coming at the Girl Scouts from all directions, challenging decades of discrimination that had been both explicit policy and quietly accepted practice. Two significant legal changes, the *Brown v. Board of Education* Supreme Court decision in 1954 and the 1964 Civil Rights Act, meant that the national organization regularly fielded questions from state and local councils regarding whether its practices—its ways of organizing troops, its (lack of) outreach to girls of color, and its differential hiring and pay scale for white and Black employees—were legal. As we have seen, the national organization had maintained itself as a cohesive national organization for years by quietly countenancing systematic discrimination both in the South and the North while voicing its ideal of being an organization for "all girls." From the beginning, it limited the number of troops open to girls of color, believing that it was important to establish Girl Scouting as a white endeavor. When the push for greater inclusion intensified from within and outside, the organization relied on a policy of incremental change so quiet and subtle that change would come without arousing white fears and animosity or without, for that matter, actually "bothering" any white people, north or south.

Brown tipped the organization's hand, revealing the extent to which Girl Scouting as a national organization had relied on the ways that white communities had segregated their school systems, thus ensuring the local segregation of troops. Indeed, memos flew back and forth between regional and national staff concerned about the flight of white girls from Girl Scouting as schools, and thus troops, began to integrate in the aftermath of the decision. From a different angle, some regional staff wondered whether it would be good for the national organization to make a public declaration of how the Supreme Court decision affected Girl Scouting. The national organization declined, hiding behind its vague and often repeated iteration of its membership criteria, that Girl Scouting was open to everyone. Such references to generalized inclusivity did nothing to actively challenge the discriminatory and exclusionary policies of individual troops and local and regional councils. Tellingly, when one staff member asked whether the national organization should contact major Black organizations regarding the Supreme Court decision, the answer was a definitive no: "It is the consensus of those consulted that, at this time, no special contact should be made at the national level with such organizations as the NAACP or the Urban League. The reason is that we would undoubtedly be asked questions to which we have poor answers."[4] Instead, the national council asked regional districts to report on the work of their local councils in the aftermath of *Brown*. Many regional districts reported that white Girl Scouts were fleeing the organization when faced with integration, a concern that rose to the top of the national memos. Other councils reported the integration of camping facilities. While on the surface this appears to be a positive move, in reality it actually meant closing African American camps, firing African American staff and leaders, and redirecting money that African American troops had saved away from the maintenance of their own camps to the new integrated ones.[5]

As the Girl Scout national organization tentatively and haltingly moved toward antiracist policies after *Brown*, the feelings of white people were often prioritized over civil rights: the fear of white families who wanted to pull their girls from troops and camps, the exhaustion of white staff who had to try to find housing for Black delegates, the sensitivity of local white people whose customs were upset, and the reluctance of white staff to raise difficult issues and thus create uncomfortable situations. These feelings often took precedence over the fact of continued segregation or over concern about inequity or attempts to rectify unfair practices of white supremacy. An exchange among staff in 1965 illuminates this overarching focus on white feelings. On a summer day, a member of the Girl Scout public relations staff, Gertrude Simpson, received a phone call from a woman who had been hired to teach folk singing and dancing to a troop in Hot Springs, Virginia. While there, this woman found out there was another troop nearby that was entirely Black; she was calling the national headquarters because she was concerned about the segregated troops and wanted to "find out our policies in this matter and to ask advice." Simpson noted:

> I talked with her at some length explaining that while Girl Scouting is open to all girls there are places where segregated troops still exist, but that progress, while slow, is considerable. She sounded intelligent, not at all belligerent and truly troubled by the situation she had found in Hot Springs. I suggested that she get in touch with the president of the council and explain her concerns. I said I was sure that the president could interpret the situation and that possibly the community was in the process of school integration for the first time and that the segregated troops might be vestiges of an old pattern.[6]

It's fascinating to see how the Girl Scout leadership deflects the caller's concerns, suggesting that she might just not have "understood" the situation, and places the responsibility for addressing the problem on the caller, not on the national organization. It's also interesting but not surprising that she says the caller was "not at all belligerent," as Black people, particularly Black people who speak up for themselves, have historically been accused of being "belligerent." The verbal confrontation over racism here is more important than the segregation that the caller had uncovered. The "problem" was the caller, possibly Black, who fails to understand the Girl Scouts. The "problem" got solved because the woman from the national office could hang up the phone after pawning the caller off on someone else. In the meantime, the reality of the continued segregation could be dismissed, "interpreted," and disregarded, all in the name of ending what Simpson described as a "difficult and touchy phone call."

The pressure on the organization from those who wanted Girl Scouting to be truly inclusive continued to grow throughout the 1960s. If the national organization was anxious about white parents who threatened to pull their girls from scouting, it was also feeling pressure from those who felt increasingly impatient with the Girl Scouts' "hands-off" approach to segregation. In 1965, Janet Jones from Prairie View, Texas, wrote to the national president of the Girl Scouts expressing concern about the "segregation and discrimination in the camping program of the San Jacinto Council. . . . As I look at their brochure 'Summer Fun at Camp 1965' and see the many statements of restriction ('open to White girls only,' 'open to Negro girls only'), I really wonder what has happened to the principles of scouting. . . . What are the Girl Scouts of 1965 supposed to stand for?" She added, "I suppose that with pressure and mass protest, the segregation and discrimination could be checked, but why should the Girl Scouts have to be pushed and pressured? Why can't they lead? . . . I've supported Girl Scout projects and have encouraged the participation of many girls in scouting until now, but I feel that to continue to do this would be to contribute to the conservation of a demoralizing system." Jones does not identify her race or ethnicity in her letter, but her disgust at seeing the continued segregation of girls is clear. Indeed, *she* is the one who is now threatening to pull girls out of scouting due to the organization's continued segregation.[7]

Girls and leaders wrote to the national organization about the near-total lack of representation of minority girls in the handbooks. Girls in Houston refused to sell Girl Scout cookies for an organization that practiced discrimination, despite their council's admonishment to be "sisterly" and tolerate the segregated camps.[8] Girl Scouts in high school convened a series of Speak Outs that emphasized the need to challenge "prejudice." And staff members continued to voice their concerns, from the two outreach staff members who urged the national organization to rethink its relationship with the Bureau of Indian Affairs ("a source of oppression for American Indians") to the senior staff member who in 1968 called the organization's bluff regarding its poor excuse for an almost all-white staff: "I have become increasingly worried and depressed about the relative absence of persons of darker-skinned minority ethnic groups in executive and other positions at National Headquarters. Such poor ethnic group balance is not healthy and gives us second-rate status as a dynamic, progressive organization." The staff member continued, "I mean *real* integration; a statement that Girl Scouting is 'open to all' in the Blue Book is not enough. *Not enough.* I have been told that there is a lack of qualified and willing Negroes to work at National Headquarters. But I do not believe it. Without casting any doubt on the integrity of the Personnel Department or any individual, I believe we have not tried hard enough to recruit."[9] The frustration within the organization at the delays, excuses, redirections, and distractions regarding integration came to a head at the 1969 convention.

After the 1969 Convention

The 1969 convention, with its glaring omission of girls and women and color, both sparked a public outcry and made at least some white board members recognize the deep, seemingly intractable racism that plagued the organization. As a result, some white board members voluntarily resigned before their terms were up, freeing up immediate space for a group of African American, Asian American, Hispanic, and American Indian women to replace them. The new members included Dr. Dorothy Ferebee (who became a vice president), Minnie Finley, Jeanne Noble, Gloria Scott, Mrs. Wilbert Ricard, and Mrs. Henry Smith. They would work with Black members of the staff, including Grace Pleasants, director of the program department, and Harriet Faulkner, recruiter in the personnel department, to launch a special national conference in Atlanta the following year on Girl Scouting for Black girls, the first of a series of special conferences that would focus on Black girls, Mexican American girls, Native American girls, and girls in migrant communities. What is significant about these specialized conferences is that they would be organized *by* and *for* the minority women and girls themselves with resources from the national board but also that they would give some bite to the new Action 70 plan.

Action 70 was an initiative that emerged after the series of Speak Outs by Senior Girl Scouts in 1968 to make Girl Scouts more of an "agent for change"; while this sounds good on the surface, the reality was that each council could choose to focus on different areas, such as "knowing individuals of different religions, races and nationalities," "caring for and defending the specialness of difference," and "being involved in my community with its needs and with its people." Severely undercutting the impact of the Action 70 plan was the fact that each council could interpret what this meant for itself, which we know historically has meant that white power and voices could continue unchecked. Even the *Seattle Daily Times* noted, "Unless the convention directs some form of compliance, the implementation or ignoring of the program will be left to individual councils."[10] The "compliance" that some advocated, particularly the group of African Americans who had come before the national board, was the addition of this important clause to the by-laws: "A girl of any race, nationality, religion, or cultural background shall be eligible for membership in any Girl Scout troop." This clause was key, as it went beyond the Girl Scout constitution, which read, "We affirm that the Girl Scout movement shall ever be open to all girls and adults who accept the Girl Scout Promise and Law," which actually de facto allowed for extensive discrimination. In other words, the proposed change would mean the end to the accepted practice of allowing individual troops to exclude girls as long as there was some troop somewhere that would take them. Glaringly, however, the addition of the "compliance" clause was defeated with a show of hands during the 1969 convention, despite the active voices of those advocating for it.[11]

Official Girl Scout histories often refer to Action 70 as a transformational plan to eliminate prejudice, but the ways that councils could tackle this was so broad and vague it was frequently meaningless, yet another point in time that the Girl Scout organization collected whatever range of information individual councils chose to share and then did nothing with it. So the insistence that there be a series of smaller conferences *by and for* girls and women of color, such as the 1970 Atlanta Conference on Scouting for Black Girls, was actually quite meaningful. The pressure of these meetings, along with a change in the board, meant that over the years the board itself bypassed a vote by the national convention and insisted on significant policy changes. In 1972, Girl Scout president Grace McNeil announced that the national board had added the clause to the bylaws regarding troop membership and race that had been voted down in the 1969 convention; there would no longer be a loophole that allowed troops to discriminate against girls of color by sending them to "other" troops across the city or town. The board had used a loophole of its own, taken from the bylaws, that allowed it to bypass votes by the general membership in order to "clarify" policy. In this case, the board chose to prioritize the experiences of girls and women of color over the apparent objections of white members.[12] Further protecting the rights of members of color, in 1982, after years of pressure, the national board approved the motion that "the practice or advocacy of racism is inconsistent with the purposes of Girl Scouting and . . . any person who acknowledges membership in an organization which advocates or practices racism cannot become or remain a leader or member of Girl Scouts of the USA."[13] For the first time in its history, the national council finally and unambiguously stated that it would remove any girl or adult who was identified as part of a racist organization. Previously, as we have seen, the national organization deflected all decisions to the local level, which generally meant that the beliefs and policies of white people in power could prevail.

Throughout the 1970s the visible face of Girl Scouting changed dramatically. In 1975, the board elected its first African American president, Dr. Gloria Scott. Only thirty-seven when she came to office, Scott had grown up as a Girl Scout in a segregated Houston council. She attributed much of her own success—as a scientist, a leader in higher education, and someone with a PhD from the University of Indiana—to scouting, despite the segregation and the prohibitive cost of the uniform and dues, which she had to earn on her own. While a college student, she met the women already heavily active in Girl Scouting who would encourage her to take on regional and national roles as well: Dr. Dorothy Ferebee, Dorothy Height, and Dr. Jeanne Noble. In 1969, Scott was elected to the national board; in 1972 she was elected as vice president and in 1975, as president. Her election brought accolades and congratulations from feminist politicians such as Bella Abzug, from Vernon Jordan at the

The first African American president of the Girl Scouts of the USA, Gloria Scott, here pictured at the National Women's Conference in 1977. Scott explicitly engaged with feminism and the civil rights movement, a reversal from decades of earlier Girl Scout policy. © Diana Mara Henry. Diana Mara Henry Collection, Robert S. Cox Special Collections and University Archives Research Center, University of Massachusetts Amherst Libraries.

National Urban League, from major Black media outlets such as *Essence* magazine, from prominent Democrats such as Hubert Humphrey, and from Black scouts, such as the former Golden Eaglet who wrote, "You know how proud I must feel about your achievement because I know that when a black woman reaches such a goal, she has prepared herself, doubly, for the position." Even conservatives, such as US senator Strom Thurmond (who had voted against the Civil Rights Act of 1964) and the director of the National Council of Catholic Women, sent their congratulations.[14]

Scott was more than just a role model and symbol of diversity. As board member, vice president, and president, she brought a perspective to Girl Scouting that encouraged an explicit engagement with feminism and the civil rights movement. She eschewed the long-standing practice in the Girl Scouts, established by Juliette Gordon Low, to ignore anything that could be construed as "political." In anticipating the Girl Scouts' role in the contemporary struggles of the nation, she explained, it was important to "understand the difference between the words political and partisan and thereby not let the decade of the international women's year and contemporary women's movement pass us by."[15] For Scott, it was crucial that the Girl Scouts challenge the practice of being "nonpolitical" that had so fully hidden power inequities and racism. Under her presidency, the Girl Scouts worked closely with the Urban League and the NAACP. Her leadership also swayed the organization to endorse the Equal Rights Amendment (ERA) in 1977, a move that created controversy but that Scott firmly embraced. The National Women's Political Caucus wrote to Scott to thank her for the help they had received from the Girl Scouts in supporting the ERA.[16] With Scott's encouragement, the Girl Scouts represented themselves at the landmark Houston Women's Conference in 1977. Indeed, as a commissioner on the President's Commission on the Observance of International Women's Year, Gloria Scott opened the proceedings using a gavel that had supposedly belonged to Susan B. Anthony.[17] These were explicitly "political" positions of the Girl Scouts, even if they weren't, as Scott noted, "partisan."

Similarly, in the 1970s the Girl Scouts pressed the public face of its feminism by nominating Betty Friedan to the national board. The author of the 1963 *The Feminine Mystique* and the founding president of the National Organization for Women in 1966, Friedan was surprised when members of the executive board asked her to serve on the Girl Scouts. But she quickly agreed, noting that she was all about shaking up mainstream organizations like the Girl Scouts. Friedan told the *Detroit Free Press* that she was "amazed" to be asked to be on the board, but then "the more I thought of it, the more interesting it became. The modern women's movement believes in restructuring institutions."[18] Recalling her own Girl Scouting days in Peoria, Illinois, Friedan said, "I liked hiking and camping badges but passed up the ones for cooking and sewing."[19] She quickly became a lightning rod for controversy. Girl Scout leaders and adult members from across the country wrote to the national organization asking it to "reconsider" its decision to appoint someone who was such a "shocking contrast to the ideals of womanhood the Girl Scout program has long promoted."[20] There appeared to be an organized effort by Catholic women, who sent in concerned letters from across the country. But many of them seemed to be writing on their own, such as the woman who wrote, "My sisters and I were all Brownies and Girl Scouts and I never dreamed the officials would allow the frustrated, sick libber faction to infiltrate the Girl Scout beliefs."[21] The angry letters poured in to such an extent that the Girl Scout national organization took an inventory, describing in detail the contents of over twenty letters and petitions that challenged Friedan's ideas about birth control, abortion, marriage, religion, and the ERA.[22] It seems that this avalanche of negativity surprised the Girl Scouts, which is somewhat odd considering that the organization itself called Friedan the "mother of feminism" in its own publicity materials noting her election to the national board.[23] Like Friedan, Gloria Scott envisioned a bolder, less tepid organization; she championed the ERA, stood firmly with the feminist Women's Conference of 1977, and fought for an organization that centered the needs and desires of girls of color. In contrast to Friedan, however, Scott was herself an active Girl Scout, understanding the methods of working within the boundaries of this mainstream organization and tempering her remarks for public consumption. She understood the "care" needed to avoid a "degree of militancy such as could turn off prospective donors who are not in sympathy with the more aggressive feminist organizations," as one internal memo reminded the staff and board regarding a national Girl Scout campaign to conduct outreach for underrepresented girls. She understood, even if she tried to methodically challenge, how the Girl Scouts could both support the ERA and sometimes step back if the organization felt too much resistance locally.[24] Friedan, in contrast, was a firebrand. She had neither understanding nor tolerance of working within an institution, despite her stated interest in "establishment" organizations. She did not choose her words carefully and frequently went off-script in interviews, even suggesting (without any support from the national board) the possibility of restructuring the Boy and Girl Scouts into a "human scout movement."[25] By the time Friedan's position came up for renewal, the national organization chose to eliminate her name from the slate of possible nominees.[26]

Constant Push and Pull

The leadership styles of Gloria Scott and Betty Friedan illuminate how the Girl Scouts did not transform into an organization of radical change in the last decades of the twentieth century but instead sometimes pushed for feminist, antiracist movement and sometimes retreated sharply. Even when the national organization explicitly supported progressive change, it usually came with a caveat. For instance, in announcing its endorsement of the ERA, a letter from the national organization to local chapters read, "Subjects which may be controversial in one community may not be so in others. It is important that the council assess carefully the community's attitudes toward certain subjects in order to avoid attacks on the effectiveness of your program. What a community thinks about whatever activity a council engages is more important to the continued support of Girl Scouting than any existing regulations."[27] In other words, if there would be outcry about support of the ERA in a community, the national organization's endorsement could be disregarded. Not everyone was happy with this process, which they (correctly) identified as a strategy that prioritized the institution over the policy. As field associate Krystal Angevine wrote to the national organization, "Let us cease our reactionary habits in the name of self-preservation. Let us stand up for what is right. I believe that such action will not be our downfall. I believe we will be reborn."[28] But, in general, self-preservation won out.

Even *Ms.*, the popular feminist magazine begun by Gloria Steinem, weighed in on some of the pressures facing the Girl Scouts. In a 1976 cover story, "Father Schmidt v. the Girl Scouts," author Peggy Anderson explained that Senior Girl Scouts had in 1970 encouraged members of the Philadelphia Girl Scout Council to develop a prototype for a new badge, To Be a Woman, that would focus on female anatomy, health issues (including abortion and mastectomies), "lifestyle" issues, careers, and family.[29] Before the Philadelphia council could even begin publicizing the new badge, Father Schmidt, the director of youth services for the Philadelphia diocese, had voiced his objection to the badge. He was particularly concerned that he had not been consulted about the To Be a Woman badge, considering that so many Girl Scout troops met in Catholic churches. Quickly becoming a regional and even national controversy, the Philadelphia Girl Scout council backed down from the badge but refused to give the Catholic Church "say" over its programming. As a result, Schmidt ordered all Catholic Girl Scouts in the Philadelphia diocese to quit the organization and join the Camp Fire Girls instead, an organization he perceived to be more amenable to his demands. While some Catholic girls did join the Camp Fire Girls, other Catholic leaders and Girl Scouts resoundingly rejected his plea, simply joining troops that met outside of Catholic churches. *Ms.* readers weighed in, chastising both Schmidt and the Girl Scouts for their tepid response. One reader noted tellingly, "The saddest part of the whole Girl Scout issues has to be that no one has asked the Scouts themselves what they would like."[30] That wasn't exactly true—it was Senior girls themselves who had asked for and begun the development of the To Be a Woman badge—but the controversy quickly moved out of their hands and into those of the Catholic Church, which wanted control over definitions of womanhood and the sharing of information about women's bodies and lives. The Girl Scouts of the USA, which eventually rejected the badge, was concerned about controversy and wanted to maintain ties with the Catholic Church. Indeed, by 1975 the national organization had signed a "plan of cooperation" with the US Catholic Conference, agreeing to submit to the church for comment anything that might have a religious bearing. Disagreements were to be worked out on a local level and move to the state, regional, or national level only if cooperation could not be achieved, according to the agreement.[31]

What this "plan of cooperation" with the Catholic Church meant in practice varied widely. Some *Ms.* readers noted that it had had an extraordinarily chilling effect on Girl Scout programming. Two professional staff members from a Midwestern Girl Scout Council, who asked that their names be withheld from publication for fear of reprisal from their council, wrote of the "gross injustice to thousands of young women when the dictatorial maneuverings of a single individual and/or religious group can cause an organization to abandon a quality program." They added, "Because of the spineless response of the national office of the Girl Scouts, staff persons from ours and other councils have had their efforts to implement programs dealing with female identity and sexuality systematically thwarted."[32] But staff members from a Colorado council wrote to emphasize the fact that "developing and implementing local programs is the responsibility of local councils," which for them meant that a robust "Sex Education program has been available to troop members (Brownies-Seniors)," with "Sex Talks" facilitated by mental health professionals that provided "honest, factual, information about human growth and sexuality." They added that they also had programs on Black culture, Chicana culture, and the importance of developing self-confidence. Father Schmidt, they pointed out, had had no effect on the programming they could develop.[33]

Indeed, at the same time that Father Schmidt was orchestrating his attack on the Girl Scouts in Philadelphia, the Girl Scouts in Atlanta were offering radical sex education. The Northwest Georgia Girl Scout Council had partnered with Vicki Gabriner, a Jewish lesbian feminist, to direct its Education for Parenthood project. A committed activist, Gabriner had years of political action and writing under her belt before she joined with the Girl Scouts. In the early 1970s she was arrested for attempting to secure false identification for another member of the Weathermen, the radical leftist group. (Her conviction was overturned in 1978.) After coming out as a lesbian, she joined a women's commune in Atlanta and worked for years on feminist organizing from the ERA to antiracist legislation. She was explicit about the incest she had experienced as a young person in her book *Sleeping Beauty: A Lesbian Feminist Fairy Tale*, which she published with the feminist collective Sojourner Truth Press.[34] Not surprising, the sex education curriculum that she designed for Education for Parenthood was neither tepid nor obfuscating. Trained facilitators led teenagers in discussions of anatomy, violence, relationships, communication, pleasure, heterosexuality, homosexuality, birth control, and abortion in their Human Sexuality for Teenage Women course. Some troops devoted entire weekend camping trips to the human sexuality program, which paid close attention to the feelings of embarrassment many young women felt and the levels of ignorance they faced. The Girl Scouts even offered the six-week program to other organizations, including schools, churches, and other youth groups.[35] It's not clear when—or whether—the program ended, but there is no evidence in the records that the Catholic Church and its attempt to squash discussion about sexuality had any effect on this program. Like so many aspects of the Girl Scouts, these two realities could coexist: the conservative shutdown of any hint of sexuality education in Philadelphia and the robust, liberal programs in Denver and Atlanta, one of which was run by a radical lesbian feminist. The primary question for the national Girl Scout organization was whether a program attracted controversy or caused white girls to withdraw; if not, the program could go on freely.

Frances Hesselbein and a Corporate Vision of the Girl Scouts

In nonprofit institutions, there are two levels of organization: the all-volunteer board and the paid staff. For the Girl Scouts, this is true at the national level all the way down to the most local level, where there is paid council and camping staff but also a plethora of troop leaders and council board members who volunteer their time prodigiously. At the national level, the highest-level professional position is today the chief executive officer, which before 2002 was known as the national executive director, the national director, or during Girl Scouts' earliest days, the national secretary. In 1976, during Gloria Scott's tenure as board president (a volunteer position), the board hired a new national executive director, Frances Hesselbein, who would shape the organization for almost fifteen years into a tighter, more corporate entity. Born in 1915, Hesselbein hailed from Johnstown, Pennsylvania, and had led her daughter's Girl Scout troop in the 1940s and '50s before becoming a member of the council board in the '60s and early '70s. She believed in hard work (the story was that she had had to drop out of college to support herself and her family when her father died during the Great Depression, which indelibly marked her with a sense of responsibility and purpose), and she had a clear sense of the importance of girls' organizations. She was no radical activist, however, and she looked and talked like the relatively conservative white woman she was. When she took over the reins of the Girl Scouts, she pushed for more emphasis on pluralism than sharp critiques of the racial history of Girl Scouting. She insisted that the Girl Scouts start tracking race and ethnicity more carefully, so that the organization could extend outreach. She insisted as well on the significance of representation, ensuring that on every Girl Scout cookie box, on every calendar, and even in the ubiquitous trefoil symbol, girls would find images that resembled them. And, indeed, looking back at the cookie boxes from this time, one begins to see that the images shift from an idealized white girl to a mix of girls, of different shapes, races and ethnicities, and abilities, with girls in wheelchairs and with obvious disabilities.

I met Hesselbein for an interview in 2017 at her offices in Manhattan, where at age 102 she still showed up multiple times a week, with carefully coiffed hair and wearing a stylish suit and Clinique lipstick, to conduct interviews and lend a hand at the consulting business she had started after she left the Girl Scouts in 1990. For almost two hours we talked about the ideas she implemented during her tenure with the Girl Scouts: a focus on pluralism, a shift from camping and nature to science and business, and above all, development of leadership skills in everyone from the girls in the littlest age groups to the high-level staff she oversaw. Even at over 100 years old, Hesselbein was forceful, engaging, and charismatic; one can see why she became a legendary director of the Girl Scouts and sought-after speaker and writer.[36] What struck me the most in our conversation was something she *didn't* say, however. When I asked her how feminism had influenced her vision of the Girl Scouts in the 1970s and '80s and the work she did there, she just looked at me and shook her head vociferously *no*. "We didn't use that word," she added (and she never did say the "f-word" in our conversation). "We had a very simple mission to help each girl reach her own highest potential" in work, in governance, and in service. She then added, "My gender does not define my leadership."[37] Under Hesselbein's leadership, the Girl Scouts continued to lean on a strategy of deflection, one that had been a trademark since the early days with Juliette Gordon Low. Her strategy: Focus on girls' empowerment, provide opportunities, but never explicitly say or name feminism. Hesselbein was the perfect leader in this way, an image of white conservatism who could push for pluralism and empowerment with a smile on her face.

It's not that the Girl Scouts rolled back gains regarding racial inclusion and feminism in the late 1970s and 1980s. Rather, they became tightly packaged in a corporate structure, with an "empowering" but simultaneously bland enough image that would arouse no "suspicions." Even when the Girl Scouts did adopt new, progressive policies they carefully maintained their historic image of American patriotism and liberalism. In 2003, the same year that Kathy Cloninger, another dynamic leader, took the helm of the Girl Scouts, the organization voted to make the word "God" optional in the Girl Scout Promise. The Promise, at the time and still to this day, reads:

> On My Honor, I will try:
> To serve God and my country,
> To help people at all times,
> And to live by the Girl Scout Law.

The Promise is key to the experience of Girl Scouting; it's the pledge that girls and adults recite in ceremonies, usually while holding up the middle three fingers of the right hand. For years, especially in the last decades of the twentieth century, the Girl Scout organization had received letters from girls who didn't want to say the word "God" in the Promise. Either their families were atheist or perhaps agnostic or they came from a religious tradition such as Islam or Hinduism that would use a word different from "God." The national organization encouraged local communities to be generous with girls, to allow them to imagine whatever kind of "spirituality" they wanted to embrace when saying the word "God." Still, however, they needed to say the Promise, including the word "God." By the early 1990s, councils across the country were finding the situation untenable, and in 1993 delegates at the national convention, held in Minneapolis that year, voted 1,560–375 to allow flexibility in the wording. Individual girls might choose "Great Spirit" or "Allah" or any other term as long as it was done respectfully. The vote made news in both the *New York Times* and the *Los Angeles Times*, which reported that the Girl Scouts voted to allow the flexibility to acknowledge "growing religious and ethnic diversity among the nation's 2.6 million Girl Scouts." The newspapers quoted LaRae Orullian, the national Girl Scout president, who opined, "It's a very strong statement that Girl Scouts continue to be on the cutting edge, and this is a continuing effort to show that we do have strength in diversity and that we are an inclusive organization."[38]

As the Girl Scouts expected, letters poured in from around the country. Many Catholics and evangelicals voiced strong opposition, even organizing letter-writing campaigns from Brownies and Junior scouts that voiced their demand "to please leave only God in. That's the Bible way." A country commissioner from Easton, Maryland, sent back her Girl Scout sash and pins to the national organization, writing that "making God optional is an invitation to tyranny."[39] Others explained they were forbidding girls to join, ejecting troops from their churches, and refusing to buy Girl Scout cookies or to donate to the United Way because it gave financial support to the organization. They voiced their concern about the Girl Scouts' supposed advocacy of lesbianism, its requirement to "tithe" to progressive causes, and the fact that cookie sales supported sexual promiscuity. The national organization responded with a reasoned voice, explaining that "God" was still in the Promise, that a diverse nation meant the Girl Scouts needed to be flexible because it was a nonsectarian organization, and that there was no "tithing" to lesbian organizations or promotion of sexual promiscuity.[40] It was indeed a very "Girl Scout" move: to maintain the structure of conservatism (keeping God in the Promise) but allowing *individuals* flexibility that supported an American belief in diversity and respect.

If the 1960s and 1970s brought an implosion from within the Girl Scouts, when the push for feminism and civil rights had found its way into the organization and shaken it up tremendously, by the 1990s the institution had reframed itself, carefully (re)constructing an image of Americanness that allowed some change from within, but on an individualized basis that allowed the organization to take cover as necessary. Compared to the Boy Scouts of America, which dug in its heels on the importance of God, the rejection (and ejection) of homosexuals, and a casual acceptance of whiteness and patriotism, the Girl Scouts looks downright radical in the last decades of the twentieth century. As it had from its origins, the Girl Scouts provided a space for girls to stretch their wings and promised a generous inclusivity in terms of race and creed; it did this, however, by maintaining a facade of patriotism and neutrality, by relying on strategies of individualism and localism, and by eschewing any kind of controversy. The organization wouldn't even use the word "feminism." In some ways, these strategies allowed many girls and women access to an organization they might not otherwise have had access to, one that gave them opportunities, encouraged confidence, and generated critical thinking. At the same time, these strategies—of containment, of hiding progressivism if it caused controversy, and of using language that was often so bland it was meaningless—really limited what the Girl Scouts could do. Depending on the council and the troop, girls could be "empowered" without understanding or learning how to challenge the sexism and violence they faced in greater society. It could mean that girls of color were given "opportunities" without the tools to really understand the oppression and discrimination their communities faced (including within the Girl Scouts). And for white girls, it could train them in a racialized innocence that created a complicity with racism and an inability to even see the racist structures that surrounded them. All of this—the empowerment and the complicity—was true for me, a young white girl in the 1970s who came from a conservative, Midwestern, middle-class family. I turn to my own story in the next chapter to illuminate how the history of this national institution worked out on the ground for one girl in Akron, Ohio.

Chapter 10

An Active Education in Forgetting

MY 1975 PILGRIMAGE TO THE JULIETTE GORDON LOW BIRTHPLACE AND THE GIRL SCOUT PLANTATION

••••••

It is the innocence that constitutes the crime.
—James Baldwin, 1962

At the end of seventh grade, when I was twelve years old, my Cadette Girl Scout troop loaded ourselves onto a "deluxe" coach bus to take an eleven-hour trip from Akron, Ohio, to Savannah, Georgia. The forty of us were going to the Juliette Gordon Low Birthplace, the national destination for Girl Scouts all over the country. At that time, there were more than 3.5 million registered Girl Scouts, over 20,000 of whom visited the Juliette Gordon Low Birthplace on a yearly basis.[1] By the time we embarked on this trip, I had been active in scouting for years, with weekly Girl Scout meetings, weekend camping trips, and longer stays at Camp Ledgewood in the summer. My experiences in Girl Scouting had really improved my life, changing me from a bullied nine-year-old into a lively, much more confident girl who was making this trip to Savannah. Girl Scouts had given me a best friend (who is still one of my very closest friends), a group of girls and women who created a community where I felt much less shy and much more confident, and a slew of badges and pins on my sash that spoke to new skills (baking, writing, ice skating, hiking, camping, traveling, hospitality, first aid). I was proud of all those pins and patches.

A few years after this trip to Savannah I'd even go on a flight by myself to Washington, DC, for a Girl Scout bicentennial, "Wider Opportunity," staying in a dorm at George Washington University with other girls from across the country. Yet it was the weeklong "pilgrimage" to Savannah that stands out in my memory, maybe because of the group photo I mentioned in the first chapter of this book, water stained and damaged but still showing us on the steps at the Juliette Gordon Low Birthplace. It is almost a replica of the publicity photo taken during the opening ceremony for the Birthplace in the 1950s. There we stand, three by three, on the stately steps to Juliette Gordon Low's home, our leaders in front, all of us in uniform, green-and-white outfits replete with sashes and pins that we had to keep sharp and crisp until this photo was taken. We look happy, satisfied, and proud—like we *belong*. The special Daisy pin we received after visiting the Birthplace cemented this feeling. We toured the house, learned about the historical furniture, and heard funny stories about the boisterous and animal-loving girl that Low had been. We took part in a pinning ceremony in the garden, seeing the iron gates Low had forged herself. We wandered the neighborhood surrounding the Birthplace, eyeing the many "Gordon" squares, street names, and historical plaques that emphasized how important this woman's family was in history. Juliette Gordon Low, we learned in so many ways, clearly came from a "fine" family, and she used that position to create something wonderful: the Girl Scouts.

As our heads were filled with details about Low's life, the history of her family, and the early days of the Girl Scouts, there was one grand omission: We learned nothing about race or slavery. Indeed, our travels to Georgia, and to South Carolina, where we stayed en route, were an explicit education in not knowing, a prime example of what historian Karen Cox, in her book *Dreaming of Dixie*, described as Lost Cause mythology. This mythology shaped itself into a burgeoning industry of twentieth-century Southern tourism and popular culture, an endless array of novels, movies, popular songs, and fashion articles that idolized the images of white Southern belles, magnolia-trimmed plantations, stately homes, and chivalrous planters. For Southerners, these cultural tropes and tourist destinations clearly worked as symbols of the Lost Cause, legitimizing the Confederacy. But, as Cox explains, Northerners were also invested in this fantasy and often were at the helm of manufacturing this imaginary of the antebellum South. White Northerners and Southerners shared an insatiable appetite for this vision of the past, one that worked as a balm against what they saw as the problems of twentieth-century life: immigration, urbanization, and above all, the threat of Black people. White supremacy was at the root of this fantastical image of the past, even though that often is

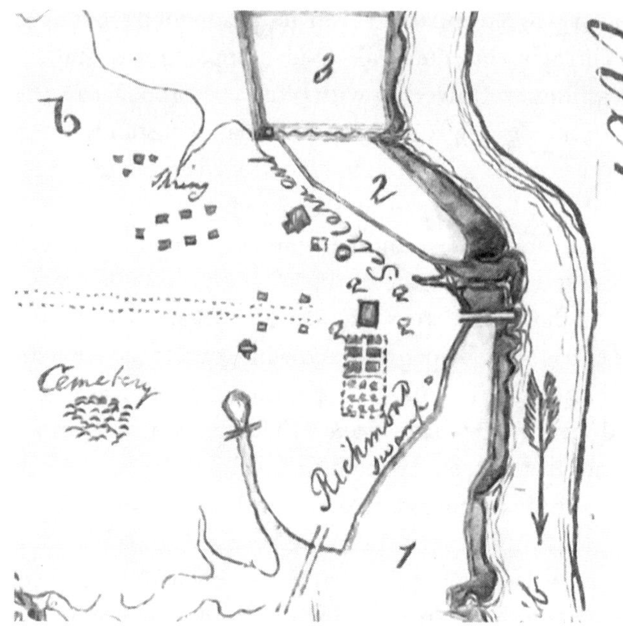

A map of the site of Richmond Plantation. My troop was camping near the slave quarters, a fact neither recognized nor acknowledged on my trip. From 1790 Charleston County Register of Mesne Conveyance, South Carolina Department of Archives and History, Charleston.

not explicitly spoken; it is a world where Black people are happy as mammy figures and childish characters and who do not make political, economic, or cultural demands. Indeed, Black people often show up only sparingly in this fantasy, an absence only recognized insofar as someone's labor produced the wealth from which the planters and rich townspeople profited, sewed the beautiful dresses, landscaped the grounds, and maintained the houses.[2]

Our entire trip was a Dixie dream. Indeed, before we even arrived in Savannah to visit the Juliette Gordon Low Birthplace, we stopped in Charleston, South Carolina. There, we spent a day wandering the cobblestoned streets, eyeing the regal townhomes, and stopping in souvenir shops. The highlight was the carriage rides; we had carefully budgeted enough money to ensure that everyone could buy a ticket to climb onto a fancy carriage seat, where we laughed at the driver's jokes and listened to his stories of Charleston lore—a little history, a few ghost stories, and some architectural references—as we toured the old town.

After we left Charleston our coach bus bumped westward toward what we excitedly referred to as the Girl Scout Plantation, an overnight camp located on the eastern branch of the Cooper River in South Carolina, where we would spend two nights before heading to Savannah. Our excitement about staying at a "real" plantation hit a wall of reality when we realized that only

A map showing all the plantations along the Cooper River in South Carolina in 1842. Richmond Plantation, on which Camp Lowcountry (or the Girl Scout Plantation, as I knew it) was built, is located at the top, center right of this map. National Register of Historic Places, Cooper River Historic District, Berkeley County, South Carolina, 2002.

a few leaders and girls would be staying in the fancy manor house; most of us would overnight in the carriage house, an extremely large concrete block building lined with bunk beds. We also didn't realize we would be sharing our space with thousands of palmetto bugs, cockroaches that scurried into our sleeping bags and suitcases when we flicked on the lights. There is something simultaneously so poignant and unsettling to me about that memory: the leaders who agreed to keep on the blazing overhead lights all night to allay our fear of the bugs, coupled with a steadfast group desire to maintain the fantasy of this as a desirable retreat. We enviously laughed about those who were lucky enough to land a spot in the "manor house" instead of the bug-infested carriage house. But nothing made us question the overall facade of this genteel, Southern past.

In writing this book, I thought perhaps I had misremembered the name, or perhaps our overactive middle school imaginations had called it the "Girl Scout Plantation." But then, in a stroke of extreme research serendipity, an archival volunteer at the Northeast Ohio Girl Scout Archives found our Troop 811 scrapbook, and I saw it for myself: a mimeographed information sheet titled "The History of the Girl Scout Plantation." I had remembered correctly; this was indeed the name of the camp where we had stayed en route to the Juliette Gordon Low Birthplace.

Its official name was actually Camp Lowcountry. The Girl Scouts of Eastern South Carolina had bought the land in the 1960s, the site of an eighteenth-and-nineteenth-century rice plantation. Included in my Troop 811 scrapbook was an information sheet about the Girl Scout Plantation, which I suspect I read scrupulously as a twelve-year-old Girl Scout. It described the place as a "153 acre fairyland rich in Carolina Lowcountry plant and animal life, where 18th century belles once strolled the terraces sweeping down to the Cooper River." It further described "an avenue of magnificent live oaks," a "13 room English Manor House, commanding a breathtaking view over lawns to the river," and "an antique mantlepiece dated 1618." The Girl Scouts of Eastern South Carolina paid for it, the article explained, with "carefully saved profits from annual Girl Scout cookie sales" so that girls could enjoy the "beauty and wonders of Carolina Lowcountry life," where people descended from an "old and illustrious family" from England once lived, some of the first settlers of South Carolina.[3] Here was nature, a beautiful landscape, historical architecture, prominent families, and British heritage, all purchased with the profits of a Girl Scout cookie sale. It was a perfect example of the imaginary of the Lost Cause that Karen Cox described. For, indeed, not only did this narrative collapse time periods into a hazy notion of the "past" (the Girl Scouts of the 1970s, the 1930s manor house, the eighteenth-century belles, and timeless "nature" all seem to occupy the same moment), but this information sheet completely erased the Indigenous people who had lived on this land before being pushed west as well as the enslaved people who had built and maintained the plantations that fueled the original wealth of these families.

While the story I learned from the information sheet we were given when we traveled to the Girl Scout Plantation constructed a mythology of beauty and prominence, it also held clues to a different narrative. Taking as inspiration Tiya Miles's breathtaking book *All That She Carried: The Journey of Ashley's Sack, a Black Family Keepsake*, in which she carefully traces the life of three generations of African American women through the found object of a nineteenth-century cotton bag, I thought I might try to find out more about the people who had worked on the plantation through this 1970s memento of my Girl Scout trip.[4] My research assistant and I pored over that sheet to find the strands of a buried history, one that would explode the Dixie myth. The Girl Scout Plantation, also known as Camp Lowcountry, was formerly Richmond Plantation. Situated on the eastern branch of the Cooper River, the plantation was one of dozens that lined the entire river. The primary crop on these plantations was rice, grown through the extraordinarily labor-intensive process of tidal irrigation. Enslaved people cleared the fields, dug ditches, and built extensive systems of levees (also known as trunks), which they had to manually open and close on a daily basis and maintain carefully to thwart the constant erosion caused by flooding. Planters relied on the expertise and knowledge of the enslaved to build and maintain these complicated systems. In addition, the rice fields required intensive weeding, as other plants also flourished in the tidal fields, threatening the health of the rice.[5] The mosquitoes were so bad on these tidal rice plantations that the white families fled to town in the summer, leaving enslaved people behind to continue tending the rice amid attacks by mosquitoes. They also grew corn, potatoes, and peas; raised horses, sheep, and cows; built bricks to be sold in town; and cut trees from the surrounding forests. Every season brought with it significant labor, as the plantation owner and overseer switched from rice and vegetables in the spring and summer to brick-building and forest clearing in the winter. And animals required tending year round.

Richmond Plantation was one of the largest and most prosperous plantations on the Cooper River in the eighteenth and nineteenth centuries.[6] The other plantations along the river were owned by interlocking groups of families, cousins, and in-laws, many of whom were descendants and relatives of the Harleston family from England, who had settled the region in the late seventeenth century and whom our mimeographed sheet referenced. Enslaved people did all the labor on this extraordinarily profitable estate. Their names and stories are absent from the Girl Scout materials and histories I read as a girl in the 1970s, but by searching for the names of the white families and historical preservation materials on the buildings, one can find glimpses into their lives.

Government records on the white owners offer some information about how many enslaved people lived at Richmond. The 1785 estate of John Harleston listed four slaves, a number that historians Louise Bailey and Elizabeth Cooper suggest should be taken as a conservative estimate, considering poor recordkeeping, the desire to quickly transfer ownership to avoid taxation, and the fact that these owners often maintained multiple plantations and moved enslaved people between them.[7] When the heir to Harleston's estate died just several years later in 1793, the number had grown tremendously, with at least 138 enslaved people living on the property.[8] The 1800 census listed at least 100 slaves living on the estate, which at that point was owned by Edward Rutledge.[9] When Rutledge's son Nicholas died, Richmond Plantation was passed to Dr. Benjamin Huger, the husband of Sara Rutledge, Nicholas's sister. The slave schedule of the 1860 US census lists Huger as owning 154 enslaved people. Their names are not listed on the schedule, but their ages are. As of 1860, Huger owned people ranging in age from a baby girl (listed as one-twelfth of a year old) to a sixty-seven-year-old man and a sixty-nine-year-old woman.[10] Huger is listed as owning an additional eleven people at his Charleston home, five women, five men, and a boy of thirteen.[11]

In this community of landowners, almost all related by blood or marriage on and around the Cooper River, the numbers are overwhelming. On the 1800 census page that lists Edward Rutledge, for instance, of the twenty-five names before and after his, every white head of family lists a small number of free white people who live in that household, usually no more than four or five. But each of these relatively small white families owned enslaved people. A few list just one or two enslaved people, most list over twenty, and many list more than 100 enslaved people. One family, for instance, owned 235 people. It takes a long time to scroll through a long list such as the one from 1860 that shows Benjamin Huger's government accounting of the 154 people he enslaved. Lingering on the sexes and ages of the people literally took my breath away, seeing in such cold detail the bedrock of brutality on which this wealth was built, so carefully erased by the publicity materials we received as visiting girls in the 1970s. That information sheet about the "153 acre fairyland" said nothing about the 154 enslaved people.

A journal kept by Huger's overseer, Anthony Weston, from 1859 to 1860 provided yet another view into the world of Richmond Plantation. Weston kept a daily accounting of the work done by enslaved people, whom he called "the Negroes" or "the hands." We learn some of the enslaved people's names, or at least the names that Weston used, as he described the ditches they dug, the babies they bore, and the punishments they suffered. The work was relentless and seven days a week for Affee, Anthony, Benego, Big Tony, Billy, Bina, Carpenter Sam, Cloe, Cornelia, Cyrus, Delia, Dina, Ellick, Ellie, Grace, Handy, Hector, Jack, Jak, John, Jose, Juda, Juiet, Margaret, Martha, Morris, Moses, Peggy, Peter, Pino, Racheal, Rock, Sally, Sarah, Simon, Thomas, Toby, and William. They dug ditches, repaired trunks (levees), cleared ground, planted crops, and butchered animals. Weston frequently moved the enslaved people between Huger's various properties or leased them to other white people. About once a week he reported giving a ration of grist (flour) to the enslaved, less frequently some rice, potatoes, or meat. Only once in the entire yearlong journal he says he gave the enslaved a day to "work for themselves"; the land was too wet for work on the rest of the plantation, which means it was a horrible day for the enslaved to work as well.

On June 15, 1859, Weston noted that he gave a cup of molasses to Dina, Delia, Peggy, Sarah, and Sally for their infants. Huger's possession of at least five women who had recently given birth puts the human picture into sharp relief of how Huger accumulated his wealth and prosperity.[12] Placing Weston's journal next to the census list, one wonders how old Dina, Delia, Peggy, Sarah, and Sally were. Were any of them one of the five thirteen- or fourteen-year-old girls that the census listed, about the same age that my Girl Scout troop was when we made our visit? Or were they eighteen-year-olds, just a few years older than we were? The contrast between the sexual violence that these girls must have faced and the protection we were accorded during our visit to the "Girl Scout Planation" is extraordinarily vivid.

Weston's journal also gives evidence of the brutal punishments the enslaved people faced on Richmond Plantation. We learn that on April 2, 1859, Weston "flogged" Cloe, and six weeks later, on May 17, "Runaway Billy" was caught, brought back to Richmond the next day, and "jailed," a likely reference to the notorious workhouses (prisons) where owners placed the enslaved to punish them. At these workhouses, the incarcerated faced starvation, flogging, paddling, and being tied to treadmills, where they had to labor continually, experiencing extraordinary injury if they stopped moving. Indeed, this may have been the infamous Charleston workhouse, where owners paid the city to punish enslaved people, a site we likely would have passed, unrecognized, on our tourist trip through the city.[13] On April 22, the overseer reported "sending Billy away," potentially meaning that he sold Billy, a way to remove anyone who might have encouraged insurrection and a punishment that painfully destroyed families. In January 1860 we read that Weston broke up a "Negro camp," a short entry that makes one wonder if a larger group of enslaved people were either organizing for resistance or creating community bonds in some other way. His mention of "breaking up" suggests but does not name the violence that surely went along with it.

All of these facts were absent in the fantasy offered to us when we visited the Girl Scout Plantation. We learned nothing of the sexual violence, the forced pregnancies, the brutal use of Black women's bodies to expand the wealth of the white owning class. While all of this formed the material basis for the "fairyland" of Richmond Plantation, it had no part in the tableau presented to and accepted by our Girl Scout troop as we drove up in our rented coach in 1975, passing by the unmarked site of the slave quarters that, according to a map of the 1790 grounds, had been situated just northwest of the carriage house where we camped.[14]

While we were active participants in this fantasy, Girl Scouts were not its creators. Besides an entire white Northern and Southern fixation on the graciousness of an antebellum South, as Cox described, this particular Richmond Plantation fantasy had been first romanticized even before the Civil War in John Beaufain Irving's 1842 *A Day on Cooper River* and then carefully maintained by George Ellis, a Yale-educated New York stockbroker, and his wife Florence in the twentieth century. After the Civil War, Richmond Plantation was sold to a number of families, who each in turn tried to maintain it as a rice plantation. Without enslaved labor, however, like most of the tidal rice plantations in the area, it ceased to function. Even the main house at Richmond was gone, burned by the time the Ellises bought it in the 1920s. George and Florence Ellis, with their extensive staff, remade Richmond Plantation into a hunting lodge and winter getaway. The Ellises built an English-style manor house, an extensive garden, horse stables, dog kennels, and outbuildings for their cars and yacht, symbols of a life of wealth and leisure reminiscent of British aristocracy and Southern planters. They entertained other Northern families who, likewise, had created faux plantations along the Cooper River.[15] After the Ellises died, their son sold the land to the West Virginia Pulp and Paper Company, as did the owners of many other of the compounds lining and surrounding the Cooper River.

And shortly thereafter, the Girl Scouts show up. In 1963, the Carolina Low Country Girl Scout Council of South Carolina (later renamed the Girl Scouts of Eastern South Carolina) purchased a portion of this land, encompassing the core of Richmond Plantation, from the West Virginia Pulp and Paper Company for $145,000. In 1973, a writer for the regional magazine *Sandlapper* wrote that "plantations have been bought and sold since the South was settled. They have been financed with the profits from cotton, rice, indigo, timber and other sources of revenue. But probably only one plantation in South Carolina was ever financed through profits from cookies." Using language that was clearly lifted almost verbatim from the Girl Scout material I had read as a young girl, the article continued: "The 153-acre fairyland was once the setting of balls and barbecues such as those from the pages of *Gone with the Wind*. Haunting melodies floated through the moss-draped live oak trees as Negro slaves trod the paths from their quarters to the cotton fields. The soil below the beautiful turf fronting the house was probably torn by horses' hooves as their riders spurred them off when leaving to join the Confederate Army." The author described the loving restoration of the "original buildings" and the rejuvenation of the splendid gardens. It is, she concluded, a tribute to "industrious girls" and the "humble cookie."[16] What is so fascinating about this article is the way it conjures up an "original" vision of a genteel Southern past, while in reality we and the thousands of other girls who went to the Girl Scout Plantation were actually visiting a replica, the remnants of an early twentieth-century Northerner reimagining an eighteenth-and-nineteenth-century plantation. This vagueness about authenticity is part of the joint Northern and Southern fantasy about preindustrial life, one in which white communities explicitly segregated and oppressed Black communities. And this story now becomes linked to a vision of wholesomeness and industriousness that further covers up the brutal process on which this country's wealth was built. The girls themselves and the Girl Scout cookies provide a veneer of innocence to gloss over centuries of enslavement.

Juliette Gordon Low Birthplace and Savannah

After our stay at the "Girl Scout Plantation" outside Charleston, we traveled south to visit the Juliette Gordon Low Birthplace and Savannah, walking through the beautiful squares and shopping for souvenirs at Factor's Row. We stayed at the Hilton DeSoto, a site of controversy, we learned, as the Hilton corporation had torn down the gracious historic building a few years earlier to make way for a modernized and air-conditioned new building. We learned nothing about race, enslavement, or the ongoing struggle for civil rights in this beautiful city and the stately birthplace of the Girl Scout founder. Much was actively ignored in the narratives we heard about Savannah and the Juliette Gordon Low Birthplace. The DeSoto Hotel, for example, was segregated through the 1960s, as were other major commercial sites in Savannah, integrated only after years of marches, sit-ins, and boycotts.[17] Even just a few years before we arrived, Black troops visiting the Juliette Gordon Low Birthplace would not have been able to stay at the hotel, and regional and national Girl

Scout offices simply ignored their complaints and requests for more information about safe and welcoming places to stay. Although the DeSoto was ostensibly desegregated by the time we arrived, I remember seeing no African American troops staying there, likely a legacy of the culture of Jim Crow that created an atmosphere of fear and violence that permeated every aspect of life in the city.

After the Civil War, the South cracked down on the promises of Reconstruction and the possibilities of integration with a system of segregation known as Jim Crow, policies, laws, and customs that were either ignored or endorsed by the North. In Savannah, poll taxes and violence at election sites prevented Black men (and then women after the passage of the Nineteenth Amendment in 1920) from voting. During Jim Crow, all Black people were excluded from city councils, juries, and the police. Housing, employment, public accommodations, and businesses all segregated or excluded African Americans. The threat of violence was continual; just six years after Juliette Gordon Low had made her call to her cousin to begin the Girl Scouts—an "organization for all girls"—a pregnant Black woman was brutally murdered by a white crowd outside of Savannah, lynched, hanged for public display, her fetus cut out and crushed. This reign of terror maintained a constant force of oppression on Black communities. Nevertheless, African Americans in Savannah continued to fight for their rights, their livelihoods, and their children. Black women were particularly important to these efforts, as clubwomen, as members of political organizations, and as founders of schools and orphanages. Even the famous Harriet Jacobs had in the early years after the Civil War lived in Savannah, working to educate young African Americans. Making our way through the mossy trees and beautiful squares, bunking pleasantly in the DeSoto Hotel, we never discussed this culture of Jim Crow or the tireless and courageous activism by African Americans to dismantle it. Indeed, we were immersed instead in the fantasy of a genteel South, a world more pleasant and beautiful than our own, where none of that struggle existed.

Some of that struggle actually surrounded Girl Scouting. Like many other cities across the United States, especially in but not limited to the South, Savannah had a tiered system of Girl Scouting, with a separate African American council that worked within, and under the direction of, the "main" council, which was all white. While Girl Scouts has liked to emphasize how diverse the original troops were in Savannah, this mainly pertained to religion, as the first troops included Protestant, Catholic, and Jewish girls. All the girls were white, however. Juliette Gordon Low's mother even urged her to explicitly exclude Black girls from the organization; while Low did not go this far, the organization had, as we saw in earlier chapters, clear policies to limit and segregate Black membership. But African American women in Savannah fought, just as they did elsewhere, for the right of their girls to participate, including in outdoor activities. Finding the local camps completely barred to them, they broke ground on their own camp, the Log Cabin Camp, in 1945.[18]

We never discussed these Jim Crow policies in my troop, or the civil rights activism that dismantled them in the 1950s and 1960s. And we never talked about the slavery that preceded segregation. Enchanted by the lovely city and busily buying souvenirs at Factor's Row, we were surrounded by the signs of enslavement to which we were blind. As a port city, Savannah was crucial to the importation and sale of enslaved people. Prior to the Revolutionary War, Governor James Edward Oglethorpe had tried to limit slavery, as he thought poor free white settlers, without African slaves, would do a better job of keeping out the Spanish and the Indians. This was a policy he eventually broke, as he relied on the labor of enslaved people, bringing them in from South Carolina, to lay out and build the gracious squares that distinguish the city, including Gordon Square, where the Juliette Gordon Low Birthplace is located. By the 1750s white settlers clamored for the right to own slaves, arguing that the economy could not grow without enslaved labor; in the years after the Revolutionary War, all restrictions had disappeared and Savannah became a robust port city, central to the slave trade. Cargo ships of enslaved people would arrive from Africa to Tybee Island, where they were temporarily quarantined and checked for disease before being moved along the Savannah River to the Port of Savannah, where they were sold either right there or on nearby plantations. In the antebellum years, Savannah was the third largest exporter of cotton in the country, just behind New Orleans and Mobile.[19] Factor's Row, where we did our souvenir shopping, was the crucial site of national and international trade in cotton, and the area where both Juliette Gordon Low's father and husband had key businesses. Every aspect of the economy in the city and its surrounding areas was explicitly grounded in a system of racialized slavery. Certainly the plantations were, as the crops in cotton, rice, and indigo were, completely dependent on enslaved labor. But so was every other aspect of the economy, from the labor to build the railroad (the other major business Low's family owned) to the work required to keep households running and the hands to staff shipping and ports.

In 1860, just a few years before Juliette Gordon Low's birth, about half of the inhabitants of Savannah were enslaved.[20] There was a small community of free Blacks—tailors, seamstresses, washerwomen, blacksmiths, seamen, barbers—who honed their skills and entrepreneurial spirit to forge a tight community that found particular strength in church, especially in Savannah's First African Baptist Church. But free Black people lived and worked under extreme white oppression: They were required to pay for work badges and have white people "oversee" and "license" their work; any white person could challenge the status of any Black person; and Black education was forbidden, which for free or enslaved Black people was punishable by whipping and imprisonment.[21] The number of freed people was dwarfed by the number of enslaved Black people in Savannah. Owners often moved enslaved people between their home in the city and the plantations as needed, and they could sell and punish the enslaved at their will. One of the most notorious sales of enslaved people happened in 1859, on a horse racecourse a few miles west of the city. Known as "the Weeping Time," the Philadelphian Pierce Mease Butler, who owned two plantations in Georgia, sold 429 enslaved people at the same time, the largest sale recorded in US history.[22] And while punishment could happen at the whim of an owner in any location, there was always the threat of the city jail for the enslaved. Just a five-minute walk from Low's home was the Chatham County Jail, where owners could pay the city to punish their enslaved with whippings, overwork, starvation, and deprivation.[23] Low's family owned a plantation just outside Savannah called Belmont, where they enslaved people, the railroad family business used enslaved labor, their businesses as cotton factors were dependent on enslaved labor, and their household on Gordon Square used enslaved people for all aspects of their lives, from nursing and caring for children and the elderly to cooking, cleaning, and tending to animals. They even served as playmates for Juliette. Early biographies of Low include "amusing" tales about these enslaved children and adults, and later the African American staff who populated Low's world, though these stories completely omit any reference to the horror of enslavement or the brutality of the system that supported it.

In laying out all that was there before us on the Girl Scout Plantation in South Carolina and at the Juliette Gordon Low Birthplace in Savannah, I can imagine some (predominantly white) readers challenging me: This was a different era! Was this information about slavery and Jim Crow even available to our troop or tour guides? And would this information have been appropriate for our ears?

I would answer thus: What did it mean that we were fed this fantasy? A Dixie myth of white Southern beauty, a fantasy that intermixed with our Girl Scout patriotism, our Girl Scout protofeminism, and our Girl Scout "innocence"? That is a powerful, dangerous conglomeration of ideologies, all of which serve to reinforce a myth of white righteousness and American purity.

Every aspect of the city we were taught to admire so much was built by enslaved people, which is consistently and conveniently forgotten (or more likely, excluded) from Girl Scout lore and history. The fact that Juliette Gordon Low's wealth came from enslavement was buried under stories of sweet summers playing with cousins and small animals, beautiful travels, and a desire to bring a boisterous energy to other girls. The fact that the Juliette Gordon Low Birthplace itself existed under a legacy of Jim Crow, so much so that the national organization had twisted the truth about the opening ceremonies, deeming them "regional" instead of "national" so that the *Blue Book* regulations about discrimination could be ignored—well, that was relatively recent history and something that the staff would have known. The details about Black life in Savannah—the Weeping Time, the lynchings, the continued push to create strong Black communities, including the Log Cabin Camp for African American girls that was built by Black people in Savannah—would have certainly been known to any local Black Girl Scouts. But we didn't meet any Black troops on our pilgrimage, a likely legacy of the segregation and practices of Jim Crow that were deeply engrained in Savannah and so many other places in the country.

As far as I remember, no one in my troop, leader or girl, asked questions about African American life, at least out loud. Instead, our heads were filled with minute details about the lives of plantation belles, historic furniture, pins and uniforms, and Gordon family ancestry. At the same time that we were developing skills and confidence to travel far from home and experiencing a visceral sense of belonging to an organization much larger than ourselves, we were also experiencing an active education in forgetting. We took the whiteness of our world at face value and believed in the oft-repeated original story about the "fine" family our founder came from, a worthy family, an accomplished family. And then an interesting slippage happened. We, mostly from working- and middle-class white Northern families, were supposed to identify with the belles of the plantation and this white, wealthy, Southern woman from the early twentieth century. She was worthy of her wealth. We were worthy of vicariously experiencing it, with the money we had earned through cookie sales and car washes. We were all innocent, a status carefully guarded by shielding us from information about race, enslavement, Jim Crow, and Black communities. We experienced an immersion in an ideology of white supremacy, white normalcy, and white erasure of history. We were being taught to actively ignore any signs—even when they were right in front of us—of the enslaved, of oppression, or of the connections between Northern racism and the history of slavery.

My pinning ceremony in the courtyard of the Juliette Gordon Low Birthplace, on our 1975 troop pilgrimage. I am third from left. Courtesy of the author.

This kind of explicit forgetting is key to understanding the entire ideology of American life and history, but it's instructive to drill down to see how it actually worked in the lives and experiences of millions of girls like me and my troop members. Our trip to Charleston and Savannah gave us skills, confidence, a powerful feeling of community, and a deep-seated trust in the beneficence of our roots and contemporary world. We were "innocent" yet proud girls who had paid for this trip with the purity of Girl Scout cookies and the hard work of car washes, in the same way that cookies had funded the purchase of the Girl Scout Plantation, in the same way that the Gordon family had financed the ownership of their plantation and the stately home on Gordon Square.

Defending the Birthplace

In 2013, the Girl Scouts of Eastern South Carolina decided to close and sell the Girl Scout Plantation/Camp Lowcountry due to the cost of keeping up the buildings and the decreased enrollment of girls in scouting. The articles and blog posts that former Girl Scouts wrote memorializing the camp, their adventures, and their friendships made no allusion to the deeper history of the plantation or the fact that this land was never the fantastical place of white Southern belles that it purported to be.[24] But in Savannah, the twenty-first century has brought about concerns about the ways girls experience the Juliette Gordon Low Birthplace. The constrained changes that the Girl Scout staff made in the home, though, generated significant resistance among those who cling to the myth of Juliette Gordon Low and her fine family.

Like it was for me and my Ohio troop, the Juliette Gordon Low Birthplace remains a crucial site of pilgrimage for girls across the nation. Indeed, one recent late afternoon, I heard a quiet knock on our front door in Pennsylvania—much too quiet to be UPS or FedEx. By the time I got to the door no one was there, but before I closed it a teenage girl popped into view, holding a bag and asking if I'd be interested in buying Girl Scout cookies. I realized the neighborhood was swarming with teen girls going up and down the street, bags of cookies in hand. As I fished out money to buy a box of Thin Mints, the bespectacled Senior Girl Scout, and then her leader, explained that they were using the money for their "trip to Savannah to see where Girl Scouts was founded." They had been saving for years, since early middle school, to pay for flights and lodging, which had now been booked. This year's cookie money was going to pay for their meals. I wished them a great trip as they rushed away to locate the other girls.

I could easily imagine their visit. Each day's activities would be carefully planned. They would spend some of it walking around the city, which would reward them with many iconic street names, monuments, and historic markers that underscore the importance of their founder's family and thus of the founder herself. The highlight of the visit would be the visit to the Birthplace. There would certainly be a picture taken of the troop on the stairs like the one I have of my troop in the 1970s. There would probably be a pinning ceremony in the garden, near the gates that Low forged herself. Inside, the visitors would walk through historic rooms, the tour guide likely stopping by the copy of Edward Hughes's 1880 portrait of Juliette, known then as Daisy, as a young woman. (The original is at the Smithsonian's National Portrait Gallery.) It's very likely that their walk up to the second floor to see Daisy's bedroom would feature stories inspired by the banister: how Daisy's energetic and lovely mom, who grew up in the frontier town of Chicago, met her father, a dashing young man from Savannah, at Yale, when she came flying down the banister into his arms, crushing his hat—or, the other one I heard when I visited in 2017, how Daisy's mom taught all the children to slide down the banister and even slithered down herself as an elderly woman, when the family thought she was on her deathbed.

There was one difference between my visit in the 1970s and the trip girls took in the twenty-first century: the library in the Birthplace. Until the mid-2010s, the library was a genteel space evoking culture and literary taste and included the very feminine youthful portrait of Daisy. When the new executive director of the Juliette Gordon Low Birthplace, Lisa Junkin-Lopez, took over, she wanted to move the Birthplace away from being a "house museum," pushing it instead to be a place of motivation, where girls could connect their present to the past, where they could be motivated by history to become the girls of "courage, confidence, and character" that the contemporary organization emphasizes. She changed programming (eliminating the tea and costume parties), worked to broaden the story (including doing archaeological work to identify where enslaved people and then servants would have worked and lived), and created interactive learning opportunities. This latter endeavor was mostly achieved by turning the family library into a space called "Girls Writing the World: The Library Re-Imagined." The bookshelves now include inspirational books by girls and women, and there are iPads to explore ideas and paper to write one's own story.

Reaction to the changes from Gordon family members was swift and fierce. Organizing themselves into a group called Defend the Birthplace, they critiqued the destruction of "sacred grounds" and the "wholesale destruction" and "desecration" of the library. In a position paper they wrote that Girl Scouts of the USA (GSUSA) "does not need to re-invent Daisy's history or dilute it with other women's histories. Lastly, we want GSUSA and the National Board to know that by alienating the Founder's family and any Girl Scout membership who support us, GSUSA stands alone in their strange defiance of what Daisy believed in and the values she held dear." The iPads and games should be moved to the "outbuildings," where they belong, the group contended. This is quite ironic when one realizes that this is the area where the slave quarters had originally been.

This is anything but a debate over iPads versus historic furniture; it's a struggle over the history that is constructed in the Birthplace, the history that I learned in the 1970s and that the teenagers showing up on my doorstep in the twenty-first century would learn on their trip. Since its origins, GSUSA has valorized its founder, turning Juliette Gordon Low into a heroine, the woman from whom young girls should gain inspiration. For Defend the Birthplace members, Girl Scouts gain their importance, their valor, by mingling with the memory of this woman of "good family," whose power, wealth, prestige, social ties, and vision are marked so clearly throughout the house and the entire city of Savannah. Yet as Junkin-Lopez explained, when an organization's myth is based on a particular founder and her family, what do we do with the difficult truths that are part of that founder's history? The money used to establish the GSUSA largely came from Low herself—from the wealth of her parents and her husband. Her mother's family possessed land and capital gained from deals made with Native Americans in the Chicago region. Her father's wealth came directly from slavery, from the plantations he owned and his cotton factor companies. Her husband's wealth, which Low inherited after his death, came from his work as an international cotton factor, with companies in both England and the United States. Low grew up with enslaved people and then impoverished freed people working for her family. And while the organization always purported to be an organization for all girls, the reality is that in its first fifty years inclusivity was separate and not entirely equal. As we have seen, Asian American, African American, and Native Americans girls were segregated into their own troops, usually under the control of a larger white council. Camping was especially segregated, either with separate facilities completely or, as was the case frequently in the North, with Black troops allowed to use the camps only during the last two weeks of the season.

In building the new library at the Birthplace, the GSUSA wanted to simultaneously address and elide its history of racial discrimination and enslavement. In emphasizing Low's creativity and intrepid spirit rather than her family, a cultural and historical asset is now perceived as a problem to be solved. Defend the Birthplace advocates recognized the threat in redirecting attention away from Low's family. A redirection, such as the new library, means that Girl Scouts' strength emerges not from the family—its wealth, power, prestige, status, and whiteness—but despite it. Defend the Birthplace advocates wanted the Birthplace to remain a pure, sacred space, with any difficult discussions about hard history being moved to the outbuildings, where the family's enslaved people and servants worked and lived. History, as this struggle shows, is not a superfluous subject but crucial to the way we see ourselves and the future we envision.

The sense of history that the Girl Scouts provided in the 1970s on our tour to Savannah and the Girl Scout Plantation created a complex education in white supremacy, girlhood power, and a distinctive ability to see things selectively. It is part of the story of how white feminism can become so complicit in racism if it doesn't clearly examine its own roots and intentions. And it is part of a larger story, of how the United States as a whole has maintained a national myth of racial innocence despite being built on a foundation of racialized oppression, discrimination, and exploitation. As James Baldwin underscored in his 1962 essay "A Letter to My Nephew," "It is the innocence that constitutes the crime."[25] This chapter is an attempt to reenact the crime itself, to drill down to see how it actually worked in the lives and experiences of millions of girls like me and my troop members. The pilgrimage to the camp and to the Juliette Gordon Low Birthplace taught us, in ways implicit and explicit, to ignore, to look away, and to discard any details that might challenge this ideological frame of whiteness, even when it was right in front of us, like in Factor's Row or the Girl Scout Plantation. It is part of the story of how the United States has maintained a national myth of racial innocence despite being built on a foundation of racialized oppression, discrimination, and exploitation. These struggles—over history, over race, over what inclusivity and feminism really mean—clearly mark the institution of the Girl Scouts of the USA in the twenty-first century, as we will see in the following chapter.

Chapter 11

Girl Scouting in the Twenty-First Century

• • • • • •

A box of Girl Scout cookies is not a political statement.
—Anna Maria Chavez

On the cusp of the twenty-first century, a group of parents from a suburb of Cincinnati became fed up with the changes the Girl Scouts had made to the Girl Scout Promise, which allowed girls reciting the words to substitute another term for "God." One of the mothers, Patti Garribay, took the lead in founding an alternative organization that looked a lot like Girl Scouts—troops, patrols, uniforms, badges, outdoor skills—but was "Christ-centered" and focused on traditional family values. The organization says it was dismayed at the way their "beloved" Girl Scouts were handling "matters of faith" and so "through a healthy helping of tears and prayer" they established the American Heritage Girls. Open to any "biological girl" and to adults who explicitly ascribe to Christianity, the organization had over 50,000 "trailblazers" (their name for members) by 2020. As Catholic dioceses, right-to-life groups, and conservative churches and schools have broken with the Girl Scouts in the last thirty years, they have frequently touted American Heritage Girls, with its explicit mix of US patriotism, Christianity, and "family values," as a potent alternative to what they see as the "woke" agenda and "indoctrination camps" of the Girl Scouts.[1]

As the American Heritage Girls were taking off, led by women antagonistic to what they saw as the left-wing agenda of the Girl Scouts, a completely different offshoot of the Girl Scouts was born in California: the Radical Brownies. In 2014 a young girl from Oakland, Coatlupe Martinez, repeatedly asked her mother, Anayvette Martinez, if she could join the Girl Scouts. Anayvette, an ethnic studies master's student at San Francisco State University, was skeptical of this predominantly white girls' organization, particularly since her daughter would be the only girl of color in the local troop. As Coatlupe remembers, "When I was in 4th grade, many of my friends began to join a local scouting troop. Naturally, I wanted to join as well. I was raised in a very politically aware and activist home, and I have been attending conferences and marches since before I could walk. So my mom felt it was important for that awareness to be reflected in any group I'd join."[2] Anayvette reached out to her friend Marilyn Hollingquest, and together they created the Radical Brownies, a new kind of girls' organization for Anayvette's daughter and other girls of color. With badges, uniforms, troop meetings, and outings, the Radical Brownies were loosely fashioned after the Girl Scouts but with a key difference: The group clearly focused on girls of color not as "charity girls" to be uplifted but as change agents themselves, with deep and important histories of their own. The Radical Brownies also explicitly claimed a political stance, challenging white supremacy, heterosexism, sexism, and the brutalities of rampant capitalism. The first badge the leaders created was Black Lives Matter, which the girls earned through attending a march, learning about Black history, and discussing violence and mass incarceration.

Not surprisingly, the Girl Scouts of the USA (GSUSA) challenged this new organization's use of the term "Brownie," the name that GSUSA has used for its younger scouts since the early twentieth century. GSUSA's chief communications officer, Kelly Parisi, gave the new organization a phone call, apparently informing the founders that the Radical Brownies were "causing some confusion among our membership about affiliation given their uniform and use of our name." Parisi explained, "They graciously offered to change their name and we graciously gave them time to discuss it with [their members]." Within a few weeks, the Radical Brownies had become the Radical Monarchs. While both sides claim that this was a friendly decision, with "no lawyers," undergirding the call was the threat of a cease and desist order, a lawsuit, and the financial power of the Girl Scouts to protect its "brand."[3] Martinez and Hollingquest's decision to form an organization that basically is a riff on the Girl Scouts is important; it suggests how culturally powerful and ubiquitous this institution is, like a piece of clay that belongs to everyone, that can be endlessly remolded to make sense for different communities. Martinez's daughter would have joined a Brownie troop if she joined the Girl Scouts;

instead, Martinez and Hollingquest formed the Radical Brownies. Lord Robert Baden-Powell chose "Brownies" as the name for the littlest Girl Guides in 1914, referring to a centuries-old European folktale retold in the late nineteenth century by Juliana Horatia Ewing, in which a "race of little people," are simultaneously silly, innocent, and helpful.[4] When W. E. B. Du Bois launched a new magazine for children in 1920 he called it *The Brownies' Book*, intentionally challenging the racism of the ubiquitous folktale, which was often used to portray Black people as servile, childlike, unthinking, and overly emotional.[5] The Radical Brownies similarly reshaped this folkloric group to belong to girls of color. But GSUSA, ever mindful of its branded ownership and eschewing anything "political," quickly moved to remind Martinez and Hollingquest of its ownership of the brand. It's an ironic moment: An organization that was working diligently to prove its diversity in the 2000s quickly shuts down an organization whose name came from a racist folktale recast by Du Bois, one of the world's leading intellectuals. While the Girl Scouts certainly had the most well-recognized use of the name "Brownie," it nonetheless feels like the Girl Scouts missed a valuable opportunity by not allowing the Radical Brownies to use the name. According to Martinez and Hollingquest, the name change was amicable, with the girls choosing Radical Monarchs, a name they especially liked because of the beauty and transformative nature of caterpillars and butterflies. But Martinez and Hollingquest kept the brown berets and clothing, in "homage to the spirits and sentiment of the Brown Beret and Black Panther movements of the past."[6] After creating the Black Lives Matter badge, they added ones such as Radical Bodies, Radical Beauty, Radical Love, and Radical Healing. Questions of power, agency, and the complexities of history take center stage as the girls explore race, body image, relationships, health, and the environment. While the materials are all age-appropriate, there is no pretense of protecting the girls' "innocence"; in a society that has historically and contemporarily hurt girls and women of color, the presumption of the Radical Monarchs is that knowledge, an ability to think critically, an understanding of the possibilities of radical change, and solidarity with other girls of color will equip them to confront sexism and racism instead of practicing a faux innocence and pretending these issues don't exist. Today, their website ends with this disclaimer: "We are in no way affiliated with the Girl Scouts of the USA."

The "Nonpolitical" Space of Girl Scouting

Studiously ignoring the American Heritage Girls and distancing itself from the Radical Brownies/Monarchs, Girl Scouts has solidly planted itself in the territory of the "nonpolitical" in the twenty-first century. This has been an explicit strategy to deal with continued conservative attacks on the Girl Scouts since the 1990s. That doesn't mean always capitulating to the Right. Early in her tenure as CEO of the Girl Scouts, Kathy Cloninger in 2004 sparred with right-wing activist John Pisciotta on *The Today Show*. An economics professor at Baylor University and the director of Pro-Life Waco, Pisciotta initiated a Girl Scout cookie boycott after the Girl Scout Council in Waco partnered with a local Planned Parenthood for a sex education program. The Waco controversy quickly blew up, with Girl Scout troops dismantling and a flurry of editorials and media campaigns. Since the origins of the Girl Scouts, councils and troops across the country could organize partnerships and plan programming with outside organizations as they saw fit, and since the 1970s this had included Planned Parenthood. When Cloninger appeared on TV, her strategy was to normalize and defend Girl Scouts' partnership with the Waco Planned Parenthood. In her Girl Scout scarf and in her clear and soft Texas accent, she smiled at the audience and said, "Girls grow up with very complex issues facing them. . . . We tackle the issues of human sexuality, body image, and all the things that girls are facing. We partner with many organizations, we have relationships with our church communities, with YWCAs and with Planned Parenthood organizations across the country to bring information-based sex education programs to girls."[7] Despite Cloninger's reasoned explanation and the fact that Girl Scout cookie sales in Texas actually went up after the Pro-Life Waco boycott (many responded to the attacks by supporting the Girl Scouts more enthusiastically), the local council canceled its relationship with Planned Parenthood. In response, Pam Smallwood, the executive director of the Central Texas Planned Parenthood, wrote in a scathing editorial that "bullying tactics are more effective than an informed democracy."[8]

Indeed, it seemed that Smallwood's words about bullies were prescient. In the first decades of the twenty-first century, the Girl Scouts faced continued attacks by right-wing media, the US Catholic Church, and conservative legislators. In addition to a national boycott of Girl Scout cookies, some activists and legislators even refused to recognize the 100th anniversary of the Girl Scouts in 2012.[9] The US Catholic Bishops' Council launched a two-year investigation into the Girl Scouts, questioning their ideas about sexuality, their support of birth control and abortion, and their ties to the international World Association of Girl Guides and Girl Scouts (WAGGGS), which officially supports full reproductive rights. While the final report did not fully condemn the Girl Scouts, it gave leeway to local dioceses to cancel Girl Scout membership and encouraged affiliation with groups like the American Heritage

Girls. Right-wing radio attacked the Girl Scouts with particular vitriol, fuming about abortion, lesbianism, transgender membership, and by the third decade of the twenty-first century, a generalized "woke" agenda. By the 2010s, GSUSA strategy had moved away from the inclusive words Cloninger had used in her *Today Show* interview. GSUSA would deny ties to anything "political" or "radical," including the mainstream organization Planned Parenthood. In 2014, the new CEO of the Girl Scouts, Anna Maria Chavez, whose Catholic faith was seen as an asset as the organization faced an organized attack by the Catholic Church and the conservative right wing, claimed the organization was completely nonpolitical: "A box of Girl Scout cookies is not a political statement." Looking into the camera, she said, "We stand for girls" to be "strong, confident, courageous adults." And then she added, "We do not now, nor have we ever, had a relationship with Planned Parenthood."[10]

That line—"We do not now, nor have we ever, had a relationship with Planned Parenthood"—will ring a bell for many readers. It is almost word for word a replica of the question Senator Joe McCarthy in the 1950s asked citizens who came before his investigatory committee: "Are you now, or have you ever been, a member of the Communist Party?" And, just as the Girl Scouts had "cleaned" the *Girl Scouts Handbook* of any references to international sisterhood, feminism, racial inclusion, or religious diversity after these McCarthy-style attacks in the 1950s and early 1960s, in the twenty-first century Chavez's words vehemently denied any Girl Scout ties to Planned Parenthood. The reality was more complicated. While the national organization had no formal tie to Planned Parenthood, on a regional and local level, troops and councils did. The attacks by right-wing groups, the Catholic Church, and pro-life forces had been so consistent and so powerful that the by the time Chavez became CEO the Girl Scouts denied these various and expansive relationships. It even subtly disavowed its relationship to the international WAGGGS, which had a more explicit policy supporting sex education and Planned Parenthood, hiding behind a technicality that it was monies from "investment income," not from active Girl Scout membership dues, that funded the membership with WAGGGS.[11] "Reproductive issues," Chavez said in her 2014 statement, "are deeply private matters, best left to families. . . . I find it unsettling that anyone would use the Girl Scout brand to have deeply adult conversations."

This was more than a rhetorical shift between Cloninger's comments on *The Today Show* that girls face complex issues (including sexuality) and Chavez's public disclaimer about any kind of sex education. It's difficult to imagine preparing girls for a future where they can plan their own destiny without having any information or control over their bodies or reproduction.

It's a fundamental human right, crucial to the ability of anyone to navigate their own life or future. Yet in making this shift, the Girl Scouts leaned into a vision of "girl leadership" that had at its center an empty space and profound silence where the information about bodies, sex, and reproduction should be. Instead of espousing access to knowledge and health care as a fundamental right for girls and women, the Girl Scouts relied on the old trope of girlhood innocence, blaming conservatives, pro-lifers, and the Catholic Church for "dirtying" the girls, asking them about abortion and sex, and demanding they have "deeply adult conversations." Just a few years earlier, Robert McCartney, a columnist for the *Washington Post*, recounted a similar story about a local girl selling Girl Scout cookies:

> When the woman answered the door, she looked at my daughter and said, "We don't support Girl Scouts because they support abortion, which kills babies," recalled Kim Douglas, who's been a troop leader as well as a Scout parent for four years.
>
> "It left my daughter very shocked, confused," Douglas said. "She said, 'Mommy, something creepy happened to me.'"
>
> Douglas's daughter didn't know what abortion was and didn't ask, which is a relief. The mother said the neighbor had a right to her views, of course, but shouldn't have shared them with a 10-year-old.[12]

While that was certainly a "creepy" encounter, to echo the ten-year-old's words, there is an obvious presumption here by McCartney that discussions about sex, reproduction, and health care should be entirely taboo around children (she didn't "know what abortion was and didn't ask, which is a relief") rather than tailored to be appropriate and not alarming. Yet we know that silence and presumptions about "innocence" being synonymous with "ignorance" have never been true: Think of the realities of sexual abuse, incest, rape, child pornography, early menstruation, and the need to access abortion. Think about the realities of sexual desire, puberty, and relationships. The future of girls, which is indeed the "business" of the Girl Scouts, is intricately wound up with sexuality, reproduction, and health care, even if no one is willing to talk about it in the name of girlhood "innocence."

In working to protect the "Girl Scout brand," as Chavez put it, the national organization has always claimed a middle-of-the-road position that sidesteps and disavows explicit connections to feminism. This was true from the first shift to the use of the word "scout" rather than "guide" to the 1950s changes in the *Handbook* and Frances Hesselbein's vehement denial of the word "feminism" itself. In the twenty-first century, the term used over and again to describe the Girl Scout mission has been "leadership." In her introduction to *Tough Cookies: Leadership Lessons from 100 Years of the Girl Scouts*, for instance, Cloninger remembers holding back a retort to someone on a plane who made a dismissive quip about Thin Mint cookies. "I wonder if he knows that the annual Girl Scout cookie sale is a unique and powerful $700 million education program that brings to life Girl Scouts' true brand: developing leadership in girls." She never names this entrepreneurship or these leadership skills as feminism but rather as something powerfully needed in a nation scarred by "poverty, inadequate education, and global market competition."[13] How exactly girls are going to lead, or where they are going to lead us, is left unsaid, as the details of that would necessitate a discussion of policy, power, and politics, all of which the national Girl Scout organization wants to sidestep in the name of protecting the brand and being an organization capacious enough to include everyone. Instead, the terms repeated over and again in Girl Scout literature in the twenty-first century are that Girl Scouts develops girls of "courage, confidence, and character"; there is never an explicit discussion of what the girls are to be courageous or confident about or what constitutes a strong character. The terms are left open, for the girls and the troops themselves to decide.

In early July 2022 I visited my former Ohio Girl Scout camp outside Peninsula, Ohio, Camp Ledgewood; I have wonderful memories of summer weeks and school-year weekends spent at Ledgewood when I was a girl. It's in a beautiful part of northeastern Ohio, nestled within the Cuyahoga Valley National Park. I met up with Jane Christyson, the CEO of the Girl Scouts of North East Ohio, who had been overseeing the Girl Scouts in this expansive region of the state for almost ten years when I spoke with her. During her tenure, she presided over a lot of change. Just a few years before she took over as CEO, the national organization had consolidated five councils (including Western Reserve, which had been mine when I was a Girl Scout) into one large region that spanned from Sandusky to Ashtabula and included Cleveland, Akron, and Canton; Christyson spent a lot of time on the road, visiting this huge region and dealing with all the mixed (largely negative) feelings that the consolidation had created. The most immediate crisis Christyson faced when she took over was the sale of many of the individual councils' camps. While the GSUSA said that it simply could not maintain so many camps due to their expense and decreasing enrollment, individual councils and Girl Scouts did not take it lightly, even suing in court to block the sales.[14] Camp Ledgewood was one of the three camps that was spared, probably because its location within the national park meant that no development would ever encroach on it.

When I met with Christyson, she could not have been more upbeat. She had already scheduled a tour of the camp for a group of young women professionals and she asked if I would like to go along. I gladly agreed and, after touring the new dining hall, she and a camp employee whisked us off on a pair of golf carts to see the rest of the camp. We saw a site with new cabins, another site with tentlike structures fashioned over what looked like Conestoga wagons, and a troop cabin that had a special room for any resident men, separate from the group dorms. We sped past the swimming pool and the lake where I had learned to canoe with my friend Laurie. As we meandered on trails through the woods, we saw the "low" and "high" ropes courses, and then we stopped in front of a large ravine to check out the zip line, which looked terrifying to me. I was happy I'd never had to deal with the ropes or the zip line, but then I thought perhaps the camaraderie and encouragement would have allowed me to conquer those. It was just the kind of physical leadership and challenge that I had been reading about in *Tough Cookies*, where Cloninger wrote that Girl Scouts defy the expectations that girls don't like taking risks: "Go watch a group of young sprites learn the high ropes challenge course at Girl Scout camp," she exhorted readers. "You'll never doubt again."[15]

Our final stop on the tour was an empty field and an old, battered clapboard house. I wasn't exactly sure what we were looking at until I realized we were looking at the future. Christyson explained it was to be the site of the new STEM Center, a state-of-the-art, all-season facility that would pull in girls from across the region. The National Science Foundation had begun to use the concept of STEM (science, technology, engineering, and math) in the early 1990s; by the 2000s this had gained such prominence that most people in the education field easily understood the shorthand and the intense focus on preparing students for careers in the field. Girl Scouts enthusiastically embraced the STEM curriculum, and between 2017 and 2021, the Girl Scouts reported a "launch of over 100 STEM projects" and over 3.5 million STEM badges earned. The group of young women professionals who were touring with me at Ledgewood that summer day in 2022 were from a local company that recruited women and minorities to STEM fields; Christyson wanted to get them excited about the work the Girl Scouts were doing and possibly even persuade them to volunteer or donate. In the summer of 2023, Camp Ledgewood finally broke ground on the STEM Center of Excellence, an event attended by local dignitaries, politicians, and representatives from various donors; funding for the center, which would be open to both girls and boys, came not only from the federal government but also from various local corporations, including the FirstEnergy Foundation and Sherwin-Williams.[16] It's important to remember that STEM is not something new to the Girl Scouts; think of that early 1918 film *The Golden Eaglet* and the way the protagonist, Margaret, saves the day (and the life of the injured man) with her knowledge of the telegraph system and Morse code. The twenty-first-century intense emphasis on STEM, however, is new. And besides being a way for the Girl Scouts to pull in monies from new sources (the federal government, corporations, and science foundations), it is also another way to "do" feminism without saying it. One can encourage girls to make inroads into male-dominated fields, to be qualified to capture the best-paying jobs, and to gain confidence and competence, all in the name of keeping the United States competitive in a global market and saving humanity from the problems that plague us. It's another stand-in for feminism, articulated and created without actually talking about feminism or power or the cultures that support inequity.

The only moment when I saw Christyson's enthusiasm level drop was at the end of the Camp Ledgewood tour. The other women were walking around the future site of the STEM Center, and I turned to Christyson and asked her how Ledgewood was dealing with the new *Dobbs v. Jackson Women's Health Organization* decision that the Supreme Court had just issued about a week before, taking away the constitutional right to abortion, allowing states to ban multiple forms of reproductive care and pregnancy terminations. It "clearly has a lot to do with science, with girls' lives, and with leadership," I offered. Christyson's face fell a bit, and she said: "You have to understand we're a nonprofit organization and we don't take political stands." And with that, she called to the other women and we gathered together on the golf carts, returning on the bumpy paths to the dining hall, where we had started. I had gotten a clear message: We don't talk about abortion, reproductive rights, sexuality, or politics.

Christyson's silence surrounding the *Dobbs* decision was deafening. Here we were, looking at a field of dreams of sorts, a new STEM Center of Excellence that would bring girls charging into the twenty-first century, side by side with boys, but we weren't going to take steps to educate girls about very real issues that could shape and sideline a girl's future: pregnancy, rape, forced birth, unplanned motherhood, unsafe medical care. At best, this was a shroud of secrecy that served only to confuse girls. At worst, this silence meant allowing girls to face a future that would force them to deny their own sexual feelings and desires, that would not protect them when faced with violence, that would not allow them control over their own bodies or even safe medical care. Clearly Christyson and the Girl Scouts of North East Ohio thought that their organization for girls, their camp that taught physical and mental confidence, and their newly planned STEM Center could be protected by a circle of silence about the political battles swirling around them. As I thought of the girls whose lives and livelihoods were at stake, who were somehow being promised that if we didn't talk about bodies, reproduction, and abortion they would be safe, I could hear Audre Lorde's words echoing loudly in my ears: "My silences had not protected me. Your silences will not protect you."[17]

Christyson's staunch reticence to discuss the *Dobbs* decision stemmed from an overall Girl Scout strategy that could be located in its origins: a strategy to be flexible and capacious enough to include everyone. In the 2014 speech where Anna Maria Chavez proclaimed that the Girl Scouts "do not now, nor have we ever, have a relationship with Planned Parenthood," she also placed Girl Scouts, their goals and ideals, in a space outside of any social, cultural, or political struggle. "True leadership," her speech concluded, "transcends politics and religion, and it transcends race and ethnicity." The national organization worked to signal this racial and ethnic inclusivity both with the multicultural pictures of the girls on the Girl Scout cookie boxes and with its choice of national leadership. In 1999, Connie Matsui became the first Asian American national board president of the Girl Scouts. In 2011, Anna Maria Chavez, whose words I quoted above, was the first Latina CEO of the GSUSA. In 2014, Kathy Hopinkah Hannan became the first woman with Native American ancestry to become the national board president. In 2020 Judith Batty became the first African American CEO of the GSUSA. And in the twenty-first century the GSUSA commissioned studies to highlight and encourage inclusivity, such as *Resilience Factor: A Key to Leadership in African American and Hispanic Girls* in 2011. It also launched programs to encourage membership outside its traditional white, middle-class base, such as the Girl Scout Border Initiative to develop Girl Scout troops on the US-Mexico border; a program to encourage Muslim membership in North Carolina and Minnesota; and a program begun at the end of the twentieth century, Girl Scouts beyond Bars, which facilitated meetings between Girl Scouts and their incarcerated mothers.[18]

One of the most publicized examples of the Girl Scouts' embrace of diversity was the 2020 book *Troop 6000: The Girl Scout Troop That Began in a Shelter and Inspired the World*. Written by *New York Times* journalist Nikita Stewart, *Troop 6000* follows the story of Giselle Burgess, an African American mother who, despite having a full-time job, faces eviction when the bills become overwhelming. She and her five children move to a homeless shelter in Queens, where Burgess launches a Girl Scout troop in an effort to bring her girls some level of stability, joy, and focus in an environment that saps all their energy and hope for a future. By the end of the book, with a new paid job at the Girl

Scouts and various government assistance programs, Burgess is able to move into a subsidized apartment with her family. Stewart points out the numerous ironies in Burgess's story, especially the fact that, though she becomes famous for her work as a leader, with guest appearances on *Jimmy Fallon*, stories on NBC and CNN, and Stewart's own book, she remains poor. As Stewart points out, the Girl Scout national organization capitalizes on her success as a troop leader in order to publicize its commitment to diversity, while Burgess herself remains on the edge of financial disaster. Real, structural inequity is never challenged. But throughout the book, we learn about the ways the girls in Burgess's troop bond, experience new challenges (including lots of STEM activities), travel to Washington, DC, and spend a weekend at a traditional Girl Scout camp. Burgess makes this happen for her troop with a ton of intrepid energy from herself and her daughters, as the odds are frequently against them, from securing a room in their homeless shelter for troop meetings to figuring out transportation to sites and camps outside their neighborhood, a feat that is quite difficult when money is extraordinarily tight (or nonexistent) and the families don't have cars. But there is a drumbeat throughout the book that suggests that scouting itself keeps the girls and the leaders from giving up, although the challenges are myriad. At the beginning of the book, we even learn that a trip the oldest daughter, Hailey, took to Savannah allowed her to connect her own mother's story to that of Juliette Gordon Low's: "While she [Hailey] knew Juliette Gordon Low had founded the Girl Scouts, she had never seemed like a real person to Hailey, making it difficult for her to relate to Juliette's experience. But inside the house on Oglethorpe Street, Juliette's troubles were on display, like the tea sets, canopy beds, quilts, and sofas too pristine and delicate for sitting. More than a century later, there were striking similarities between Juliette's troubles and her mother's plight, her mother's struggle." In Low's health challenges and marital discord, Hailey saw some of her mother's own life—and like Low, the book seems to suggest, her mother Giselle could find new momentum with the Girl Scouts.[19]

Yet even if Giselle Burgess and her daughters could connect with the Girl Scouts in ways that were meaningful, useful, and joyful, GSUSA continued to have difficulty in the first decades of the twenty-first century in reaching girls of color. In 2017, GSUSA reported that approximately 71 percent of Girl Scouts (adults and girls) identified as white, 13 percent as African American, 16 percent as Hispanic, 5 percent as Asian American, and 1 percent as American Indian.[20] In other words, it remained a white organization despite public language—from its national publicity materials to the words of Jane Christyson, who lamented the stagnant membership of girls of color in Northeast

Ohio Girl Scouting. The 2023 GSUSA *Stewardship Report* gives us some more detail about girls of color's reluctance to join. GSUSA hired a research firm to ascertain the state of diversity in the Girl Scouts, which found that "individuals who identify as Black, Indigenous, and People of Color (BIPOC) are at the 'periphery of Girl Scouting'—meaning that the needs, interests and priorities of BIPOC Girl Scouts and potential BIPOC girl members have not always been the first or central factor when making Movement decisions." And, because BIPOC girls and their families perceived that their needs were at the periphery of the organization, they shied away from joining the organization. The report went into greater detail, pointing out GSUSA's "tendency to be fierce protectors of the norms and rituals of Girl Scouting, which leads to exclusion of those who have not traditionally been part of the stories we tell." In other words, unlike Hailey Burgess, most girls of color could neither find inspiration in the origin stories of the Girl Scouts nor connect with stories about generations of girls camping and building camaraderie around the firepit. The findings further detailed that the reliance on volunteers meant that a leader with a narrow point of view had an outsize effect on BIPOC girls, who would understandably avoid the organization if they felt unwelcome at the troop level, which is really the only way most girls ever experience the Girl Scouts. And, finally, the report spoke to the overall policy of remaining neutral on political issues; while things such as the *Dobbs* decision, Black Lives Matter, or Donald Trump's presidency weren't specifically cited, certainly those come to mind as pressing topics affecting contemporary girls that the organization avoided discussing. The report noted that "fear of addressing some of the issues and concerns that our young people are going to address with or without us—including those related to potentially controversial issues—is preventing full engagement with communities of color." The risk, the report concluded, was an organization that not only was unwelcoming to BIPOC girls but that, in general, was "less representative, less attractive, and less relevant to new generations." Significantly, the Girl Scout *Stewardship Report* laid out a plan to address these issues by focusing on a fair pay structure for staff and a commitment to "racial reconciliation," goals that had been articulated since the 1940s though never achieved. In addition, what exactly this racial reconciliation would mean was not spelled out in the report. The generalized apolitical stance of the organization, however, which the research had pointed out was the crucial area of concern, remained untouched in the recommendations.[21]

Considering the history of the Girl Scouts—the homage given to a woman whose wealth came from enslavement, the waffling the organization had done over racial inclusion, the explicit discrimination in outdoor activities and camping, and the idealization of a particular kind of intrepid yet innocent white girl—it's not surprising that girls and adults of color would mistrust the Girl Scouts in the ways that the *Stewardship Report* described. In her poignant 2003 short story "Brownies," ZZ Packer touches on just these issues of distrust and (un)belonging in the Girl Scouts. In the story, a group of Black fourth-grade girls from an Atlanta suburb travel to Camp Crescendo with their two leaders. In many ways, the protagonist, Laurel, connects to the camp in the ways Girl Scouting literature usually highlights: She's in awe of the stars, the smell of the pine trees moves her, and the latrines are a challenge. But the tension of the story revolves around Laurel's troop's relationship with the other troop at the camp, a group of white girls. A girl from Laurel's troop apparently hears one of the white girls use the N-word and, in retaliation, Laurel and her friends plan an ambush in the bathroom, a plan that engenders more confusion than retaliation. It turns out the white girls are in a troop for intellectually and developmentally disabled girls, so it's not clear whether the young white girl could actually have said the offensive word. The white leader offers yet another explanation, defending her troop members by saying that many of the girls are "echolalic," meaning they repeat what they hear, and they may have heard that word from their (un)progressive parents. Even if someone said it, it would not have been "intentional," she insists.

The story is so powerful, twisting us along as Laurel tries to figure out *how* to respond in a world in which the actions of adults are often inscrutable and the cultures of whiteness and racism permeate everything. Among the many things to talk about in this story, two stand out in relation to the Girl Scouts. The first is when Laurel's friend Octavia, in lamenting how wrong the camping trip went, wonders, "You know, why *did* we have to be stuck at a camp with retarded girls?" "*You* know why," another girl in the troop, Arnetta, responds. Packer wants us to cringe at the word "retarded"; indeed, the whole short story works up to the protagonist's conclusion that that there is "something mean in the world." But Octavia's question also probes at a deep factual truth in the history of the Girl Scouts, the exclusion of Black girls from camps or, if they were "allowed" to come, their placement at the most undesirable times: during the offseason, after the white girls had used the camp during the best months. Octavia and Arnetta both know why their troops—the Black one and the disabled one—would have been put together, even if no adult is willing to acknowledge it: They are unwanted, "foreign," as Arnetta puts it.

The white leader's defense of the girl who may (or may not) have used the N-word also touches on a raw nerve in the history of the Girl Scouts. The leader never fully denies the plausibility that this slur may have been said, she just deflects responsibility. It's a striking claim: If the white girls are disabled, their culpability is questionable. But, then, who can be held responsible? Is everyone actually innocent? Does the white leader apologize? Does the camp leadership apologize? Is there any discussion with the white girls that using these slurs is unacceptable, hurtful, oppressive? Or is this something that is just allowed to be, swept under the rug, too much to address with the white girls and their parents, who the white leader seems to suggest are conservative? It's the righteously angry Black girls who are kept under tight surveillance by their leaders for the rest of the trip. Packer's short story illuminates so many of the issues that the *Stewardship Report* would relay twenty years later, above all the lack of connection and the aura of distrust that infiltrates the experiences of girls of color with the Girl Scouts.[22]

The Boy Scouts Take a Different Route

Even as this chapter outlines the limitations of Girl Scout tactics—the "apolitical" stance that gives girls no protection over their bodies, their reproduction, or their sexuality and the reach for "diversity" that fails to address historic and contemporary racism and discrimination—it's crucial to underscore how different its goals have been from the Boy Scouts' in the same era. As we know, from their origins the Boy Scouts and Girl Scouts have taken different routes. While Boy Scout and Girl Scout troops may have paired up on a local level for parades and public events, while their name similarity conjoins the two in much of public imagination, and while both originated at the behest of Lord Robert Baden-Powell in England, the organizations have had distinctly different trajectories. The Boy Scouts has embraced conventional ideas about masculinity, which has meant a rejection of anything that hints at girls' empowerment—thus, its continued lawsuits against the Girl Scouts for decades after Juliette Gordon Low changed the name from "Guides" to "Scouts" and Boy Scouts' endorsement of Camp Fire Girls, an organization that more clearly hewed to ideals of domesticated femininity.[23] As the Girl Scouts faced continued backlash from the Catholic Church and fundamentalist groups for its more open (but by no means radical) stance on reproductive rights, inclusion of LGBTQ members, religious and racial diversity, and girls' rights, the Boy Scouts fought to remain an organization that was aggressively masculinist, heterosexual, and conservatively Christian and patriotic. Throughout the late twentieth and into the twenty-first century the Boy Scouts stood by its decisions to bar atheists and gay membership. Actively excluding boys who refused to take a religious oath and adults who were openly gay, the Boy Scouts faced multiple legal cases at the local, state, and even federal level. In a 2000 case, *Boy Scouts of America v. Dale*, the Supreme Court ruled that the New Jersey Boy Scouts had the right to exclude James Dale, an assistant scoutmaster, when he came out publicly as gay. As the Boy Scouts' 2004 Youth Policy Statement read, Boy Scout membership was contingent on being "morally straight and clean in thought"; being gay by this logic was both sexually perverse and dirty. Despite the carte blanche given by the US Supreme Court, pressure from within and without the organization forced Boy Scouts to redraw its policies, so that by 2015 it rescinded its general restrictions on gay membership. It still allowed troops sponsored by religious organizations to maintain heterosexual-only policies, which meant that the Catholic Church, the Church of Jesus Christ of Latter-Day Saints, and conservative Protestant groups continued to support the Boy Scouts, even as they railed against the Girl Scouts and chose new groups to support, like the American Heritage Girls.

Boy Scout membership fell dramatically from the mid-1980s through the twenty-first century, pushed, as political scientist Barbara Arneil argues, by the organization's conservative stances on masculinity, religion, and sexuality.[24] Even longtime champions of the Boy Scouts found their support for the organization fraying. Jay Mechling, a longtime scout himself and the author of *On My Honor: The Boy Scouts and the Making of American Youth*, found himself deeply troubled, writing in an editorial for *USA Today*, "I love Scouting, but I have not always loved the policies of the Boy Scouts of America." In particular, within a context of mass shootings endangering schoolchildren all over the country, he was fed up with the Boy Scouts' relationship with the National Rifle Association (NRA), one that is physically represented by the close proximity of the NRA's Whittington Center to the Boy Scout National Museum in New Mexico. The NRA, Mechling argued, was using the Boy Scouts as an "educational cover for its real mission of lobbying for the firearms and ammunition industry," and the Boy Scouts was dependent on the NRA's financial contributions, $335 million in 2016.[25]

Indeed, the Boy Scouts was likely feeling particularly dependent on the NRA's contribution, even if it was a cowardly move, as Mechling asserted, because its coffers were being significantly depleted by the regular payouts it was making in the twenty-first century to victims of sexual abuse. Since the end of the twentieth century, men had been coming forward regularly to report that they had been sexually abused as children by scoutmasters. According to journalist Savannah Walsh, the Boy Scouts of America had known for decades about the abuse it was covering up; indeed, from its origins in the United States, it had kept a "Red Flag List" (also known as a list of "ineligible volunteers" or "perversion papers") of men who had been identified as abusing victims within the organization. The Boy Scouts was a particularly good cover for sexual abuse, as the male predators could hide behind a veneer of wholesomeness, patriotism, and upright masculinity, a mask that made it particularly difficult for victims to come forward. The atmosphere of shame for the boy victims was particularly rampant in an organization that prized masculinity to such an extent. Even as the Boy Scouts organization was aware of the abuse (and it clearly was, as the "perversion papers" demonstrated), the organization would fight accusers in court rather than address the problem, apologize to the victims, or willingly provide compensation. As the extent of the rampant sexual abuse became publicly apparent, and more and more men came forward, the Boy Scouts hired Michael Johnson as youth protection director in 2010. Johnson left the organization ten years later in disgust, however, arguing that the new policies were weak and meaningless, simply a public relations facade. By 2023, over 80,000 men had come forward to report abuse, and the courts ordered the organization to pay $2.46 billion in compensation, the largest sexual abuse settlement in US history.[26]

Amid these formidable challenges in the 2010s—declining membership, disastrous public relations, plummeting finances, and bankruptcy—the Boy Scouts made a bold decision in 2017 to accept girls as members, starting with Cub Scouts (the youngest group), and in subsequent years to create a program for older girls as well. The national board of the Boy Scouts of America voted to change its name, dropping "Boy" and becoming simply "Scouts." This was an ironic move—both the decision to include girls and the name change—considering that since its origins the Boy Scouts had railed against the encroachment of girls into boys' spheres, had argued that the very name of Girl Scouting "sissyfied" boys, and had done everything to discourage Girl Scouting and to encourage alternative groups more amenable to Boy Scouts' ideas of strict masculinity and separate gender roles. Michael Surbaugh, the chief Boy Scout executive, defended the decision: "The values of Scouting—trustworthy, loyal, helpful, kind, brave and reverent, for example—are important for both young men and women. We believe it is critical to evolve how our programs meet the needs of families interested in positive and life-long experiences for their children."[27]

Most critics doubted these virtuous goals, including the Girl Scout national organization itself, which viewed it as an attempt by the Boy Scouts to siphon off membership from the Girl Scouts, whose membership had actually been holding solid or growing in the twenty-first century.[28] To add to the irony, the Girl Scouts began to sue the Boy Scouts for the name change, arguing that it was causing marketing confusion, tricking girls and their families who didn't know what they were joining, and hurting the name of the Girl Scouts with the problems that the Boy Scouts brought with them, above all the public image disaster caused by the decades of sexual abuse cover-up.[29] Sylvia Acevedo, CEO of the Girl Scouts, who had previously equivocated on issues of "politics" when it came to reproductive rights, race, and politics, spoke directly to this point, drawing a solid line separating the Girl Scouts from the Boy Scouts and disparaging the Boy Scouts for trying to steal girl members. In a swing at the declining membership of the Boy Scouts, she wrote in a *USA Today* op-ed, "We are disappointed that the Boy Scouts have chosen to open its membership in contravention of its charter, rather than focusing on the 90% of American boys not being served by Boy Scouts." Then, in a not so veiled reference to the sexual abuse cover-up, she added, "We believe strongly in the importance of the *safe, all-girl, and girl-friendly* environment that Girl Scouts provide." And finally, Acevedo reminded readers that the Girl Scouts had always been about *girl* empowerment, about creating opportunities for *girls*, about centering and focusing on the needs and experiences of *girls*: "At Girl Scouts, girls aren't the ancillary tag-along or supporting player—they are the central character. For more than a century, Girl Scouts has delivered unparalleled experiences that allow girls to discover their passions, develop leadership and people skills, explore their worlds, and embark on new adventures."[30] Though Acevedo was not using the word "feminism" here (as the Girl Scouts never does), that's what her words implied—that Girl Scouts has always understood we live in a patriarchal world, and that if we are to encourage girls to be leaders, to have adventures, to "discover their passions," we need a program that recognizes this unequal playing field and creates a context where girls can flourish. In 2022, after five years of litigation, a federal judge dismissed the Girl Scouts' case over the name, and the Girl Scouts and Boy Scouts (now Scouts) agreed to a settlement (with no financial payment) that ended all litigation.[31]

Taking a Bolder Stance

It's crucial to underscore that, even if the GSUSA equivocated on most political issues and frequently took feminist stands without explicitly naming them as feminist, some Girl Scouting avenues were indeed taking bolder political stands on feminism, reproduction, sexual abuse, and transgender and queer rights. This was happening at both the local and the international level. For instance, in its frequently asked questions on social issues, noted above, the GSUSA described its policy on transgender youth:

> Girl Scouts is proud to be the premiere leadership organization for girls in the country.
>
> Placement of transgender youth is handled on a case-by-case basis, with the welfare and best interests of the child and the members of the troop/group in question a top priority. That said, if the child is recognized by the family and school/community as a girl and lives culturally as a girl, then Girl Scouts is an organization that can serve her in a setting that is both emotionally and physically safe.[32]

The GSUSA national policy, then, is that local councils and troops have the ultimate authority over whether to accept a transgender child, who will be accepted only if she lives culturally as a girl and is recognized by her family and community as a girl. This is not a wholehearted welcoming of nonbinary children or transgender girls by any means. Local troops or councils could decide to exclude transgender children, and the national policy allows the possibility that recognition by families and communities is a prerequisite.

In contrast, some local chapters took a much more explicitly inclusive stance. The Girl Scouts of the Northwestern Great Lakes, which comprises northern Wisconsin and the Upper Peninsula of Michigan, unequivocally stated: "We are building Girl Scouts of courage, confidence, and character who make the world a better place. To do that, we must first provide a space that is inclusive, equitable, and accessible for all Girl Scouts, across many diverse identities." Using the ubiquitous words of the GSUSA ("building girls of courage, confidence and character"), the chapter establishes that this means creating an environment that is safe and welcoming for LGBTQ Girl Scouts. "Supporting LGBTQ+ Girl Scouts requires special care and attention," the seven-page, brightly colored, rainbowed document reads. Importantly, this local council insists on maintaining the child's privacy, guiding leaders to understand how "outing" their choice of name or identity neither respects the child nor protects their safety. That is, the council policy is that leaders should only share name and identity choice with the parents if the child gives permission to do so. This council also explicitly states that all girls and nonbinary children (whether living as girls or boys) are to be welcomed to the Girl Scouts.[33]

In terms of education regarding sexuality and reproduction, the GSUSA adopts, as Acevedo outlined, a "hands-off" policy, almost making the subject itself taboo. The social issues FAQ on the GSUSA's position on "human sexuality, birth control, and abortion" is short and vague and gives all power to the parents: "Girl Scouts of the USA (GSUSA) does not take a position or develop materials on these issues. We feel our role is to help girls develop self-confidence and good decision-making skills that will help them make wise choices in all areas of their lives." The explanation concludes, "Parents or guardians make all decisions regarding program participation that may be of a sensitive nature. Consistent with that belief, GSUSA directs councils, including volunteer leaders, to get written parental permission for any locally planned program that could be considered sensitive."[34] Yet even in a cultural climate where individual troops and councils continued to face harassment and backlash about supposed ties to Planned Parenthood, individual Girl Scouts, both girl members and staff members, moved forward. Jinath Tasnim, a program coordinator from the Girl Scouts River Valleys (a region that includes Minnesota, Wisconsin, and Iowa), wrote an essay titled "The Joys of Teaching Consent." In a world where girls face extensive sexual harassment and assault, she wrote, it's important to start early teaching girls what it means to consent to or reject touch; she encouraged leaders and parents to find a way to discuss everything from hugs to hand-holding as a way to pave the way for girls to speak up for themselves about their bodily integrity.[35] And numerous individual Girl Scouts—usually Seniors earning the highest award in Girl Scouting, the Gold Award—have forged programs in sex education: Emmeline L., for instance, a high school Girl Scout in Atlanta, won the Gold Award for her project "Advocating for Sex Education in Schools." Chicago suburb Girl Scout Emma Costello-Wollage designed a comprehensive sex education curriculum for middle school youth.[36] But these are individual actions, not programs sponsored by entire troops or councils, and certainly not the national organization. On the whole, Girl Scouting has decided that it is simply too dangerous to the institution to support sex education—the cost too great, the backlash too fierce, the public relations too much of a quagmire.

Yet it's extremely important to note that, even within this national Girl Scout atmosphere that encourages a strategy of silence and vagueness when it comes to the politics of sexuality, sex education, race, and LGBTQ inclusion, some councils have chosen a much different tactic. In June 2023, the Girl Scouts of Eastern Massachusetts published their "Camp Culture Code." Rather than taking cover behind a vague statement and aiming to placate the more conservative members of their communities, they explained that their camps would be places that welcomed "all youth who identify with the girl experience," they would actively work to dismantle racism, and they would place controversial issues on the table for discussion. (This would, presumably, include abortion, sexuality, race, and politics.) They wrote, "The Girl Scout Movement strives to be a safe place to stand against hate and discusses issues that divide our nation. If you are someone who is not open to participation in anti-racism and LGBTQIA+ allyship work, our camp programs are not a good fit for you and your child."[37] Creating a camp for "all girls" meant creating an antiracist context where anyone—nonbinary children, girls of color, or anyone wanting to discuss sex, race, or LGBTQ issues—who identified with the "girl experience" was welcome. If someone was uncomfortable with that expansive position, so uncomfortable that they could not tolerate the expansiveness, the uncomfortable person could be excluded. It's an interesting, important choice, as the Girl Scouts of Eastern Massachusetts took a stand that there were perhaps some identities and positions that were simply incompatible. Inclusivity, or as their Camp Code described it, an expansive "understanding of who belongs at Girl Scouts," might not mean everyone can come. Camp might not be a "good fit" in the language of the Camp Code.

The World Association of Girl Guides and Girl Scouts

The international organization World Association of Girl Guides and Girl Scouts (WAGGGS) has been more outspoken about girls' and women's rights than the Girl Scouts of the USA, which has consistently worked to placate white, conservative groups. On a 2018 visit to Switzerland's Our Chalet, the first world center for Girl Scouting and Girl Guiding, I attended a session for older middle school girls on body image. As the facilitator raised questions about beauty and the media, the girls' responses included talk about fat and body size, social media, gossip, sexual assault, relationships with boys, lesbian relationships, and unequal standards between girls and boys. None of these issues was off the table, and the young adult facilitators skillfully encouraged the girls to reflect on their experiences and to think about what would make their lives safer, more fun, and fairer. In 2023, when I visited Pax Lodge in London, the program manager for the center, Liz Tranter, took a group of visiting scouts and guides on a tour of the building, which I followed attentively. The group of Brownies for the "Jambrownie" weekend had just left the building to go on their adventures for the day, but I had a sense Tranter's talk would have largely followed the same direction had the littlest girls been there too. This group was mostly middle school and high school girls from the United States, Scotland, and England, and it included their leaders and parents, women and men. Gesturing to the row of flags on a dining hall shelf, each of which represented a country from which the volunteers came, Tranter asked the girls what country each stood for: the United States, Ireland, Canada, Australia, Tunisia. Then she picked up the flag that held center place, a Pride flag.

"What is this?" she asked. "It's a Pride flag," someone answered. "Yes," she said, "because June is Pride Month, and we think it's really important that *everyone* knows they are welcome here and that they have an important place in the world." As I wandered the halls of Pax Lodge, I saw lots of walls of flags, "swaps" from troops around the world, memorabilia from Lady Olave Baden-Powell, and posters from WAGGGS. The bulletin board across from my dormitory room encouraged girls to take part in U-Report, a UNICEF program that asked for the opinions of youth across the world. Sixty-seven percent of the responses come from boys or young men, the bulletin board explained, and WAGGGS was trying to change that imbalance. The bulletin board noted that questions included ones on pressuring girls and women to have sex, on how sexual diseases were transmitted, and on violence that girls and women faced. "Girls' voices matter!" the board exhorted.

The focus at both Our Chalet and Pax Lodge on girls' voices, body positivity, and ending gender violence are all in line with initiatives by the United Nations, especially ones that have emerged since the Beijing Declaration and Platform for Action, which the UN Fourth World Conference on Women produced in 1995.[38] As a nongovernmental organization with consultative status with the United Nations, WAGGGS encourages its delegates, many of them young women, to get involved with United Nations policymaking, volunteer initiatives, and especially the work necessary to promote gender equality.[39] Interestingly, even within WAGGGS, the discussion of abortion and reproductive rights is much less explicit than the programs on ending violence, promoting girls' education (including sex education), and encouraging the democratic participation of girls and women in policymaking.[40] Nevertheless, in the United States, conservative groups continually bring up a relationship between Planned Parenthood, radical gender ideas, and WAGGGS, accusations that boil to the surface from time to time and that both the national GSUSA and the local and regional councils have chosen to deflect. In general, rather than a wholehearted endorsement of the world organization or its girl advocacy, GSUSA has generally diminished its role in the global organization. In its informational material, GSUSA explains that, as one of 145 members, "GSUSA does not always take the same positions or endorse the same programs as WAGGGS." In addition, no money from membership dues or Girl Scout cookie sales goes to GSUSA's WAGGGS membership; it comes "solely from investment income."[41] That is a technical difference, as the overall "pot" of money is the same—it is all Girl Scout money. But when GSUSA feels the pressure from right-wing, conservative groups who threaten to boycott cookie sales, pull their girls from membership, and spread ideas that are reminiscent of 1950s anticommunist accusations about Girl Scouting, the GSUSA will work to appease everyone. In this case, it means keeping its international membership but downplaying the more progressive and inclusive goals, programming, and relevance that international membership entails.

Returning to Juliette Gordon Low

Amid the pressures GSUSA has felt in the twenty-first century—with calls for accountable antiracist efforts and contemporary relevance on the one hand and accusations of pushing a "woke" agenda of abortion rights, Black history, and LGBTQ inclusivity on the other—what has the national Girl Scout organization done with the woman at the center, Juliette Gordon Low? Her image, her story, and her mythology have always been fundamental to the way this organization thinks about itself and projects itself to the world. As I discussed at length in chapter 2, almost immediately after Low's death in 1927, the national Girl Scout organization began mythologizing its founder. The 1928 collection of remembrances *Juliette Low and the Girl Scouts* identified the source of Low's intrepid spirit in the merging of two of the "finest families" (wealthy, white, powerful) of the North and South. The never-ending stream of children's and young adult biographies extended this mythology to tell of her innocent yet energetic childhood, her love of animals, and her indomitable and joyful spirit that allowed her to overcome ear illnesses and hearing problems. Gladys Shultz and Daisy Gordon Lawrence's 1958 biography *Lady from Savannah* begins by telling the story of Low's difficult marriage, a tale that had, up to this point, been mostly hidden. The retrieval of this unhappy marriage story may have been a way to ward off accusations of lesbianism, particularly in a historic moment that focused incessantly on the dangers of homosexuality and its connection to communism. By the 1990s, the myth of the woman at the center had transformed again, to tell the story of Juliette Gordon Low as a general badass, a woman who shook off her abusive marriage, sought meaningful work, and envisioned a truly diverse organization for all girls, emblemized in that ubiquitous quote, "I have something for all the girls of America!"[42]

By the 2020s, there was some backpedaling in the Girl Scouts' representation of Juliette Gordon Low as someone consistently inclusive and staunchly antiracist. Under Lisa Junkin-Lopez's tenure as the director of the Juliette Gordon Low Birthplace, the national organization began scrutinizing the records and sifting the archaeological evidence to ascertain the names and numbers of enslaved people who had lived and worked in the house and the outbuildings.

While I was visiting the Birthplace in 2017, the docents continued to talk about the "servants" who had lived in Juliette's home (even when talking about the years before her birth and during her early childhood, when those would have been enslaved workers), but Junkin-Lopez was working with the staff to dislodge the stories that created images of happy enslaved people and to speak honestly about enslavement and what GSUSA knew and didn't know. As of 2023, the executive director of the Juliette Gordon Low Birthplace is Shannon Browning-Mullis, a public historian known for facing difficult histories, as her previous work was as curator of the Telfair Museums, where she emphasized the life and experiences of the enslaved people at the Owens-Thomas House in Savannah. Browning-Mullis's appointment signifies a particular commitment on the part of the Girl Scouts to face honestly the history of the founder and the organization.[43]

Yet a specific linguistic shift indicates that the Girl Scouts did not want to stray too far from the heroic myth of Juliette Gordon Low, even after Junkin-Lopez's intervention. When I began my research in the 2010s, the Girl Scout department I applied to for access to the archival records was the National Historic Preservation Center. That title suggests that one wants to preserve history, which could mean both preserving the past in perpetuity (as the Defend the Birthplace activists wanted to do) or simply preserving the records with care and clarity, for historians and future generations to interpret. In 2021 that department had changed dramatically, however, with the records moved to off-site storage centers and a new director, Page Harrington. At that point, the name of the archive had changed from the National Historic Preservation Center to Cultural Assets; Harrington explained that the organization's motto regarding its archival record was to "leverage the history to grow the movement."[44] Focusing on the history of the Girl Scouts as an "asset" is corporate lingo, making it a resource to be mined, to be "leveraged," to "grow" the business. One of GSUSA's most profound and long-lasting "assets" is the story of Juliette Gordon Low, a crucial resource to be honed and used for membership and financial growth. Any challenge to the uplifting nature of her story—a clear telling of her upbringing, the family wealth that came from enslavement and settler colonialism that provided the seed money for the organization, and Low's own antipathy regarding racial inclusion—would turn this asset into a liability. Indeed, the model of drawing from history for organizational and corporate growth presumes a particular selectivity and exclusion of details. It's certainly not about looking at the records carefully to come to terms with the difficult racial histories and political compromises and obfuscations the Girl Scouts of the USA has made to establish and maintain itself as the largest organization for girls in the United States. While I was writing this book, the organization changed the name of the archive once again, to a more neutral term, GSUSA Collection and Archive, signaling perhaps a shift to a more scholarly and open approach to its own records.

In 2023, the US Mint announced that in 2025 it will issue a new quarter featuring Juliette Gordon Low as part of its American Women Quarters series. This is a formidable achievement for the Girl Scouts of the USA, as it solidifies the role this organization has played in the history of the United States, its shaping, and its future. The GSUSA wrote that the new Juliette Gordon Low coin would honor the "unstoppable founder" whose "visionary spirit" is a "beacon of hope for every girl."[45] Alongside the schools and the naval ship that have been named in her honor and her posthumous receipt of the Presidential Medal of Freedom, this coin places Low at the center of this movement for girls in the United States. But in valorizing her in this manner, it also asks us not to question who this woman was or how this organization has actually worked, or not worked, for girls, women, and the complex and destructive ways that race and gender have shaped our history and our future. When an institution organizes a sense of itself around a heroic story of an individual, there is always a looming problem: What if that story falters?

As the twenty-first century progresses, the organization will face difficult questions about how to move forward. The lure of coeducational "scouting" is strong for those who see Girl Scouting as a second-class institution compared to Boy Scouting and for those skeptical of the power of Girl Scouting to advocate for the particular needs and cultures of girls. One potential avenue is that taken by the more radical Girl Scout council in Massachusetts that explicitly stands by its feminist politics and creates deliberately inclusive communities. But that approach comes into direct conflict with the long-standing tactics of deflection that the Girl Scouts have used for over a century to bridge differences and make space in a world hostile to racial equality, gender equity, and girls' and women's empowerment. The final chapter will ask us to consider the costs of this long-standing strategy of what I have, in the end, come to call a "dangerous innocence."

Chapter 12

A Dangerous Innocence

As I conclude this book, I end with two moments that speak deeply to the tensions inherent in the history of Girl Scouting: one is a trip to an art exhibit, the other a letter I received from a former colleague. In 2017 I was walking through an exhibit of the artist Kerry James Marshall at the Met Breuer in New York City. Marshall's paintings, many of them very large mixed-media collages, evoke the joy and complexity of African American communities and histories in the United States; we see hair salons, children riding bikes, the interiors of homes, and the pain and joy of Black life in the twentieth century within the institutions, neighborhoods, and businesses that make up the fabric of everyday life. As I turned a corner in the exhibit I came to a standstill in front of a row of portraits: distinguished-looking young people in Girl Scout and Boy Scout uniforms. I later learned that Marshall had had his original portraits turned into patches, mirroring the badges scouts would wear on their own uniforms. The collection includes a Brownie, a Girl Scout, a Cub Scout, a Boy Scout, a scoutmaster, and a den mother, all staring forward with a dignified gaze, all silhouetted on the background of an image of a shooting star. These six Black scouts, adults, children, and teens, are stars of their own lives, stars of scouting. Girl Scouting and Boy Scouting, Marshall reminds us, have been crucial to African American life, a space Black adults claimed for their girls and boys, and girls and boys claimed for themselves, so that they could experience some measure of childhood safety and could learn the skills and confidence necessary to survive and flourish in a world that thrust upon them pain, inequity, and oppression.[1]

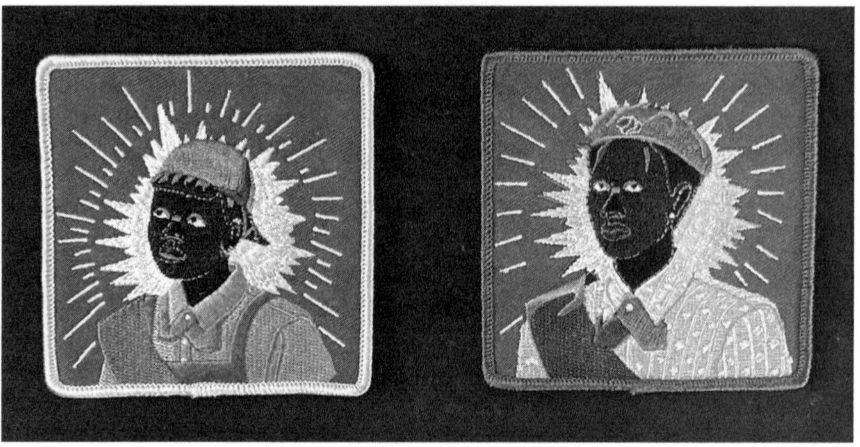

In the mid-1990s, artist Kerry James Marshall painted a series of portraits of African American Boy and Girl Scouts, which were later turned into patches similar to scouting badges. Here are two, of a Brownie and a Senior Girl Scout. Courtesy of the author.

The email I received from Janet Wright, a former colleague at Dickinson, underscored how much Black American girls and women had to fight for their rights and places within Girl Scouting. Wright had seen a notice about my research and wanted to share her own experience growing up as a white Girl Scout in the 1960s. She wrote:

> I was big in Girl Scouts in high school in Greensboro, NC in the early sixties, and I competed to be a delegate to the Girl Scout Roundup in Vermont in 1962. The schools were not integrated in those days, so I knew no black Girl Scouts; they even had a separate camp from "ours." A group of local leaders was designated to choose the Roundup delegates, and to our surprise they said we would be sending integrated patrols, and the competition weekend would take place at the "white" camp, Old Mill. That weekend was the first time I had met any Black Scouts. We camped in different units but were all together for activities, so we did get to know them. When our patrol was chosen for the Roundup, we elected one of the Black Scouts as our patrol leader and that was the group that attended the Roundup. . . .
>
> After we got home to Greensboro, I thought maybe things would be different; but the two Girl Scout camps, Old Mill and Douglas Long, remained separate (there was even a brochure, which didn't explicitly

> mention race, but it was clear from the photographs of campers). That year the Scouts said they would offer a LifeSaver swimming class, and my mother volunteered to teach it. We didn't have a pool, so they contracted with the Greensboro YWCA to hold the class there. Shortly before it began, we learned that one of the Black Scouts had applied for the class. I'm not sure whether it was the YWCA or the Scouts that found this objectionable, but it was proposed that they tell her that the class had been canceled (and then hold it anyway). My mother refused to teach it under that lie, so the class actually was canceled. I wrote a letter to the Council objecting to the decision, and received a reply that my letter was "ill timed" and implying I wasn't old enough to understand. But it appeared that sending an integrated group to Vermont was not the same as letting the same Scouts swim together in North Carolina.[2]

What struck me so powerfully about the story Wright remembered, and why I think she chose to share it with me, is the institutional duplicity that it underscores. On the one hand, the Greensboro Girl Scout council was willing to allow the girls, Black and white, to democratically vote for a Black patrol leader and to send an integrated group to Vermont, a picture of the inclusivity that by the 1960s the Girl Scouting was supposed to not only endorse but also facilitate. But when it came to more fundamental change, the council encouraged Wright's mother to lie and, when that did not work, chose to cancel the swimming lessons entirely. Wright's objections were met with derision, mocking her maturity and accusing her of being "ill timed." "Ill timed" for what? For whom?

As these chapters have explored, Girl Scouts promised a democratic, racial inclusivity without wanting to challenge white supremacy and encouraged girls to become strong, confident women without fundamentally wanting to upset normative concepts of femininity or challenge patriarchy explicitly. We have seen this in Juliette Gordon Low's first dreams about the organization, based on Lord Robert Baden-Powell's vision, in films such as *The Golden Eaglet*, and in the convoluted inroads of Girl Scouting into American Indian boarding schools and Japanese American incarceration camps. We have seen this in the ways the organization handled discrimination against African American girls. We have seen this in the ways it vacillated between championing women's rights and racial equity and then hiding behind a mask of childhood sweetness, especially when it dealt with accusations of communism and blackballing by the Catholic Church and right-wing organizations. This approach gave the organization enough "cover" and sufficient flexibility to exist for over a century and to stretch across the North and South, deep racial division, and conflicting ideas about womanhood. But this approach also led to a thwarted form of silent feminism and to the reinforcement of a dangerous and incorrect myth of a benevolent nation where the enduring legacy of slavery, Indigenous genocide, and the ongoing brutality of white nationalism and imperialism simply did not exist. This book has asked us to face directly the way this extraordinarily mainstream organization was both a force for progressive change and an institution where many white women wielded significant power in the shaping and development of our colonial state. It has asked us to understand the ways that the Girl Scouts' trailblazing has always occurred with forces pressing on it from every side. On the one hand, the organization exuded patriotism and acquiescence to the standards of white femininity, a sweetness that seemed beyond reproach; on the other hand, it created space for women and girls who were rebels on every level, in their individual deportment, in their racial politics and international worldview, in their sexual identities. And usually, the ability of girls and women to act as those rebels was tolerated only insofar as they stayed carefully inscribed within the boundaries of white nationalism and a certain kind of normative womanhood. When Janet Wright spoke up, her voice was rejected as "ill timed." When African American cultural critic Tressie McMillan Cottom tried to join the organization, she found herself unwelcome, "too much" for "white Girl Scout troops."[3]

This book, then, has asked us to look at the tangled roots of white supremacy, imperialism, and a tepid, white protofeminism that gave birth to this organization and to the ways that it allowed girls to be "loud" and "competent" only insofar as they didn't challenge the status quo too much. It asks us to look directly at the "innocence" that so framed my own experience of Girl Scouting. In her book *Breathe: A Letter to My Sons*, Imani Perry writes, "Americans are addicted to innocence. That is part of its parsimoniousness when it comes to democracy. They are never held to account, like the child with donut crumbs around her mouth who is so cute we pretend to believe she didn't swallow the sugar."[4] There is so much that Americans claim innocence about: the genocide that "cleared" the land for the project of American nationalism; the enslavement of Africans that fueled the economic engine that created the economic powerhouse of the United States; the enduring racism—in Jim Crow laws and their aftermath, in the incarceration of Japanese Americans, in hostility to immigration—that continually strengthened and re-created social and political white supremacy; and the cultural and military imperialism that annexed territories and maintained markets throughout the world. Girl Scouting narratives about itself certainly fit into this rhetoric of innocence: a girls' organization that promised inclusivity and brought its useful, engaging program to everyone who wanted it. And the national organization reinforces this "innocent" history every time it pulls out pictures of racially mixed groups (which were a rarity) to demonstrate its wide-open approach. This narrative of innocence both obscures the fact that Girl Scouts were never entirely inclusive, that girls and women of color had to struggle long and hard to claim a place in this organization, and it masks the way that Girl Scouts foisted itself on non-white groups, serving as a vehicle for the race-based imperialism that our national ideology also rewrites as the spread of democracy.

Girl Scouts have drawn from this narrative of innocence in yet another way: to mute the ways that it was frequently involved in progressive, antipatriarchal, antiracist work. When Juliette Gordon Low claimed the masculinist term "scout" rather than "guide," saying it was just more "fun" and "fit American girls better," she eluded the accusation that she was part of the New Woman movement. It was a useful strategy, a deflection so she could continue her work that was indeed creating new opportunities for and challenging so many of the restrictions imposed on girls and women. Girl Scouts used this technique throughout the twentieth century whenever difficult issues arose. The organization could deny lesbianism, saying that many of its leaders were simply single. It could allow troops of color to exist, but only under the control and jurisdiction of white councils. When the American Legion brought on its full attack against the organization, claiming it was part of an internationalist communist plot, it could say, "We are simply a girls' organization." It might move in progressive directions, but Girl Scouts knew how to take cover quickly, to protect themselves from conservative forces by never explicitly "saying" "antiracism" or "feminism." Indeed, as I've studied the Girl Scouts, I've learned that one of the most powerful ways the organization has been able to maintain its narrow tightrope across the battle lines of feminism and civil rights is through careful "cover-up" work, shrouding the aspects of its organization that were protofeminist and antiracist in a veneer of innocence so powerful that no one who might be critical would look too closely. As Girl Scout CEO Anna Maria Chavez said so vehemently in denying any ties to Planned Parenthood or to any progressive causes, "A box of Girl Scout cookies is not a political statement." Girl Scouts have reverted to the "sweet girl" image whenever the risks of using one's voice or explicitly fighting for civil rights and feminism appeared too great, and it has been doing that from the origins of the organization through today.

These strategies of innocence—claiming innocence of the sins of American hegemony of which Girl Scouting was completely a part, and using innocence to convey that scouting is "just a girls' organization"—created a flexibility that allowed Girl Scouting to survive for over a century. But they have also created great damage, allowing the organization to support policies and practices that hurt girls and women, that undercut the possibilities of a truly inclusive girls' organization, and that limit their ability to really work for change that would support a better world. Innocence also encouraged a white complacency and a way of thinking about and living in feminism that was brutally incapable of examining its own imbrications in racist structures and beliefs.

As the Girl Scouts move further into the twenty-first century, it's unclear where the organization will go. Will it be able to withstand pressure from the Boy Scouts, which has become the "Scouts"? Will it be able to survive in a world that gives girls so much else to be interested in, from sports to digital worlds? It is clear that the world needs organizations that protect children and that provide opportunities free of sexism, racism, and ableism, free of the constrictive forces of unbridled nationalism, authoritarianism, capitalism, and rising fascism. Can Girl Scouting help do this? It might, but only if it claims its politics squarely, eschewing the prevarication that has so silenced and weakened it before.

Whatever the future of Girl Scouting, however, it behooves us to look clearly back at its tangled and complex history. For over a century this major US institution has coupled women's empowerment—mostly white women's empowerment—with a deep racism and colonialism that has been largely unexamined or unearthed. That legacy of white women's empowerment braided together with racism and colonialism helps explain both the limits of mainstream feminism today and the ways that cultural, social, political, and economic inequity have continued to flourish despite a vocal rhetoric to the contrary. Each of us has personal, everyday histories that are bound up in greater national and international stories. For me, it's the Girl Scouts. As I said in the beginning of this book, Girl Scouts saved my life. But while Girl Scouting taught me to be an intrepid girl, it also taught me a dangerous "innocence." Undoing the "innocence" of that history is a first step to imagining, and creating, a more just and equitable society for everyone.

Notes

CHAPTER 1

1. Jennie Vasarhelyi, "Exploring Black History in Cuyahoga Valley," National Park Service, accessed November 30, 2024, www.nps.gov/articles/000/exploring-black-history-in-cuyahoga-valley.htm. I particularly want to thank Hazim Abdullah-Smith, postdoctoral fellow at Cuyahoga Valley National Park, for his 2024 American Studies Association presentation on Camp Mueller.

2. Celeste Ng, *Little Fires Everywhere* (New York: Penguin Books, 2017), 3.

3. Some excellent sources on the Boy Scouts include Jay Mechling, *On My Honour: Boy Scouts and the Making of American Youth* (Chicago: University of Chicago Press, 2001); Benjamin Rene Jordan, *Modern Manhood and the Boy Scouts of America: Citizenship, Race and the Environment, 1910–1930* (Chapel Hill: University of North Carolina Press, 2016); and Mischa Honeck, *Our Frontier Is the World: The Boy Scouts in the Age of American Ascendancy* (Ithaca, NY: Cornell University Press, 2018).

4. Key works on the history of Girl Scouts include Mary Degenhardt and Judith Kirsch, *Girl Scout Collector's Guide: A History of Uniforms, Insignia, Publications, and Memorabilia*, 2nd ed. (Lubbock: Texas Tech University Press, 2005); Betty Christiansen, *Girl Scouts: A Celebration of 100 Trailblazing Years* (New York: Stewart, Tabori, and Chang, 2017); and children's biographies celebrating the originality and pluck of Juliette Gordon Low, such as Ginger Wadsworth, *First Girl Scout: The Life of Juliette Gordon Low* (New York: Clarion Books, 2012). There is a cohort of scholars with work on the Girl Scouts, including Stacey Cordery's substantive and beautifully written biography *Juliette Gordon Low: The Remarkable Founder of the Girl Scouts* (New York: Penguin Books, 2012); Nancy Manahan, ed., *On My Honor: Lesbians Reflect on their Scouting Experience* (Northboro, MA: Madwoman, 1997), a moving collection of personal essays exploring lesbian identity and experiences in Girl Scouting; Tammy Proctor, *Scouting for Girls: A Century of Girl Guides and Girl Scouts* (Santa Barbara, CA: Praeger, 2009), which identifies the modes of flexibility that allowed Girl Scouting and Girl Guiding to survive for so long; and a number of studies that place Girl Scouting within a cohort of girls' organizations and popular culture. These include Kristine Alexander, *Guiding Modern Girls: Girlhood, Empire and Internationalism in the 1920s and 1930s* (Vancouver: UBC Press, 2017); Susan Miller, *Growing Girls: The Natural Origins of Girls' Organizations in America* (New Brunswick, NJ: Rutgers University Press, 2007); Renée M. Sentilles, *American Tomboys, 1850–1912* (Amherst: University of Massachusetts Press, 2018); and Jennifer Helgren, *American Girls and Global Responsibility: A New Relation to the World during the Early Cold War* (New Brunswick, NJ: Rutgers University Press, 2017).

5. Hard Histories at Hopkins project, https://hardhistory.jhu.edu; Robin Pogrebin,

"Roosevelt Statue to Be Removed," *New York Times*, June 22, 2020, www.nytimes.com/2020/06/21/arts/design/roosevelt-statue-to-be-removed-from-museum-of-natural-history.html.

6. See, e.g., Susan Ware, *Why They Marched: Untold Stories of the Women Who Fought for the Right to Vote* (Cambridge, MA: Belknap, 2019); and Elisa Camiscioli and Jean Quataert, eds., "Suffrage and Beyond—Celebrating Women's History," special issue, *Journal of Women's History* 32, no. 1 (2020).

7. Ibram Kendi, *How to Be an Antiracist* (New York: Random House, 2019).

8. Sara Ahmed, *The Cultural Politics of Emotion* (New York: Routledge, 2015).

9. The work of Saidiya Hartman, such as *Scenes of Subjection: Terror, Slavery, and Self-Making in Nineteenth-Century America* (New York: Oxford University Press, 1997) and *Lose Your Mother: A Journey along the Atlantic Slave Route* (New York: Farrar, Straus and Giroux, 2007), and the work of Tiya Miles, such as *All That She Carried: The Journey of Ashley's Sack, A Black Family Keepsake* (New York: Random House, 2021), provide powerful examples of scholarship that works creatively with the absences in the traditional archives.

CHAPTER 2

1. "Juliette Gordon Low," Girl Scouts, accessed July 2, 2021, www.girlscouts.org/en/about-girl-scouts/our-history/juliette-gordon-low.html.

2. Anne Hyde Choate and Helen Ferris, eds., *Juliette Low and the Girl Scouts: The Story of an American Woman, 1860–1927* (New York: Girl Scouts, Incorporated, 1928), 102.

3. To trace the use of this quotation, note that Mildred Pace quotes Johnston in Mildred Pace, *Juliette Low* (New York: Scribners Sons, 1947), 135. Gladys Denny Shultz and Daisy Gordon Lawrence then quote Pace (who quoted Johnston) in their *Lady from Savannah: The Life of Juliette Low* (Philadelphia: J. B. Lippincott, 1958), 305; and Stacey Cordery cites Lawrence and Shultz (who quoted Pace, who quoted Johnston) in her *Juliette Gordon Low: The Remarkable Founder of the Girl Scouts* (New York: Penguin Books, 2012), 202. The quotation shows up—usually without any citation—in every children's biography of Juliette, including Pace, *Juliette Low*, 135; Ely List, *Juliette Low* (New York: Girl Scouts of the USA, 1928 and 1960), 37; Kathleen Kudlinski, *Juliette Gordon Low: America's First Girl Scout* (New York: Viking Penguin, 1988), 50; June Behrens, *Juliette Low: Founder of the Girl Scouts of America* (Chicago: Childrens Press 1988), 3; and Ginger Wadsworth, *First Girl Scout: The Life of Juliette Gordon Low* (New York: Clarion Books, 2012), 113. Of all these works, Stacy Cordery's carefully researched scholarly biography stands out as the exception.

4. Edith Johnston, "My Work with the Girl Scouts and Juliette Low," August 6, 1952, box 1, folder 9; Johnston to Choate, November 27, 1928, box 1, folder 11; and Choate to Johnston, October 10, 1928, box 1, folder 11, all in Edith Johnston Collection, Georgia Historical Society, Savannah.

5. Corrine McConnaughy, *The Woman Suffrage Movement in America: A Reassessment* (Cambridge: Cambridge University Press, 2013).

6. Low to Johnston, n.d., MS 318, Gordon Family Papers Collection, Georgia Historical Society, Savannah.

7. Nellie Kinzie Gordon to Low, March 17, n.d., MS 318/42/3, Gordon Family Papers Collection, Georgia Historical Society, Savannah; Cordery, *Juliette Gordon Low*, 206.

8. From Diversity Timeline: Kat White, internal GSUSA memo, "Historic Fact for DEI," 2 (in author's possession), 2; Cordery, *Juliette Gordon Low*, 249; Low to Montague Gammon, January 12, 1917, folder "JGL Bio-1920," Girl Scouts of the USA National Historic Preservation Center, New York.

9. Cordery, *Juliette Gordon Low*, 2012, 248–49; "President's Wife Gives Colors Here to Girl Scout Unit," *Philadelphia Inquirer*, June 27, 1918.

10. Betty Christiansen, *Girl Scouts: A Celebration of 100 Trailblazing Years* (New York: Stewart, Tabori, and Chang, 2017), 96, 152.

11. Charles Johnson, "William Washington Gordon," New Georgia Encyclopedia, last modified September 25, 2014, www.georgiaencyclopedia.org/articles/history-archaeology/william-washington-gordon-1796-1842; Jeffrey Young, "Slavery in Antebellum Georgia," New Georgia Encyclopedia, last modified September 30, 2020, www.georgiaencyclopedia.org/articles/history-archaeology/slavery-in-antebellum-georgia.

12. Cordery, *Juliette Gordon Low*, 4.

13. Slave schedules, series M653, Eighth Census of the United States, 1860, Records of the Bureau of the Census, RG 29, National Archives, Washington, DC.

14. "Biographical Note: Gordon Family," Georgia Historical Society (website), accessed April 26, 2025, https://7063.sydneyplus.com/archive/final/Portal.aspx?lang=en-US; Young, "Slavery in Antebellum Georgia"; Cordery, *Juliette Gordon Low*, 5.

15. For a comprehensive account of white settlement and Indigenous resistance and survival, see Roxanne Dunbar-Ortiz, *An Indigenous People's History of the United States* (Boston: Beacon, 2015).

16. The Kinzies are credited in popular discourse as the "founders" of Chicago.

17. See Dominic A. Pacyga, *Chicago: A Biography* (Chicago: University of Chicago Press, 2009), 12–13.

18. Nina Baym, introduction to *Wau-Bun: The Early Day in the Northwest*, by Juliette M. Kinzie (1856; Champaign: University of Illinois Press, 1992).

19. Karen Bell, "Atlantic Slave Trade to Savannah," New Georgia Encyclopedia, last modified September 24, 2020, www.georgiaencyclopedia.org/articles/history-archaeology/atlantic-slave-trade-to-savannah.

20. Anastatia Hodgens Sims, "Juliette Gordon Low," in *Georgia Women: Their Lives and Times*, ed. Ann Short Chirhart and Betty Wood (Athens: University of Georgia Press, 2009), 370–89.

21. Shultz and Lawrence, *Lady from Savannah*, 184.

22. Cordery, *Juliette Gordon Low*, 184.

23. For a full discussion on the fears of emasculation in the late nineteenth and early twentieth centuries, see Gail Bederman, *Manliness and Civilization: A Cultural History of Gender and Race in the United States, 1880–1917* (Chicago: University of Chicago Press, 1995).

24. Cordery, *Juliette Gordon Low*, 184.

25. Kristine Alexander, *Guiding Modern Girls: Girlhood, Empire and Internationalism in the 1920s and 1930s* (Vancouver: UBC Press, 2017), 27.

26. In *Juliette Gordon Low*, 178, Cordery notes that she was unbothered by others' judgment of her as quite "quirky." Sometimes this focus on action could be construed negatively. For instance, Shultz and Lawrence, in *Lady from Savannah*, describe the "natural

naivete and impulsiveness into the downright eccentricity for which she became famous" (199); in Choate and Ferris's *Juliette Low,* her brother Arthur describes her as someone whose "reasoning power was often faulty and common sense appeared to be lacking" (76).

27. For a thorough discussion of early twentieth-century US girls' organizations, see Susan Miller, *Growing Girls: The Natural Origins of Girls' Organizations in America* (New Brunswick, NJ: Rutgers University Press, 2007).

28. Mary Degenhardt and Judith Kirsch, *Girl Scout Collector's Guide: A History of Uniforms, Insignia, Publications, and Memorabilia,* 2nd ed. (Lubbock: Texas Tech University Press, 2005), 546.

29. Cordery, *Juliette Gordon Low,* 295.

30. "Mrs. Arthur Choate Dies at 80; a Long-Time Girl Scout Leader," *New York Times,* May 18, 1967; "Helen Josephine Ferris," Nebraska Authors, accessed December 7, 2021, https://nebraskaauthors.org/authors/helen-josephine-ferris.

31. "Gladys Denny Shultz," *New York Times,* June 22, 1984; "Daisy G. Lawrence, 81, First Girl Scout in U.S.," *New York Times,* April 28, 1982.

32. Shultz and Lawrence, *Lady from Savannah.*

33. This is the general outline of Juliette Gordon Low that resurfaces in nearly all the texts that focus on her life. These range from many children's biographies, such as Pace, *Juliette Low* (published originally in 1947 and reissued in 1975 and 1997); to works in the genre of "important American women," such as Kudlinski, *Juliette Gordon Low*; to the many books published during the 100th anniversary of the Girl Scouts, such as Wadsworth, *First Girl Scout.* Significantly, most of the details and stories in these biographies come from the two early aforementioned sources written by Low's relatives and friends. Only Stacy Cordery's well-researched 2012 *Juliette Gordon Low* deviates from these stories and often works to seek out the truth behind such myths as Low saving a kitten or selling her pearls.

34. Robin Bernstein, *Racial Innocence: Performing American Childhood from Slavery to Civil Rights* (New York: New York University Press, 2011), 8.

35. This detail shows up first in Low's autobiographical essay in Choate and Ferris, *Juliette Low,* and then is repeated in Pace, *Juliette Low.*

36. Bernstein, *Racial Innocence*; Tressie McMillan Cottom, *Thick: And Other Essays* (New York: New Press, 2019).

37. Helen Boyd Higgins, *Juliette Low: Girl Scout Founder* (New York: Bobbs-Merrill, 1951), 7.

38. Margaret Mitchell, *Gone with the Wind* (New York: Macmillan, 1936).

39. Cordery, *Juliette Gordon Low,* 26.

40. Cordery, *Juliette Gordon Low,* 39, 217.

41. For instance, Cordery (*Juliette Gordon Low,* 3) writes, "Eighteen-year-old Nellie Kinzie slid gleefully down the banister at the Yale library and landed with a self-assured bounce directly in front of the astonished Southerner."

42. The stories often include additional details of place and time. The occasion of Nellie's slide down the banister was a visit to Yale, where Willie was a student; Nellie was visiting from her New York finishing school with her friend Eliza, Willie's sister.

43. David Blight, *Race and Reunion: The Civil War in American Memory* (Cambridge, MA: Belknap, 2002).

44. "The engagement lasted for over three years. . . . They had several things to straighten out between themselves. . . . There was also the matter of slavery to which Nellie, as a good Northerner, objected. . . . In a later letter she says, 'I don't like your remarks on puritanism. . . . Our church and our religion do not forbid innocent enjoyment. . . . Do you think you've caught a Tartar? I may express myself strongly but remember, I feel anything *like* a slur on my church far more than you ever did my remarks on *slavery*.' Apparently they reached a compromise. Willie bowed to Nellie's Episcopalianism, later on joining Christ Church in Savannah, and Nellie forbore to criticize slavery." Shultz and Lawrence, *Lady from Savannah*, 53–54.

45. Shultz and Lawrence, *Lady from Savannah*, 18.

46. Janie Lynn Panagopoulos, *Little Ship under Full Sail: An Adventure in History* (Spring Lake, MI: River Road, 2013).

47. For a full discussion of why the Fort Dearborn battle should not be considered or labeled a "massacre," see Ann Durkin Keating, *Rising Up from Indian Country: The Battle of Fort Dearborn and the Birth of Chicago* (Chicago: University of Chicago Press, 2012).

48. Cordery, *Juliette Gordon Low*, 229.

49. For a full exploration of the attacks on Girl Scouts in the 1950s, particularly regarding communism and by extension lesbianism, see Susan H. Swetnam, "Look Wider Still: The Subversive Nature of Girl Scouting in the 1950s," *Frontiers* 37, no. 1 (2016): 90–114.

50. Nancy Manahan, ed., *On My Honor: Lesbians Reflect on their Scouting Experience* (Northboro, MA: Madwoman, 1997).

51. See, e.g., Wadsworth, *First Girl Scout*, 2. This work also features the banister story.

52. Shultz and Lawrence, *Lady from Savannah*, photograph inset.

53. Shultz and Lawrence, *Lady from Savannah*, 316.

54. Shultz and Lawrence, *Lady from Savannah*, 11.

55. Choate and Ferris, *Juliette Low*, 4, 14, 5, 58. I have used the spelling "Eliza" Hendry, which Stacy Cordery also uses, despite the various spellings found in Choate and Ferris's work, such as in Arthur's memories on p. 58.

56. Josephine Daskam Bacon, dir., *The Golden Eaglet* (New York: Girl Scouts of the USA, 1918).

57. Choate and Ferris, *Juliette Low*, 59, 143.

58. Choate and Ferris, *Juliette Low*; Pace, *Juliette Low*.

59. For instance, neither Ruby Radford nor June Behrens mentions slavery or servants in her biography. Ruby Radford, *Juliette Low: Girl Scout Founder* (Champaign, IL: Garrard, 1965); Behrens, *Juliette Low*.

60. Choate and Ferris, *Juliette Low*, 163; "A Gift from the Girl Scout to our Boys in Service," *Rally*, November 1918; "Camping Days Are Coming," *Rally*, April 1919.

CHAPTER 3

1. Josephine Daskam Bacon, dir., *The Golden Eaglet* (New York: Girl Scouts of the USA, 1918).

2. Louise Paine Benjamin, "Filming the Girl Scouts," *Rally*, September 1918, 1.

3. Edwin S. Porter, dir., *The Great Train Robbery* (New York: Edison Manufacturing, 1903).

4. Sherrie A. Inness, ed., *Nancy Drew and Company: Culture, Gender and Girls' Series* (Bowling Green, OH: Bowling Green State University Press, 1997).

5. Josephine Daskam Bacon, "Here and There with Juliette Low in Girl Scouting," in *Juliette Low and the Girl Scouts: The Story of an American Woman, 1860–1927*, ed. Anne Hyde Choate and Helen Ferris (New York: Girl Scouts, Incorporated, 1928), 163, 166. The image of the cook can be seen in Choate and Ferris, *Juliette Low*, 163; "A Gift from the Girl Scout to our Boys in Service," *Rally*, November 1918; "Camping Days Are Coming," *Rally*, April 1919.

6. See Brian Rouleau, *Empire's Nursery: Children's Literature and the Origins of the American Century* (New York: New York University Press, 2021), 1.

7. Susan A. Miller, *Growing Girls: The Natural Origins of Girls' Organizations in America* (New Brunswick, NJ: Rutgers University Press, 2007); "Early Girl Scouting Organizations in the United States," February 2013, from Girl Scouts of the USA National Historic Preservation Center, New York (hereafter cited as NHPC) in author's possession. GSUSA has changed the name of its archives many times in recent years; as of the publication of this book, GSUSA calls it the GSUSA Collection and Archive. Many of the materials have been moved off the New York site since I completed my research. Considering that I conducted my research when all the materials were stored in New York City, I have chosen to retain the name the National Historic Preservation Center to clarify the site of my research.

8. Low to Jane Rippin, July 31, 1919, box "American Indian Girl Scouts," folder "Girl Scout Organizations," NHPC.

9. For an excellent study of the Camp Fire Girls, see Jennifer Helgren, *The Camp Fire Girls: Gender, Race, and American Girlhood, 1910–1980* (Lincoln: University of Nebraska Press, 2022). In a letter to Dean James Russell of the Teachers College of Columbia University, Lou Henry Hoover, the president of the Girl Scouts and future First Lady of the United States, wrote that the "Campfire Girl program contains certain features which their church cannot recommend," such as "ceremonies and principles" that made the Girl Scouts more attractive to Catholics. Camp Fire Girls executive director Lester Scott complained in another letter that the "beads" used in Camp Fire Girls did not remind Catholics of the rosary. Hoover to Russell, March 31, 1924; and Scott to Mrs. Oliver Harriman, January 26, 1925, both in box "Campfire Girls, Proposed Amalgamation Controversy Reports," NHPC.

10. For an early and thorough discussion of the "guide"-versus-"scout" controversy, see Mary Aiken Rothschild, "To Scout or to Guide? The Girl Scout–Boy Scout Controversy, 1912–1941," *Journal of Women Studies* 6, no. 3 (1981): 115–21.

11. Lord Robert Baden-Powell, "Girl Scouts or Girl Guides," *Jamboree*, October 1921.

12. Baden-Powell to Anne Hyde Choate, January 1922, box "Boy Scouts of America," folder "Correspondence/Comments," NHPC.

13. "Report Re Girl Scout Situation," March 19, 1924, box "Boy Scouts of America," folder "Reports by Boy Scouts," NHPC.

14. "Report Re Girl Scout Situation."

15. Adrienne Rich, "Compulsory Heterosexuality and Lesbian Existence," *Signs* 5, no. 4 (1980): 631–60.

16. For an introduction to the range of feminist activisms of the time, see Miriam Schneir, ed., *Feminism in Our Time: The Essential Writings, World War II to the Present* (New

York: Vintage Books, 1994); and Beverly Guy-Sheftall, ed., *Words of Fire: An Anthology of African-American Feminist Thought* (New York: New Press, 2011).

17. "Nature of Complaints," in "Report Re Girl Scout Situation."

18. All these quotations collected in "Report Re Girl Scout Situation."

19. Eleanor Roosevelt, "I Hope Girl Scouts and Camp Fire Girl Groups Will Merge," *Washington Daily News*, September 24, 1946, 29.

20. Girl Scout memorandum summarizing the Boy Scout report, April 14, 1924, box "Boy Scouts of America," folder "Reports by Boy Scouts," NHPC.

21. Christina Kotchemidova, "From Good Cheer to 'Drive-By Smiling': A Social History of Cheerfulness," *Journal of Social History* 39, no. 1 (2005): 5–37.

22. Juliana Horatia Ewing, *The Brownies and Other Tales* (London: Society for Promoting Christian Knowledge, 1871, www.gutenberg.org/files/16052/16052-h/16052-h.htm.

23. "A Gift from the Girl Scouts to Our Boys in Service," *Rally*, November 1918.

24. Mrs. Theodore H. Price, "Girl Scouts," *The Outlook*, March 6, 1918.

25. Walter J. Hoxie, *How Girls Can Help Their Country: Handbook for Girl Scouts* (Bedford, MA: Applewood Books, 1913), 70–71.

26. Hoxie, *How Girls Can Help*, 168–69.

27. For discussion of Boston marriages, see Lillian Faderman, *Odd Girls and Twilight Lovers: A History of Lesbian Life in 20th-Century America* (New York: Columbia University Press, 1991).

28. For a fine collection of essays on the Nancy Drew series, its racism, and its ideal of a new kind of girl, see Carolyn Stewart Dyer and Nancy Tillman Romatov, eds., *Rediscovering Nancy Drew* (Iowa City: University of Iowa Press, 1995). See also Rosemary Garland Thomson, *Extraordinary Bodies: Figuring Physical Disability in American Culture and Literature*, 20th anniversary ed. (New York: Columbia University Press, 2017).

29. Lillian C. Garis, *The Girl Scout Pioneers* (New York: Cupples and Leon, 1920).

30. Edith Lavell, *The Girl Scouts Good Turn* (New York: A. L. Burt, 1922), 80, 82.

31. For a full listing of early Girl Scout novels, see Mary Degenhardt and Judith Kirsch, *Girl Scouts Collector's Guide* (Lubbock: Texas Tech University Press, 2005), 449–51.

32. Lavell, *Girl Scouts Good Turn*, 56. For a discussion of how fatness is connected to concepts of the uncivilized body, see Amy Erdman Farrell, *Fat Shame: Stigma and the Fat Body in American Culture* (New York: New York University Press, 2011), 59–81.

33. Miller, *Growing Girls*; Leslie Paris, *Children's Nature: The Rise of the American Summer Camp* (New York: New York University Press, 2008).

34. Gail Bederman, *Manliness and Civilization: A Cultural History of Gender and Race in the United States, 1880–1917* (Chicago: Chicago University Press, 1995).

35. In her book *American Tomboys, 1850–1915*, Renée Sentilles describes the tomboy as a figure who could play with the freedoms of boyhood, dabbling in the "wildness" of outside activities. Novels and cartoons often painted tomboys as white girls who were dirty, even dark. As the tomboy grows into adulthood, however, those masculine and "savage" features are erased, digested into a figure who would be an active, healthy, white woman. As Sentilles writes, "The term sanctioned girls behaving like boys while still separating them by gender, granting girls freedom to temporarily own a boyish identity while denying that same freedom to girlish boys." The construct of the tomboy allowed

girls access to the "humanness" of a masculine-oriented childhood, though for a limited time, sufficient only to allow them to become future robust mothers of the nation. In other words, being a "tomboy" was a transitional moment, one that would "naturally" end with marriage and motherhood; there was no parallel for boys, as this would mean dabbling in the inferior state of girlhood. Significantly, the "tomboy" identity developed out of and was ensnared in the construction of white supremacy. Only white, middle-class girls, whose femininity was firmly established, could be imagined as or live as a "tomboy." Working-class girls and all girls of color rarely to never emerged in tomboy literature, Sentilles points out. Their claims to femininity and even to the state of childhood, which was required for the tomboy status, were so weak within dominant, white culture that they were excluded from the liminal phase of "tomboy." As Sentilles puts it, "Although the tomboy was widely understood to embody female liberation, she also rendered her freedoms as white privilege." Renée Sentilles, *American Tomboys, 1850–1915* (Amherst: University of Massachusetts Press, 2018), 2.

36. *Campward Ho! A Manual for Girl Scout Camps* (New York: McGraw Phillips, 1920).

37. "History," Edith Macy Center, accessed April 27, 2025, www.edithmacy.com/about-us/history.

38. "Report on Girl Scouts and the Camping Experience," 1987, box "Camp and Camping: General to All American Camp," NHPC.

39. Elin Lindberg, "Report on Girl Scout Camping," August 1956, box "Camp and Camping: General to All American Camp," NHPC. Emphasis in the original.

40. The myth of the pioneer extended across US organizations that emphasized youth camping, as Leslie Paris so beautifully explores; Paris, *Children's Nature.* It was indeed crucial for the Girl Scouts.

41. "Report on Girl Scouts and the Camping Experience."

42. John Archer, ed., *Girl Scout Songs* (New York: Girl Scouts of the USA, 1925).

43. For the groups of people excluded from camping, see Paris, *Children's Nature.*

44. Miller, *Growing Girls.*

45. See Miller, *Growing Girls*, 196. For a discussion of the eugenics movement, see Wendy Kline, *Building a Better Race: Gender, Sexuality, and Eugenics from the Turn of the Century to the Baby Boom* (Berkeley: University of California Press, 2001).

46. *Campward Ho!*, 150.

47. *Campward Ho!*, 19.

48. Ann Campbell Duncan, "Health Report, Camp Andree," 1924, box "Camp and Camping: General to All American Camp," NHPC.

49. Hoxie, *How Girls Can Help*, 28.

50. Hoxie, *How Girls Can Help*, 28.

51. Lindberg, "Report on Girl Scout Camping."

52. Jessica Rippin, "Report of Camp Andree," 1925, box "Camp and Camping: General to All American Camp," NHPC.

53. Nancy Manahan, ed., *On My Honor: Lesbians Reflect on their Scouting Experience*, (Northboro, MA: Madwoman, 1997). See also Judith McDaniel, "The Juliette Low Legacy," in *Lavender Mansions: 40 Contemporary Lesbian and Gay Short Stories*, ed. Irene Zahava (Boulder, CO: Westview, 1994), 242–50.

54. *Campward Ho!*, 15.

55. *Campward Ho!*, 63.

56. *Campward Ho!*, 15.

57. For a discussion of Girl Scout camping, see Paris, *Children's Nature*, 220–23.

58. "Camp Andree Advisory Committee Meeting," May 21, 1940, box "Camp and Camping: General to All American Camp," NHPC.

59. Miya Carey, "Becoming 'a Force for Desegregation': The Girl Scouts and Civil Rights in the Nation's Capital," *Washington History* 29, no. 2 (2017): 54–55.

60. "Camp Andree Advisory Committee Meeting."

61. "Girl Scout News," *Pittsburgh (PA) Courier*, July 5, 1947, 2.

CHAPTER 4

1. Whitebead to Committee on Awards, February 2, 1938, box "American Indian Girl Scouts," folder "1929–1950," Girl Scouts of the USA National Historic Preservation Center, New York (hereafter cited as NHPC).

2. "Report on Indian Scouting," n.d., box "American Indian Girl Scouts," folder "1929–1950," NHPC.

3. David Wallace Adams, *Education for Extinction: American Indians and the Boarding School Experience, 1875–1928* (Lawrence: University of Kansas Press, 1995).

4. Riverside Indian School actually predated Carlisle Indian Industrial School, but Carlisle nevertheless became the prototype for schools across North America and Australia. Pamela Koenig, "Riverside Indian School," Encyclopedia of Oklahoma History and Culture, accessed April 27, 2025, www.okhistory.org/publications/enc/entry.php?entry=RI015.

5. "From the Commission of Indian Affairs," *Girl Scout Leader*, May 1932, 51.

6. "Help Toward Indian Study," *Girl Scout Leader*, May 1932, 61, 62.

7. Marguerite Twohy, "American Indian Girl Scouts," *Girl Scout Leader*, May 1932, 1.

8. Oleda Schrottky, "Famous American Women," *American Girl*, January 1940, 28–29.

9. George W. Knepper, *Ohio and Its People* (Kent, OH: Kent State University Press, 2003), 49.

10. Information about Tomochichi's boulder comes from two sources: "Brief Biography," Georgia Historical Society, accessed April 27, 2025, https://georgiahistory.com/education-outreach/online-exhibits/featured-historical-figures/tomochichi/tomochichi-brief-bio, and "Tomochichi Monument," Great American Treasures, accessed April 27, 2025, www.greatamericantreasures.org/destinations/tomochichi-monument/.

11. "Settler colonialism" is a term, coined by Patrick Wolfe, used to explain the processes by which a colonial power seeks to establish itself on new territories, living on the land and pushing out Indigenous people, whether by force, annihilation, or assimilation. The term provides a way of understanding conquest that is different from resource colonialism, where the plan of the conquering entity is to extract resources for the homeland but not permanently reside except as necessary or in the continued control of the resources. Interesting and important to this project, the logics of settler colonialism often seek to maintain some aura of "indigeneity" in order to differentiate the new state from the former one; thus, one can see how both Australia and the United States often appear

to valorize "Indians" even as the state has sought to destroy them. See Patrick Wolfe, "Settler Colonialism and the Elimination of the Native," *Journal of Genocide Research* 8, no. 4 (2006), 387–409.

12. Mary Degenhardt and Judith Kirsch, *Girl Scout Collector's Guide: A History of Uniforms, Insignia, Publications, and Memorabilia*, 2nd ed. (Lubbock: Texas Tech University Press, 2005), 96.

13. Degenhardt and Kirsch, *Girl Scout Collector's Guide*, 162.

14. Degenhardt and Kirsch, *Girl Scout Collector's Guide*, 277; Girl Scouts of the USA, *1963 Junior Girl Scout Handbook* (New York: Girl Scouts of the USA, 1963), 238.

15. Mary Levey to Jo Bloom, April 17, 1992, box "American Indian Girl Scouts," folder "American Indian Girl Scouts," NHPC.

16. Charlotte Moton Hubbard, "Report," November 21, 1946, box "American Indian Girl Scouts," folder "1929–1950," NHPC.

17. Marjorie Kirk interview by unidentified interviewer, n.d., transcript, box "American Indian Girl Scouts," folder "1954–," NHPC.

18. Lillian S. Williams, *A Bridge to the Future: The History of Diversity in Girl Scouting* (New York: Girl Scouts of the USA, 1996), 11.

19. For examples of the flurry of correspondence on this topic, see Mary White to Sibyl Newell, April 11, 1937; William Beatty (Office of Indian Affairs) to Newell, 1938; Newell to White, April 21, 1937; White to Emelia Thoorsell, February 25, 1937; and J. E. Shields to John Collier, April 11, 1936, all in box "American Indian Girl Scouts," folder "1929–1950," NHPC. On the 1947 name change to Bureau of Indian Affairs, see "Native American Heritage," National Archives, accessed April 27, 2025, www.archives.gov/research/native-americans/bia.

20. Jacqueline Fear-Segal and Susan D. Rose, eds., *Carlisle Indian Industrial School: Indigenous Histories, Memories, and Reclamations* (Lincoln: University of Nebraska Press, 2016). For an example of the complex and often fond feelings students had toward their schooling, see Amanda Cobb-Greetham, *Listening to Our Grandmothers' Stories: The Bloomfield Academy for Chickasaw Females, 1852–1949* (Lincoln: University of Nebraska Press, 2000).

21. "An Indian Girl Scout Camp," *Girl Scout Leader*, August–September 1934, 1; Williams, *Bridge to the Future*, 15.

22. "Report on Indian Scouting."

23. For an example of this correspondence, see Shields to Collier, April 11, 1936.

24. Ivalee Hobden to Burlington, Iowa, Girl Scout Council, March 13, 1950, box "American Indian Girl Scouts," folder "1929–1950," NHPC.

25. "An Indian Girl Scout Camp," 1; "Girl Scouting and the American Indian Girl," March 1963, *Girl Scouts Professional Newsletter*, in box "American Indian Girl Scouts," folder "American Indian Girl Scouts to 1966," NHPC.

26. For examples of overburdened staff, see "Conference with Miss Charlotte Mangseth, Head of Girls' Counselor Service, Intermountain Indian School," n.d.; and Juanita Oviatt, memorandum, June 4, 1952, both in box "American Indian Girl Scouts," folder "1951–1953," NHPC.

27. Michael P. Taylor and Terence Wride, "Indian Kids Can't Write Sonnets: Remembering the Poetry of Henry Tinhorn from the Intermountain Indian School," *American Quarterly* 72, no. 1 (2020): 25–54.

28. Hobden to the Burlington, Iowa, Girl Scout Council, March 13, 1950.

29. "Notes on Indian Work since Dec. 1952 Report," May 4, 1953; Boyce to Miss Thomas, March 10, 1953; and "Intermountain Indian School Community Visitation and Student Exchange Program," memorandum, 1953, all in box "American Indian Girl Scouts," folder "1951–1953," NHPC.

30. "Informal Group Meeting on American Indian Affairs," November 25, 1953, box "American Indian Girl Scouts," folder "1951–1953," NHPC.

31. On the pen pal scheme, see Eleanor Thomas to Helen Person, October 26, 1954, box "American Indian Girl Scouts," folder "American Indian Girl Scouts," NHPC. On the international fund, see "Meeting Concerning Girl Scouting for American Indians," February 19, 1951, box "American Indian Girl Scouts," folder "1951–1953," NHPC.

32. Twohy, "American Indian Girl Scouts," 52.

33. *Blue Book on Girl Scout Policies and Procedures* (Girl Scouts of the USA, 1957), 29; Letter to Diana Wilson, September 27, 1950, box "American Indian Girl Scouts," folder "American Indian Girl Scouts," NHPC.

34. Ivalee Hobden, "Field Activities Report," October 4–9, 11–13, 1950, box "American Indian Girl Scouts," folder "American Indian Girl Scouts to 1966," NHPC.

35. Diana Wilson to Miss C. Miller, August 24, 1950, box "American Indian Girl Scouts," folder "American Indian Girl Scouts to 1966," NHPC.

36. Skewes to George Boyce, November 25, 1944, box "American Indian Girl Scouts," folder "1929–1950," NHPC.

37. Hill to Sally Stickney, December 20, 1946, box "American Indian Girl Scouts," folder "American Indian Girl Scouts to 1966," NHPC.

38. Marguerite Twohy interview by Mrs. Dermady, February 12, 1966, transcript box "American Indian Girl Scouts," folder "American Indian Girl Scouts to 1966," NHPC; "Indian Name Given to Girl Scout Leader," n.d., box "American Indian Girl Scouts," folder "1929–1950," NHPC.

39. Mary White, "A Contemporary Pioneer," *Girl Scout Leader*, August–September 1934, 75.

40. For a discussion of the possibilities that life as a white female missionary provided, see Barbara Reeves-Ellington, Kathryn Kish Sklar, and Connie A. Shemo, eds., *Competing Kingdoms: Women, Mission, Nation, and the American Protestant Empire, 1812–1960* (Durham, NC: Duke University Press, 2010).

41. Hill to Stickney, December 20, 1946.

42. Ivalee Hobden to Miss Hotelling, March 15, 1950, box "American Indian Girl Scouts," folder "1929–1950," NHPC; Margaret Chapman, "Navajo Country: A Report on Girl Scouting in the Indian Schools," *Girl Scout Leader*, May 1953, 16.

43. "An American Indian Girl Scout Camp," *Girl Scout Leader*, August–September 1934.

44. "Famous American Women," 28–29. Emphasis is mine.

45. "Indian Girl Scout Camp," 74; Chapman, "Navajo Country," 15–16.

46. Loraine Morley Reynolds, "Navajo Nuggets—The Pinon Nuts," *Girl Scout Leader*, May 1932, 52.

47. For a discussion of "cheerfulness" as a mandatory affective state in dominant American culture, see Christina Kotchemidova, "From Good Cheer to 'Drive-By Smiling': A Social History of Cheerfulness," *Journal of Social History* 39, no. 1 (2005): 5–37.

48. Twohy, "American Indian Girl Scouts," 1. White to Newell, April 11, 1937.

49. Mary Littlefield, "Field Report on Crowe Indian Agency," November 18, 1942, box "American Indian Girl Scouts," folder "1929–1950," NHPC.

50. Boyce to GSUSA, May 19, 1947, box "American Indian Girl Scouts," folder "1929–1950," NHPC.

51. "Field Report: Girls at Kin-Li-Chee Day Ganado Mission School," December 6, 1946, box "American Indian Girl Scouts," folder "1929–1950," NHPC.

52. Marguerite Twohy, "The Weekend Camp, May 6–10, 1954, M. E. Rawley's Report," June 4, 1954, box "American Indian Girl Scouts," folder "1954–," NHPC.

53. Ivalee Hobden, "Field Report on Visit to Navajo Coordinating Council," October 1950, box "American Indian Girl Scouts," folder "1929–1950," NHPC; "Excerpts from Quarterly Reports on Indians, Region I," n.d. [ca. 1961], box "American Indian Girl Scouts," folder "–1966," NHPC.

54. Twohy, "American Indian Girl Scouts," 50.

55. Katharine Shankland, "Field Report," December 5, 1940, box "American Indian Girl Scouts," folder "1951–1953," NHPC.

56. "Meeting Concerning Girl Scouting for American Indians."

57. "Indian-Anglo Tensions," box "Civil Rights," folder "Integration," NHPC.

58. John Bloom, *To Show What an Indian Can Do: Sports and Native American Boarding Schools* (Minneapolis: University of Minnesota Press), 111–12.

59. "Indian Girl Scout Camp," 74.

60. Mrs. Edward L. Hughes, "The Great Adventure," March 20, 1953, box "American Indian Girl Scouts," folder "1951–1953," NHPC.

61. "Indian Girl Scout Camp," 74.

62. Katharine Shankland, "Field Report for Taos, New Mexico," May 1–3, 1941, box "American Indian Girl Scouts," folder "1929–1950," NHPC.

63. "Excerpt from Quarterly Report," November 15, 1957, box "American Indian Girl Scouts," folder "1954–," NHPC.

64. "Memoir from Eunice Prien and Mary Frances Biering," July 5, 1957, box "American Indian Girl Scouts," folder "1954–," NHPC.

65. Margaret Archuleta, Brenda J. Child, and K. Tsianina Lomawaima, *Away from Home: American Indian Boarding School Experiences, 1879–2000* (Phoenix, AZ: Heard Museum, 2000), 48.

66. Archuleta et al., *Away from Home*, 74.

67. Field Department to Field Staff, March 3, 1961, box "American Indian Girl Scouts," folder "American Indian Girl Scouts to 1966," NHPC.

68. The report "Girl Scouting and the American Indian Girl" included an excerpt from the 1963 *Girl Scouts Professional Newsletter*, which I quote here at length in this section. The newsletter article summarized the Girl Scout emphasis on integration: "As of 1962, the best and most exciting news about American Indian girls in Girl Scouting is that we do not know exactly who they are or how many of them are registered. This is not the result of poor statistical work, but the happy outcome of integrating American Indian girls into regular Girl Scout troops wherever possible."

69. "Girl Scouting and the American Indian Girl."

70. Twohy to Thompson, August 27, 1951; and Thompson to Margaret [*sic*] Twohy,

September 6, 1951, both in box "American Indian Girl Scouts," folder "1951–1953," NHPC; letter from National Congress of American Indians, November 4, 1954, box "American Indian Girl Scouts," folder "American Indian Girl Scouts to 1966," NHPC. In many GSUSA records, Thompson's name is spelled "Hildegarde," though in all her published materials it is spelled "Hildegard." I have used her published spelling in this book.

CHAPTER 5

1. Kristine Alexander, *Guiding Modern Girls: Girlhood, Empire, and Internationalism in the 1920s and 1930s* (Vancouver: UBC Press, 2017), 24, 27.

2. Tammy Proctor, *Scouting for Girls: A Century of Girl Guides and Girl Scouts* (Santa Barbara, CA: Praeger, 2009), 52–53.

3. "Philippines," World Association of Girl Guides and Girl Scouts, accessed July 12, 2024, www.wagggs.org/en/our-world/asia-pacific-region/member-organisations/philippines.

4. Rudyard Kipling, *Kim* (London: Macmillan, 1901). The first handbook for Girl Scouts explains that, "like Kim, a Scout should be 'Little friend to all the world.'" Walter J. Hoxie, *How Girls Can Help Their Country* (Bedford, MA: Applewood Books, 1913), 5.

5. Rudyard Kipling, "The White Man's Burden," *McClure's Magazine*, February 1899, 290–91.

6. For a full discussion of the Philippine-American War, see Daniel Immerwahr, *How to Hide an Empire: A History of the Greater United States* (New York: Farrar, Straus and Giroux, 2019), esp. chap. 6. See also Eric Foner, Kathleen DuVal, and Lisa McGirr, *Give Me Liberty! An American History*, 7th ed. (New York: W. W. Norton, 2023), 2:684–85.

7. Proctor, *Scouting for Girls*, 43.

8. "Who We Are," USA Girl Scouts Overseas, accessed July 12, 2024, www.usagso.org/en/discover/our-council.html. Lone Troops on Foreign Soil was renamed USA Girl Scouts Overseas. Today there are over 12,000 members in ninety countries.

9. Stacy A. Cordery, *Juliette Gordon Low: The Remarkable Founder of the Girl Scouts* (New York: Viking Books, 2012), 285.

10. Proctor, *Scouting for Girls*, 132.

11. Proctor, *Scouting for Girls*, 43.

12. Immerwahr, *How to Hide*, 400.

13. Immerwahr, *How to Hide*.

14. Storrow and her husband shared an interest in scouting; he became the second president of the Boy Scouts of America.

15. "The Founding of Our Chalet," World Association of Girl Guides and Girl Scouts, accessed March 17, 2022, www.wagggs.org/en/our-world/world-centres/our-chalet/about-our-chalet/history/our-chalet-story.

16. Wetherill's narrative explains that she actually was kicked out of her position as a Virginia troop leader—where she had hoped to fulfill her dream of going to Our Chalet—for being a lesbian. Rachel Wetherill, "Beneath One Roof," in *On My Honor: Lesbians Reflect on Their Scouting Experience*, ed. Nancy Manahan (Northboro, MA: Madwoman, 1997), 145–54.

17. "Our Council History," Girl Scouts of Hawai'i, accessed July 14, 2024, www.gshawaii.org/en/discover/our-council/Our-Council-History.html; "About Us," Guam Girl Scouts,

accessed July 14, 2024, http://guamgirlscouts.org/about-us; "About Us," Girl Scouts Farthest North Council, accessed July 14, 2024, www.fngsc.org/en/about/council_history.html.

18. "Girl Scouts of the USA Corporate Records," Girl Scout Archive Management System, accessed July 15, 2024, https://archives.girlscouts.org/Detail/collections/1.

19. Proctor, *Scouting for Girls*, 66, 67, 113.

20. Jennifer Helgren, *American Girls and Global Responsibility: A New Relation to the World during the Early Cold War* (New Brunswick, NJ: Rutgers University Press, 2017).

21. Helgren, *American Girls*, 61.

22. Helgren, *American Girls*, 15.

23. Proctor, *Scouting for Girls*, 126, 135.

24. Helgren, *American Girls*, 159.

25. Marcia Chalelain, "International Sisterhood: Cold War Girl Scouts Encounter the World," *Diplomatic History* 38, no. 2 (2014): 261.

26. Helgren, *American Girls*, 10.

27. Helgren, *American Girls*, 90.

28. Natalie Grace Merritt, "I Live on Okinawa," *American Girl*, November 1947.

29. Okinawa scrapbooks, 1957–59, Archives of the Girl Scout Council of the Nation's Capital, Frederick, Maryland. The 1960s numbers and details come from a sheet, dated 1969, inserted into the 1959 scrapbook.

30. Mary Bard, "Girls' Big Swap," *Reader's Digest*, June 1960, 117–20.

31. Mrs. Rittenhouse from Special Assigned Committee, memorandum re: "Outline of Plan for International-Intercultural Work," June 14, 1945, box "Diversity," folder "Intercultural," Girl Scouts of the USA National Historic Preservation Center, New York.

CHAPTER 6

1. "Girl Scout Troop Certificate," Japanese American National Museum, Los Angeles, California. A note on terminology: Following the work of scholar Yoosun Park, I use the term "Nikkei" to refer to all Japanese-born immigrants and US-born Japanese Americans, unless the original source uses a different term. As Park explains, "'Nikkei' is a Japanese term used generally to refer to all Japanese emigres and their descendants." Yoosun Park, "Facilitating Injustice: Tracing the Role of Social Workers in the World War II Internment of Japanese Americans," *Social Service Review* 82, no. 3 (2008): 447–83, quote on 482. This also avoids the contrast between "Japanese aliens" and "Japanese American citizens," which obscures the fact that the 1882 Chinese Exclusion Act and the 1924 Asian Exclusion Act made Asians ineligible for citizenship. Likewise, I use the terms "imprisonment" and "incarceration" rather than the euphemistic "relocation" or "internment" except when the original source uses those terms. "Internment" is a term that not only obfuscates the reality of imprisonment but also proves confusing, as there were additional internment centers that held political prisoners (and sometimes their family members) who were identified as particular security risks. Also important to note is that there were sixteen temporary "assembly centers" along the West Coast, where Nikkei were first taken before being sent to the ten permanent "relocation centers."

This chapter draws from archival sources from the Girl Scouts of the USA National

Historic Preservation Center, the National Archives/War Relocation Authority, the Japanese American National Museum, and the online repositories Densho and ReGeneration.

2. "World War II: Girl Scout Citations," box "Defense—General," folder "Japanese Relocation Camps," Girl Scouts of the USA National Historic Preservation Center, New York (hereafter cited as NHPC).

3. "Operating Agreements and Statements of Joint Policy: Statements of Relationships: Girl Scouts and War Relocation Authority," BANC MSS 67/14 c, folder E2.09, Japanese American Evacuation and Resettlement Records, 1930–74, Bancroft Library, University of California, Berkeley.

4. Ayako Noguchi, ed., *Vignette: A Pictorial Record of Life in the Fresno Assembly Center* (Fresno, CA: Fresno Assembly Center, 1942), in Guy and Marguerite Cook Nisei Collection, University of the Pacific, Stockton, California.

5. "World War II: Girl Scout Citations."

6. National board minutes, February 1943, box "Defense—General," folder "Japanese Relocation Camps," NHPC; Mary Degenhardt and Judith Kirsch, *Girl Scout Collector's Guide: A History of Uniforms, Insignia, Publications, and Memorabilia*, 2nd ed. (Lubbock: Texas Tech University Press, 2005), 144.

7. Yoosun Park, "The Role of the YWCA in the World War II Internment of Japanese Americans: A Cautionary Tale for Social Work," *Social Service Review* 87, no. 3 (2013): 477–524, quote on 479. Despite its voiced critique of the incarceration centers, the YWCA's Girl Reserves nevertheless showed up regularly in the centers.

8. Degenhardt and Kirsch, *Girl Scout Collector's Guide*, 144.

9. Tammy Proctor, *Scouting for Girls: A Century of Girl Guides and Girl Scouts* (Santa Barbara, CA: Praeger, 2009), 85. While national Girl Scout records do indicate that every prison had Girl Scouts, when I visited the Granada Internment Camp in Colorado (also known as Amache) I saw a lot of archival evidence of the YWCA Girl Reserves' presence and of Boy Scouts but none of Girl Scouts. This doesn't mean that the Girl Scouts weren't there, but it does mean that some of the prisons had a stronger presence of Girl Scouts than others.

10. "Japanese-American Incarceration during World War II," National Archives (website), accessed July 22, 2024, www.archives.gov/education/lessons/japanese-relocation.

11. For more information on Poston, see Thomas Fujita-Rony, "Poston (Colorado River)," Densho Encyclopedia, last modified September 11, 2024, https://encyclopedia.densho.org/Poston%20(Colorado%20River); and Brian Niiya, ed., *Japanese American History: An A-Z Reference from 1868-Present* (New York: Facts on File, 1993).

12. *Poston (AZ) Chronicle*, February 4, 1943. I also wish to thank Valerie J. Matsumoto, in whose work I first read about the brickmaking; Valerie J. Matsumoto, *City Girls: The Nisei Social World in Los Angeles, 1920–1950* (New York: Oxford University Press, 2014), 158.

13. Fujita-Rony, "Poston." In 1943, the WRA took sole control.

14. Alexander H. Leighton, "Community Planning," in *Governing of Men* (Princeton, NJ: Princeton University Press, 1945), 104–5.

15. Leighton, "Community Planning," 100.

16. Niiya, *Japanese American History*, 285.

17. "Block 215 Tops Week's Adobe Production," *Poston Chronicle*, February 21, 1943.

18. "Women Lauded for Adobe Work," *Poston Chronicle*, February 9, 1943.

19. "Lumber Missing from School Project," *Poston Chronicle*, February 25, 1943, 6.

20. Noguchi, *Vignette*, 21, 39.

21. Bud Aoyama, "INCOMING—Arrivals leaving train assisted by Girl Scout with their baggage," Heart Mountain, Wyoming, War Relocation Authority Photographs: Japanese-American Evacuation and Resettlement, BANC PIC 1967.014 v.66 HG:103—PIC, Bancroft Library, University of California, Berkeley.

22. "Envelope and letter to Dr. Keizaburo 'Kei' Koyama from Teru Koyama," Densho Digital Repository, accessed April 28, 2025, https://ddr.densho.org/ddr-one-5-43.

23. For instance, a 1945 scrapbook from Minidoka in Idaho, collected in the Densho Digital Archive, includes a newspaper article, "Girl Scouts Play Prominent Role in Center Activities," which details the induction of six troops in 1942, their visits to summer camps, and their fundraising sales for disabled veterans. "Scrapbook Page," Densho Digital Repository, accessed April 28, 2025, https://ddr.densho.org/ddr-densho-35-395.

24. Matsumoto, *City Girls*, 156–61.

25. The Japanese American National Museum's 2023 exhibit *Don't Fence Me In: Coming of Age in America's Concentration Camps*, curated by Emily Anderson, provides an excellent exploration of how crucial Girl Scouting was to many imprisoned girls.

26. Janet (Jeannette) Sui Matarai Misaka, interview by Emily Anderson, n.d., in *Don't Fence Me In* exhibit.

27. Noguchi, *Vignette*, 21.

28. Noguchi, *Vignette*, 12.

29. "A Salute to the Scouts" and "First Girl Scout Troop Invested," *Heart Mountain Sentinel* (Cody, WY), February 6, 1943, 4, 3. One-third of all girls and women who were incarcerated at Heart Mountain were Girl Scouts; Evelyn Haskell, "Japanese American Girl Scouts: Heart Mountain, Wyoming, 1942–45" (master's thesis, University of Wyoming, 2009), 31.

30. Mary Taukamoto, "Facing the Future," in Noguchi, *Vignette*, 43.

31. Sam Nakano, "Our Life Is What We Make It," in Noguchi, *Vignette*, 70.

32. Marion I. Masada, interview by Kristen Luetkemeier, September 10, 2014, Fresno, California, video recording, Manzanar National Historic Site Collection, Densho Digital Archive (Densho ID: denshovh-mmarion-01-0021).

33. Margaret Saito, interview by Kirk Peterson, December 17, 2009, Fresno, California, video recording, Manzanar National Historic Site Collection, Densho Digital Archive (Densho ID: denshovh-smargaret_2-01-0012).

34. "Envelope and Letter to Dr. Keizaburo 'Kei' Koyama from Teru Koyama."

35. Yasuko Ikeda, interview by Sojen Kim, February 19, 2021, audio recording, in *Don't Fence Me In* exhibit.

36. Matsumoto, *City Girls*.

37. "World War II: Girl Scout Citations."

38. Shimako "Sally" Kitano, interview by Alisa Lynch, October 15, 2008, video recording, Manzanar National Historic Site Collection, Densho Digital Archive (Densho ID: denshovh-ksally-02-0016).

39. Levey to Jo Bloom, April 17, 1992, box "American Indian Girl Scouts," folder "African American Girl Scouts," NHPC.

CHAPTER 7

1. "Girl Scouts of America: Interracial Organization Celebrates Its 40th Anniversary This Month," *Ebony*, March 1952, 46–50.

2. W. E. B. Du Bois, *The Souls of Black Folk* (1903; reprint, Mineola, NY: Dover, 1994), v. See, e.g., the 1944 campaign to "extend the program to all racial groups." "1944 Annual Report," box "Diversity," folder "Diversity 1940–1941"; "Extending Scouting to Other Races," box "Diversity," folder "Diversity 1942–1943"; "Negro Workers on the National Staff," April 26, 1944, box "Diversity," folder "Diversity"; and "Report to the National Girl Scout Board of the Special Committee on Girl Scout Racial Policy," box "Diversity," folder "Diversity," all in Girl Scouts of the USA National Historic Preservation Center, New York (hereafter cited as NHPC).

3. Eduardo Bonilla-Silva, "The Invisible Weight of Whiteness: The Racial Grammar of Everyday Life in Contemporary America," *Ethnic and Racial Studies* 35, no. 2 (2012): 173–94.

4. For a discussion of how racism threaded itself through the North as well as the South, see Thomas Sugrue, *Sweet Land of Liberty: The Forgotten Struggle for Civil Rights in the North* (New York: Penguin Random House, 2009).

5. Letter from Girl Scout National Headquarters, New York City, July 21, 1916, box "General History," folder "General History, Beginning, Savannah, 1916," NHPC.

6. Girl Scouts Commonwealth Council of VA, Inc., "Girl Scout Commonwealth Council to Celebrate and Honor First African-American Troop in the South," press release, May 19, 2008, accessed April 28, 2005, https://web.archive.org/web/20090326055255/http://www.comgirlscouts.org/News%20Room/vuu.pdf.

7. Council minutes, February 12, 1932, Commonwealth Council of the Girl Scouts of Virginia Records, 1910–2012, collection no. M 400, Special Collections and Archives, James Branch Cabell Library, Virginia Commonwealth University, Richmond.

8. Negro Troop Committee minutes, April 11, 1932, Commonwealth Council of the Girl Scouts of Virginia Records, 1910–2012, collection no. M 400, Special Collections and Archives, James Branch Cabell Library, Virginia Commonwealth University, Richmond.

9. Council minutes, November 2, 1933, Commonwealth Council of the Girl Scouts of Virginia Records, 1910–2012, collection no. M 400, Special Collections and Archives, James Branch Cabell Library, Virginia Commonwealth University, Richmond.

10. "Sarah Randolph Bailey," Georgia Women of Achievement, accessed August 22, 2024, www.georgiawomen.org/sarah-randolph-bailey.

11. Barbara Hallman to Rittenhouse, January 25, 1946; and Rittenhouse to Hallman, January 28, 1946, both in box "Interracial," NHPC.

12. "Purpose and Policy and Five Important National Policies of the Girl Scout Organization with Which Every Member of the Board of Directors; Every Commissioner and Council Member; and Girl Scout Captain Should Be Familiar," April 1, 1929, box "Diversity," folder "Diversity 1912–1939," NHPC; "History of Girl Scout Policies Regarding Intergroup Relations, from Blue Books, 1919–1958," box "Diversity," folder "Diversity, 1950s," NHPC.

13. See, e.g., Miya Carey, "Becoming 'a Force for Desegregation': The Girl Scouts and Civil Rights in the Nation's Capital," *Washington History* 29, no. 2 (2017): 54.

14. "Information on Girl Scout Policies and Requirements for Prospective Leaders and All Others Interested in Starting a Lone Girl Scout Troop," box "Diversity," folder

"Diversity, 1940–1941," NHPC; "History of Girl Scout Policies," box "Diversity," folder "Diversity, 1950s," NHPC; Girl Scouts, Inc., *Blue Book of Girl Scout Policies and Procedures* (New York: Girl Scouts, Inc., 1940), 76.

15. "Information on Girl Scout Policies."

16. Mrs. H. Plant Osborne, "Recommendations on Negro Work," October 1940, box "Diversity," folder "Diversity, 1940–1941," NHPC.

17. Mrs. Gerald de Westfelt to Joan B. Thompson, March 20, 1940, box "Diversity," folder "Diversity, 1940–1941," NHPC.

18. "International-Integrated Project," October 3, 1946, box "Diversity," folder "Diversity, 1945–1949," NHPC.

19. "1944 Annual Report"; "International-Integrated Project."

20. "Extending Scouting to Other Races."

21. "History of Requests for Negro Girl Scout Lone Troops," June 1941, Box "Diversity," folder "Diversity, 1940–1941," NHPC.

22. "Marie Trego Report," August 11, 1942, box "Diversity," folder "Diversity, 1942–1943," NHPC.

23. Dixie Regional Committee to Girl Scout National Organization, memorandum, January 27, 1928, box "Civil Rights: General Correspondence," folder "Civil Rights—General Correspondence, 1928–1933," NHPC.

24. "History of Requests for Negro Girl Scout Lone Troops."

25. Elisabeth Israels Perry, "The Very Best Influence: Josephine Holloway and Girl Scouting in Nashville's African-American Community," *Tennessee Historical Quarterly* 52, no. 2 (1933): 76.

26. Girl Scouts of the USA (@Girl Scouts), "Throwback Thursday Women's History edition! [flower emoji] This virtual bouquet of flowers is for Josephine Holloway for her duty, dedication, and creating opportunities for Black Girl Scouts," Facebook, March 3, 2022, www.facebook.com/photo/?fbid=10166921311785393&set=a.10150331202525393.

27. Perry, "Very Best Influence," 73–85.

28. "History of Requests for Negro Girl Scout Lone Troops."

29. Carey, "Becoming 'a Force,'" 52–60.

30. Leslie Paris, *Children's Nature: The Rise of the American Summer Camp* (New York: New York University Press, 2008), 221.

31. Perry, "Very Best Influence," 73–85.

32. "Report to Council 1941"; and "Narrative Report," n.d., both in box 12, folder 4, Pinoaka Reports, 1940–51, Commonwealth Council of the Girl Scouts of Virginia Records, 1910–2012, collection no. M 400, Special Collections and Archives, James Branch Cabell Library, Virginia Commonwealth University, Richmond.

33. Racial Relations Committee meeting minutes, October 15, 1942, box "Diversity," folder "Diversity, 1942–1943," NHPC.

34. Rittenhouse to Newell, September 10, 1942, box "Diversity," folder "Diversity, 1942–1943," NHPC.

35. Newell to Alice Wagener, September 10, 1942, box "Diversity," folder "Diversity, 1942–1943," NHPC.

36. "Extending Girl Scouting to Other Races," n.d. [ca. mid-1940s], memorandum, box "Diversity," folder "Diversity, 1942–1943," NHPC.

37. Racial Relations Committee meeting minutes, November 1, 1942, box "Diversity," folder "Diversity, 1942–1943," NHPC.

38. "Plan for the Operation of the Gainesville Colored Girl Scout Troops, 1940," box "Diversity," folder "Diversity, 1940–1941," NHPC.

39. De Westfelt to Mrs. Ralph Morgan, March 29, 1940, box "Diversity," folder "Diversity, 1940–1941," NHPC. Emphasis added.

40. For a discussion of the way white Northerners and Southerners came together after Reconstruction by allowing a memory of the Civil War to take hold that erased Black people and slavery, see David Blight, *Race and Reunion: The Civil War in American Memory* (Cambridge, MA: Belknap, 2002).

41. Teresa Carter to Edith Sinnett, March 13, 1941, box "National Conventions, 1947," folder "National Conventions 1947, Housing Racial Policy," NHPC.

42. Teresa Carter to Mrs. John Russell, March 19, 1941, box "National Conventions, 1947," folder "National Conventions 1947, Housing Racial Policy," NHPC.

43. Teresa Carter to Mrs. John Russell, April 20, 1941, box "National Conventions, 1947," folder "National Conventions 1947, Housing Racial Policy," NHPC.

44. Katie Lee Johnson to Mrs. Paul Rittenhouse and Mrs. C. Vaughan Ferguson, March 19, 1947, box "National Conventions, 1947," folder "National Conventions 1947, Housing Racial Policy," NHPC.

45. Johnson to Rittenhouse and Ferguson, March 19, 1947.

46. Rittenhouse to Murray, April 10, 1947, box "National Conventions, 1947," folder "Housing Racial Policy," NHPC.

47. Murray to Katie Lee Johnson, April 21, 1947, box "National Conventions, 1947," folder "Housing Racial Policy," NHPC.

48. Margaret Murray, interview report, Lafayette Hotel, May 23, 1947, box "National Conventions, 1947," folder "Housing Racial Policy," NHPC.

49. Charlotte Moton Hubbard to Katie Lee Johnson, April 4, 1947; and to Murray, May 13, 1947, both in box "National Conventions, 1947," folder "Housing Racial Policy," NHPC.

50. William V. Keenan to Rittenhouse, June 20, 1947, box "National Conventions, 1947," folder "Housing Racial Policy," NHPC.

51. Murray to Constance Rittenhouse, n.d. [ca. 1947]; and Margaret Murray, "Public or Private Organization Interview Report," April 18, 1947, both in box "National Conventions, 1947," folder "Housing Racial Policy," NHPC.

52. Murray, "Public or Private Organization Interview Report."

53. Murray, "Public or Private Organization Interview Report."

54. Murray to Bernard Ross, May 28, 1947; and to Constance Rittenhouse, May 28, 1947, both in box "National Conventions, 1947," folder "Housing Racial Policy," NHPC.

55. "Excerpt from Convention Program Committee Meeting," May 2, 1947, box "National Conventions, 1947," folder "Housing Racial Policy," NHPC.

56. "Regional Committee Meeting Held at Mrs. Martin's," memorandum, May 14, 1947, box "National Conventions, 1947," folder "Housing Racial Policy," NHPC.

57. Katie Lee Johnson to Charlotte Moton Hubbard, April 4, 1947, box "National Conventions, 1947," folder "Housing Racial Policy," NHPC.

58. "Regional Committee Meeting Held at Mrs. Martin's."

59. Rittenhouse to Murray, September 23, 1947; and Leonard Lathrop to Rittenhouse, memorandum, September 23, 1947, both in box "National Conventions, 1947," folder "Housing Racial Policy," NHPC.

60. Rittenhouse to Murray, September 23, 1947; Lathrop to Rittenhouse, September 23, 1947.

61. Rittenhouse to Murray, September 23, 1947.

62. Hubbard to Mrs. Louis B. Martin, June 13, 1947, box "National Conventions, 1947," folder "Housing Racial Policy," NHPC.

63. Hubbard to Murray, September 18, 1947, box "National Conventions, 1947," folder "Housing Racial Policy," NHPC.

64. Mrs. Louis Martin to Hubbard, June 6, 1947, box "National Conventions, 1947," folder "Housing Racial Policy," NHPC.

65. Rittenhouse to Murray, June 13, September 23, 1947, box "National Conventions, 1947," folder "Housing Racial Policy," NHPC.

66. "Racial Harmony, World Food Aid, Backed at Girl Scout Convention," *New York Times*, November 4, 1947.

67. "Racial Harmony, World Food Aid."

68. "Girl Scout News from Los Angeles," *Pittsburgh (PA) Courier*, October 11, 1947.

69. "Girl Scouts, from All Over Nation, Plan National Convention," *Chicago Defender*, November 1, 1947.

70. "Summary Report of Work on West Coast in Connection w/1947 National Convention at Long Beach, CA," December 22, 1947; and Leonard Lathrop and Johnson to Mrs. Vaughn Ferguson, and Lathrop and Katie Lee Johnson to Constance Rittenhouse, ca. 1947, both in box "National Conventions, 1947," folder "National Conventions, 1947, Publications/Report," NHPC.

71. A series of news clippings on Hubbard's work with the Girl Scouts, including the Thirty-Fifth Anniversary International Girl Scout Encampment, can be found in folder 46, Charlotte Moton Hubbard Collection, Girl Scouts of America, Moorland-Spingarn Research Center, Howard University, Washington, DC. Hubbard's commentary on her work at the Girl Scouts can be found at Records of the Women in the Federal Government Oral History Project, 1981–91, Schlesinger Library on the History of Women in America, Radcliffe Institute, Cambridge, Massachusetts.

72. Alice Wagener to Regional Directors, memorandum re: desegregation in public schools, July 1, 1954, box "Civil Rights, General Correspondence," folder "Civil Rights, General Correspondence, 1953–1961," NHPC.

73. "Progress Report of Inter-Group Relations, Guide for National Staff Use," May 1950, box "Civil Rights, General Correspondence," folder "Civil Rights, General Correspondence, 1949–1953," NHPC.

74. Homer Bishop to Isobel Crowe, October 10, 1955, box "Diversity," folder "Diversity, 1954–1959," NHPC; "History of Girl Scout Policies Regarding Intergroup Relations."

75. Stella Lackey to Margaret Delano, memorandum re: training in Richmond, Virginia, October 9, 1953, box "Diversity," folder "Diversity, 1950–1953," NHPC.

76. "A Southern Town," October 19–21, 1954, box "Diversity," folder "Diversity, 1954–1959," NHPC.

77. Memphis-Selby County Council of Girl Scouts, "Scouting among Negroes in Memphis," April 1952, box "Diversity," folder "Diversity, 1950–1953," NHPC.

78. Mrs. Joseph Bottler to Olivia Layton, November 24, 1954, box "Civil Rights, General Correspondence," folder "Civil Rights, General Correspondence, 1953–1961," NHPC.

79. Layton to Bottler, December 8, 1954, box "Civil Rights, General Correspondence," folder "Civil Rights, General Correspondence, 1953–1961," NHPC.

80. Alice Wagener and Alice Carney to Field Staff Members, "Strengthening Councils in Intergroup Relations," memorandum re: relation of Girl Scouts to desegregation in public schools, June 25, 1954, box "Diversity," folder "Diversity, 1954–1959," NHPC.

81. "Case Study for Community Relations Discussion with Region VIII National Staff," December 1954, box "Diversity," folder "Diversity, 1954–1959," NHPC.

82. Alice Freeman, Bertha Smith, Thelma Johnson, Rosetta Mackel, Rhetaugh Dumas, and Patricia White to Stratton, July 19, 1955, box "Civil Rights, General Correspondence," folder "Civil Rights, General Correspondence, 1953–1961," NHPC.

83. "Excerpt from Field Activities Report by Julia Peterkin, Wheeling, WV," May 13–14, 1954, box "Diversity," folder "Diversity, 1954–1959," NHPC.

84. This was the same area that had seen complaints by white families when Senior Girl Scouts organized a Boy Scout–Girl Scout dance that included white and Black troops. See memorandum, n.d. [ca. 1955]; and "An Experimental Workshop in Intercultural Relations," March 1955, both in box "Civil Rights," folder "Civil Rights, 1953–1961," NHPC.

85. "Excerpt from Field Activities Report by Julia Peterkin." Oglebay is still a park today; see "Experience Oglebay," Oglebay, accessed April 28, 2025, https://oglebay.com/experience-oglebay.

86. Kranz to Eleanor McKay, March 31, 1954, box "Diversity," folder "Diversity, 1954–1959," NHPC.

87. "Camp Deer Creek Narrative Report," October 5, 1955, box "Diversity," folder "Diversity, 1954–1959," NHPC.

88. Girl Scouts of Memphis and Shelby County, "Report on Integration, 1950–52," box "Diversity," folder "Diversity, 1950–1953," NHPC.

89. *Girl Scout Leader*, June 1954, front cover.

90. "Let Us Build," *Girl Scout Leader*, June 1954, 16, 14.

91. While the photograph was removed from the Girl Scout website at some point, one can still see it in many publications. See Alexis Orgera, "Looking Back, Moving Forward at the Juliette Gordon Low Birthplace," *Savannah Magazine*, September 11, 2018, https://savannahmagazine.com/culture/looking-back-moving-forward-juliette-gordon-low-birthplace.

92. "Confidential: Use of House," May 4, 1954, box "Diversity," folder "Diversity, 1954–1959," NHPC.

93. Law Offices of Lawyona and Cunningham to Anne Choate, box "Civil Rights–Councils to Regions to Position Statement," folder "Civil Rights, Integration, 1953," NHPC.

94. Rev. T. James McNamara to Miss Hetznecker, February 24, 1956, box "Diversity," folder "Diversity, 1954–1959," NHPC.

95. Leahy to Margaret Chapman, March 23, 1954, box "Diversity," folder "Diversity 1954–59," NHPC.

96. "Confidential: Use of House."

97. For instance, Kathrine Park writes in an April 2 letter to Margaret Chapman that she "knows the [proposed party] will leave out all negroes." Earlier, she wrote about the "Interracial Situation as it affects Program-planning at the Birthplace." In addition, a note from Agnes Leahy to Chapman makes it very clear that the Girl Scouts national organization was aware that its policies should have prevented the Birthplace from operating as a national site, considering the level of discrimination Black troops would experience there. Park to Chapman, January 15, April 2, 1958; and Leahy to Chapman, March 23, 1954, all in box "Diversity," folder "Diversity, 1954–1959," NHPC.

98. Excerpt from Lora Skilton to Mrs. Mobley, August 1954, box "Diversity," folder "Diversity, 1954–1959," NHPC.

99. See, e.g., Mrs. Silver to Mrs. Copeland, March 25, 1957, box "Diversity," folder "Diversity, 1954–59," NHPC: "Now rumors are flying! Milford and Ansonia have asked me if it is true that there will have to be segregation and discrimination at the Birthplace to Negros. I certainly hope your answer will be 'no.' I can understand it in Savannah but at the 'Birthplace' it will be hard for many in this area to accept that and I know it will have some bearing on our drive. I imagine this has been a question you have been asked before. . . . Will you answer in writing the National policy concerning this very vital issue."

100. Marguerite Dixon to Miss Wood, October 7, 1963, box "Civil Rights, Correspondence to Councils, Region IV," folder "Civil Rights, General Correspondence 1963–1965," NHPC; Julia Campbell (Juliette Gordon Low Birthplace) to Appalachian Girl Scout Council, July 19, 1957, box "Diversity," folder "Diversity, 1954–1959," NHPC. Campbell explained that a troop needed to be contacted because they seemed to be "illiterate," so therefore probably Black, and they would not be able to stay at the beach motel they had reserved.

CHAPTER 8

1. For other scholars' work on this controversy, see Jennifer Helgren, *American Girls and Global Responsibility: A New Relation to the World during the Early Cold War* (New Brunswick, NJ: Rutgers University Press, 2017), 125–56; Sara Fieldston, *Raising the World: Child Welfare in the American Century* (Cambridge, MA: Harvard University Press, 2015), 87–88; and Susan Swetnam, "Look Wider Still: The Subversive Nature of Girl Scouting in the 1950s," *Frontiers* 37, no. 1 (2016): 90–114.

2. Jonathan Yank, "The Cracker Barrel," *Los Angeles Herald and Express*, June 24, 1954.

3. Anne New to Dorothy Stratton, June 6, 1954, American Legion Controversy Records, National Historic Preservation Center (hereafter cited as ALCR).

4. "Just What You Wanted: Books, Pamphlets and Films to Help You," *Girl Scout Leader*, February 1953, 24.

5. "Believe It or Not, Girl Scouts Are Advised to Read Books of Langston Hughes and Dorothy Canfield Fisher," *Southern Conservative* (Fort Worth, TX), May 1, 1953, 5.

6. Michael Denning, *The Cultural Front: The Laboring of American Culture in the Twentieth Century* (New York: Verso Books, 2011).

7. Alice Carney to Leonard Lathrop, January 21, 1948, ALCR.

8. Rittenhouse to National Staff, memorandum re: "Questions on Un-American Activities," January 19, 1948, ALCR.

9. Ruth Schroeder to Field Staff, March 18, 1949, ALCR.

10. "Guide on the Release of Leaders," March 18, 1949, ALCR.

11. Bernice Hess to Elizabeth Mundie, "Problem Re: Communism in Albany," September 30, 1953, ALCR.

12. Summary of Evelyn Loch interview by Margareth Chemore, April 21, 1953, ALCR.

13. Alice Carby to Ruby Simpson, n.d., ALCR.

14. See Mary L. Dudziak, *Cold War Civil Rights: Race and the Image of American Democracy* (Princeton, NJ: Princeton University Press, 2011). For a particular study of how the Southern Negro Youth Congress was completely shut down by government harassment, see Donnae' Hampton, "Preceding Footsteps in Revolution: The History of the Southern Negro Youth Congress" (master's thesis, University of Alabama, 2023).

15. Ruth Kenny to Gertrude Campbell, January 11, 1952, ALCR.

16. Elizabeth Mundie to Alice Carney, Anne Marie Schindler, Gertrude Campbell, December 10, 1951; Alice Wagener field report, March 6, 1953; and Alice Wagener to Eunice Prien, March 11, 1953, all in ALCR.

17. Minutes, all-executive staff meeting, September 17, 1954, ALCR.

18. Though taking place twenty years later, Rachel Wetherill's essay "Beneath One Roof" is a good example of someone "quietly" forced to leave the Girl Scouts because she was a lesbian. Rachel Wetherill, "Beneath One Roof," in *On My Honor: Lesbians Reflect on Their Scouting Experience*, ed. Nancy Manahan (Northboro, MA: Madwoman, 1997), 145–55. See also the section "Disillusionment" in Manahan's book for more stories.

19. Raymond Currier, Gerti Dooneief, Ruth Eisenberg et al. to Girl Scouts of the USA, November 11, 1951, ALCR.

20. On questioning Shepard's "emotional stability," see phone conversation between Alice Carney and Elizabeth Mundie, March 14, 1952, transcript. On "practically saying nothing" and accepting her resignation, see Virginia Robbins to Mundie, December 13, 1951. On controversial activity, see Raymond Currier, Gerti Dooneief, Ruth Eisenberg et al. (executive board of the Westchester Committee for Human Rights) to Girl Scouts of the USA, December 11, 1951. On the Roger Smith Hotel, see Dorothy Wright to Girl Scouts of the USA, December 10, 1951. On "cause célèbres," see summary of Mrs. Geoffrey Robbins interview by Jane Lounsbury, Jane Lounsbury interview with Mrs. Geoffrey Robbins, November 7, 1951. On Shepard's refusal to sign the letter and protest letters rolling in, see Mundie to Alice Wagener, December 14, 1951. All in ALCR.

21. "But, Adlai, That 1953 Girl Scout Manual Needed Pruning!," *Saturday Evening Post*, June 9, 1956, 10.

22. Marguerite Twohy, Western Union telegram, August 7, 1954, ALCR.

23. Lillian Gilbreth, "Girl Scouting: One Answer to Communism," *Girl Scout Leader*, October 1954, 5.

24. Eleanor Roosevelt, My Day, August 11, 1954, Eleanor Roosevelt Papers Digital Edition, accessed April 8, 2022, www2.gwu.edu/~erpapers/myday/displaydocedits.cfm?_y=1954&_f=md002930.

25. Mrs. John Kraus (Racine, WI) to Olivia Layton and Florence Otto, May 13, 1954; and Layton to Mrs. Windes (Winnetka, IL), June 23, 1954, both in ALCR.

26. *Girl Scout Handbook: Intermediate Program* (New York: Girl Scouts of the USA, 1953), 190; *Girl Scout Handbook: Intermediate Program*, rev. ed. (New York: Girl Scouts of the USA,

1953), 191. All these changes are discussed in "Editorial Changes in the Fifth Impression of the Girl Scout Handbook," ALCR.

27. *Girl Scout Handbook*, 204; *Girl Scout Handbook*, rev. ed., 204.

28. *Girl Scout Handbook*, 431; *Girl Scout Handbook*, rev. ed., 431.

29. *Girl Scout Handbook*, xvi; *Girl Scout Handbook*, rev. ed., xvi.

30. *Girl Scout Handbook*, 210.

31. *Girl Scout Handbook*, 211; *Girl Scout Handbook*, rev. ed., 211.

32. *Girl Scout Handbook*, 221; *Girl Scout Handbook*, rev. ed., 221.

33. Twohy, Western Union telegram, August 7, 1954, ALCR.

34. Charlotte Hartman interview by Florence Otto and Lucile Cannon, May 12, 1954, summary; and Marguerite Twohy, "Refusal of Removal of Membership," May 14, 1954, both in ALCR.

35. Alice Wagener to Gertrude Simpson, June 28, 1954, ALCR.

36. Alice Wagener to Eleanor McKay, September 17, 1954, ALCR.

37. The director of public relations for GSUSA, Mary Shelly, wrote about her attempts to stop the *Atlantic Monthly* from publishing Bagdikian's article. Mary Shelly to Swift Newton, January 28, 1955, ALCR.

38. Ben H. Bagdikian, "What Happened to the Girl Scouts?," *Atlantic Monthly*, May 1955, 63–64.

39. Louis Lyons, "The New Handbook: A Close Look," *Christian Register* (Boston), February 1955.

40. "Berserk Patriotism," *Chicago Daily News*, August 8, 1954.

41. "Big Bullies," *Denver (CO) Post*, August 10, 1954; "How Screwy Can the Legion Get?," *Chicago Daily Sun-Times*, August 9, 1954.

42. Bernard DeVoto, "The Easy Chair: Peter and Wendy in the Revolution," *Harper's Magazine*, July 1955, 10.

43. Layton to Gertrude Simpson, July 13, 1955; and DeVoto to Layton, July 23, 1955, both in ALCR.

44. Marjorie Haldeman to Girl Scouts of the USA, May 23, 1955, ALCR.

45. Clarence Cortner to Robert Wick, January 11, 1961; and Elizabeth Whitten to Mary Duffy, January 12, 1962, both in ALCR.

46. Herb Block, "Stand Fast, Men—They're Armed with Marshmallows," *Washington Post*, August 11, 1954.

47. AnnEditorWriter, "Margarite Hall," YouTube video, November 6, 2014, www.youtube.com/watch?v=TgCBUW_CAcA&t=139s. In the archival record, her name has been spelled Margarite and Marguerite.

CHAPTER 9

1. Stephen H. Dunphy, "Girl Scout 'Tokensim' Hit," *Seattle Daily Times*, October 22, 1969, 7.

2. "Girl Scout Act to Eliminate Prejudice," *Chicago Daily Defender*, November 8, 1969, 10.

3. Dunphy, "Girl Scout 'Tokensim' Hit," 7.

4. Mary Shelly to Louise Wood, July 1, 1963, box "Civil Rights, General Correspondence

to Councils–Region IV," folder "General Correspondence, 1963–1965," Girl Scouts of the USA National Historic Preservation Center, New York (hereafter cited as NHPC).

5. Girl Scouts of Memphis and Shelby County, "Report on Integration, 1950–52," box "Diversity," folder "Diversity 1950–1953," NHPC.

6. Gertrude Simpson to Mary Burch, August 18, 1965, box "Civil Rights, General Correspondence to Councils–Region IV," folder "General Correspondence, 1963–1965," NHPC.

7. Jones to Mrs. Holton Price, March, 25, 1965, box "Civil Rights, General Correspondence to Councils–Region IV," folder "General Correspondence, 1963–1965," NHPC.

8. Charisse Lillie to Jeanne Noble, February 19, 1967, box "Civil Rights–Councils," folder "Integration," NHPC.

9. "Memoir from Eunice Prien and Mary Frances Biering," July 5, 1957, box "American Indian Girl Scouts," folder "1954–"; "1969 National Senior Girl Scout Speak Out Report," box "Civil Rights–Councils," folder "Councils, Region VII"; and Gerald Schneider to Louise Wood, May 14, 1968, box "Civil Rights–Councils," folder, "Councils, Region VII," all in NHPC.

10. "Understanding among People Aim of New Scout Program," *Seattle Daily Times*, October 22, 1969, 19.

11. Virginia Greene, "Awareness-Action," *Girl Scout Leader*, January 1970, 10.

12. Grace M. S. McNeil, "The Specialness of Difference," *Girl Scout Leader*, January/February 1972, 12.

13. National board meeting notes, January 20–21, 1982, quoted in Lillian S. Williams, *A Bridge to the Future: A History of Diversity in Girl Scouting* (New York: Girl Scouts of USA, 1996), 37.

14. Abzug to Scott, January 2, 1976; Jordan to Scott, November 20, 1975; Amelia Anderson (personnel director of *Essence*) to Scott, December 3, 1975; Humphrey to Scott, November 11, 1975; Laurette Hinkson to Scott, November 21, 1975; Mrs. Arthur Horsell and Margaret Mealey (National Council of Catholic Women) to Scott, December 16, 1975; and Thurmond to Scott, December 15, 1975, all in Gloria D. Scott—Personalities File (Letters of Congratulations, Speeches/Writings), NHPC.

15. Gloria D. Scott, "The Challenge of Possibility: Revisited," speech delivered at the Presidents' and Executive Directors' Meeting, October 1976, transcript, Gloria D. Scott—Personalities File (Letters of Congratulations, Speeches/Writings), NHPC.

16. Mildred Jeffrey to Scott, June 18, 1979, Gloria D. Scott—Personalities File (Letters of Congratulations, Speeches/Writings), NHPC.

17. A caption for the image of Scott using the gavel notes that she used the gavel that Susan B. Anthony had used at the 1848 Seneca Falls ceremony. It may have been Anthony's gavel, or it may have been used at the Seneca Falls convention, but it could not have been both, as Anthony was not at the 1848 Seneca Falls convention. More important, however, the caption gestures to the history and lineage of feminism that the Girl Scouts were working to invoke. For the many ways that girls' organizations in the 1970s used the historic moment to represent powerful women, see Jennifer Helgren, "Finding 'Hidden Heroines': Girls' Organizations, Public History, and the 1976 Bicentennial," *Public Historian* 43, no. 1 (2021): 102–22.

18. Patricia McCormack, "Betty Friedan: Girl Scout," *Detroit Free Press*, November 24, 1974, 5C.

19. "About Women: Betty Friedan Rejoins Girl Scouts," *Los Angeles Times*, November 17, 1974, pt. 5.

20. Ellen Pekarna (St. Paul and Minneapolis Archdiocesan Council of Catholic Women) to Dr. Cecily Selby, November 18, 1974, Betty Friedan—Personalities File, NHPC.

21. Barbara Wilson to Richard Knox, March 14, May 17, 1975, Betty Friedan—Personalities File, NHPC.

22. "Public Relations and Chronology of Events on Betty Friedan," April 10, 1975, Betty Friedan—Personalities File, NHPC.

23. "News from GSUSA," October 23, 1974, Betty Friedan—Personalities File, NHPC.

24. Julie Kammerer, "Report to the National Board Meeting and Concept for a National Fund-Raising Campaign," October 24, 1975, Papers of Betty Friedan, 1933–85, Schlesinger Library on the History of Women in America, Radcliffe Institute, Cambridge, Massachusetts (hereafter cited as SL); Gloria Scott to Betty Friedan, April 1, 1977, Betty Friedan—Personalities File, NHPC.

25. "About Women: Betty Friedan Rejoins Girl Scouts," *Los Angeles Times*, November 17, 1974, pt. 5.

26. On not being renominated, see Mrs. Howard Sprague (chair, National Nominating Committee) to Friedan, February 6, 1981, Girl Scout Files, Papers of Betty Friedan, 1933–85, SL.

27. On the Girl Scout endorsement of the ERA, see Marjorie Ittman to Council Presidents, February 14, 1975, Girl Scout Files, Papers of Betty Friedan, 1933–85, SL.

28. Angevine to Marjorie Ittman, Cecily Selby, and Betty Friedan, February 28, 1975, Girl Scout Files, Papers of Betty Friedan, 1933–85, SL.

29. Peggy Anderson, "Father Schmidt v. the Girl Scouts," *Ms.*, March 1976, 16–18.

30. Letters to the editor, *Ms.*, July 1976, 12.

31. "Plan of Cooperation United States Catholic Conference Girl Scouts of the USA," May 13, 1975, Girl Scout Literature, Papers of Betty Friedan, 1933–85, SL.

32. Anonymous to *Ms.* magazine, March 2, 1976, "Letters to Ms. 1970–1998, MC 331, box 7, folder 76, "Girl Scouts, Postpartum Blues," SL.

33. Mile Hi Council to *Ms.* magazine, March 5, 1976, Letters to Ms. 1970-1998, MC 331, box 7, folder 76, "Girl Scouts, Postpartum Blues," SL.

34. Rochelle Goldberg Ruthchild, "Vicki Levins Gabriner," Jewish Women's Archive, accessed July 11, 2023, https://jwa.org/weremember/gabriner-vicki.

35. "Scouts Offer Teen Program," *Atlanta Journal*, November 24, 1975, 5SD. For further materials on the program, see Vicki Gabriner Papers, Northwest Georgia Girl Scouts, 1975–76, SL.

36. Frances Hesselbein, *My Life on Leadership* (San Francisco: Jossey-Bass, 2002); Frances Hesselbein, interview by the author, January 17, 2017, New York.

37. Hesselbein interview.

38. "Girl Scouts Revising Pledge to Accept Religious Diversity," *New York Times*, October 25, 1993; "Vote Allows Changes in the Girl Scout Oath," *Los Angeles Times*, October 24, 1993.

39. Peter Howell, "Caroline Commissioner Breaks with Scouts over New Oath Policy," *Star-Democrat* (Easton, MD), October 29, 1993, 1A.

40. These responses found in box "Promise and Laws," folders "Promise and Laws—God—Negative—Petitions" and "Promise and Laws—1993—God—Background/Summary," NHPC.

CHAPTER 10

1. Girl Scouts of the USA, "Girl Scouting Now," 1973, inside cover and p. 7, box 120, folder 1446a, Girl Scouts 1974–79, Papers of Betty Friedan, 1933–85, Schlesinger Library on the History of Women in America, Radcliffe Institute, Cambridge, Massachusetts (hereafter cited as SL).

2. Karen Cox, *Dreaming of Dixie: How the South Was Created in American Popular Culture* (Chapel Hill: University of North Carolina Press, 2011).

3. Leola Roberts, "History of the Girl Scout Plantation," n.d. [ca. 1960s–'70s], in possession of author.

4. Tiya Miles, *All That She Carried: The Journey of Ashley's Sack, a Black Family Keepsake* (New York: Random House, 2021).

5. Joyce E. Chaplin, "Tidal Rice Cultivation and the Problem of Slavery in South Carolina and Georgia, 1760–1815," *William and Mary Quarterly* 49, no. 1 (1992): 33, https://doi.org/10.2307/2947334.

6. Andrew Chandler, Mary Edmonds, Valerie Marcil, J. Tracy Power, and Stephen W. Skelton, preparers, "National Register of Historic Places Nomination Form," 2002, 24, www.nationalregister.sc.gov/berkeley/S10817708004/S10817708004.pdf.

7. N. Louise Bailey and Elizabeth Ivey Cooper, *Biographical Directory of the South Carolina House of Representatives*, vol. 3, *1775–1790* (Columbia: University of South Carolina Press, 1981), 317, estimates on 7.

8. Walter B. Edgar and N. Louise Bailey, *Biographical Directory of the South Carolina House of Representatives*, vol. 2, *The Commons House of Assembly 1692–1775* (Columbia: University of South Carolina Press, 1977), 307.

9. N. Louise Bailey, *Biographical Directory of the South Carolina House of Representatives*, vol. 4, *1791–1815* (Columbia: University of South Carolina Press, 1984), 496; Second Census of the United States, 1800, M32, Records of the Bureau of the Census, National Archives, Washington DC.

10. Eighth Census of the United States, 1860, series no. M653, Records of the Bureau of the Census, RG 29, National Archives, Washington, DC.

11. Eighth Census of the United States, 1860, series no. M653, Records of the Bureau of the Census, RG 29, National Archives, Washington, DC.

12. Anthony Weston, "Richmond Plantation Journal 1859–1869," Low Country Digital Library, South Carolina Historical Society, Charleston; John Beaufain Irving, *A Day on Cooper River* (Charleston, SC: A. E. Miller, 1842), https://archive.org/stream/adayoncooperrivooirvigoog/adayoncooperrivooirvigoog_djvu.txt. "Every thing about the premises is in the same excellent order and condition. The accommodation for the domestics—the stables—the negro houses—the barn, are all painted and whitewashed, and as seen from

the river, have a very imposing appearance. Dr. Benjamin Huger, the present proprietor, is regarded as one of the most diligent planters on the river" (54).

13. Emma Whalen, "Charleston Unveils Plaque Describing the Punishment House for Slaves," *Post and Courier* (Charleston, SC), July 13, 2022.

14. Hillary Nicole King, "Building Preservation Plan Richmond Plantation Manor House, Cordesville, South Carolina" (master's thesis, Clemson University, 2008), maps on 7, 20; Chaplin, "Tidal Rice Cultivation," 29–61.

15. King, "Building Preservation Plan"; details on the Ellis family on 13–15.

16. Jackie Odem, "A Plantation Financed with Cookies," *Sandlapper*, May 1973, 37–39.

17. Hosea Williams, "Segregation Southern Style: A Recollection from the 1950s," *Object of History* (blog), National Museum of American History, accessed May 1, 2025, https://objectofhistory.org/objects/show/lunchcounter/70.html; Tony Cope, *No Reservations: Savannah's Forgotten Hotels* (Savannah, GA: Abercorn Press, 2021).

18. "First Unit to Be Built for Girls Scout Camp," *Savannah (GA) Tribune*, February 8, 1945, 1.

19. Susan Eva O'Donovan, "At the Intersection of Cotton and Commerce: Antebellum Savannah and Its Slaves," in *Slavery and Freedom in Savannah*, ed. Leslie Harris and Daina Berry (Athens: University of Georgia Press, 2014), 48.

20. Leslie Harris and Daina Berry, "Slave Life in Savannah: Geographies of Autonomy and Control," in Harris and Berry, *Slavery and Freedom*, 104.

21. Janice L. Sumler-Edmond, "Free Black Life in Savannah," in Harris and Berry, *Slavery and Freedom*, 130–39.

22. O'Donovan, "At the Intersection," 66. See also Anne Bailey, *The Weeping Time: Memory and the Largest Slave Auction in American History* (New York: Cambridge University Press, 2017).

23. Harris and Berry, "Slave Life in Savannah," 99.

24. Cathy Miller, "Lingering One Last Time at the Girl Scout Plantation," *Pluff Mud Perspectives* (blog), July 15, 2013, http://pluffmudperspectives.blogspot.com/2013/07/lingering-one-last-time-at-girl-scout.html.

25. James Baldwin, "A Letter to My Nephew," *Progressive Magazine*, December 1, 1962.

CHAPTER 11

1. American Heritage Girls, "Girl Scouts Indoctrination Camps; American Heritage Girls Founder Calls Out GSUSA's Camp Culture Code," news release, July 12, 2023, https://americanheritagegirls.org/wp-content/uploads/2023/07/071223-Girl-Scouts-indoctrination-camps-American-Heritage-Girls-founder-calls-out-GSUSAs-Camp-Culture-Code.pdf; "Missouri Right to Life Policy on Girl Scouts USA," Missouri Right to Life, accessed September 12, 2023, https://missourilife.org/policies/girl-scouts-usa; American Heritage Girls, accessed September 12, 2023, https://americanheritagegirls.org; "American Heritage Girls Named Christian Alternative to the Girl Scouts," Catholic Online, January 18, 2012, www.catholic.org/prwire/headline.php?ID=10404.

2. Coatlupe Martinez, "Dream to Your Future: Radical Monarchs," *New Moon Girls*, January/February 2020.

3. "Oakland's 'Radical Brownies' Troop to Change Name after Getting a Call from

the Girl Scouts," February 24, 2015, CBS News, www.cbsnews.com/sanfrancisco/news/oakland-radical-brownies-troop-change-name-girl-scouts.

4. Juliana Horatia Ewing, *The Brownies and Other Tales* (London: Society for Promoting Christian Knowledge, 1871).

5. Anna Holmes, "The Magazine That Helped 1920s Kids Navigate Racism," *Atlantic*, February 12, 2021, www.theatlantic.com/culture/archive/2021/02/how-w-e-b-du-bois-changed-black-childhood-america/617952.

6. "FAQ," Radical Monarchs, accessed September 19, 2023, https://radicalmonarchs.org/faq.

7. CNSNews, "The Girl Scouts and Planned Parenthood," YouTube video, June 15, 2011, www.youtube.com/watch?v=uZKiQuboZnA.

8. "Girl Scout Cookies, and Troops, Crumble in Texas," NBC News, March 3, 2004, www.nbcnews.com/id/wbna4441006.

9. "Bob Morris, Indiana Lawmaker, Calls Girl Scouts a 'Radicalized Organization,'" *HuffPost*, February 20, 2012, accessed May 1, 2025, www.huffpost.com/entry/bob-morris-indiana-law-ma_n_1289489; Brigid Ayer, "Concerns over Girl Scouts Persist Following USCCB Investigation," *National Catholic Register*, July 16, 2014, www.ncregister.com/news/concerns-over-girl-scouts-persist-following-usccb-investigation.

10. Girl Scouts of the USA, "Anna Maria Chavez Sets the Record Straight," YouTube video, February 27, 2014, www.youtube.com/watch?v=NkB6YygHXkE.

11. "Social Issues: FAQ," Girl Scouts, accessed September 23, 2023, www.girlscouts.org/en/footer/faq/social-isues-faq.html.

12. Robert McCartney, "Girl Scouts' Critics: Too Extreme to Succeed," *Washington Post*, February 22, 2012, www.washingtonpost.com/local/girl-scouts-critics-too-extreme-to-succeed/2012/02/22/gIQAiFF9TR_story.html.

13. Kathy Cloninger, *Tough Cookies: Leadership Lessons from 100 Years of the Girl Scouts* (Hoboken, NJ: John Wiley and Sons, 2011), vi, 3.

14. James Ewinger, "Jane Christyson New Girl Scouts of North East Ohio Leader," March 8, 2013, www.cleveland.com/metro/2013/03/jane_christyson_new_girl_scout.html.

15. Cloninger, *Tough Cookies*, 34.

16. "Girl Scouts of North East Ohio Breaks Ground on Stem Center of Excellence on Camp Ledgewood," Girl Scouts of North East Ohio, August 17, 2023, www.gsneo.org/en/discover/our-council/news-media-press-announcements/girl-scouts-of-north-east-ohio-breaks-ground-on-stem-center-of-e.html; Girl Scout Research Institute, *The Impact of Girl Scout STEM Programming* (New York: Girl Scouts of the USA, 2022), www.girlscouts.org/content/dam/gsusa/forms-and-documents/about/research/GSUSA_GSRI_2022_The-Impact-of-Girl-Scout-STEM-Programming-Full-Report.pdf.

17. Audre Lorde, "The Transformation of Silence into Language and Action," in *Sister Outsider: Essays and Speeches* (Berkeley, CA: Crossing, 2007).

18. Bianca Vazquez Toness, "The New Girl Scouts," Minnesota Public Radio, July 11, 2005, http://news.minnesota.publicradio.org/features/2005/06/30_tonessb_girlscouts/; "Muslim Girl Scouts Extend Fun and Friendship across Cultures," Girl Scouts, accessed October 2, 2023, www.girlscouts.org/en/our-stories/girl-scouts/take-action/muslim-girl-scouts-host-open-mosque-role-models.html; Girl Scout Research Initiative, *The Resilience Factor: A Key to Leadership in African American and Hispanic Girls* (New York: Girl Scouts of the USA, 2011);

Kathleen J. Block and Margaret J. Potthast, "Girl Scouts beyond Bars: Facilitating Parent-Child Contact in Correctional Settings," *Child Welfare* 77, no. 5 (1998): 561–78.

19. Nikita Stewart, *Troop 6000: The Girl Scout Troop That Began in a Shelter and Inspired the World* (New York: Ballantine Books, 2020), 31.

20. Girl Scouts of the USA, *2017 Annual Report* (New York: GSUSA, 2017), 27.

21. Girl Scouts of the USA, *2023 Stewardship Report* (New York: GSUSA, 2023), 11, www.girlscouts.org/content/dam/gsusa/forms-and-documents/members/ncs-con23/GSUSA_Stewardship-Report-2023.pdf.

22. ZZ Packer, "Brownies," in *Drinking Coffee Elsewhere* (New York: Riverhead Books, 2003), 1–28.

23. In her richly researched book *The Camp Fire Girls: Gender, Race, and American Girlhood, 1910–1980* (Lincoln: University of Nebraska Press, 2022), Jennifer Helgren explores the complexities of the Camp Fire Girls, including girls' experiences that often went far beyond stereotypically "feminine" pursuits.

24. Barbara Arneil, "Gender, Diversity, and Organizational Change: The Boy Scouts v. Girl Scouts of America," *Perspectives on Politics* 8, no. 1 (2010): 53–68.

25. Jay Mechling, "The NRA Helped This Boy Scout to Shoot a Gun, but It's Time for a Friendly Divorce," *USA Today*, October 11, 2018, www.usatoday.com/story/opinion/voices/2018/10/11/boy-scouts-america-should-sever-ties-nra-lobbying-guns-column/1578027002.

26. Savannah Walsh, "The Boys Scouts' Sexual Abuse Scandal No Longer Lives in the Shadows," *Vanity Fair*, September 6, 2023, www.vanityfair.com/hollywood/2023/09/the-boy-scouts-sexual-abuse-scandal-no-longer-lives-in-the-shadows; Dietrich Knauth, "US Boy Scouts Exits Chapter 11 after Abuse Settlement," Reuters, April 19, 2023, www.reuters.com/legal/boy-scouts-emerges-chapter-11-bankruptcy-2023-04-19. Two powerful documentaries about the Boy Scouts and its sexual abuse cover-up include *Leave No Trace: Child Sexual Abuse in Boy Scouts of America* and the 2023 *Scouts Honor: The Secret Files of the Boy Scouts of America*. See also Natalia Winkelman, "Scouts Honor: The Secret Files of the Boy Scouts of America," *New York Times*, September 8, 2023, C6.

27. Bart Jansen, "Boy Scouts to Allow Young Girls into Cub Scouts, Parallel Program for Older Girls," *USA Today*, October 11, 2017, www.usatoday.com/story/news/2017/10/11/boy-scouts-girls-admitted-into-cub-scouts/754605001.

28. Arneil, "Gender, Diversity," 53–68.

29. Christian Berthelsen, "The Girl Scouts Just Sued the Boy Scouts over Use of the Term 'Scout,'" *Time*, November 6, 2018, https://time.com/5446540/girl-scouts-boy-scouts-lawsuit.

30. Sylvia Acevedo, "Girls Are Stars in Girl Scouts: They'd Be Supporting Players in Boy Scouts," *USA Today*, October 24, 2017, www.usatoday.com/story/opinion/2017/10/24/girls-star-in-girl-scouts-supporting-players-again-in-boy-scouts-sylvia-acevedo-column/790244001. Emphasis added.

31. Johnny Diaz, "Lawsuit Accusing Boy Scouts of Muddling the Girl Scouts Brand Is Dismissed," *New York Times*, April 7, 2022, www.nytimes.com/2022/04/07/us/girl-scouts-suit-dismissed.html; Dietrich Knauth, "Boy Scouts of America and Girl Scouts Settle Trademark Dispute over Co-Ed Scouting," Reuters, July 23, 2022, www.reuters.com/legal/litigation/boy-scouts-america-girl-scouts-settle-trademark-dispute-over-co-ed-scouting-2022-07-23.

32. "Social Issues: FAQ."

33. "Supporting LGBTQ+ Youth in Girl Scouts," Girl Scouts of the Northwestern Great Lakes, accessed May 1, 2025, www.gsnwgl.org/en/members/for-volunteers/forms-and-documents/supporting-lgbtq--youth-in-girl-scouts.html. www.gsnwgl.org/content/dam/gsnwgl-redesign/documents/program/Supporting%20LGBTQ.pdf.

34. "Social Issues: FAQ."

35. Jinath Tasnim, "For Volunteers," Girl Scouts River Valleys, accessed October 17, 2023, https://volunteers.girlscoutsrv.org/2018/11/29/the-joys-of-teaching-consent.

36. Girl Scouts of Greater Atlanta, "Meet Emmeline! Emmeline developed a workshop, website, and pamphlet to address the rising rates of teen pregnancies and STD rates in her community due to the lack of Sex Education taught in our school systems," Facebook, December 12, 2018, www.facebook.com/46268322786/posts/meet-emmeline-emmeline-developed-a-workshop-website-and-pamphlet-to-address-the-/10156491620987787; Elizabeth Short, "Prioritizing Inclusion: Girl Scout Focuses on LGBT+ Sex Ed in Service Project," *Forest Park Review* (Oak Park, IL), June 27, 2023, www.forestparkreview.com/2023/06/27/prioritizing-inclusion-girl-scout-focuses-onlgbtq-sex-ed-in-service-project.

37. "Camp Culture Code," Girl Scouts of Eastern Massachusetts, June 2023, www.gsema.org/content/dam/girlscoutseasternmass-redesign/documents/outdoor-program/gsema-camp-culture-code.pdf.

38. *Summary Report: The Beijing Declaration and Platform for Action Turns 20*, UN Women, 2015, accessed May 2, 2025, www.unwomen.org/en/digital-library/publications/2015/02/beijing-synthesis-report; "CSW59 / Beijing+20 (2015)," UN Women, accessed October 21, 2023, www.unwomen.org/en/csw/previous-sessions/csw59-2015.

39. "Economic and Social Council," United Nations, accessed October 21, 2023, www.un.org/ecosoc/en/ngo; "Young Women's Advocacy Forum @Women Deliver 2019," World Association of Girl Guides and Girl Scouts, accessed October 21, 2023, www.wagggs.org/en/what-we-do/young-womens-advocacy-forum-women-deliver-2019.

40. "WAGGGS Position Statement: Girls and Young Women's Sexuality Education," World Association of Girl Guides and Girl Scouts, accessed October 21, 2023, https://duz92c7qaoni3.cloudfront.net/documents/WAGGGS_position_statement_MDG45_sexuality_education.pdf.

41. "Social Issues: FAQ."

42. See chapter 2 for more on this story.

43. "Telling Our Origin Story," Girl Scouts, accessed October 1, 2023, www.girlscouts.org/en/our-stories/alumnae/telling-our-origin-story.html; Shannon Browning-Mullis, phone conversation with author, September 26, 2023 (notes in author's possession).

44. Page Harrington, phone conversation with author, December 3, 2021 (notes in author's possession). For the GSUSA's description of the Cultural Assets Department, see "About the Cultural Assets Department," Girl Scout Archive Management System, accessed November 28, 2023, https://archives.girlscouts.org/index.php/About/Collection.

45. "American Women Quarters Program," US Mint, accessed May 2, 2025, www.usmint.gov/coins/coin-programs/american-women-quarters-program; "Coining History: Juliette Gordon Low Takes Her Place on the Quarter," *GSBlog*, October 17, 2023, https://blog.girlscouts.org/2023/10/coining-history-juliette-gordon-low.html.

CHAPTER 12

1. Another artist, Deborah Roberts, also suggested for me the importance of Girl Scouting for Black girls. Roberts creates intricate collages of Black girlhood—"very Black Norman Rockwell," she says—that evoke an innocent world from which Black girls have traditionally been excluded, faced with so much racism, caregiving responsibilities, and a white culture that sexualizes them at a too-early age. When she draws Black girls, she says she generally makes their hands and feet larger than normal, to give them power to deal with what will be thrust at them. See Aruna D'Souza, "Self-Representation, Play and Power," *New York Times*, February 26, 2022, C1.

2. Janet Wright, email correspondence with author, September 15, 2023.

3. Tressie McMillan Cottom, *Thick: And Other Essays* (New York: New Press, 2019), 7.

4. Imani Perry, *Breathe: A Letter to My Sons* (Boston: Beacon, 2019).

Index

Page numbers in italics refer to illustrations.